MICHAEL SCHNEIDER
A Brief History of the German Trade Unions

Translated by Barrie Selman

Verlag J.H.W. Dietz Nachf.

ISBN 3-8012-0161-9
English translation © 1991 Verlag J.H.W. Dietz Nachf. GmbH
In der Raste 2, D-5300 Bonn 1
Originally published as „Kleine Geschichte der Gewerkschaften.
Ihre Entwicklung in Deutschland von den Anfängen bis heute".
© 1989 Verlag J.H.W. Dietz Nachf., Bonn
Cover: Karl Debus, using a banner of the woodworkers' union (office Stuttgart) from
1901. Original in the central office of the Gewerkschaft Holz und Kunststoff in Stutt-
gart.
Pictures: Archiv der sozialen Demokratie, Bonn-Bad Godesberg.
Typesetting: satz+druck gmbh, Düsseldorf
Printing: Fuldaer Verlagsanstalt GmbH
All rights reserved.
Printed in Germany 1991

Contents

Introduction 11

I. Industrialization, the development of the working class and the
    beginnings of the trade union movement around the middle of
    the nineteenth century 15
    1. Industrialization and the emergence of the working class:
       the development of the "social question" 15
    2. Towards the formation of the first trade unions 20
    3. Organizational setbacks in the reactionary 1850s 28

II. The rise of the labour movement in the 1860s and 1870s . . . 30
    1. The emergence of class society 30
    2. The breakthrough 36
    3. The trade unions and the struggle between the parties . . . 40
    4. Crisis in the trade unions and the beginnings of centrali-
       zation 45

III. Illegality: the trade unions under the Socialist Law
     1878–1890 51
     1. Political disenfranchisement and social policy:
        the Bismarckian state and the working class 51
     2. The trade unions go underground 54

IV. The unions under the Wilhelminian Empire: the breakthrough
    of mass organization 1890–1914 62
    1. The organization of industrial capitalism: the economic and
       social development of the Wilhelminian Empire 62
    2. Organizational problems on the road to the mass union . . 69
         The Free trade unions 69 – The Hirsch-Duncker trade
         associations 75 – The Christian trade unions 77 –
         Structural obstacles to organization 80 – Ideological
         and political divisions within the working class and
         the split in the trade union movement 84
    3. Conflicts over the independence of the trade unions 87
         Free trade unions and the SPD: from subordination to
         equality 87 – The Christian unions, the Catholic
         Church and the Centre Party: interdenomination-
         ism and party political neutrality put to the test 94

4. Industrial struggle, collective agreements and social reform: trade union work under the Empire 97
5. Trade union reform policy under the authoritarian state: a balance sheet 105

V. Upheaval: the trade unions in the First World War 1914–1918 109
1. Beginnings of the political truce: for defence of the realm, peace through victory and social reform 109
2. Towards political integration 114
3. The trade union mass movement and non-union mass protest 123

VI. The struggle for a new political order: the trade unions in the early years of the Weimar Republic 129
1. The trade unions in the revolution of 1918–19 129
2. Policy changes and union reorganization, 1919–20 139

The Free trade unions 140 – The Christian-national unions 147 – The Hirsch-Duncker associations 150 – International trade union confederations 150 – Membership trends 151

3. Back on the defensive: from the Kapp Putsch to inflation . 153

VII. The trade unions' role in constructing the social state 1924–1930 159
1. Heading for the "social state"? The middle years of the Weimar Republic 159
2. The unions' organizational consolidation 168
3. The beginnings and limits of a joint programme of all the national union federations 170
4. Into the crisis: the Ruhr iron dispute 1928 176

VIII. In the shadow of the Depression: the dissolution of the trade unions 1930–1933 180
1. The Depression and the weakening of the trade union organizations 180
2. Powerless in the crisis 185

The collapse of the Grand Coalition in March 1930 185 – The "Brüning Era": fruitless tolerance and loyalty 186 – Against the Papen Cabinet: powerless opposition 197 – The Schleicher cabinet: a last-minute attempt at stabilization 201

3. The trade unions in the Weimar Republic: a balance sheet . 202

IX.   Under the National Socialist dictatorship: persecution, resistance and exile 1933–1945 204
    1. Between protest and compliance: the end of the trade unions under the National Socialists 204
    2. The social order of the "Führer state" 210
    3. Trade unionists in the resistance and in exile 216

X.   Between hopes of reconstruction and restoration: the re-establishment of the trade unions 1945–1949 224
    1. From local beginnings to national organizations 224
    2. Trade union work under occupation law 231
    3. The foundation of the German Trade Union Federation . . 241
    4. The post-war period – a "wasted opportunity"? 245

XI.   Social successes and political defeats: the trade unions in the years of the "economic miracle" 1950–1965 247
    1. The disputes over the Law on Co-determination in the Coal and Steel Industry and the Company Statute Law 247
    2. The unions' share in the "economic miracle": policy on wages, working hours and social welfare 258
        The economic trend 259 – Pay policy: a fair wind 260 – Heading for the 40-hour week 267 – Strike policy 270 – Decisions of principle on social policy 273
    3. The trade unions as a political opposition 276
        Against rearmament and the issue of nuclear equipment to the Bundeswehr 278 – The start of the conflict over the emergency laws 283
    4. Under the impact of the "economic miracle": social change, organizational problems and a new policy direction 290

XII. A new departure: the trade unions in the years of social reform 1966–1974/76 302
    1. Trade unions in politics: shared responsibility and a share in shaping events 303
        The Grand Coalition: fighting the crisis, social policy initiatives and the adoption of the emergency laws 304 – The first years of the Social-Liberal coalition: social reforms – aims and realities 313
    2. Collective bargaining: from a low profile, via spontaneous strikes to a more aggressive approach 323
    3. Good times for trade union organization: increase in membership and heyday of the "co-operative economy" 329

XIII. Power and impotence of the trade unions in the crisis of the
1970s and 1980s 336
    1. Cyclical and structural crises, mass unemployment and
organizational stagnation 336
    2. On to the political defensive 341

        The "Schmidt Era": the start of an uphill struggle 342 –
        After the "watershed" of autumn 1982: on the side-
        lines 346

    3. The unions fall back on their own strength: collective bar-
gaining on a collision course 357
    4. A phase of reorganization: problem areas in trade union
policy 368

Conclusion: an appraisal of the achievements and prospects of trade
union policy 375

Appendix

I. *Tables*

1. Membership of the national trade union federations
    a) The Free, Christian and Hirsch-Duncker trade unions, 1868–1932 383
    b) Free, Christian-national and Hirsch-Duncker salaried employees' federations 1920–1931 386
    c) German Trade Union Federation (DGB) and German Salaried Employees' Union (DAG) 1951–1987 387
2. Industrial action
    a) Industrial disputes in 1848, 1869, 1871–1882 and 1884–1890 388
    b) Industrial disputes conducted by the Free trade unions, 1890–1898 388
    c) Industrial disputes (strikes and lockouts) affecting workers in trade and industry 1899–1933 389
    d) Industrial disputes 1949–87 390
3. Wages and salaries
    a) Real wages of workers in trade and industry under the Empire 1871–1913 391
    b) Real wages of workers in trade and industry under the Weimar Republic and the "Third Reich" 1925–39 391
    c) Real gross hourly and weekly wages of workers in West German industry, 1950–78 392
    d) Average gross wages of workers in industry in 1913–14 and 1925–86 393
    e) Wage differences between the sexes in the textile industry, 1913–78 394
4. Working hours
    a) Length of the working day and working week in industry, 1800–1918 395
    b) The length of the working week in industry, 1919–83 397
5. Unemployment
    a) Unemployment rates, 1887–1939 398
    b) Unemployment rates, 1950–87 399
6. Structure of the labour force
    a) Persons in paid employment by economic sector, 1882–1987 . 400
    b) Employment categories 1895–1987 401

II. *Bibliography*
1. Bibliographies 402
2. Trade Union History 402

III. *Abbreviations* 412

IV. *Glossary of other organizations* 417

V. *Index of Names* 419

The Author 423

Introduction

For some time now, the trade union convoy has been contending with "heavy seas", in the words of the periodical "Gewerkschaftliche Monatshefte". Who can forget the loss of credibility caused by the "Neue Heimat" scandal? The circumstances surrounding the management and sale of the "flagship" of co-operative enterprise were bound to increase the suspicion encountered by large bureaucratic organizations on all quarters today. Calls for cuts in working hours without loss of wages and for safeguarding the position of wage earners in industrial law meet with a more subdued response now; in an age of mass unemployment they are liable to be condemned as symptoms of narrow sectional politics, benefiting only those fortunate enough to be "in work".

If it is the unions themselves and their policies that are chiefly to blame for this loss of credibility, there are also a number of problems besetting them from without that reinforce the impression that the unions are in crisis. Firstly, the unions' influence and freedom of action are severely restricted by economic problems and mass unemployment. Then there is the political defensive against the champions of supply-side economic policies. Finally, there are the difficulties of finding a negotiable path away from an outmoded industry-based growth ideology, in the direction of an environment-friendly goods-and-services society. As if this were not enough, many contemporary observers see the "end of the labour movement' looming up, maintaining that it (and the trade unions) have lost their core support with the disintegration of the industrial working class in the wake of technological and cultural change.

There is no overlooking the symptoms of crisis. But do they really justify the assumption so often made that the trade unions, the "dinosaurs of the industrial age", have outlived their usefulness and that, like the industrial society that spawned them, they have no future? Such prognostications, delivered in the tone of utter conviction used to such effect by the media pundits – stemming from bitter disappointment or malicious glee according to political stance – are somewhat premature. But the questions they raise about the present and hence future importance of the trade unions are valid ones. Which aspects of the trade unions and their policies are outdated and which are here to stay? Where is there potential for development? Answers to these questions can only be found by looking back into history and, as we do so, three issues in particular will attract our attention:

- How have the unions contributed to social and economic development – especially to the improvement of workers' conditions, the formation of the "social state" and the construction, defence and stabilization of democracy?
- What were (and are) the necessary conditions for union success, and the factors behind union defeats?
- How have the trade unions' importance and role changed in the course of almost 150 years of German social history? Or, to put it another way, are the unions really "finished", as is often claimed?

My concern in this book is with the background conditions and self-imposed aims of union policy, the effort expended and the results achieved. Following my historical survey, the unions' achievements are assessed in a kind of closing "balance sheet", thus enabling us to view the current union crisis in perspective and pick out more clearly the novel features of the present situation. Can a look back at history do more than that? True, history offers no specific guidance for current political decision-making. But it teaches us how important it is to analyse both one's own and one's opponents' interests, strategies and weapons. It gives us a better eye for the unchanging pattern of argument and action, thus helping us to explore new issues in all their complexity. The history of the trade unions is a rebuff to sceptics who claim that all that can be learned from history is that history has nothing to teach us; for the birth and development of joint workers' action by and through organization was and still is a continuing learning process, a manifestation of the continuous assimilation of historical experience.

Even though change, as we shall see, is virtually the only stable element in union history, we must be clear in our minds about what trade unions are, exactly. Let us define them as follows: democratic organizations with long-term aims, formed by workers who have joined of their own free will, which, independently of employers, state, Church and political parties, represent their members' economic, social and political interests, inter alia by means of the strike. Although every union has not always met the "requirements" of this abstract description, for an historical account it is a necessary guideline, enabling us to distinguish trade unions from other organizations of wage earners (i.e. manual or white-collar workers). For instance, religious workers' associations, even if they do represent their members' interests vis-à-vis the employers, are not real trade unions because of their commitment to the church concerned. This also applies to the employer-backed "sweetheart unions" dedicated to maintaining industrial peace by expressly renouncing the strike weapon. The early history of trade unionism shows, however, that it is not always easy to draw a clear line between the various forms of workers' organization – say, between a political party and a trade union, or even between employers' and employees' associations.

The author would like to thank the staff of the Archives of Social Democracy and the Archives of the German Trade Union Federation for their kind assistance in the preparation of this book. I am indebted to my colleagues at the Department of Social and Contemporary History and the Institute of Social History for my stimulating discussions with them, particularly Beatrix W. Bouvier, Dieter Dowe and the late Kurt Klotzbach. I am particularly grateful to Heike Spanier and Andrea Mesecke for turning my handwritten manuscript into a legible typescript, and to Barrie Selman for translating it into English.

I. Industrialization, the development of the working class and the beginnings of the trade union movement around the middle of the nineteenth century

In order to understand what was "new" about the labour movement, and the trade union movement in particular, and to appreciate the achievement of the union pioneers, it is necessary to form a picture of the economic, political and social situation in the first half of the nineteenth century. After all, the formation of trade unions was a response by sections of the working class to the challenge of the Industrial Revolution and the "social question", which left their stamp on the first, tentative moves to form unions.

1. Industrialization and the emergence of the working class: the development of the "social question"

The emergence of the working class and the development of the "social question" were the direct consequences of industrialization, which in the nineteenth century began to transform the face of Germany and the lives of its people. Although paid labour, poverty and distress existed in pre-industrial society, too, they were formerly accepted as the will of God, whereas the wage labour and mass impoverishment of the nineteenth century triggered off demands for (radical) social change. Unlike its consequences, the causes of industrialization have not been fully clarified; at best it is possible to point to a number of interlocking conditions that are cause and effect simultaneously.[1]

The prerequisite and driving force of industrialization were above all the technical innovations that transformed the exploitation of mineral resources and increased the productivity of labour. The great novelty was, more than anything else, the introduction of machines to generate power and their use as machine tools. Important stages in the process of mecha-

---

1 See: Friedrich-Wilhelm Henning: Die Industrialisierung in Deutschland 1800 bis 1914 (Paderborn, 1976); Gerd Hohorst, Jürgen Kocka, Gerhard A. Ritter: Sozialgeschichtliches Arbeitsbuch. Materialien zur Statistik des Kaiserreiches 1870–1914 (Munich 1975); Jürgen Kocka, Lohnarbeit und Klassenbildung. Arbeiter und Arbeiterbewegung in Deutschland 1800–1875 (Berlin and Bonn 1983)

nization, which began in England, were the invention and construction of the steam engine (1765), the spinning machine (1769), the power loom (1786) and the steam locomotive (1803–4 and 1814). However, these were slow to reach Germany, where their spread was patchy. If one places the entire emphasis on the introduction of new technologies, as far as Germany is concerned the decades from 1830 to 1850 may be regarded as the prelude to industrialization, which developed from the middle of the century onwards – thus somewhat later than in England, but more rapidly.

A few facts will suffice to illustrate the course of events. Whereas in 1849 there were only 651 permanent steam engines with an output of 18,775 horsepower throughout the Rhineland and Westphalia, a quarter of a century later there were 11,706 producing 379,091 horsepower. Railway construction was both a consequence of and a spur to economic growth: it not only created jobs in the iron and steel industry but also brought a whole new system of transport into being, giving many areas access to a nationwide market for the first time. Whereas Prussia had 3,869 km of railway in 1850, by 1870 this had risen to 11,523 km, and the number of locomotives had increased in the same period from 498 to 3,485. Railway construction – for the whole of the German Reich – also highlights the acceleration of industrialization after the formation of the Reich (1871): the railway network expanded from 28,000 km in 1875 to 65,000 km by 1913.

The way in which Germany lagged behind England on the one hand, and the pace of industrialization after the formation of the Reich on the other, are evident from the example of German pig iron production – which may also serve to illustrate the development of heavy industry, the leading sector in turning Germany into a highly industrialized nation. Between 1850 and 1871 it rose from 200,000 to 1.6 million tonnes, reaching some 14 m tonnes in 1910; whereas in England, with an output of 6.7 m tonnes in 1871, it had "only" risen to a little over 10 m tonnes by 1910. The rapid increase in iron manufacturing, which was even exceeded by steel production, was also due to technical innovations that did not change the working patterns of heavy industry until the second half of the nineteenth century. Steam engines had been used since the 1840s for pumping water out of the coalmines and transporting men and materials, making it possible to open deeper coal seams and increase output. A rise in coal output was a precondition for the growth in the production of iron and especially steel, which was given a boost by the Bessemer converter in 1861 and the Thomas process in 1878–79.

The effects of mechanization in the first half of the nineteenth century are clearly illustrated by the textile industry, which in Germany – unlike

England – was in the vanguard of industrialization only in its early stages. In 1800, 77 spinners were still needed to operate every thousand spindles; in 1865–69, only 14. As, moreover, machine work was considered light work, it was increasingly women and children that were recruited. In 1830, children under fourteen comprised almost one third of the Saxony cotton mill workers, and more than half were women.

Industrial growth was greatly stimulated and favoured by general political and legal conditions. Let us recall the "liberation of the peasants" in Prussia, which in the decades after 1807 encouraged the emergence of a rural underclass of former serfs, now made available as "free" labourers. Another crucial factor was the legal backing given to the freedom to conclude contracts of employment; for instance, Article 134 of the Prussian Trade Regulations of 17 January 1845: "The relations between independent tradesmen and their journeymen, assistants and apprentices shall be laid down by an agreement freely arrived at by the parties."[2] The text is based, of course, on the illusion that employers and employees are economically equally powerful parties in negotiations. In addition, mention should be made of the dissolution of the craft guilds and the gradual introduction of freedom to practise a trade in the period 1810–45, resulting in overmanning in some trades and a consequent increase in competition. Again, it should not be forgotten that the foundation of the Zollverein (customs union) under Prussian leadership brought some 23 million people together into a united customs and trading area in 1833–34. The creation of a uniform exchange and commercial law in the early 1850s and 1860s and the standardization of the currency and coinage systems and the postal service following the foundation of the Reich in 1871 did much to facilitate economic activity in the long term. Government reforms thus created favourable legal and political conditions for economic development on the one hand; on the other, by "liberating" the peasants and guaranteeing the freedom to conclude contracts of employment, they led directly to the formation of the "modern" working class.

Finally, it was of major importance that capital was required to set industrialization in motion and to keep it moving. The nineteenth century saw the triumph of industrial capitalism as an economic system, with its stress on private ownership and private access to capital. This capital is invested in companies that produce and sell goods for profit. Capitalism's profit-mindedness – epitomized ideologically by Manchester liberalism – unleashed tremendous forces for economic development. On the one hand, it brought about the rise of the bourgeoisie, which became the lead-

---

2 Preussische Gesetzessammlung 1845, p. 41 ff.

ing economic stratum, and before long the leading social stratum, too. But, on the other hand, it created or exacerbated social evils on a scale not seen before. It thus gave rise to the clash of interests between capital and labour, between the employer as the owner of the means of production and the wage-earner who owned neither the machines and tools nor the raw materials, still less the finished products made by him.

There were soon growing numbers who were bitterly aware of their economic and social situation and saw the employers as their adversaries; but the contradiction between capital and labour by no means created a united "working class" that thought and acted as one man. The workers were and remained split and divided – by social origin, sex, trade, industry, income, religion, political conviction, age, marital status, domicile and so on. It is all these factors taken together that comprised, as they still do, the individual's political consciousness, which is moulded not by one basic contradiction alone but by many different social and political influences, personal experiences and so forth. The labour movement would time after time reflect the divisions within the working class; for at no time – least of all in the early years around the middle of the nineteenth century – was the working class consciousness as unified as many theoreticians and politicians expected, in view of the opposing positions of the "workers" and the "employers".

Alongside the triumphal progress of technical innovations, the changes in the overall legal and political conditions and the advance of capitalist economic forms, another significant feature of the nineteenth century transformation of society as a whole was population growth. The population of Germany rose from 24 million in 1800 to more than 36 m in 1856 and to 56 m in 1900. The chief reason for this population increase, which not only provided manpower but also created a market for mass-produced goods (albeit limited by restricted purchasing power), was declining mortality due to improved hygiene, medical treatment and nutrition.

∗

What did industrialization mean to the people concerned? Work, the environment and every aspect of human life was affected. A rough idea of the advance of industrial capitalism can be gained from changes in the numbers of those employed in the various sectors of the economy. Although continuing to rise in absolute terms, the number of those engaged in agriculture as a proportion of the entire working population fell from 59 per cent in 1825 to 55 per cent in 1850 and 38 per cent in 1914. By way of contrast, the proportion of those engaged in trade and industry rose over the same period from 21 to 24 to 37 per cent, and those working in the service sector of the economy increased from 17 to 21 to 25 per cent.

From the mid-nineteenth century on it was already possible to see which were to be the key industrial centres. Heavy industry, dependent on iron and coal deposits, began to set its stamp on entire regions: Upper Silesia, the Ruhr and Saar areas became industrial landscapes to which people streamed in their thousands. The population of the Ruhr district grew from 360,000 in 1850 to 3.5 m by 1914. The number of major cities increased rapidly. Whereas in 1800 there were only two German cities with a population exceeding 100,000 – Berlin (172,000) and Hamburg (130,000) – there were three in 1850 (Berlin, Hamburg and Munich), eight in 1871, and 48 by 1914.

Just as industrialization and urbanization changed the human environment, the industrial mode of production transformed working life. The operatives "served" the machines, whose operating speed and "capabilities" determined the course and duration of the work process. Division of labour and the fragmentation of production to the point of routine monotony; filth, noise, stench and health hazards; the separation of workplace and home; subjection to the dictates of the "millowner" in all matters of time and work – these phrases must be sufficient description of the process of "alienation" that the industrial mode of production imposed on growing numbers of working people.

The surplus of labour – former farmers and serfs, journeymen and craftsmen from trades in decline – had noticeable effects on the labour market. Owing to the competition between workers, the burdens of economic competition could be shifted on to the working people in the shape of more ruthless exploitation. Despite differences between occupations, companies and regions, the thirteen-hour day was the norm until the middle of the nineteenth century. Until the early 1870s, real wages had been pushed below the level of the early years of the century. In fact, the wage situation had in many cases been made worse by the truck system, that is, payment in goods instead of in money. Housing conditions also reflected social distress: it was by no means unusual for whole families of six or more persons to inhabit one or two rooms.

*

The working class – male and female workers and their families – were largely defenceless against the disastrous social phenomena that accompanied the rise of capitalism. The beginnings of state intervention were first seen in the protection of children and young people. Prussia was first to restrict child labour in 1839, partly at the insistence of army officers who feared that their "recruitment material" might be harmed. It was no longer permitted to employ children between nine and sixteen for more than ten hours per day in factories and mines; night work and working on Sundays and holidays were prohibited. But as these regulations were not always complied with, under the Prussian Trade Regulations of 17 January 1845 the local police were instructed to ensure that where journeymen and apprentices were employed due heed was paid to the "preservation of health and morals".

These measures to protect workers, particularly children and young people, from the worst excesses of industrialization were, however, confronted by political and legal obstacles designed to prevent any independent, organized defence of the workers' interests. Article 182 of the Prussian Trade Regulations forbade any agreement by trainees, journeymen or factory hands to strike on pain of up to one year's imprisonment; the "formation of associations by factory hands, journeymen, trainees or apprentices without police permission is punishable by fines of 50 Talers or up to four weeks' imprisonment for the instigators and leaders, and fines of up to 20 Talers or a fortnight's imprisonment for other participants, unless more severe penalties are laid down in law."[3] As growing numbers of workers became aware that their position was determined by economic and political factors and hence open to change, their readiness to get together and organize increased – but so did the determination of the employers and the State to resist.

2. Towards the formation of the first trade unions

There was a long way to go before the emergence of the first workers' organizations. This reflected the arduous learning process that culminated in the realization by journeymen and workers – prompted by earlier experiences and supported by socially committed people from outside the working class – that their interests would be best represented by organizations of their own.

In the first decades of industrialization, that is the 1830s and 1840s, there were seldom any moves towards more permanent forms of organization in associations. Earlier forms of organization were the friendly societies (Unterstützungskassen), designed to provide mutual help in

---

3 Preussische Gesetzessammlung 1845, p. 41 ff.

cases of sickness and death, and support for members "on tramp" (Wanderunterstützung). There were also the educational associations (Bildungsvereine) – for example, those of Berlin (1844), Hamburg (1844–45) and Hanover (1845) – and strike associations formed for specific cases. These educational associations gave impetus to the idea of autonomous organization, even though it was representatives of the middle classes and the Church who were often instrumental in setting them up and running them. The protest movements of the years preceding the March revolution of 1848 showed through countless petitions to employers and the authorities the people's growing discontent with social and political conditions. It was not so much the hunger riots, isolated cases of machine-wrecking and the protests of craftsmen and home workers against distributors and merchants, as in the Weavers' Revolt of 1844, that new, trend-setting forms of militancy emerged, but in the strikes and boycotts organized by journeymen and railway navvies. Organization and social protest – these were the two elements of social development around the middle of the century that were to bind the labour movement together.

But it was not the poorest of the poor who became the champions of organization as an idea. Rather, it was the artisans and journeymen. Day labourers and home workers had neither the organizational tradition and experience nor the self-esteem; neither did they have the financial resources to lend permanence to sporadic and short-lived revolt by means of expensive organizations. Even taking into account the numerical weakness of the industrial working class around the middle of the century, it is not surprising that skilled manual workers were the chief advocates of organization. With their professional self-esteem rooted in the pride of the pre-industrial craftsman, they felt the capitalist version of the employment relationship and the change in working conditions to be an attack on their own hopes and expectations. While in the old days the journeyman could assess the appropriateness of his wage by comparing it with the price of the commodity, and the demand for a "fair wage", allowing a "reasonable" standard of living, was perfectly realistic, the calculations behind modern industrial production were impenetrable. Furthermore, work became fragmented by the increasing use of machines and craft skills were devalued. Finally, whereas the journeyman had previously risen to be an independent master craftsman as a matter of course, for most journeymen this was now unattainable. It was not workers but journeymen who set up the first associations, the aims of which were partly professional and partly radical and democratic.

*

A professional awareness of tradition in combination with social and political experience of the present thus favoured the emergence of workers' organizations. That is shown by the journeymen's associations (Gesellenbünde), which, while harking back to a medieval tradition of combination and militancy, would have been unlikely to arise had it not been for the fear of social decline and the liberal, democratic ideas with which itinerant journeymen came into contact, particularly in Switzerland and France. Worth mentioning is the secret, radical democratic "League of Outcasts" (Bund der Geächteten), formed in Paris in 1834 by emigrated intellectuals and journeymen. It was from this that the "League of the Just" (Bund der Gerechten) split away in 1837. The League of the Just was initially dominated by the social revolutionary ideas of the Magdeburg journeyman tailor Wilhelm Weitling. Later, in 1847, under the influence of Karl Marx and Friedrich Engels, it renamed itself "The Communist League" (Bund der Kommunisten).

The importance of this League and its basic principles to the subsequent development of (not only) the labour movement cannot be overestimated. February 1848 saw the publication in London of the Communist Manifesto. Taking as their starting point the materialist conception of history, according to which the "history of all hitherto existing society is the history of class struggles", Marx and Engels – with developments in England before their very eyes – laid bare the workings of modern capitalism. The basis of man's dependence on man, the basis of exploitation and oppression, the basis also of the political hegemony of the bourgeoisie was the private ownership of the means of production. As it developed, society would split up into "two great hostile camps, into two great classes directly facing each other: Bourgeoisie and Proletariat". But "the development of Modern Industry [. . .] cuts from under its feet the very foundation on which the bourgeoisie produces and appropriates product". For as capitalism becomes increasingly established, the working class becomes ever stronger. And so the bourgeoisie "produces, above all, its own grave-diggers. Its fall and the victory of the proletariat are inevitable".

The Communists' aim was to bring about this victory by "formation of the proletariat into a class, overthrow of the bourgeois supremacy, conquest of political power by the proletariat". Hence the necessity of abolishing private ownership of the means of production, and the "forcible overthrow of all existing social conditions".The concluding sentences resounded like a clarion call: "Let the ruling classes tremble at a Communistic revolution. The proletarians have nothing to lose but their chains. They have a world to win. Working men of all countries, unite!"

Although the Communist Manifesto was later to achieve major political significance, in the mid-nineteenth century it was out of step with the political and social situation in Germany. The proletariat was not yet a mass, there were no proletarian mass organizations, and the nascent working class had yet to develop an awareness of its common interests. Without doubt, the 1848 revolution speeded up this process of consciousness-raising by politicizing the people.

With its main aims of national unity, parliamentary democracy on a constitutional basis and equal suffrage, the revolution of March 1848 was essentially a bourgeois revolution. The accession of Friedrich Wilhelm IV in Prussia in 1840 had awoken hopes among the liberally minded middle class of an end to absolutist supremacy. Then, against the background of the 1840s famine crises, disappointment at the lack of reform allowed the February revolution in France to spread to Germany. But the revolution was chiefly enacted by artisans and workers, who took to the barricades not only for democracy but also for their own social and economic objectives. The direct result of the revolution was the convening of the Frankfurt Parliament in spring 1848, which drew up a constitution in St Paul's Church. The few months of the revolution and the pre-revolutionary period, when it appeared as though the monarchies could be turned into democracies, were sufficient to give the idea of organization its breakthrough.

*

And so in 1847–48 the first Catholic and Protestant workers' associations were set up, linking up with early socially critical reflections by Christian laymen and clerics and the tradition of devout and charitable associations. They were under clerical leadership and thus caught up in the Church hierarchy, and were intended to promote faith, culture and conviviality and to raise the worker's class awareness, thus helping to find a solution to the "social question".

Concurrently with the development of the first working men's associations, Adolph Kolping's idea, first achieved in 1847, of Catholic journeymen's associations, designed to provide bachelors with religious instruction, occupational training and a comradely home atmosphere, gained ground; in 1855 the journeymen's associations had 12,000 members, and by 1870–71 some 70,000.

Efforts of this kind to attract the workers, in particular, found favour with the Catholic Church. Special mention should be made of Bishop Wilhelm Emmanuel Baron von Ketteler, who, beginning with his Advent sermons of 1848, repeatedly came out with growing vehemence in favour of improving the social and political position of the working class. The Protestant Church, on the other hand, tended to stand back; Johann Heinrich Wichern's support for social welfare as part of his "Inner Mission" programme was almost an exception to the rule. But in the mid-1800s, both Catholic and Protestant social reformers were agreed that the "social question" was above all a question of morality, regarding the reform of people's hearts and minds as a task for the Church. Their plan was to establish associations *for* the workers.

∗

But the revolution brought home to growing numbers of workers the need for organizations of their own. This realization was encouraged by the March revolution, which created the necessary legal conditions for the expansion of workers' and journeymen's organizations by establishing freedom of the press, association and assembly. Furthermore, the Frankfurt Parliament was "discovered" as the right address for demands to include democratic and social reform in the constitutional discussions.

Here we might point to the initiative taken by the typesetter, Stephan Born, who in April 1848, with the Berlin Central Committee for Working Men, called a General Congress of German Workers to meet in Berlin in late August and early September that year, when the "Fraternity of Working Men" (Arbeiterverbrüderung) was founded. This, the first German working class "mass movement", derived its support chiefly from journeymen and skilled workers and partly also from master craftsmen. The September 1848 social policy programme of the Fraternity not only recommended the traditional ways of social self help – support for journeymen on the tramp, death and sickness benefits – but in addition to calling for the introduction of a certificate of employment, also stated its aims of establishing producer and consumer cooperatives and obtaining legal backing for the ten-hour day. It also published its own journal, "The Fraternity".

In any case, as early as June 1848 the Berlin Central Committee for Working Men had approached the Frankfurt National Assembly with pioneering demands. These included: the setting of minimum wages and fixing of working hours by committees of workers and master craftsmen or employers; regulation of the number of apprentices a master was allowed to take on by similar committees; a commitment by the workers to adhere to the agreed wage; the abolition of indirect taxes, the introduction of progressive income tax with exemption for those with only the barest necessities of life; free schooling and free public libraries; the repeal of all special travel laws for working men, the general right of domicile

Fighting on the barricades in the Alexanderplatz, Berlin, on 18 March 1848

anywhere, freedom to move and safeguards against official highhanded-ness; the employment of the jobless in state-run institutions, the creation of model workshops by the state and state support for the destitute and all those disabled at work; reduction of the minimum age of candidates for the Prussian Chamber to twenty-four. But this initiative foundered, like other proposals for social reform, on Parliament's liberal-minded major-ity, whose sole aim (and the importance of this should not be underrated) was to win the bourgeois freedoms and achieve national unity. At any rate, social affairs were given short shrift in the constitutional discussions.

The Fraternity of Working Men did, however, break new ground in another, more wide-ranging sense. Under the slogan "One for all, and all for one", it turned the principles of self help, solidarity and social reform into cornerstones of the labour movement. Self help and unity were the watchwords of the early labour movement. Everywhere – for instance, in the appeal by the Central Committee of the Fraternity of Working Men to all workers and workers' associations of 18 September 1848[4] – the mess-

---

4 Quot. Horst Schlechte, Die Allgemeine Deutsche Arbeiterverbrüderung 1848–1850. Dokumente des Zentralkomitees für die deutschen Arbeiter in Leipzig (Weimar, 1979), pp. 338–40

age was: "We workers must help ourselves." And here, too, we find the call to close ranks: "Be united, then you will be strong." The dividing lines between association, political party and trade union were very fluid around the middle of the nineteenth century. Thus it was that at different times not only did a number of local trade societies, such as that of the Berlin mechanical engineers, belong to the Fraternity, but in 1850 the cigar-makers' association, which along with the printers' association was one of the first German trade unions, was also affiliated to it.

*

The first national trade union was established at the initiative of status-conscious journeymen printers and printing office proprietors. They – that is, the delegates of 12,000 printers and typesetters – founded the National Printers' Association (Nationaler Buchdrucker-Verein) at a congress held in Mainz from 11 to 14 June 1848. Their purpose, according to their petition to the Frankfurt National Assembly[5], was to defend themselves against "being forced into factory work", which they feared would be the outcome of the introduction of the steam engine and high-speed printing press. The association's main aims were protection from social relegation and other risks, especially the consequences of seasonal employment and falling wages. These aims were emphasized in its petition to the National Assembly, which also called for the setting up of a ministry of labour, the abolition of all laws discriminating against workers, the supervision of apprentices' training, the regulation of machinery and the creation of a comprehensive insurance scheme. The demand for agreed national rates of pay for typesetters and printers met with the opposition of the proprietors and led to a number of industrial disputes. As a result the wage agreement decision was amended at a second congress – held in Frankfurt in late August 1848 – which prompted the journeymen to leave the General German Printers' Association and set up the Gutenberg League in Berlin in late September–early October 1849.

According to the League's constitution of October 1849[6], its aim was to "justify, improve and secure the material and spiritual welfare of printers and typefounders, and also that of proprietors and trainees". So this association, too, initially derived its support from status-conscious printing workers and proprietors. In October 1849 the League had 3,000 members

---

5 Reprinted in: Willi Krahl, Der Verband der deutschen Buchdrucker, vol. 1 (Berlin, 1916), p. 219 f.
6 Gutenberg No. 51 of 22 December 1849, p. 202 f.

in 148 places. Headed by Karl Fröhlich, it demanded not only a curb on apprenticeships but also the setting of standards rates of pay and working hours to reduce competition between workers. The League also succeeded, at least initially, in building up a system of benefits that included travelling, sickness, disability and life insurance. It was never a militant organization; like the working men's associations, it was more concerned with solving problems within the trade by putting its demands to the employers and government bodies in negotiations. But this in itself, together with the offer of further vocational training measures, the democratization of society and the setting up of benefit schemes, pointed the way ahead to trade unionism.

*

1848 also saw the setting up of the Association of German Cigar Workers (Assoziation der Zigarren-Arbeiter Deutschlands) at the first congress of cigar workers, held in Berlin from 25 to 29 September. Unlike the printers, who wished to defend their status, the cigar workers were principally concerned with improving their position and the respect in which they were held. Although the work was unhealthy, it was considered light, and cheap labour – women, children and prison inmates – was employed, which did little to boost the cigar workers' reputation in a highly status-minded society. The fact that cigar production was concentrated in certain regions – Westphalia, Saxony and Baden – obviously helped the idea of organization to gain acceptance; the silence of the work process was conducive to conversation; and the workers' distress was such that relief was urgently required.

The formation of this association again shows quite clearly the importance of the guild as a model, even when there was no such tradition within the trade. Thus one of the association's main aims was regulation of the labour market; it sought a ban on all child, female and prison labour. Furthermore, in the rules of 13 September 1849 the founders believed that they could oblige all cigar workers to join their association[7].

On the other hand, looking at the democratic structure of the organization, the system of self-financing through contributions and the demand for collective wage agreements, with courts of arbitration in cases of conflict with the employers, the beginnings of trade unionism were also in evidence. Industrial action was also one of the means whereby members' interests were to be defended, although the trade union formations of

---

7 Printed copy in the Hauptstaatsarchiv, Düsseldorf (Reg. Düsseldorf Präs. 861)

the revolutionary period can hardly be considered militant organizations. The Cigar Workers' Association also attempted to build up a benefits system and widows and orphans fund. Another of the aims set out in the constitution was further vocational training for members. The need for organization among the cigar workers may be gauged from the fact that under the leadership of Wenzel Kohlweck the association rapidly acquired 1000 members and by September 1849 it had 12,800 members in 77 places.

3. *Organizational setbacks in the reactionary 1850s*

Scarcely had the first working class organizations come into existence when they were banned in the period of reaction that set in. The nobility, the army and a compliant bourgeoisie prevented the implementation of political rights and liberties. True, the Prussian Association Law (Vereinsgesetz) of 11 March 1850 and the federal decision of 13 July 1854 guaranteed freedom of association and assembly; but on the other hand a blanket ban was introduced on all workers' associations with "political, socialist or communist aims". Also, all associations classified as political were forbidden to recruit women, schoolchildren and apprentices, and they were also prevented from setting up organizational links with one another. The Fraternity of Working Men, which in February 1850 had pressed for cooperation between political and trade union organizations with some success, at least amongst the cigar workers, the Gutenberg League and the Cigar Workers' Association all suffered political persecution in Prussia as early as 1850, and by 1854 in other parts of Germany, too. But the idea of organization was kept alive in the funds and benefit schemes until these, too, were dissolved or turned into state-controlled insurance schemes in 1853–54. Only individual schemes continued to run at company or local level, and these provided a jumping-off point in the 1860s.

The continuity of the trade union idea was thus not entirely broken in the 1850s. It was simply not possible to "prohibit" clandestine organizations, the experiences of union founders and members and, least of all, the everyday clash of interests with the employers, which led to "strike waves" in the 1850s, particularly in 1855 and 1857. But while the independent labour movement was smashed, there developed organizations which either appealed expressly to workers and journeymen or pressed for associations that bridged class and social strata. The co-operative idea, which also played a part in the Fraternity of Working Men, should be mentioned here. As Friedrich Wilhelm Raiffeisen, mayor of a village in Westerwald, did for agriculture, Hermann Schulze-Delitzsch had been advocating co-operative mergers between traders and artisans since the 1850s; as a convinced liberal, he hoped to protect the lower middle class against the advance of (large-scale) industry in this way. Although Schulze-Delitzsch also appealed to factory workers, they had little to gain from the formation of credit co-operatives, for they lacked not only money but also experience and training.

The 1850s showed the two-faced attitude of the authorities towards the working class: the independent organizations of the labour movement were crushed – at the same time as (very modest) efforts were made to alleviate the worst manifestations of the "social question". May 1853 saw the introduction in Prussia of government factory inspectors, whose prime duty it was to protect young people. Further, the minimum age for factory work was reduced to 12; minors between 12 and 14 years were no longer permitted to work more than seven hours a day. In 1854 the first steps towards sickness and disability insurance were taken. But measures of this nature achieved precisely nothing; the state was still overwhelmingly inclined to see the "social question" primarily as a policing problem.

It was not merely social discrimination against working people but also the legal obstacles, and in particular the ban on all their efforts to organize, that forced the labour movement to become politicized. For any demand for social improvements presupposed political rights which first had to be won. So long as there was no guaranteed freedom of assembly or association and no freedom of the press, any workers' organization had to give political demands a central place in its programme.

The period of reaction and its authoritarian legacy thus helped the labour movement to develop with all the more vigour and political motivation later on. It was possible to put the brakes on the labour movement for a while – but not on the process of economic and social change that produced it and to which it was a response. In a single decade, 1851–60, industrial production doubled, the railway network increased from 5,870 to 11,150 km, and the output of Germany's steam engines rose from 260,000 to 850,000 horsepower. Industrialization was proceeding apace – and with it the emergence of the working class.

II. The rise of the labour movement in the 1860s and 1870s

Industrialization did not really gather momentum in Germany until the 1850s, but in the decades that followed it proceeded at an ever increasing pace. This was a decisive factor in making the "social question" the dominating issue of the 1860s, alongside the problem of national unity, in the confrontations between the major ideological tendencies of the day – Christianity, liberalism and socialism – which were all to exert a lasting influence on the development of the trade union movement in Germany.

1. *The emergence of class society*

In the 1850s and 1860s it became perfectly clear that the future belonged to industry. Even in 1870 there were still more people employed in agriculture and handicraft than in industry, but their proportion of the working population was declining; mechanization was increasing its hold on small businesses and on small-scale manual production. Although Germany was still an agrarian country in 1870, it was by now firmly on course to become an industrial power. The nationalist fervour resulting from the Franco-Prussian War of 1870 and the proclamation of the Reich in 1871 certainly gave general impetus to economic development; but the freedom of trade (Gewerbefreiheit) taken over from the North German Confederation and the standardization of the monetary, stock market and postal systems and the French reparations gave rise to a "foundation boom", which soon – in 1873–74 – turned into a protracted economic downturn.

With the advent of industrial capitalism the bourgeoisie became the dominant class in economic terms. Although the bureaucracy, diplomatic service and military professions were still dominated by the Prussian nobility from the provinces east of the Elbe, it was the rising industry, the large trading companies and the banks that formed the foundation of the grande bourgeoisie's economic influence. But as in the 1850s, the bourgeoisie largely acquiesced, as far as its political aspirations were concerned, in the authoritarian monarchy; full of admiration for the policy of a strong Germany incorporated by the Chancellor, Otto von Bismarck, and swept away by visions of Germany's greatness and world stature, large sections of the bourgeoisie adopted Prussian concepts of virtue and supremacy: discipline, diligence, subordination, inculcated at home, at school and in the armed forces, became the dominating values. The same values – translated into a sort of entrepreneurial head-of-the-household outlook ('Herr-im-Hause-Standpunkt') – also held sway in working life.

In the 1870s – probably owing to the recession – economic power became increasingly concentrated. Cartels and large concerns formed. Names such as Alfred Krupp and Carl Ferdinand Baron von Stumm-Halberg became symbols of entrepreneurial success and the patriarchal, authoritarian treatment of the workers. Patriarchal attitudes and company welfare policies developed over these decades, denying the workers any say in economic matters and immunizing them against the blandishments of radical political or trade union organizations. This viewpoint could not have been better put than in Krupp's "Message to my dependents" of February 1877: he said that everyone must "do his duty in peace and harmony and in accordance with our directions". And addressing "his workers", he urged: "Enjoy what is given to you. When work is done, remain amongst your nearest and dearest, your parents, your wife, your children, and consider household and education. Let this be your politics and you will enjoy many a happy hour. But do not allow yourselves to become excited by national politics. Matters of state require more spare time and knowledge of conditions than the worker has. You will be doing your duty if you elect those recommended to you by persons whom you trust. But you will do nothing but harm if you seek to intervene in the lawful order. Playing politics down at the pub is expensive, too – you can find better things to do at home."[1]

In the 1850s and 60s the directors of large companies were generally also their owners; the same person thus wore both the employer's hat and the proprietor's. From the 1870s onwards, with the development of the stock market, these two roles grew apart, gradually at first and then more rapidly. The consequences were the growing anonymity of capital and the rise of the manager, answerable to the proprietors. Further, the 1870s saw the rise of entrepreneurs' organizations, representing the economic, social and political interests of their members. This period jolted both sides of industry into organizing: a number of anti-strike societies were founded, the first factory-owners' associations appeared, and 1875 saw the formation of the Central Association of German Industrialists, dominated by heavy industry.

---

1 Quot. Wilhelm Berdrow (ed.), Alfred Krupps Briefe 1826–1887 (Berlin, 1928), p. 342 ff.

Hand-in-hand with the advance of industrial capitalism, the above changes in the world of work and the workplace became more pronounced in the decades around the proclamation of the Reich, in particular the ruthless exploitation of the working class, continued urbanization with the attendant housing shortages, social uprooting and frequently appalling living conditions, exacerbated by low wages, undernourishment, unemployment and disease. Of course, it should be remembered that pay varied greatly according to industry, occupation, qualifications, age, sex and even region. In 1863 the weekly earnings of a worker in the Saxony textile industry around Crimmitschau were 1–1¼ Talers, of a Leipzig printer 6–7 Talers, and a Berlin mechanical engineer 12–13 Talers. These enormous wage differentials certainly hampered the development of a uniform worker consciousness, which was almost inevitable, given the experience of exploitation common to all workers and their marginalization and the discrimination against them in law and politics. This patronizing Big Brother attitude towards the working class was most obvious in the Prussian electoral system, which laid down three classes of voter, depending on income. In Berlin, for example, a voter belonging to the first class had 21 times as many votes as a third-class voter; in Wattenscheid, 1,100 times as many; and in Essen, Krupp was able to appoint one third of the town councillors with his vote alone.

Yet despite the evident trend in the 1860s and 70s towards a class society, the picture was not all black: there were also progressive, democratic forces at work in politics and society. Successive waves of legal reform in the 1860s, originating in the states of southern Germany, created a new political climate. With the dawn of the "New Era", democratic and social reform bills were expected and for this reason the old laws were applied less rigorously – in anticipation, as it were. Crucial to the development of trade unionism was the lifting of the ban on associations – first in Saxony (1861) and Weimar (1863) and finally throughout the North German Confederation (1869). But this was still a far cry from a guaranteed *freedom of association,* as is evident from Article 152 of the trade regulations of 21 June 1869[2]: "All prohibitions and penal sanctions against tradesmen, trainees, journeymen and factory hands for concluding agreements or forming associations for the purpose of obtaining improved wages or working conditions, in particular through the withdrawal of labour or the

---

2 Bundesgesetzblatt des Norddeutschen Bundes No. 26, 1869, p. 281

The power hammer "Fritz", inaugurated on 16 September 1861, made the Krupp cast steel works one of the largest forges in the world.

Krupp's Bessemer steelworks about 1900

locking out of workers," were lifted. On the face of it this sounded quite good – but it put a ball and chain around the workers' feet. For firstly the "right of association' did not apply to agricultural labourers, seafarers and canal-workers, railwaymen or state officials; secondly, Article 152 recognized not only the strike but also the lockout, even granting employeers the right to terminate the contract of employment (that is, sanctioning dismissal). Thirdly, it was still possible to declare the trade unions political associations, thus providing grounds for the application of legal restrictions on the right of association (including an all-out ban). Finally, Article 153 expressly limited the unions' freedom of action: for instance, recruiting members, picketing and even shouting "blackleg" were considered punishable acts: "Anyone who by the use of physical force, threats, insults or slander compels or seeks to compel others to subscribe to such agreements (Article 152) or to comply with them, or by similar means prevents or seeks to prevent others from withdrawing from such agreements, shall be liable to three months' imprisonment, unless the general criminal law lays down a more severe penalty."

But as we have already pointed out, the working class was by no means faced with a "united front" of exploiters and political adversaries. Growing numbers of more perceptive people were devoting their attention not only to the question of nationhood but also to the "social question" and proposing various different solutions.

Let us first turn to the Church, and the Catholic Church in particular. Although many advocates of social reform still had outdated ideas of a status-based social order, by championing and founding working men's associations on the one hand and by urging brotherly love and charity on their fellow-men on the other, they preached a balance between employers and workers. The mood of a new beginning in matters of social welfare not only took hold of individual areas, such as the Essen and Aachen districts, but also seized the biennial assemblies of Catholic churchmen. Before long, the Centre, the party of political Catholicism, was obliged to draw up a social policy programme and in 1877 a lathe-operator from Essen, Gerhard Stötzel, became the first worker to be admitted into its parliamentary group.

The leading figure of "social Catholicism" was, however, Bishop Ketteler, who advocated social reforms with a Christian flavour, a more energetic state social policy and organized self help for the working class. The fact that he turned to Ferdinand Lassalle, the founder of the Social Democratic General Association of German Working Men (Allgemeiner Deutscher Arbeiterverein – ADAV), for advice on some points of social reform shows how fluid the boundary between the camps was in the

1860s, even if any organized form of co-operation between the Church and Social Democracy or the trade unions was unthinkable. The description of social misery and exploitation and the criticism of labour's character as a commodity and of untrammelled economic liberalism contained in Ketteler's key work "The Worker Question and Christianity" (1864) come close to Lassalle's ideas. Like Lassalle he recommended as a solution the setting up of producer associations, though funded by voluntary contributions rather than the state, as proposed by Lassalle. In his speeches in 1869 at the Liebfrauenheide in Offenbach and at the Episcopal Conference in Fulda, Ketteler advocated wage rises, shorter working hours and a ban on child labour and factory work for mothers and girls. He gave his backing not only to the Catholic working men's associations but also to the interdenominational Christian-social associations, which in 1870 formed a federation in Elberfeld and at this time had some 200,000 members. The influx of new members enjoyed by the Catholic workers' and journeymen's associations and the Christian-social associations shows that religion still exercised an influence over large sections of the working class. Rapid industrialization and Bismarck's *Kulturkampf* against the Catholic Church helped to ensure that many workers, especially Catholic ones, retained their religious commitment and their ties with the Church.

There were also sections of the liberal bourgeoisie that showed some understanding of contemporary social problems – especially as they often saw the growing explosiveness of the issue as a threat to their own social position. Support for social reform – for example, in the shape of the Association for Social Policy (Verein für Socialpolitik) formed in 1872 by scientists, politicians, employers and clergymen – and the provision of educational associations and liberal trade unions were intended to check the build-up of radical protest movements. Under the motto "education and thrift" the idea was to enable the working class to move up in the world and become integrated into existing society. At the same time there were no doubt hopes that workers organized in liberally inclined associations would support the bourgeoisie in its confrontation with the nobility and the absolutist state, particularly in the constitutional clash with Bismarck, and come out in favour of national unity and the parliamentary system. In fact, this idea did catch on with some of the workers, who not only acquired specialist know-how through these educational associations but could also practise the principles of organization: the development and expression of informed opinion, and the representation of interests.

Finally, the 1860s saw the first stirrings of social democracy, which, though far from being a unified movement, at least derived most of its support from the workers themselves. It was within the ambit of these organizations that in the 1860s, and above all in 1868–69, a number of trade unions emerged, favoured by the lifting of the ban on association and the upturn in the economy.

2. *The breakthrough*

Even in the reactionary 1850s the continuity of the labour movement was not entirely broken; the experience of political suppression and worsening capitalist exploitation may have helped to show up the clash of interests between employer and employee, which still seemed surmountable to the founding fathers of trade unionism in 1848–49, in a harsher light. Furthermore, the shortcomings of government social policy confirmed the assumption that the main way of curing social ills was self help. Backed by sections of the liberal bourgeoisie and the Catholic Church, this idea won increasing support from the workers themselves, who had begun to organize into political parties and trade unions in the 1860s. These parties and unions developed in tandem; and in any case the demarcation lines between progressive liberal organizations and social democratic ones were by no means clearly defined.

So the continuity of the trade unions was not completely destroyed by the bans of the 1850s. This is illustrated most clearly by the fact that it was again the printers and cigar workers that were among the first occupational groups to make use of the "new freedoms" of the 1860s and form new associations. Commencing with the Leipzig Printers' Assistants' Association, set up in 1861–62, the idea of trade unionism quickly spread to many other cities. The merger of local associations was undoubtedly encouraged, more than anything, by experience of conflict with the employers. That is demonstrated by the "Threepenny Strike" (Dreigroschenstreik) in Leipzig in the spring of 1865 over the introduction of better piece rates. Even though the strike as a whole was a defeat for the printers, resulting only in small wage rises, the solidarity movement, reaching far beyond Leipzig itself, was a step in the direction of a new, common worker consciousness, as the basis of a wider organization; not only the printers but also workers in other trades supported the Leipzig strikers by collecting money for them.

Two immediate results of the Threepenny Strike are of special importance. The Printers' Association left the liberal Assembly of German Working Men's Associations, demonstrating its desire to break with the political and philosophical ideas of the bourgeoisie. Secondly, in autumn

1865 the Leipzig printers announced a congress of German printers, to be held in Leipzig at Whitsun 1866, to discuss the experiences of the strike. There, in May 1866, the German Printers' Union (Deutscher Buchdruckerverband) was founded. The main aim of the union – headed by Richard Härtel from 1867 on – was to achieve standard rates of pay for printers. It was above all experience of conflict and solidarity that had led to a clarification of the position: independence from political parties and supraregional combination – these were the lessons the printers learned from developments in the mid-1860s.

As for the importance of experience of conflict and strikes for the emergence of a sense of working class solidarity, the development of the printers' association was fairly typical of the early stage of trade union history. This is underlined by the example of the miners. After thousands of miners had submitted a petition in 1867 to the ministry responsible, seeking an amelioration of their wretched plight, in 1872 they proceeded to stage the first "mass strike", their resentment fuelled by disappointment at the failure of their petition. This strike, too, ended in defeat, but the strike committee that had been set up became the embryo of a miners' trade union.

Experience of industrial conflict was of major importance in virtually all the unions that were founded in rapid succession in the late 1860s and early 70s, profiting from the strength of the economy. It would be no exaggeration to speak of a wave of strikes from 1865 to 1873 (Table 2a), in which the textile and garment workers, engineering workers, printers and, in particular, the miners were the leading participants. This wave of strikes was accompanied by a trade union "foundation boom". In 1868–69 alone the trade associations of the tailors, bakers, carpenters, shoemakers, building workers, woodworkers, engineering workers and textile and garment workers all came into being. As the occupations indicate, these associations were by no means centred on industrial wage labour. Though trade unions did emerge in that sector, too, with the associations of miners, iron and steel workers, engineering workers and manufacturing workers, it was the craft-based trade associations that initially dominated, such as those of the printers, joiners and shoemakers. So to begin with, the unions were not very well represented in the centres of heavy industry; rather, they arose in the commercial regions of central Germany, the Rhine–Ruhr area and, above all, the major cities – Berlin, Hamburg, Hanover, Leipzig, Munich and Nuremberg.

The setting-up of trade unions in the 1860s was by no means a uniform process: there were major differences according to occupation and industry and also on a regional basis. The unions soon sought other recruits, too, such as semi-skilled and unskilled workers and women. But this proved difficult. Often it meant the formation of separate associations, as in the cases of the Manufacturing, Factory and Manual Workers' Association and the Manual and Factory Workers' Association. This shows the difficulty of bringing together craftsmen and skilled workers with considerable professional pride and less qualified labourers in *trade associations*. Thus the founding years of the 1860s and 70s were also a period of seeking, in which organizations both local and supraregional, both segregated by occupation and gender and all-embracing, short-lived and more permanent, co-existed. While the dominant trend even in the 1870s may have been the formation of central trade associations, it was by no means the only path taken.

The first few years after the formation of a trade union were naturally a time of constant efforts to set up a permanent executive and administration and to ensure efficient press relations and recruitment; in addition, all the associations sought to establish a stable system of benefits, partly as the best argument when joining up new members. Finally, with the following wind of a flourishing economy, they all attempted to formulate their economic and social demands and to achieve them through numerous cases of industrial action. Higher wages and shorter working hours (down to ten hours a day) were certainly the most important "material" goals of the unionized workers. But equally important were probably their efforts to resist the "bosses'" attempts to debase them and deny them their rights; again and again, strikers would call for an end to the "gagging" regulations in force in the factories and demand humane treatment by superiors and the right freely to join a trade union.

Disregarding political parties, the labour movement took two forms in the 1860s: temporary strike coalitions, which were rallying movements for specific conflicts, and local, but more long-term trade union associations, based on the principle of representative democracy through the election of delegates. These two forms of organization were often born out of industrial disputes with the employers, although naturally once the dispute was over only the trade unions were able to monitor the employers' compliance with the agreements reached and, if necessary, take the required action, or threaten to do so, without losing valuable time. Unions enjoyed another great advantage over strike coalitions: they were able to provide funds for industrial disputes and their existence as permanent organizations enabled them to "learn" – "storing" information on the tactics to use when taking militant action, for instance. Moreover, it swiftly became clear that strikes could not be an end in themselves: the cost to the workers was simply too high. Furthermore, major industrial disputes, especially defeats, repeatedly turned out to be the undoing of the organization involved. In fact, carefully devised objectives and methods soon became standard trade union policy. A resolution adopted by the Leipzig Social Democratic Workers' Association in May 1871 stated that a strike should only be called "if there is a compelling necessity and the necessary resources are available". The "establishment and maintenance of works cooperatives (Gewerksgenossenschaften)" was recommended as the "best way of acquiring money and organizations".[3] The unions were, then, a response to specific industrial disputes, which they turned into formal conflicts of interest. With the strike wave of 1865–73, industrial action superseded the traditional forms of protest such as complaints and petitions as the workers' means of defending their interests.

Simply in view of the risks which strikes entailed, the inclination of most union members to aim for regional and national forms of organization as quickly as possible is quite understandable. It was the best way to build up funds, to finance industrial action and to prevent strike breaking through the transfer of workers from areas not affected by a strike. Moreover, the benefits system was also a major argument for achieving the maximum level of organization.

While these were undoubtedly sensible reasons, the importance of which cannot be exaggerated, there is no overlooking the fact that unionization provided a way of keeping worker militancy and spontaneous protest under control and ultimately snuffing them out. Before long, absenteeism, go-slows and "wildcat" strikes were subject to disciplinary measures by the unions as well as the employers. The decision to centralize the unions marked the first step on a road that was ultimately to lead to administration, order and discipline becoming the essential characteristics of everyday trade unionism.

If experience of industrial action is to be considered the most important precondition for establishing unions, there were considerable differences when it came to party political allegiance. Unlike the Printers' Union, the first national union, the General German Cigar Workers' Association, founded in 1865, was close to Lassalle's ADAV; by autumn 1867 it had roughly 6,500 members and by the summer of 1869, some 10,000. Its chairman, Friedrich Wilhelm Fritzsche, was a committed Lassallean. And the trade associations that emerged in the late 1860s and early 70s by no means attached as much importance to stressing their party political independence as did the printers. Although the early trade

---

3 Quot. Arno Klönne/Hartmut Reese, Die deutsche Gewerkschaftsbewegung. Von den Anfängen bis zur Gegenwart (Hamburg, 1984), p. 40

union movement arose from the workers' desire to defend their social and economic interests against the employers without depending on anyone else, the unions were very much involved in the various political tendencies and parties to which they subscribed; these, however, sought to use the unions for their own ends. What did this party political spectrum look like?

3. *The trade unions and the struggle between the parties*

Let us first look at social democracy. Ferdinand Lassalle broke new ground with the formation of the General Association of German Working Men (ADAV) on 23 May 1863 in Leipzig. The ADAV manifesto, Lassalle's "Open Letter of Reply" to the central committee for the convocation of a general German workers' congress in Leipzig on 1 March 1863[4] not only painted a vivid picture of the wretched conditions of the day but also pointed the way ahead to a better future. The key words of this plan were equal suffrage and state-aided producer associations; the trade unions had no place in it. Union work was bound to appear pointless: in tackling the issue of consumer associations, Lassalle had expounded the "iron law of wages", whereby pay could not rise above subsistence level for any length of time, since higher wages would lead to an increase in the working population, whereupon the increased supply of labour would push wages down again. Lassalle did see that the organization of the working class was a precondition of obtaining political influence; but it was party political organization he had in mind – in the ADAV, the membership of which was growing but slowly, reaching 4,600 in the summer of 1864. Under pressure from reality (that is, the trade unions' success in attracting members), the ADAV, now headed by Johann Baptist von Schweitzer following Lassalle's death, finally brought itself to recognize this branch of the German labour movement. As mentioned above, an ADAV official, F.W. Fritzsche, even took over the leadership of a trade union, the Cigar Workers' Association. The possibility cannot be ruled out that von Schweitzer, who never made any secret of his reservations on the subject of unions, encouraged the setting up of unions partly because the supporters of the International Working Men's Association, founded in London in 1864, would shortly be forming their own associations.

---

4 Reprinted in Dowe and Klotzbach (eds.), Programmatische Dokumente der deutschen Sozialdemokratie, 2nd edition (Berlin and Bonn, 1984), pp. 112–44

Be that as it may, at the ADAV general assembly, which met in Hamburg from 22 to 26 August 1868, Schweitzer moved that a congress be convened to set up an umbrella organization for trade unions with Lassallean leanings. Although this proposal was rejected by the majority, who still retained the old hostility towards the unions, Schweitzer and Fritzsche were authorized to arrange a congress in Berlin in their capacity as members of the Reichstag. Accordingly, on 26 September – with Schweitzer in the chair – the General Federation of German Workers (Allgemeiner Deutscher Arbeiterschaftsverband) was founded; true to the centralist principles of the ADAV, it organized itself into trade sections – for coal and iron ore miners, engineering workers, dyers, shoemakers and so on. Nine of the twelve sections planned were set up immediately.

In its rules the General Federation of German Workers[5] stated that its aim was "the preservation and promotion of the honour and the material interests of the working class". In accordance with the ADAV's centralist ideas, Article 2a laid down that each section was to "give its president or some other individual the unconditional authority to take part in the negotiations and decisions of the Central Committee of the General Federation of German Workers on behalf of the section". This Central Committee, consisting of the presidents of the individual sections, was the body which decided whether or not to support a strike (Article 8f). If one looks at the strike movements of those years, this rule meant that the route from a local or company-wide protest to the support of the Central Committee was a very long one. Certainly, it was a contribution to planned, sensible union action and represented a way of organizing industrial disputes; but for the workers concerned it must have been hard to grasp at times that they had to shelve a strike for "overriding" reasons.

The second largest tendency within social democracy, the "Eisenachers", led by August Bebel and Wilhelm Liebknecht, accepted the idea of trade unions from the start. They were thus following the principles of the International Working Men's Association, which were influenced by Karl Marx. Marx's Inaugural Address at the IWMA's Geneva congress recog-

---

5 See Satzung für den (Schweitzerschen) Allgemeinen Deutschen Arbeiterschaftsverband, beschlossen vom ersten Deutschen Arbeiterkongress 1868, in Hermann Müller: Die Organisationen der Lithographen, Steindrucker und verwandten Berufe, reprint of the first edition of 1917 (Bonn and Berlin, 1978), pp. 425–30

nized the necessity of the "economic emancipation of the working class"[6]. Marx therefore endeavoured to commit the unions to a revolutionary policy. In his view, which he put to the General Council of the International on 26 June 1865, the trade unions "completely miss their purpose as soon as they confine themselves to a guerilla war against the effects of the existing system, instead of simultaneously trying to change it, instead of using their organized forces as a lever for the final emancipation of the working class, that is to say, the ultimate abolition of the wages system".[7]

The effect of these ideas was indirect rather than direct and was seen above all when the Union of German Workers' Associations cut loose from its mentors in the liberal movement at its Nuremberg Congress of 7–9 August 1868. Several union leaders took part in this "General Congress of German Social Democratic Workers" out of opposition to Schweitzer's authoritarian style of leadership and the ADAV's centralist concept of trade unionism – chief among them being Fritzsche, the leader of the Cigar Workers' Union and Vice-President of the ADAV, Heinrich Schob of the Tailors' Union, Louis Schumann of the Shoemakers' Union and Theodor Yorck of the Joiners' Union. Led by August Bebel, the President of the Union of German Workers' Associations, the majority of the delegates passed a resolution stating that the emancipation of the working class had to be the work of that class itself; the Congress also resolved to join the IWMA and recommended the establishment of works co-operatives (Gewerksgenossenschaften), for which Bebel submitted "model rules" on 28 November 1868[8].

With this draft constitution, the "Eisenachers", as they were called from 1869 on, after the town where the Social Democratic Workers' Party (SDAP) was founded, came out in favour of democratically structured trade associations. The main power of decision-making – for example, on whether or not to give backing to an industrial dispute – was to be given to the union executive (Article 38) and not, as advocated by the Lassalleans under Schweitzer's leadership, to the "umbrella organization". The aim of the trade unions was to "preserve and promote the dignity and the material interests of its members' (Article 1). To this end, they were to introduce

6 Karl Marx, Inauguraladresse der Internationalen Arbeiterassoziation, gegründet am 28 September 1864, in Karl Marx/ Friedrich Engels: Werke (MEW), vol. 16, (Berlin, 1962), p. 5 ff.

7 Karl Marx, Lohn, Preis und Profit (1865) in MEW, vol. 16, p. 152; originally written in English and reprinted in Marx/ Engels, Collected Works Vol. 20 (London, 1985) p. 149

8 See (Bebels) Musterstatuten für Deutsche Gewerksgenossenschaften, in Müller, pp. 441–450

assistance in the event of a strike or disciplinary action and a comprehensive system of welfare benefits, carry out statistical surveys and start their own newspaper (Article 2). Express provision was made for female membership (Article 3). In early 1869, a number of unions were founded in conformity with Bebel's recommendations, including the International Bookbinders' Association, the Coal and Iron Ore Miners' Union and the International Manufacturing, Factory and Manual Workers' Union headed by Julius Motteler.

While the Eisenachers were thus far more sympathetic towards trade unions than the Lassalleans, both assigned the unions a subordinate part in the emancipation of the working class. The unions were supposed to school the proletariat for the decisive political struggle, which was to be waged by the party. Thus both trends inside social democracy tried to gain the support of the trade unions in the 1860s. From the very outset they turned the unions into battlefields for competing party political interests, which undoubtedly weakened them. This probably applied most of all to Schweitzer; after all, he made sure that the Federation of German Workers barred its members from joining the "Eisenacher" SDAP. This made it obvious that the Federation was the ADAV umbrella organization. In view of later developments, there is no denying that the trade unions' clear links with the Social Democratic movement provided a welcome pretext for setting up the liberal Hirsch-Duncker trade associations (Gewerkvereine) and, at a later stage, the Christian trade unions.

*

Even the inaugural congress of Schweitzer's Federation of German Workers in Berlin saw a break with the liberal trade unions, represented by a delegation of mechanical engineers from Berlin led by Max Hirsch. Hirsch had just toured England and in his "Social Letters" in the "Berliner Volkszeitung", a newspaper published by Franz Duncker, a deputy of the liberal German Party of Progress, he tried to enlist support for trade unions on the English model. Furthermore, he had opposed the appeal by the General Congress of Workers because it mentioned striking. One may assume that the idea of hitching the planned Federation to the ADAV also disturbed him. Hirsch's conception of trade unions was dominated by ideas about the amicable settlement of disputes and independence from political parties, which in fact meant giving implicit support to the liberal Progress Party (*Fortschrittspartei*), of which he was a member.

When the mechanical engineers from Berlin led by Hirsch put forward these ideas at the congress, they were expelled from the hall for seeking –

as a resolution put it[9] – "to cause disquiet and disturbance among the workers in the interest of the capitalists". In response Hirsch called for the establishment of trade associations (Gewerkvereine) 'on the English model'. In November 1868 the Trade Association of the Mechanical Engineers of Berlin was set up, becoming in December the Trade Association of German Mechanical Engineers and Engineering Workers (H-D), the first national, liberal trade union organization. In May 1869 the Federation of German Trade Associations (H-D) was formed as an umbrella organization of eight trade associations whose memberships were growing rapidly. By the end of 1869 some 30,000 members were organized in 250 local associations along the lines of the model rules drawn up by Hirsch and Duncker[10]. These laid down that a trade association was intended to "protect and promote the rights and interests of its members in a lawful fashion", in particular by setting up a comprehensive system of benefits (Article 2) and the improvement of working conditions (Article 3) – from wage levels and working hours to the establishment of courts of arbitration. Rooted in the tradition of liberal thought, the H-D trade associations rated the principle of self help more highly than state aid. They envisaged their organization as a negotiating counterweight to the employers, from whom they did not consider themselves divorced by any unsurmountable clash of interests. Equal rights for workers, the amicable settling of differences through negotiation, social reforms on the basis of existing conditions and their own benefits system – these were, in their opinion, the way to solve the "social question", which they approached with purely moderate demands.

However attractive the idea of trade associations was initially, resistance to equal rights for workers and a thorough-going policy of social reform on the part of the government and the liberal bourgeoisie soon dashed their hopes for the peaceful settlement of differences. Disillusionment was probably hastened, too, by the defeats suffered by the associations in two strikes in 1869–70 – in the Waldenburg coal district (Lower Silesia) and the Niederlausitz textile industry around Forst. They confirmed the view born of experience that the unions had nothing to gain by adopting a conciliatory policy in the face of the employers' intransigence. The failures of union policy and the Franco-Prussian War of 1870–71 combined to inflict severe membership losses on the H-D associations, whose numbers declined to less than 20,000.

*

9 Quot. Müller, p. 157
10 See Musterstatuten der Deutschen Gewerkvereine (Hirsch-Duncker) in Müller, pp. 431–41

What was the situation at the end of the 1860s? There were the Arbeiter-schaften allied to Schweitzer's ADAV; there were the International Gewerksgenossenschaften, which looked to the "Eisenacher" SDAP headed by August Bebel and Wilhelm Liebknecht; and finally there were the liberal Hirsch-Duncker Gewerkvereine. This political spread reflected social as well as political differences. Those sections of the working class that enjoyed higher status, such as the glove-makers, gold and silversmiths and mechanical engineers, were obviously drawn to a liberal democratic or social liberal vision of society, at least in the early stages of trade union-ism in the 1860s and 70s. Those who had formerly practised a trade under the old guild system and since come down in the world – such as shoemak-ers, tailors, weavers, spinners and joiners – seem to have been more recep-tive to social democratic ideas.

The roughly equal attraction of liberal and social democratic ideas is reflected in their membership statistics. When the founding phase of the unions was interrupted by the Franco-Prussian War in 1870, the Hirsch-Duncker associations had about 35,000 members, the Arbeiterschaften about 18,500 and the International Gewerksgenossenschaften about 18,000; on top of this there were the 6,600 members of the Printers' Asso-ciation, which did not take a definite political line. The strength of the H-D associations and the Social Democratic unions' occupational orient-ation reinforce the impression that trade unionism was initially more popular with the more skilled workers, artisans and craftsmen.

4. *Crisis in the trade unions and the beginnings of centralization*

The Franco-Prussian War signified a major setback for the young trade union movement. The Federation of German Workers lost the majority of its members in 1870–71, a trend that was strengthened by Schweitzer's plan to turn the Federation into a cross-occupational organization called the "General German Federation for the Support of Working Men" (All-gemeiner Deutscher Arbeiterunterstützungsverband). The purpose of this new federation was laid down in Article 2 of the rules adopted by the gen-eral assembly on 12–15 June 1870: "To preserve and promote the honour and the material interests of its members by adopting a firm and united stance, particularly – if necessary – by the organized withdrawal of labour."[11] This national union, headed by a three-man Bureau and a cen-

---

11 Satzung des Allgemeinen Deutschen Arbeiterunterstützungsverbandes, beschlossen von der Verbandsgeneralversammlung vom 12. bis 15. Juni 1870, reprinted in Müller, pp.450–56

tral committee of twelve, brought together workers and artisans, both male and female, organized not by trade or industry but by district. This decision met with so much internal resistance that it was relaxed in 1871. None the less, several occupational unions, including the carpenters and joiners, left the Federation, whose membership had fallen from a pre-war figure of more than 18,000 to 4,200 in May 1871. The "Eisenacher" International unions also suffered heavy losses: four of the ten occupational unions folded in 1870, and the remaining ones had been weakened so badly that they were unable to convene a general assembly.

The economic boom of 1871–73 did enable the unions to recover to a certain extent. They achieved greater stability, and during the outbreak of strikes in this period they began to secure for the first time a small share in the benefits of growth for their members. A few examples will suffice.In 1871 the Berlin bricklayers achieved the ten-hour day after several strikes; in Chemnitz 6,500 engineering workers came out on strike in the autumn of 1871; and lastly there was the strike of 21,000 miners in the Essen district mentioned above.

But the crisis in the union movement triggered off by the war soon deepened with the onset of the depression of 1873. The poor economic situation sapped union power and lessened their chances of success. In almost every industry workers were forced to accept wage cuts. It was not only in heavy industry that the employers' crisis plan was in evidence. To bring down costs working hours were increased and wages cut; at the same time, the formation of cartels and entrepreneurs' associations was stepped up. The employers' position, which was evident enough from numerous cases of industrial action, became much more rigid. The "factory bosses" devised their own response to the rash of strikes and the spread of the trade union movement in general. With a call for state assistance against the "subversive movement" and through their own organizational efforts they sought to maintain their supremacy.

Moreover, most employers refused to negotiate with union representatives at all. The employers were determined to cling on to personal contracts, in accordance with the dictum "divide and rule". In spite of this, the first collective agreement was reached in 1873, the General German Printers' Agreement. Remaining in force for three years, it made the ten-hour day compulsory, regulated permitted overtime and stipulated the setting up of arbitration services. But it was to be a while yet before the idea of collective agreements gained general acceptance within the trade union movement, let alone with the employers.

*

In this situation, the determination of trade unionists to meet the crisis with unity grew. Some years earlier, in 1870, Theodor Yorck, the chairman of the Woodworkers' Union, had come up with a plan to bring the unions together. At the Erfurt Trade Union Congress from 15 to 17 June 1872 this idea was unanimously approved: "Considering that the power of capital oppresses and exploits all workers equally, regardless of whether they are conservative, progressive-liberal or social democratic, Congress declares it the workers' sacred duty to set aside all party discord and, on the neutral ground of a united union organization, create the right conditions for powerful and successful resistance, safeguard livelihoods under threat and secure an improvement in their class position."[12] But the attempt to set up a "union of trade unions' planned for Whitsun 1874 at the trade union congress in Magdeburg, as an umbrella organization of "German trade co-operatives, trade and craft associations, which are concerned to achieve the material betterment and spiritual edification of the working class"[13], ultimately foundered on the reservations of the local organizations, which rejected any centralization of decision-making as undemocratic undermining of their own position. The strength of these local associations is shown by the size of their membership: of the 11,300 trade unionists represented in Erfurt by 50 delegates, approximately 6,100 belonged to national trade unions, 3,700 to local associations and 1,500 to free or "mixed" trade unions.

The crisis in the young trade union movement favoured such attempts at unification – albeit only in the case of unions with a social democratic tendency. However, it was only when the political parties achieved unity that the way was clear for a merger between the trade unions. With the founding of the empire in 1871 one of the bones of contention between the Lassalleans and the Eisenachers had lost its relevance: the question of whether German unity should be achieved under Prussian domination, as advocated by the Lassalleans, or whether a "greater-German" solution – including Austria – was preferable had been decided in favour of the former. The two parties were agreed on basic principles – radical reform but not revolution – and had, after all, received 6.8 per cent of the vote in the general election of 10 January 1874. And as stated above, it also seemed advisable to unite Social Democratic factions in view of the weakness of

---

12 Quot. Müller, p. 301
13 Satzungen der „Gewerkschafts-Union", nach den Beschlüssen des Gewerkschafts-Kongresses vom 15. bis 17. Juni 1872 in Erfurt, in Müller, pp. 456–62; revised version, based on the decisions taken at the congress in Magdeburg, 23–25 May 1874, ibid. pp. 463–65

the trade unions, and therefore the decision was taken at the Gotha party conference from 22 to 27 May 1875 to found the Socialist Workers' Party of Germany. One encouraging result of the party merger was an increase in the socialist vote to 9.1 per cent at the general election of 10 January 1877; another was the unification of the Social Democratic union movement, a decision taken on 28–29 May 1875, also in Gotha, at a trade union conference immediately after the party conference.

The merger arose from a resolution by Friedrich Wilhelm Fritzsche, making it the duty of all trade unionists "to keep politics out of the trade union organizations". The resolution called on the trade unionists in the newly created Socialist Workers' Party to join, "as they are the only ones fully able to make the political and economic position of the workers fit for human beings". This formulation was undoubtedly intended to get round the law on association with regard to "political associations". At the same time, however, it expressed the idea of a division of labour between union and party, with the latter having precedence over the former. After all, the conference resolution stated most modestly: "Although the workers' trade union organizations cannot improve the workers' situation radically and permanently, they are nevertheless capable of raising their living standards periodically, promoting education and making them conscious of their class position."[14]

The low level of self-assurance among trade unionists was without a doubt due to the recent economic crisis, with all its adverse effects on organization and setbacks in industrial disputes. The willing recognition of the party's leading role was, however, also a symptom of the political situation, for the unions' position in law and equality for the working class as a whole still had to be fought for and won.

Putting the decision to unite into practice turned out to be rather a slow process, as many of the occupational trade unions were very reluctant to carry out the merger. Overall union membership was slow to recover from the setbacks of wartime and crisis. The trade union movement grew steadily but was far from being a mass movement: by the end of 1877 the Social Democratic unions had a total of some 50,000 members. Thirteen unions had over a thousand members: the bookbinders, printers, factory workers, kid glove makers, joiners, hatters, bricklayers, engineering work-

14 Beschlüsse der Gewerkschaftskonferenz zu Gotha am 28/29 Mai 1875, in Müller, p. 380 ff.

ers, ships' carpenters, tailors, shoemakers, tobacco workers and textile workers. The strongest unions were the tobacco workers with 8,100 members, the printers with 5,500, the joiners with 5,100, the engineering workers with 4,000, the shoemakers with 3,600 and the carpenters with 3,300[15]. These membership figures show that even in the Social Democratic union movement the unions of artisans dominated the picture.

But the unification of the trade union movement slowly went ahead. In February 1878 the trade union conference in Gotha agreed on the need for greater concentration of the trade union newspapers and more co-operation between them. Membership dues were to be standardized (and raised). Lastly, the issue of greater mutual support in union administration and agitation was debated[16]. But a joint conference of trade unions on these plans due to take place in Magdeburg at Whitsun 1878 could no longer be held, with the imminent enactment of the Socialist Law and the prohibitions contained therein. The spread of the union movement and the Social Democratic Party, the reconciliation between Lassalleans and Eisenachers in Gotha, and the strikes and elections won by the movement as a whole strengthened the cohesion of their adversaries' defensive front, comprising both employers and state. As political pressure on the unions grew, so too did the political divergence in the trade union movement between Social Democrats and Liberals. At their Leipzig congress of 1876, the Hirsch-Duncker trade associations decided to introduce a signed declaration, whereby every member stated that he opposed Social Democracy. This was, however, not merely a response to the advances and radical policies of the Social Democrats; it was also, and principally, an attempt to evade the increasingly severe legal restrictions being placed on the labour movement.

The first attempts "to stem the Social Democratic tide" occurred in the mid and late 1870s, and certainly by the outbreak of the economic crisis. The breach of contract bill which Bismarck laid before Parliament in late 1873, making it a punishable offence to go on strike, was voted down in 1874 thanks to the National Liberals. But the same year a decree by the Prussian Ministry of the Interior made "pernicious agitation and incitement directed against the employers or against the owning classes" in the press or at a public meeting an offence. 1874 also saw the start of the "Tessendorf Era", so called after a Berlin public prosecutor, when every legal

---

15 Statistics from Willy Albrecht, Fachverein – Berufsgewerkschaft – Zentralverband. Organisationsprobleme der deutschen Gewerkschaften 1870–1890 (Bonn, 1982), p. 534 f.
16 Beschlüsse der Gewerkschaftskonferens zu Gotha vom 24. und 25. Februar 1878, in Müller, p. 466–68

possibility of harrassing the labour movement was employed. On 19 October 1878, the "law against the efforts of Social Democracy to endanger society" was passed by the Reichstag, hitting both party work and the trade unions very hard. With this step, Bismarck's Reich helped provide tangible proof that the picture of a class state painted by the Social Democratic labour movement was correct.

III. Illegality: the trade unions under the Socialist Law 1878–1890

The obstacles placed in the way of the trade union and political labour movement, which came to a head with the economic depression from 1873 onwards, culminated in the passing of the Socialist Law (also known as the Anti-Socialist Law), which placed social democracy under emergency law and made it illegal, forcing it to go under ground. What was state policy on these matters?

1. *Political disenfranchisement and social policy: the Bismarckian state and the working class*

It was not the policy of the government under Chancellor Otto von Bismarck to treat the "enemies of the Reich", which is how he dubbed his political adversaries, with kid gloves. This had been evident back in the early 1870s during the *Kulturkampf* against the Catholic Church, political Catholicism and its party, the Centre. The many restrictions placed on Social Democratic activities, particularly in the "Tessendorf Era", also attested to the fundamental tendency of Bismarck's policy: internal unity through the marginalization and suppression of critics. Two attempts on the life of the Kaiser, Wilhelm I, – falsely attributed to the Social Democrats, though Bismarck knew full well that they were not involved – provided the pretext in 1878 to deliver the "final blow" to the "subversive movement of socialism". With the votes of the Conservative Party and most of the National Liberals, the Reichstag passed the Socialist Law on 19 October 1878, against the opposition of the SPD, Centre and liberal Progress Party, by 221 votes to 149.

This "law against the Social Democrats' efforts to endanger society"[1], which came into force on 21 October and was renewed four times before expiring on 1 October 1890, introduced a number of measures intended to prevent social democracy, now emerging as a political force, from developing into a mass movement. A ban was placed on "associations with the purpose of overthrowing the existing state and social order by working for social democratic, socialist or communist ideas" (Article 1). The law went

---

1 Reichs-Gesetzblatt No. 34, 1878, pp. 351–58

on to say that "combinations of any kind shall be considered equivalent to associations", thus including the trade unions. Furthermore, the law banned meetings and publications "in which social democratic, socialist or communist ideas aimed at the overthrow of the existing state and social order are expressed". Membership of banned associations or attendance at banned meetings was punishable by fines up to 500 Marks or imprisonment up to three months. More severe punishments were laid down for those who organized or spoke at banned meetings; in addition to imprisonment, agitators were also liable to have restrictions imposed on their place of abode, that is, they could be deported. Finally, a minor state of emergency could be declared in towns or districts that were threatened by socialist activities "endangering public safety". In such cases, meetings could only be held with police permission, the public distribution of printed material was prohibited, and "persons who are likely to constitute a danger to public safety or public order" could be "denied leave to stay in the town or district". "Meetings relating to an election for the Reichstag or the state legislature" were excepted from the ban; that is to say, Social Democratic party work was prohibited but not the activity of the parliamentary group, nor was it prevented from standing in elections.

Thus a long list of measures that were a severe blow to the Social Democratic Party and allied trade unions (though not to the liberal Hirsch-Duncker associations) now had legal force. The background to this emergency law was undoubtedly a widespread fear of the socialists that was out of all proportion to the real strength of the Social Democratic labour movement. Of importance at the time was also the fact that the downturn in the economy left less scope for wealth distribution, so that gagging the workers' organizations was seen as a means of avoiding industrial disputes. Finally, a compromise was in sight between the interests of heavy industry and large landowners detrimental to the export-based manufacturing industry and particularly, in the longer term, to the working class. In 1879 – after the enactment of the Socialist Law – the protectionism that resulted from this compromise made corn imports more expensive, thus leading to a rise in living costs and, until 1881–82, a decline in real wages.

*

While the Socialist Law, by pushing the Social Democratic working class on to the sidelines, supported the ideology of harmonious co-operation across the classes by all "decent Germans of good will", that is, "nationally minded" Germans, the Bismarck government tried to take the wind out of the Social Democrats' sails by pursuing an active social policy. Of course, many bourgeois politicians advocated social reform for thoroughly honourable motives. But political disenfranchisement and the sudden interest in social policy were not unconnected with considerations of political strategy, which Bismarck openly expressed in Parliament on 26 November 1884: "Were it not for Social Democracy and the fact that many people are afraid of it, the modest advances in social reform that we have hitherto made would not have been achieved."[2]

The fact that social insurance was being used as an instrument of politics – to steal the Social Democrats' thunder – cannot detract from its importance in substantially diminishing the risks of life. In 1878 an amendment to the trade regulations released mothers from work for three weeks after the birth of a child, prohibited the truck system (the payment of wages in the form of goods) and made factory inspections compulsory. On 17 November 1881, the Kaiser announced further improvements in social welfare. The introduction of sickness insurance (1883), accident insurance (1884) and old age and disability insurance (1889) may indeed be regarded as thoroughly progressive and pioneering measures, compared with the position in comparable industrialized, capitalist countries. Although the benefits payable were very limited, the Bismarck government demonstrated an ability to embark on reform that was in glaring contrast to the way in which it clung on to pre-parliamentary decision-making structures – which were actually strengthened by the reforms. With their stabilizing effect on the system, the social insurance laws of the 1880s were a major step on the way to the modern interventionist state, which – in contrast to the liberal, laissez-faire state – seeks to take an active part in shaping economic and social conditions.

The Socialist Laws revealed the Bismarckian state's Janus face particularly clearly. On the one hand, the Social Democratic working class was marginalized, suppressed and deprived of political rights; on the other, a start was made on a state social policy. In the eyes of a growing number of workers, however, the withdrawal of political and trade union rights greatly overshadowed these tentative signs of the state's readiness to introduce reforms. And yet it was precisely this Janus face which set a permanent stamp on the development of the labour movement.

---

2 Otto von Bismarck in the Reichstag on 26 November 1884, published in Stenographische Berichte über die Verhandlungen des Deutschen Reichstages, VI. Legislaturperiode, 1. Session, Vol. 1, p. 25

2. *The trade unions go underground*

As late as 9 October 1878, just ten days before the Socialist Law was passed, Bismarck had assured the Reichstag that he personally would encourage any effort that was "designed to improve the lot of the workers, including an association for the purpose of improving the position of the workers, to obtain for the workers a larger share in the profits of industry and to reduce working hours as far as is feasible"[3]. Trade unionists who saw this as a tribute to and as recognition of their work, were soon bitterly disappointed to find that they had been wrong. Like the Social Democratic Party, the unions were soon steamrollered by a wave of prohibitions. In the first few weeks of the Socialist Law's existence, 17 trade unions, 63 local associations and 16 friendly societies had to stop work; as a result, about 55,000 workers had lost their organization. But the Hirsch-Duncker associations were not dissolved, and nor were the Printers' Union, the Senefeld Union of Lithographers, the Ships' Carpenters' Union and the Union of Saxon Coal and Iron Ore Miners. These unions had already declared their party political neutrality, and thus their detachment with regard to the SPD, or they quickly made good the omission; in addition they renounced trade union aims and forms of action in order to ensure their survival as organizations.

In the first two years after the Socialist Law was passed, the Social Democratic trade union movement was almost destroyed. Conscious of the swift victory they had won, in the years after 1881 the authorities and the police no doubt felt that they could afford to adopt a "milder approach" in applying the Socialist Law. But by the end of 1880 there were already first signs that the unions were being rebuilt: local associations, sickness and death benefit schemes, travel assistance (to provide against the financial consequences of strikes and unemployment) and employment exchanges were set up, which in addition to their stated aims were primarily intended to preserve the political cohesion of the Social Democrats under the emergency law. In this period, the shared experience of suppression and persecution brought many trade unionists and party members together – many workers were, after all, both. Although, in the first few

---

3 Otto von Bismarck in the Reichstag on 9 October 1878, in Stenographische Berichte über die Verhandlungen des Reichstages, IV. Legislaturperiode, 1. Session, Vol. 1, p. 125

years after the enactment of the Socialist Law, the trade union movement was once more reduced to the organizational level of the early days, a succession of unions were soon started up, or rather re-started. In 1884 there were already 13 national unions, in 1886 there were 35, and by 1888 as many as 40; here we shall mention but a few, such as the unions of the printers, hatters, manufacturing workers, tailors, stonemasons and joiners. The fact that the shoemakers and tobacco workers met at "friendly societies" was in compliance with the dictates of the Law on Associations and the Socialist Law, which they thus sought to circumvent. In addition, there were countless local benefit clubs that put the idea of self help into practice, thus indirectly facilitating the advance of the unions.

The dominant form of organization was probably the occupational trade association at local level, with its members drawn from the ranks of the skilled workers or journeymen. These local associations, which thus represented a traditional branch of the German trade union movement, jealously guarded their independence of central authority. The local attachment was far from being an antiquated relic of the past. This organizational model was a lesson that police persecution had taught the unions: it was much easier to shield local organizations from bans and other restrictions, and also – because the members knew one another – from informers, than large national unions. The latter's aim was to co-ordinate strikes across the country, to safeguard their funds by sharing the risk and, above all, to organize a mobile working class nationwide; the local associations kept up the tradition of direct democracy. Demands were formulated and a strike committee elected at a meeting, so that "preventive intervention" by the police was made difficult. While national unions had to rely on a system of representative democracy, with responsibility delegated from level to level, local associations often followed the principles of spontaneous and direct grassroots participation – an idea that was to be taken up again and again, particularly in the notion of "councils" current during the revolutionary period of 1918–19, the so-called *"Rätebewegung"*.

The main emphasis in the trade union movement continued to be on skilled workers and artisans, both in the national unions and the local associations. Few unions (among them the tobacco workers and the manufacturing workers) attempted to organize both skilled and unskilled workers, both men and women, as early as the 1880s. A move in this direction by the engineering workers' union in the summer of 1885 was stopped by an order to disband. Another factor that was equally important as the beginnings of cross-occupational organization, which was soon – in the 1890s – to be extended, was the change of generations that took place during the period of the Socialist Law. For the first time, men who were "born" workers appeared in the top positions of the unions, men such as Carl Legien and Theodor Leipart of the woodworkers, Carl Kloß of the joiners, August Brey of the factory workers and Alexander Schlicke of the engineering workers. Their political views and their attitude to the state and society had been shaped by the Socialist Law, a fact that made itself felt in the decades to come. Whereas the state was initially considered to be a ruling class instrument for oppressing the workers, the unions soon came to see the state social policy launched in the 1880s as a means of reforming the capitalist system, and hence an important field of action for the labour movement. From being the "bourgeoisie's agent of domination", the state became the means whereby the working class might hope to achieve economic and social liberation. These attempts to influence social policy and, in particular, co-operation with the employers in administering the social insurance schemes were to have a lasting effect on the unions' attitude to the state and the employers.

Evidently the Social Democratic workers' determination to organize and take action took the authorities by surprise. Not only did the Social Democratic Party fail to disappear; despite all the obstacles placed in its way by the state, its work flourished. From taking 7.5 per cent of the vote in the general elections of 1873, it maintained its share of the vote, even under the Socialist Law, at a respectable level, polling 6.1 per cent in 1881, 9.7 in 1884 and 7.1 in 1887, before leaping to 19.7 in 1890. And the trade union movement also continued to expand. This by no means applied solely to the Hirsch-Duncker Gewerkvereine, which commenced a slow but steady upward movement in the 1880s: their membership, often organized in cross-occupational unions, rose from just over 16,500 in 1878 to about 52,000 in 1886 and about 63,000 four years later. Moreover, the associations' benefits scheme profited by the introduction of a compulsory state insurance scheme in 1883, which people could opt out of by joining a private scheme. But if one takes into account the measures designed to suppress them, the upswing experienced by the Social Democratic unions was far more impressive: the membership of the national unions increased from 53,000 at the end of 1877 to more than 230,000 by the end of 1889.[4]

Moreover, it should not be forgotten that under the Socialist Law the Church's efforts to organize the workers were stepped up, later to result in the Christian trade unions. One of the main organizations was *Arbeiterwohl* (worker welfare), founded in 1880 by the cloth manufacturer Franz

---

4 See W. Albrecht, Fachverein, pp. 529 and 534 ff.

Brandts and headed from 1881 on by Franz Hitze, the general secretary; it was this organization that gave rise in 1890 to the People's Association for Catholic Germany (Volksverein für das katholische Deutschland), which came out firmly in favour of extending the Catholic workers' associations and founding and strengthening Christian unions. Pope Leo XIII's 1884 encyclical "Humani generis" also encouraged the Catholic workers' associations, which were supposed not only to tie the workers to the Church but also to render them invulnerable to social democracy. There were similar reasons behind the setting up of the Protestant workers' associations from 1882 on; following the merger into a national union (Gesamtverband) in 1890, they could boast some 40,000 members. The Protestant associations combined the idea of a harmonious settlement of disputes through co-operation between the two sides of industry on the one hand with support for emperor and fatherland on the other.

*

The Socialist Law was not even able to completely eliminate industrial action, as shown by the strike movement of 12,000 Berlin bricklayers in the summer of 1885. It seemed to be time for another clampdown, as signalled in 1886 by the Strike Decree of the Prussian Ministry of the Interior, Robert von Puttkamer: between 1886 and 1888, 15 trade union organizations and 6 friendly societies were dissolved. This took the number of trade union organizations banned since 1878 to 17 national unions, 78 local associations, 23 friendly societies, 106 political associations and 108 recreational clubs. In addition to these, almost all trade union newspapers and periodicals were banned. In view of the overwhelming dominance of the bourgeois press, these papers were of an importance that is hard to comprehend today. A total of 1,299 publications were forced to close under the Socialist Law. One of the harshest consequences of the law was the persecution of large numbers of labour movement activists: some 1,500 people were imprisoned and about 900 were expelled from their home districts. Many were forced into political exile, and others emigrated for good[5].

Neither the advance of the Social Democratic Party and unions nor the industrial struggle could be halted in this way. Against the background of a slight upturn in the economy from 1888 on, there was a marked increase in strike action (Table 2a). Even by international standards the following

---

5 Ignaz Auer, Nach zehn Jahren. Material and Glossen zur Geschichte des Sozialistengesetzes (Nuremberg, 1913), p. 354 ff.

years were notable for a spate of strikes, culminating in the miners' strike of 1889. It started spontaneously, without union involvement. The miners were demanding a wage rise of 15 per cent and the introduction of eight-hour shifts (including travelling time). These demands, which were made in several areas, were handed to the pit managements in writing – but elicited no response. At this, the strike started on 1 May, at first in scattered pits, but soon spreading to the whole Ruhr district. On 5 May, at the command of the Westphalian Supreme President, troops were used against the strikers. But the strike continued to spread – to the Saar district, Upper and Lower Silesia, Aachen, Lorraine and Saxony (Zwickau, Lugau and Plauen), eventually involving more than 150,000 men. It ended in partial victory after the Kaiser, Wilhelm II, had received a miner's delegation.

Precisely because the strike developed spontaneously there was a lack of coordinated planning behind the industrial action. This fact, together with the attitude of the pit managements and, above all, the use of state coercion seemd to permit only one conclusion to be drawn from this partial success: in August 1889 a Social Democratic-inspired miners' union called the "Old Union" was set up.

So this struggle, too, showed the mobilizing effect of a strike. And the wave of 670 strikes between 1888 and 1890 did their bit to boost the number and membership of the unions quite sharply: at the beginning of 1889 there were 41 unions with 174,000 members; by the end of the year, this had increased to 58 unions with 230,000 members. Under the Socialist Law the unions were already well on the way to becoming a mass movement, a trend that was to lead to a breakthrough in the decades prior to the First World War.

However slight the impact of the Socialist Law on the organizational development of the SPD and the unions, its effect on matters of policy could hardly have been greater. The Janus face of Bismarck's policy – suppressing the party while allowing it to continue its parliamentary work, depriving the working class of political rights while pursuing social policies designed to aid it – had a lasting influence on the Social Democrats' attitude to the state. It was precisely the results of political persecution that paved the way for the acceptance of Marxist ways of interpreting reality. The economic depression was seen as proof of the theory of the impoverishment of the working class. The repressive measures confirmed that the state was the instrument of the wealthy, a class state belonging to

The 1889 miners' strike: young people attack an army patrol

Cartoon about the Socialist Law's failure to have the desired effect. The captions read: Fired up, not blown out! and Thank you for your kind support!

the bourgeoisie. And the workers' ghetto situation favoured the formation of a radical outlook of their own, to which SDP propaganda tried to give content and direction in order to make them "class-conscious". Being proscribed and excluded by bourgeois society forced the Social Democrats – both its leaders and the workers – to adopt a radical stance in policy matters that manifested itself in the recognition of the Marxist analysis of society and future developments. The most prominent champion of Marxism within the party was Karl Kautsky, with his theoretical review "Die Neue Zeit" (The New Age). The struggle against the contemporary capitalist class state and the vision of the socialist society of the future popularized by August Bebel's book "Die Frau und der Sozialismus" (Women and Socialism) of 1879, were greeted eagerly, but the SPD remained a party of democratic reform, precisely because it was allowed to continue its parliamentary work. Under the Socialist Law, Parliament was the sole legal forum for agitation, the parliamentary party was the real party leadership – and the ballot paper was considered the sole means of achieving political power. The SPD's political methods remained " lawful" even though the Wyden party congress of 1880 had deleted this word from the Gotha Programme, precisely because the party considered that it was being forced to act illegally. At the 1887 party congress in St. Gallen, Wilhelm Liebknecht asserted that it was "not by coups and outrages" that the victory of the SPD would be hastened, "but only by means that increase our power", by which he meant the recruitment of new members and voters[6].

The experience of repression and, above all, success in the parliamentary elections of 1890 had the effect of entrenching the assumption familiar from the 1860s and 70s that the political struggle took precedence over the trade union struggle. Moreover, this period strengthened internationalism. Exile and contact with the socialists of other countries and the realization that action had to be co-ordinated internationally both helped the German Social Democrats to see themselves as part of an international labour movement, which rallied round the call for the eight-hour day at the International Workers' Congress held in Paris in 1889[7]. The idea of demonstrating every May Day for this specific objective turned into a

---

6 Wilhelm Liebknecht, in Verhandlungen des Parteitages der deutschen Sozialdemokratie in St. Gallen, abgehalten vom 2. bis 6. Oktober 1887 (Hottingen–Zürich 1888), p. 42

7 See Arbeiterschutz-Resolution, in Protokoll des Internationalen Arbeiter-Congresses zu Paris, abgehalten vom 14. bis 20. July 1889. German translation (Nuremberg, 1890), p. 121 f.

headache for the German labour movement, with opinions in the party and in the trade unions divided.

Even under the Socialist Law, the accession of Wilhelm II on 15 June 1888 had aroused hopes of a period of political and social reform. The Reichstag was not unaffected by this "new" mood. When the government proposed extending the Socialist Law on 25 January 1890 it was voted down, with the result that the law lapsed on 30 September 1890. Partly because of the failure of his domestic policy, which had been designed to halt the advance of social democracy, Bismarck resigned as Chancellor on 20 March 1890. The end of the Bismarck era and the expiry of the Socialist Law marked the onset of a new period in the life of the trade unions.

IV. The unions under the Wilhelminian Empire: the breakthrough of mass organization 1890–1914

From Bismarck's point of view, the Socialist Law turned out to be a dismal failure. Its repressive provisions had put a brake on the development of the SPD and the unions but failed to halt it. Despite – or because of – the government's emergency legislation the Social Democratic labour movement was stronger and above all more radical than before. As the pace of industrialization quickened in the 1880s and 1890s – and it never stood still even in times of recession – the nation's social and political problems worsened. At the same time, the working class grew in size and importance, bringing the trade unions their breakthrough as a mass movement.

1. *The organization of industrial capitalism: the economic and social development of the Wilhelminian Empire*

The economic depression that started in 1873 continued into the mid-1890s, interrupted only by feeble upturns; it was not until 1895 that the economy revived. Apart from temporary crises in 1901–2 and 1907–8, the revival lasted until 1912–13. Heavy industry had been heavily favoured by Bismarck's protective tariffs and its importance was soon reinforced by the arms race, particularly by the naval shipbuilding programme under Alfred von Tirpitz from 1898 on. In 1890 England's output of iron, at 8 m tonnes, was almost double Germany's (4.1 m tonnes); by 1910 the German output of 14 m tonnes far exceeded England's (just over 10 m). Even more dramatic was Germany's steel output, which grew from 2.1 m tonnes in 1890 to 13.1 m twenty years later, whereas English steel production rose from 3.6 m tonnes to only 6.4 m over the same period. While these statistics chart Germany's development into an industrial nation, industry underwent significant changes in the 1890s. As a result of new inventions and the development of pioneering technical processes, the German electrical engineering and chemical industries achieved world rank alongside mechanical engineering.

The picture of Germany as a highly industrialized society emerged during this period. The process of concentration continued steadily: in industry, the number of firms employing less than six people accounted for 59.8 per cent of the working population in 1882; by 1907 this had fallen to 31.3 per cent. Over the same period the number of companies with a workforce of more than a thousand rose from 1.9 to 4.9 per cent of the total. Cartels increased in number and importance. While a large proportion of the cartels of the depression were short-lived (as was evident in the 1880s), the age of cartels had now arrived. In 1893 the Rhenish-Westphalian coal syndicate was formed; by 1910 it embraced almost every pit in the Ruhr district. In 1897 the iron ore mines combined to form the Rhenish-Westphalian Pig Iron Syndicate. Electrical engineering was dominated by the giants AEG and Siemens, and the chemical industry by four or five large concerns. Five major banks – including the Deutsche Bank and the Dresdner Bank – held almost half of all bank deposits. The banks exerted considerable influence on economic development, not merely as lenders but also as shareholders. Industrial and banking capital began to merge, one of the typical signs of the "organization" of the capitalist economy.

In addition a network of economic syndicates emerged. The Central Federation of German Industrialists, founded in 1875, was joined in 1895 by the League of Industrialists (Bund der Industriellen), which laid more stress on the needs of the processing industry. The employers were chiefly concerned with asserting their interests in the face of the rising trade unions, as evidenced by the Crimmitschau textile strike in 1903–4. Witnessing the solidarity displayed by the workers of different regions, the employers set up the Central Organization of German Employers' Associations (Hauptstelle Deutscher Arbeitgeberverbände), which was dominated by heavy industry, and the Union of German Employers' Associations (Verein Deutscher Arbeitgeberverbände), in which the processing industry was heavily represented. In 1913 the two organizations merged to form the Federation of German Employers' Associations (Vereinigung der Deutschen Arbeitgeberverbände). This emphasized the trend on both sides of the industrial divide to organize in ways that cut across trades and regions. This was reflected in the development of the trade unions, which in turn was a consequence of the changes in the labour market.

*

As industrialization proceeded, the proportion of the working population engaged in agriculture fell from 43.5 to 35.2 per cent between 1882 and 1907, while the proportion of workers employed in industry rose from 37.7 to 40.1 per cent (Table 6a). Over the same period the number of industrial workers grew from about 3 m to 5.8 m. Urbanization continued apace: in 1871, 65 per cent of the population lived in villages and small towns, by 1910 only 40 per cent, while the number of city-dwellers rose from 4.8 per cent to more than 20 per cent over the same period. Furthermore, the population continued to grow rapidly, soaring by 60 per cent between 1871 and 1914 to 68 million.

Urbanization brought a number of social problems in its train. It was a symptom and a consequence of migration away from the countryside, particularly from the poor areas on the fringes of Germany, such as the rural districts of East Prussia or the Eifel. Many of the people torn from their traditional ties found it hard to adjust to life in the cities of the industrial conurbations; others, especially Catholics, found that, when everything around them had changed, all they had to fall back on was their religious faith. Besides differences in occupation and income, it was regional or ethnic origin and religion that hampered – without preventing – the emergence of a unified class consciousness, in the sense of a united political will. In particular, the influx of workers from the east and from Poland, caused or exacerbated breaches within the working class, not only in the form of ethnic and religious differences but also social ones. For as long as there was a readily available "reserve" of unskilled and undemanding workpeople, the greater the chances of promotion for the better trained German workers, and the greater the opportunity to develop an awareness of their status. It is hardly surprising that these social and cultural differences among the working class should have had an impact on their political and trade union organizations. The high degree of mobility, the migration from place to place, also meant that the trade unions found recruiting and particularly keeping members extremely difficult.

The growing numbers of unskilled workers and women posed particular problems for the unions when it came to propaganda and recruitment, as did the increase in white-collar workers. Having such firm roots among skilled male workers who were proud of their professional skills, it was difficult for the unions to penetrate the ranks of unskilled and female workers, while the latter often took the view that they were not adequately represented by the unions. Of course, women's union activities were limited by other factors apart from the legal restrictions placed on associations, namely traditional gender roles and the double burden of paid employment and work in the family. As for the white-collar workers, they comprised a stratum of wage-earners that was developing an awareness of self and class all of its own, prompting it to set up its own organizations with strong nationalist and bourgeois leanings.

Regardless of these splits, life was hard for all workers. The housing situation in the towns was abysmal: overcrowding, rack renting and sub-

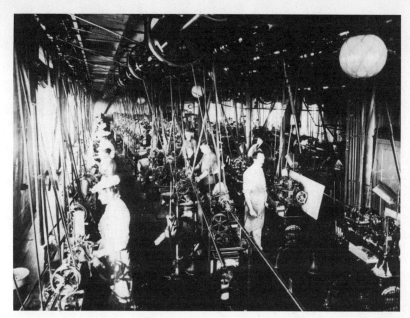

Workers at the lathes in the Siemens factory circa 1900

Making aprons – home working circa 1910

letting to one or more persons were commonplace. The high cost of food and less chance of making the family at least self-sufficient in some things by growing their own produce in their spare time forced workers' living standards down, particularly in the towns and cities. Even making allowances for differences due to industry, occupation, qualifications, area and sex, wages were often terrible; in sickness and old age, destitution was inevitable. It was often necessary for wife and children to go out to work, too, if the family was to have enough to live on. Despite the drawbacks, home working was considered a way of combining paid employment with work in the family.

But in the 1890s there were also signs that things were getting better. Between 1890 and 1913 the average annual wage of workers in industry, commerce and transport went up from 650 to 1,083 Marks. Taking into account the rise in living costs over the same period, average wages rose in real terms (in 1895 prices) from 636 to 834 Marks (Table 3a). These figures, however, conceal differing trends: for instance, while incomes in the printing industry went up substantially, conditions in the textile industry continued to be appalling.

In the same period, working hours in industry went on getting shorter. In 1890, 11 hours per day and 66 hours per week were the norm; in the years up to 1913 the workers won a cut to 10 hours per day and – as they started getting Saturday afternoons off – 54–60 hours per week (Table 4a). Individual firms such as the Carl Zeiss works in Jena and the Freese Venetian blind factory introduced the eight-hour day of their own accord as early as 1889 and 1892 respectively. This illustrates how the process of shortening the working day varied from one industry to another and from one firm to another. As with wages, this development would certainly not have taken place had it not been for the generally favourable economic situation, improvements in productivity and the struggles of the trade unions. But it should not be forgotten that these achievements were accompanied by the progressive intensification of work: technically, manufacturing became increasingly complex while the work process itself was rationalized. With the division of labour and the introduction of fixed times – that is, detailed stipulations governing the production process as a whole – the trend towards rationalization became a central element in employers' efforts to improve productivity and thus increase production.

*

At this point, mention should be made of industrial safety legislation. In the February decrees, Kaiser Wilhelm II announced the setting up of workers' committees and the introduction of industrial safety laws. And in fact the following years saw a succession of laws affecting worker welfare come into force. On 1 June 1891 an amendment to the trade regulations (Lex Berlepsch) provided for the creation of worker committees, made Sunday a day of rest, limited maximum working hours for women and young people to 10–11 hours per day and banned night work, prohibited child labour by minors younger than thirteen and improved protection for women following childbirth. The same year, a law on industrial tribunals (Gewerbegerichte) set up "special courts" with lay magistrates and worker representatives to deal with cases of industrial strife; these were the fore-runners of the labour tribunals (Arbeitsgerichte) created in 1926. In 1900 the industrial safety provisions of the trade regulations were revised and the rules protecting women and children improved. The same year also saw new regulations governing the closing times of shops and rest periods for employees, and an amendment to the Bavarian Mining Law laid down that pits employing more than twenty men had to set up worker com-mittees, a rule that was also adopted by Prussia in 1905 – after a major industrial dispute – for pits with more than a hundred employees. After the reform of the Law on Associations in 1908, young people under 18 years of age continued to be barred from political meetings and associa-tions but the rules were relaxed for women. The road to "social interven-tionism", linked with the names of the Prussian Trade Minister, Hans Hermann Baron von Berlepsch, and the Secretary of State of the Interior Ministry, Arthur Duke von Posadowsky-Wehner, demonstrated a willing-ness to carry out a measure of cautious social reform, though the general aim remained the same: to curb the growth of social democracy. The main impression was, nevertheless, still of a working class exploited and margi-nalized.

Government policy in the Wilhelminian Age continued to display the twin faces of social reform and political repression. Wilhelm II repeatedly spoke out, for example in a speech in Königsberg in 1894, against the "parties of subversion", to which he opposed religion, morals and order, which he wished to see upheld and strengthened. The assassination of the President of France by an Italian anarchist provided the pretext for polit-ical intervention: it prompted the submission of a Bill in 1894, the "Sub-version Bill", laying down harsher penalties for subversion, which was defined in terms of opinions as well as actions. The Bill did not receive the required majority in Parliament. The same fate was shared by the "Prison Bill" announced by Wilhelm II in 1898 in Bad Oeynhausen, whereby anyone attempting to prevent strike breakers from working during a strike would be sentenced to imprisonment. The Bill was laid before the Reichstag in June 1899, caused a storm of protest and was defeated in November 1899.

Despite the failure of these attempts to force through sanctions against the Social Democratic Party and the trade unions, the Kaiser's speeches and the Bills mentioned above created a climate of uncertainty and menace that was often felt to be a political buttress for the economic exploitation and the social marginalization of the workers. In addition, there were the measures for suppressing union activity devised by the employers, especially in the heavy industry sector: from blacklists and lockouts to the setting up of works associations (Werkvereine) devoted to maintaining industrial peace. They refused even to listen to trade unionists, let alone negotiate with them. In accordance with their authoritarian, paternalistic outlook, most employers continued well past the turn of the century to see trade union demands for a say in matters as unwarranted interference by outsiders in their private affairs or as trouble-making, upsetting the "harmonious" relationship between the employer and the individual employee. Apart from government policy and the employers' hostility to the Social Democratic labour movement, the parts played by the bureaucracy, police and judiciary, as well as the use of troops in industrial disputes, could all in all scarcely be interpreted as anything but proof of the reality of the class state and its role as the protector of the propertied classes.

Finally, due consideration should be given to the overall social climate, in which the idea of international solidarity was seen as a betrayal of Germany's Great Power aspirations. It was not only the Social Democratic labour movement that managed to become a mass movement; other organizations were equally successful in attracting support. In April 1891 the General German League (Allgemeiner Deutscher Verband) was founded, renamed the Pan-German League (Alldeutscher Verband) in 1894. The aims of this association were to cultivate patriotic awareness, conduct anti-semitic agitation and lend support to nationalist domestic and foreign policies, above all on behalf of Germans abroad and the German colonies. In its imperialist propaganda it was supported, from April 1898, by the German Naval Association (Deutscher Flottenverein), which by 1913 could boast 1.1 million members.

Moreover, since the 1890s efforts had been made to rally all bourgeois, conservative forces around an anti-Social Democratic "coalition policy", whose most conspicuous manifestations were the Imperial Association against Social Democracy (Reichsverband gegen die Sozialdemokratie), founded in 1904, and the Cartel of the Productive Classes (Kartell der schaffenden Stände), formed after the Social Democrats' election successes of 1912. It was certainly no coincidence that from 1904–5 onwards there was a lull in social welfare policy. Those rules which discriminated most harshly against the working class – the restrictions on the right of association, the Prussian three-class electoral system and the entrepreneur's absolute power as the "lord and master" of the company – remained in force right up to the end of the Empire. The beginnings of a social welfare policy were overlaid by the picture of a class society that sought to realize the dream of worldwide German influence by means of protective tariffs at the expense of the consumer, colonialist policies and the scramble to rearm, national hubris and an aggressive ideological stance. Both these factors – the beginnings of social reform and repressive measures designed to secure domestic backing for imperialist aims abroad – left their stamp on the programmes, self-image and policies of social democracy, of which the great mass of the union movement considered itself a part. Both factors, but probably more than anything the experience of being excluded from bourgeois society, contributed to the development of a ghetto mentality among large sections of the working class – a sense of rejection and solidarity – that caused them to view social democracy as a "home", giving the ghetto stance an ideology of its own and thus reinforcing it. This feeling of exclusion and isolation characterized not only the Social Democratic sections of the working class but also the Catholic ones, in which the two largest trade union federations were rooted.

2. *Organizational problems on the road to the mass union*

The Free trade unions

Although the trade union movement had survived the repressive measures of the Socialist Law, it did not mean that henceforth – after 1890 – it was able to develop unhindered. The feeling of being under constant threat from the Law on Associations and a stream of proposed new laws, from the police and judiciary and the action taken by the employers to defend their position was enough in itself to make trade union policy uncertain and prompt cautious manoeuvring. More than anything else it was due to the defeats suffered since 1894 on account of the troubled state of the economy that trade unionists were far from looking to the future with confidence. Innumerable lost battles were a painful reminder to trade unionists of how limited their influence was. The strike and lockout of 3,000 Hamburg tobacco workers in 1890, the strike by 20,000 Ruhr miners in 1891, the strike in the Saar region in 1891–92 and the printers' strike of 1891–92 – defeats such as these constantly raised doubts about the prospects of success of trade union work. Furthermore, strikes that ended in defeat often led directly to the weakening of the organizations, as many workers left their unions when they had been financially bled to death. The number of trade union members declined from over 290,000 in 1890 to 215,000 in 1892.

But the strike movements of 1889–90 also prompted the merger of the Social Democratic unions, thus laying the foundation of the modern trade union movement. Major and protracted industrial disputes in which the employers, as in Hamburg in 1890, resorted to a punitive lockout over the May Day celebrations, made the workers aware that they needed nation-wide, cross-occupational solidarity to defend them. This repeated experience lay behind the formation of a trade union umbrella organization. On 16–17 November 1890 the Conference of Trade Union Executives in Berlin decided to set up the General Commission of German Trade Unions (Generalkommission der Gewerkschaften Deutschlands), under the leadership of Carl Legien, who remained in place until his death in 1920.

Born in Marienburg in 1861, Carl Legien had a rapid rise in the union movement behind him. The story of his life was typical of the trade union leaders of his generation. After the death of his parents he was raised in an orphanage, apprenticed as a turner at the age of fourteen and then set out on his travels as a journeyman until doing his military service from 1881 to 1883. After travelling around for a few more years he settled in Hamburg in 1886. The same year, with the Socialist Law still in force, he joined the Turners' Union and a year later attended the Turners' Congress in Naumburg as a delegate, where he was elected chairman of the newly founded German Association of Turners. At the Berlin meeting of union representatives in mid-November 1890 he was elected chairman of the General Commission, on the policies of which he had a major influence as editor of the journal "Correspondenzblatt" – more on account of his personal acumen than any formal rights laid down in the rules and regulations.

How did the General Commission see its duties?[1] Its first aim, for obvious reasons, was to defend the right of association. The Commission also had to carry on propaganda work in areas where there were no unions; it had to fund defensive strikes; it had to prepare and convene the congresses of the trade union umbrella organization; and finally it had been

---

1 See Paul Umbreit, 25 Jahre Deutscher Gewerkschaftsbewegung 1890–1915. Erinnerungsschrift zum fünfundzwanzigjährigen Jubiläum der Begründung der Generalkommission der Gewerkschaften Deutschlands (Berlin, 1915), pp. 155–62

instructed to draft an organizational plan for the trade unions. The very nature of these duties showed that the General Commission was not really an instrument for leading the Free Unions; it was handed the jobs that the individual occupational associations were unable or unwilling to take on – and there was plenty of room for argument on that point.

So much was evident at the first Congress of German Trade Unions, held in Halberstadt from 14 to 18 March 1892. The plan to set up a central fund to provide backing for defensive strikes was once again dropped because it would probably have entailed too great a concentration of power in the hands of the umbrella organization. A step of crucial importance for the future of the trade union movement was the decision, after a good deal of heated discussion, to encourage the formation of national unions (Zentralverbände). A majority of the delegates thus came out against the local form of organization and the "shop steward" system, which had both proved their worth under the Socialist Law and were in tune with the ideals of grassroots democracy. There were a number of things in favour of national unions: greater financial power, better coordination of administration, propaganda and press, a wider spread of the risk in industrial disputes and stronger benefit schemes. But those who supported the principles of local organization did not find these reasons convincing enough and left the congress in protest.

The decision to work for the formation of industrial unions for appropriate trades was a pioneering one[2]; the unions of allied trades were to move closer together by entering into "cartel agreements". But there was no clear decision on the issue of industrial unions versus occupational unions. Basically, this was in keeping with the actual situation, with large and small companies coexisting side by side. While the occupational approach reflected the position in the skill-based small and medium-sized companies, the growth of the large corporation, in which members of quite different trades and workers with greatly varying qualifications worked together, tended to support the idea of industrial unions. But in the early 1890s, with the dominant position of the big companies only just becoming apparent, there was no definitive solution in sight. It was to be decades before the union movement as a whole followed the example of the engineering workers' and woodworkers' organizations, which both overcame the limitations of the occupational approach at an early stage – 1891 and 1893 respectively. It was largely this step that ensured that the

---

2 Protokoll der Verhandlungen der Ersten Kongresses der Gewerkschaften Deutschlands, abgehalten zu Halberstadt vom 14. bis 18. Marz 1892 (Hamburg, 1892), pp. 68–70

unions in question grew more rapidly than the others in the years to come, especially as they were able to compensate for the decline and disappearance of individual trades by recruiting other workers, particularly unskilled ones.

In the eyes of the General Commission, trade union policy was principally organizational policy. Recruitment and the provision of services to members were among its most important tasks. On 1 January 1891 it started publication of its own newspaper, the "Correspondenzblatt der Generalkommission". By expanding the benefits system, the trade unions were responding not only to the current plight of the working class but they were also trying to reduce fluctuations in membership by relating benefits directly to length of membership and the amount paid in dues. Furthermore, the General Commission consistently advocated the standardization and the raising of dues to ensure the strength of the organization. If one considers that in 1895 the average dues of the Printers' Union were 57.75 Marks, while in the Raftsmen's Union they were only 1.44 Marks, it is hard to dismiss such efforts. Lastly, the General Commission developed into a sort of trade union statistical bureau: data on membership, funds, strike action, the economic situation, wages, working hours and prices were collated and published to provide a firm foundation for union work.

The 1890s saw a tremendous expansion in the trade unions' benefit schemes. Nearly all the unions set up strike funds, travel funds, sickness and death benefits, and compensation schemes for workers penalized by the employers. The establishment of a trade union unemployment benefit scheme, on the other hand, was considered too risky for trade unions organized on occupational lines and often concentrated in one region; some unions also feared that the movement would overstretch itself financially, leaving no money available for industrial disputes.

At the same time, the trade unions began amalgamating the payments offices of the individual unions into local groups in order to exert greater influence on the local labour market. In addition, from 1894 local labour secretariats were set up, offering advice to wage earners (not only members) and representing them free of charge in matters of insurance and industrial law. Following the formation of eleven district secretariats at the seats of the Higher Insurance Offices of the National Workers' Insurance scheme, a central labour secretariat was created in 1903 at the supreme tribunal in Berlin; by 1914 there were a total of 150 local labour secretariats.

*

The possibility cannot be ruled out that this emphasis on the local level was intended to take the wind out of the sails of local activists. The supporters of local forms of organization, who had been in a minority in Halberstadt in 1892, were initially able to enjoy the indirect support of the Law on Associations, which prohibited "political associations" from establishing links that extended outside the locality – and every response to government action was seen as "political", for instance the demand for laws laying down shorter working hours, improving industrial safety and so on. So the unions were confronted by a choice: should they address political issues or link up nationally? The fact that this internal dispute went on smouldering after the Law on Association was amended indicates that it really centred on differences of opinion about union organization and tactics.

The "localists" advocated a radical, revolutionary trade union policy; according to the journal "Der Bauhandwerker" in 1893, a success by the trade union movement would be regarded as proof that "on the foundation of the existing order the worker could get by to his satisfaction", whereupon "the need for a social revolution would be shelved". The trade union movement could only have a revolutionary effect "by arousing hopes which it cannot fulfil"[3]. This is why the localists opposed the established division of labour and duties between the party and the trade unions. They rejected the model of representative parliamentary democracy and proclaimed their belief – influenced by the French labour movement – in "direct action", the syndicalist idea of the unity of economic and political struggle forged at local level.

The localists, who got together in 1897 under the name of the "Free Association of German Trade Unions" (Freie Vereinigung deutscher Gewerkschaften), were at their peak around 1900, with about 20,000 members. The centre of the movement was clearly in Berlin, particularly among the bricklayers, carpenters and engineering workers. As far as the building trade was concerned, this was mainly due to the favourable conditions for local strike movements in Berlin, especially as during the building boom in the capital the often irreplaceable craftsmen did not have a strong employers' federation to contend with. After the turn of the century the localist movement rapidly lost ground, partly due to the deci-

---

3 "Der Bauhandwerker" No. 37 of 16.9.1893, quot. Dirk H. Müller, Der Syndikalismus in der deutschen Gewerkschaftsbewegung vor 1914, in Erich Matthias and Klaus Schönhoven (eds), Solidarität und Menschenwürde. Etappen der deutschen Gewerkschaftsgeschichte von den Anfängen bis zur Gegenwart (Bonn, 1984), pp. 57–68; this quot. p. 61

sion by the SPD party congress in 1908 that membership of the SPD was incompatible with membership of the Free Association.

*

The question of which organizational model the trade unions should choose was not resolved before 1914. Up to the beginning of the First World War the number of unions affiliated to the General Commission fell to 46, with traditional trade associations alongside new industrial unions. Craft-based organizations such as the bookbinders, printers, coopers, hatters and coppersmiths continued to maintain their position. But the strongest unions – as emerges from a glance at the membership figures for 1914 – were the cross-occupational organizations of the rising industries: the German Engineering Workers' Union with over 500,000 members, followed by the building workers', miners', woodworkers' and textile workers' unions. One of the fastest growing unions was the Factory Workers' Union, which organized semi-skilled and unskilled workers in almost a hundred trades. The building labourers', retail workers' and transport workers' unions also recruited members among the unskilled. In any case, there were tremendous differences of size even between the various craft-based unions: the union of the note engravers had less than a hundred members, that of the printers more than 50,000. But overall the importance of the true craftsmen's unions dwindled because of their limited catchment area, the increasing proportion of unskilled workers and the declining importance of many crafts, such as those of the kid glove makers, hatters and ships' carpenters. But if one considers the degree of unionization, the "old" occupational unions do not come out badly: while about 30 per cent of the printers, coppersmiths and glove makers – all highly skilled trades – were unionized, the corresponding figure for bricklayers, for example, was only about 7 per cent.

While skilled male workers were the backbone of the unions prior to the First World War, their importance declined with the development of large-scale industry and the devaluation of skilled labour in favour of unskilled. This was one of the main reasons why cross-occupational national unions, organizing skilled and unskilled workers, both male and female, proved to be the organizational form of the future.

Even before the First World War, we can see the emergence of the organizational principles and structures that were to survive right up to the present day: personal membership of a specific union, which in turn belonged to an umbrella organization; delegation from the local level by way of the regional level to the central level through democratic elections;

the elected executive's accountability to congress at all levels; payment offices of the individual unions at the local level, merging to form local groups (later replaced by local committees of the umbrella organization); strike decisions taken at the centre; the construction of a central machinery of professional union officials, taking charge of administration, funding, propaganda work, public relations and so forth. Between 1900 and 1914 the number of central union employees increased tenfold, from 269 to 2,867. But, particularly in the light of the controversy over "localism", the drawbacks of this development should not be overlooked. The system of delegating decisions upwards through a number of tiers to the top meant that there was a large gap between the union leadership and the shopfloor. The bureaucratization of decision-making – for instance, on strike action – fostered apathy and passivity in members, or led to spontaneous strikes bypassing the unions altogether. All these problems were being discussed in the trade union press well before the turn of the century; but they did not – before 1914 – give rise to a serious crisis of confidence between membership and leadership.

The fact that large sections of the working class were content with the trade unions as they were is best illustrated by the rise in membership that reflected the sound economic trend after 1895 and the trade union victories that this made possible. From 215,000 in 1892, the membership of the Social Democratic Free Trade Unions rose to more than 1.1 million in 1904 and to 2.5 m the year before the First World War (Table 1a), leaving the Hirsch-Duncker associations and the Christian unions trailing in their wake.

The Hirsch-Duncker trade associations

Despite their privileged position under the Socialist Law, the liberal trade associations lost more and more ground. Like the Free Trade Unions, their success in attracting members was largely dependent on the economic situation and successful strike action: from over 65,000 in 1891, their membership fell to 45,000 a year later and then rose slowly and with fluctuations to 106,000 in 1913 (Table 1a). The Hirsch-Duncker associations thus only benefited to a very limited extent from the trend towards a mass movement.

This was partly due to internal tensions. The first issue was the representation of the individual associations within the umbrella organization. In view of the great variations in strength between the individual associations, which were not given adequate consideration by the Central Council of the umbrella organization, the mechanical engineers and the factory workers were repeatedly outvoted by the smaller associations. After a long and heated controversy, proportional representation on the Central Council was introduced in 1889, giving the associations influence commensurate with their size. This reform assisted the smaller associations in their efforts to carry out cross-occupational mergers, thus gaining in strength and importance. But members had a good deal of respect for the occupational principle – in accordance with the ideas of the founder, Max Hirsch – and such efforts quickly came to naught; indeed, they may even have frightened away many members. The concept of trade thus continued to dominate, and this fact – together with the associations' political outlook – succeeded in deterring the fast-growing group of semi-skilled and unskilled workers from joining the Hirsch-Duncker Gewerkvereine.

The strike issue was also a controversial one – in fact, a central one for all unions. The H-D associations had not merely paid lip service to the strike as the ultimate means of defending their members' interests; time and again they were involved in industrial struggles, even though it entailed great sacrifices. But there was no question of pursuing a policy of offensive strikes. It was for this reason that as early as 1891 the porcelain workers' association, with its 4,000 members, switched its allegiance to the Free Trade Unions. Particularly in Düsseldorf there was resistance to this reluctance to strike, which Hirsch continued to defend until his death in 1905, still at the helm of the associations. His opponent on this fundamental issue was Anton Erkelenz, who later became one of the leaders of the Gewerkvereine. In contrast to Hirsch, he came from the skilled artisan class, which was typical of the H-D associations. He was born in 1878, the son of an independent master fitter. After learning his father's trade, he joined the engineering workers' association at the age of eighteen. By the time he was 24 he had been elected workers' secretary of the Hirsch-Duncker associations of the Rhineland and Westphalia. In this post he strengthened the "Düsseldorf tendency", adding a clear nationalist tinge to its social-liberal outlook.

Such internal disagreements about organizational structure and, more than anything, strike policy were certainly detrimental to the image of the H-D associations; but it was the vagueness of their political line that was probably crucial. In the document "Basic Principles" adopted in 1907[4], the associations professed party political and religious neutrality, though they could not deny their close connections with leftwing liberalism. They

---

4 Reprinted in Anton Erkelenz, Arbeiter-Katechismus. Eine Erklärung des Programms der freiheitlich-nationalen Arbeiterschaft (Berlin-Schönberg, 1908), pp. 7–11

demanded a firm policy of social reform, which did nothing to distinguish them from the Free Trade Unions nor – in view of their allegiance to liberalism – to improve their credibility. The Gewerkvereine tried to cope with this curious intermediate position by stressing their distinct profile – in 1901 incompatibility with membership of the SPD was confirmed – and nationalist ideals. In 1907–8 they described themselves – in the words of Karl Goldschmidt, union chairman from 1907–16 – as "popular-libertarian"[5] and from 1910 as "libertarian-national", in a pithy phrase of Erkelenz's[6]. The position became extremely difficult for the H-D associations when a third union movement appeared on the scene and soon laid claim to the label "national" in the phrase "Christian-national". The Gewerkvereine thus became "piggy in the middle" within the trade union movement, with major chunks of their programme being put across more trenchantly and more credibly by their rivals.

The Christian trade unions

Encouraged by the upturn in the economy from the mid-1890s on, a third union movement quickly developed, soon overtaking the H-D associations to become the second largest branch of the union movement. The first Christian trade unions were set up in those parts of Germany that already had a well-developed network of Catholic workers' associations, above all the Aachen area, the industrial district of the Lower Rhine (Mönchen-Gladbach, Krefeld), the Ruhr district and the areas around Munich and Stuttgart in southern Germany. Invitations to the inaugural meetings of Christian trade unions were often issued by clergymen; at any rate, they were the main speakers, particularly the members of the Popular Association for Catholic Germany. Also, the clergy were often initially involved, via the institution of the honorary council, as mediators or overseers of the union leadership, though – unlike the denominational workers' associations and the occupational sections, which were intended to act as non-striking substitutes for proper trade unions – the unions themselves were not under Church leadership. The way had been cleared for the Catholic Church's involvement by the papal encyclical "Rerum novarum", in which Pope Leo XIII had come out firmly in favour of social

---

5 Karl Goldschmidt, Das Programm des Verbandes der Deutschen Gewerkvereine und die Forderungen der einzelnen Gewerkvereine (Berlin, 1910)
6 Anton Erkelenz, Freiheitlich-nationale Arbeiterbewegung (Munich, 1910)

reform born of Christian charity and the establishment of Christian workers' associations.

The model for most of the subsequent Christian unions was the Union of Christian Miners, formed in October 1894 at the instigation of the miner August Brust and initially covering the mining district of Dortmund. In particular, the objective set out in Article 2 of its rules[7] served as a model for others: "The purpose of the trade union shall be to improve the miners' moral and social position on a Christian and lawful basis and to initiate and maintain a peaceful accord between employers and wage earners." In addition it was emphasized that "the Association shall be loyal to the Kaiser and Empire and shall not discuss denominational and political party matters". According to Article 8, joining the association amounted to a declaration that the new member was an "opponent of Social Democratic principles and aspirations".

In the years that followed a number of Christian unions were set up at local and regional level. They quickly moved towards a merger. At the first congress of the Christian unions, held in Mainz at Whitsun (21–22 May) 1899, the "Mainz principles" were adopted as a basic programme[8]. The unions' interdenominational character and party political neutrality were the key principles enshrined in it. For this reason, both denominations should be appropriately represented in the selection of delegates and officers. The comments on the Christian unions' attitude to strikes were also important: it should "not be forgotten that workers and employers have common interests" – as the producers of goods, vis-à-vis the consumers. For this reason "the entire activity of the unions should be pervaded and inspired by a conciliatory spirit. Demands must be moderate but put forward with firmness and determination. The strike must be used solely as a last resort and if likely to be successful".

Thus unlike the Free Trade Unions, the Christian unions very definitely had a programme setting our their basic principles. This, of course, was indispensable, as the Christian federation had been expressly founded in opposition to social democracy, whose "class struggle mentality", "materialism" and "godlessness" were rejected. In the programme of the Christian unions, the social question appeared to be mainly one of

---

7 Quot. Heinrich Imbusch, Die Saarbergarbeiterbewegung 1912/13 (Cologne, 1913), p. 2 f.
8 Reprinted in Geschichte und Entwicklung der Christlichen Gewerkschaften Deutschlands nebst Protokoll des III. Gewerkschaftskongresses zu Krefeld (Mönchen Gladbach, 1901), p. 10 ff.

morality that could be solved with good will, particularly on the part of the employers.

*

It is a remarkable fact that the Christian unions set out on the road to a national union even before they had built up a system of individual unions. The congresses in Mainz (1899) and Frankfurt (1900) were by no means full stops in the story of the birth of the Christian unions; instead, they triggered off the establishment of new local, regional, and ultimately national unions. The fact that the creation of the federation ran parallel with the formation of numerous national unions is best illustrated by the following data: 1899 saw the formation of the Christian-Social Union of Engineering Workers, the Central Union of Christian Woodworkers, the Union of Christian Tobacco and Cigar Workers and the Central Union of Christian Building Workers; on the other hand, the Union of Christian Shoe and Leather Workers of Germany, the Union of Christian Tailors and Allied Trades and the Christian-Social Union of Non-Industrial Workers and Sundry Trades of Germany were not set up until 1900 – the year after the Mainz congress. But the federation undoubtedly derived its main support in the pre-war period from the miners' and textile workers' unions, which together accounted for one half of all the federation's members in 1905; five years later they still made up 42 per cent of the membership. Of all female Christian trade unionists, in 1905 60 per cent belonged to the Textile Workers' Union; in 1910, 46 per cent.

So although the formation of central (national) unions was by no means completed, as early as 1899 a central committee of the entire Christian trade union movement was set up in Mainz, though it ran out of money and ceased to function. But a little later, the Krefeld congress of 1901 adopted the rules of the national federation; at the time of its foundation, it had 23 affiliated organizations with some 84,000 members. With the formation of the federation, the debate about the organizational principles of the Christian unions was, in theory, decided. It was built up as follows: the individual unions soon all had central general assemblies that elected the executive; the next tier down consisted of regional or area unions, and finally there were the local payment offices, which – especially in the cities – were merged to form area groups. These area groups saw themselves as the local representatives of the federation and ensured that the individual unions took concerted action in matters of propaganda and also in the elections to the management committees of health insurance funds and industrial tribunals.

The federation also managed to put out a number of periodical publications – just as quickly as most of the national unions. On 15 April 1901 it commenced publication of "Bulletins from the Federation of Christian Trade Unions of Germany", which changed its name in 1905 to the "Central Journal of the Christian Trade Unions of Germany" (Zentralblatt der Christlichen Gewerkschaften Deutschlands). From 1 October 1901, the chairman of the Union of Christian Woodworkers – and later Secretary General of the Federation – Adam Stegerwald edited the "Christian Trade Union Journal" for individual unions that could not support a journal of their own.

Like Legien, Adam Stegerwald was a tough character, perhaps even more hardbitten than Legien. He was born on 14 December 1874 in Greussenheim near Würzburg. His family were poor smallholders; Stegerwald sought to escape by completing an apprenticeship as a cabinetmaker. During his travels he came into contact with the Catholic journeymen's movement. In 1899 he was one of the founders of the Central Union of Christian Woodworkers. He was an energetic supporter of the merger of the Christian trade unions into a federation, becoming its secretary general on 12 January 1903.

This institution continued to grow rapidly, so that it is accurate to say that by 1906 the Christian trade unions had been consolidated locally, regionally and centrally. They had a rich and varied press, union officials and an extensive benefits system. Because of this, the dues had been raised sharply year after year. The steady increase in membership, despite some setbacks – due to internal disputes (1902) and trouble in the economy (1907–9 and 1913) – is a sure sign of a stabilization process that was undoubtedly helped along by the overall favourable trend in the economy since 1894. It should be emphasized that the Christian trade unions – contrary to their own trade-centred outlook – pushed hard for the formation of unions covering groups of trades or whole industries, though the occupational trade union remained the prevailing form of union organization of the pre-war period.

Structural obstacles to organization

Their breakthrough as a mass movement certainly did not mean that the trade unions had now achieved wall-to-wall coverage, as it were. Owing to the restrictions placed on agricultural workers, messengers, state railway employees and so on, these occupations were anyway untouched by unionization. Home workers were also hard to organize since they often clung on to an illusory independence.

The size of the company also directly affected opportunities to organize. In small craft-based companies the masters' social control over the journeymen in his employ was frequently complete, while in large companies, effective action by the employers often made union membership difficult. Blacklists on the one hand, welfare measures such as company accommodation, company shops, health care and so forth on the other, together with the support given to works associations dedicated to preserving industrial peace, serving as blacklegs and thus reducing the union's ability to fight and win a dispute, long hampered union expansion in the big companies. In 1910 only 3,000 (4.3 per cent) out of 70,000 Krupp workers in Essen were unionized. At BASF in Ludwigshafen, three-quarters of the workforce belonged to a "sweetheart" union. In 1910 the "sweethearts" merged to form a federation, which in 1913 became the "Head Committee of National Labour and Trade Associations", with a total of 173,000 members. The crucial role played by the strength and policies of the employers in the spread of these organizations is shown by the heavy industrial regions such as the Rhine, Ruhr, Upper Silesia and the Saar. In collaboration with the regional administration and the Church, authoritarian, patriarchal employers could slow down the advance of the unions considerably. And this applied not only to the notoriously revolutionary Free Trade Unions, but also to the liberal unions and even to rival Christian organizations.

Another factor that should be borne in mind is the differing extent to which the various regions were industrialized. The trade unions were strongest in cities with rising industries, such as Augsburg, Berlin, Bremen, Hamburg, Hanover, Nuremberg and the central German towns; their position was conspicuously weak in predominantly agricultural regions like East and West Prussia, which is an indication not only of the restrictions on the right of association but also of the social control exercised by the large landowners, reminiscent of the patriarchal attitudes of the early industrial barons.

The increase in female labour was another obstacle to the steady expansion of the trade unions. The occupational survey of 1907 showed that as a proportion of the working population women now accounted for 35.8 per cent. But the unions had little success in attracting female members. At the first congress of the Free Trade Unions in Halberstadt in 1892, it was seen as an "act of self-preservation" to step up agitational work among women. No special women's organizations were to be set up; if necessary, the rules of the existing unions should be altered to enable women to be admitted.[9] This decision only bore fruit, however, in cases where men and women had roughly the same qualifications, for instance, in the bookbinders', printers' assistants', gold and silver workers' and tobacco workers' unions. Unions in trades or industries in which men were often better qualified than women, such as the textile and clothing industry, were less successful in recruiting female members.

Disregarding the restrictions set out in the Law on Associations, which ceased to apply in 1908, women's reservations about unionization were due to several factors. To many women paid employment was simply a temporary phase in their lives, whose main duty was considered to be raise a family. Working mothers struggled under the dual burden of jobs and housework, especially since the latter was often left to them alone, even by convinced Social Democrats, in line with the traditional gender roles. Moreover, the wages paid to female workers, who were often unskilled, were so low – though much needed, indeed relied upon, as extra income for the family – that it was impossible to pay the still quite high union dues out of them. Lastly, many women were more deeply attached than the men to their rural, and hence often religious backgrounds, and these ties prevented them from backing the "aggressive" policy of defending one's interests embodied by the male-dominated unions.

Thus women were rarely represented at the top of the union movement. The only woman to be elected on to the General Commission at the Halberstadt congress was Wilhelmine Kähler of the Female Factory and Manual Workers' Union; Emma Ihrer, who founded the Association for the Defence of the Interests of Women Workers in Berlin in 1885, was not elected. Kähler was re-elected once only, in 1896. From 1899 to 1905 there was not a single woman on the General Commission. Although the Fifth Trade Union Congress (1905) decided to step up the recruitment of women and build up a system of female union representatives to this end, even setting up a secretariat for female workers the same year, the impression remained of male dominance at union congresses and on executive committees. For all these reasons the proportion of female members of the Free Trade Unions rose exceedingly slowly – from 2 per cent in 1892, to 3.3 per cent in 1900 and 8.8 per cent in 1913.

In the Christian trade unions things were not much different. There, too, the number of women members was a long way behind the proportion of women in work. From 5.8 per cent in 1903 it rose slowly and unevenly to 8.1 per cent by 1913. Even this could be seen as surprising, since the

---

9 Protokoll der Verhandlungen des 1. Kongresses der Gewerkschaften Deutschlands, p. 73

Christian unions never missed an opportunity to refer to women's "true" role as mothers and to play on their reservations about employment outside the home, which were fuelled by Catholic ideas about the proper order of things. The fact that the proportion of women in the Free and Christian trade unions was about the same is even more remarkable if one takes into account the dominant position of the Miners' Union in the Christian trade union movement; otherwise, in view of the high proportion of women in the Textile Workers' Union, the average would have been even higher.

The trade unions found it hard to make headway among the white-collar workers, a group that was growing fast. Although they differed greatly in function and income, the white-collar workers developed an independent mentality that was chiefly characterized by the wish to be distinguished from manual workers. Whether office-workers or shop assistants, technicians or clerks – the most important thing for them was their status as "non-workers". The launching of a special insurance scheme for white-collar workers in 1911 heightened their awareness of their status, which obviously ruled out membership of a proletarian mass movement. Although the Free Unions set up a clerical assistants' union in 1907, it was not able to report a great measure of success. White-collar workers often preferred the nationalist associations, as they felt less of a need for organizations of their own, not considering themselves rejected by Wilhelminian society in the way the workers did. In any event, the "bourgeois" white-collar associations were more successful in recruiting members than unions belonging to the trade union movement proper.

That much is revealed by a look at the membership statistics. When the National Union of Salaried Staff (Zentralverband der Angestellten) was formed in 1897 with 522 members, the Clerical Assistants' Association of 1858 (headquarters: Hamburg) already had some 54,000, the Union of German Clerical Assistants in Leipzig 47,000, and the German Nationalist Union of Clerical Assistants (DHV) 7,700. By 1913 the situation had changed in favour of the DHV, which now had 148,000, while the 1858 association had 127,000, the Leipzig union 102,000 and the nationalist union only 24,800. These figures illustrate how the white-collar workers' strong status awareness affected their decision to join a professional organization or trade union. The leading position of the DHV, which recruited members with its nationalist and anti-semitic propaganda, showed where the political sympathies of many white-collar workers lay – a problem that was to become particularly acute under the Weimar Republic.

At this point another problem should be mentioned: the rise in membership figures would have been more impressive, if it were not for the huge turnover in members. For example, between 1892 and 1913 2.1 million workers joined the German Engineering Workers' Union – but 1.6 m left it again. Even the job of simply managing the ever-growing membership records made it necessary to build up a superstructure of regularly paid officials. Membership fluctuations forced the unions constantly to consider how best to tackle the problem: benefits schemes and more frequent contact with members via regular collection of dues were considered the best means, but they did not really provide a successful solution.

The administrative needs of a mass movement, the growing numbers of trade union duties and the trend towards centralization of union powers – all combined to change the face of trade unionism, which came to be increasingly dominated by the "union machinery", or the "union bureaucracy". One trend that was bound to affect the relationship between the members and the paid union leadership was the emergence of professional union officials, who – naturally – developed "class interests" of their own. Through their various tasks – for instance, as representatives and lay assessors on arbitration and self-management bodies – union employees had become incorporated into the society of the Reich. In consequence, anything that jeopardized the trade unions, which after all were their life's work and livelihood at the same time, was viewed with the utmost suspicion. True, this had not yet led to a profound credibility gap between the rank and file and the leadership; but there were the makings of a problem that was to flare up during the Great War and later, especially during the revolution of 1918–19.

Ideological and political divisions within the working class and the split in the trade union movement

The breakthrough of the unions as a mass movement does not present a coherent picture. There was a steep rise in the number of union members in the 25 years between the end of the Socialist Law and the outbreak of the First World War. The strength of the unions also increased as a result of the centralization of the individual unions and the formation of umbrella organizations. Yet there was an obvious risk of membership and leadership drifting apart. Furthermore, there were large areas that remained out of bounds to unions of all tendencies. The fragmentation of the union movement and the resultant rivalry also tied up a good deal of energy that could have been expended more usefully on other things. Of course, the formation of trade union federations on political lines was not entirely a bad thing. The different ideological and political ties of the unions were precisely what won over to trade unionism many people from sections of the working class that emphatically rejected it in its Social Democratic guise.

We should remember, however, that the splits in the trade union movement were not artificial ones: they corresponded to divisions in the working class itself, though admittedly these were initially deepened and entrenched by the various different organizations. The rival unions were both an expression and a consolidation of the old division of the working class into different socio-cultural milieux that shaped the lives and attitudes of the workers who belonged to them at any given time. The Free Trade Unions were part of the "Social Democratic milieu" that was also held together by the SPD, the benefit schemes and co-operatives, press, libraries, cultural societies and joint festivals. The Christian trade unions derived their surest support from the Catholic working class, most of whom tended towards the Centre Party politically and were politically and ideologically "at home" with their "own" insurance, their "own" co-operatives, the Catholic press and the cultural activities offered by the workers' associations and the Church.

It was not only the rival organizations that were affected by the various working class milieux – they made their mark on everyday life. They determined how people voted – but also where people lived and shopped, what insurance they took out against the vicissitudes of life, what they read, how and what they celebrated, whether they attended the May Day parade or the Corpus Christi procession. These different milieux were a consequence of the marginalization of the working class under the Empire; but at the same time they were a voluntary means of demarcation, enabling people to dissociate themselves from outside influences and thus promoting unity within the milieu.

The ideological and political division of the working class, the mass base for the various trade unions movements, thus extended to other levels. This is true of the co-operation between the trade union and co-operative movements, for instance. Since the 1890s the trade unions had seen the co-operative movement, formed under the influence of Schulze-Delitzsch's ideas, as a possible partner in improving the lot of the working class. The trade union members of the General Co-operative Association (Allgemeiner Genossenschaftsverband) broke away in 1903 to set up the Central Union of German Consumer Associations (Zentralverband deutscher Konsumvereine). At the Cologne trade union congress in 1905, Adolf von Elm, who had founded the Bulk Buying Company of the German Consumer Associations in Hamburg in 1893, sought backing for co-operation between the two movements in his speech on "Trade Unions and Co-operatives"; after all, the latter were a "weapon in labour's struggle against capital". Congress decided that trade unionists should join the co-operatives[10].

Despite all the internal conflicts (between, for example, model but costly working conditions, on the one hand, and higher dividends on the other) the co-operatives throve (partly owing to trade union support) and founded or took over a number of companies of their own, such as factories producing cleaning materials and food. In 1911 there were 1,142 local co-operatives with 1.3 m members and a turnover of 335 m Marks. On 1 July 1913, the consumer co-operatives and Free Trade Unions co-founded the People's Care (Volksfürsorge) insurance scheme, which was to have its heyday in the Weimar period. The Hirsch-Duncker and Christian unions collaborated with their own consumer co-operative movements, which also flourished. In 1913 the Christian trade unions established the German Popular Insurance Company (Deutsche Volksversicherungs AG).

There was a schism in the trade union movement internationally, too. Since the 1890s, a network of contacts had been built up, initially by unions organizing the same trades. Delegates attended the congresses of sister organizations abroad, international trade or occupational conferences were arranged and, finally, the first international occupational associations were formed, the Social Democratic and Christian unions doing this separately. Since the turn of the century, preparations had been in train to establish international federations of the Socialist and the Christian umbrella organizations. In view of the German trade unions' strength, they were given a leading role in these international efforts to achieve unity. Their work was rewarded with executive posts: Carl Legien, former secretary of the International Bureau of Socialist Trade Unions (founded 1902), was appointed president of the International Trade Union Federation, set up in Zürich in 1913. Adam Stegerwald was made leader of the International Trade Union Commission, which evolved into the International Federation of Christian Trade Unions.

10 Protokoll der Verhandlungen des Fünften Kongresses der Gewerkschaften Deutschlands, abgehalten in Köln a. R. vom 22. bis 27. Mai (Berlin, 1905); A. von Elm, Gewerkschaften und Genossenschaften, pp. 158–70, this quot. p. 170; resolution p. 35 f.

3. Conflicts over the independence of the trade unions

The period between the lifting of the Socialist Law and the First World War not only witnessed the emergence of the basic structures of the modern trade union mass organizations; these were also years in which the nature of the trade unions was clarified and they asserted their independence from their ideological and political mentors. Though the unions had not actually been founded by the parties or by the Catholic Church, these institutions continually tried to control them or to use them for their own ends. But as the unions grew stronger and scored successes in the day-to-day struggle to better the lot of the working class, they developed their own self-awareness, which was scarcely compatible with their allies' claims to leadership. This is why the Free Trade Unions clashed dramatically with the SPD, and the Christian unions fell out with sections of the Catholic Church.

Free trade unions and the SPD: from subordination to equality

The unity between the Free Trade Unions and the Social Democratic Party that had developed under the pressure of the Socialist Law and was almost taken for granted lived on, but it was troubled if not effaced by a series of conflicts. The Social Democratic Party laid claim to unlimited powers of leadership, as set out in the 1891 Erfurt party programme[11], which stated that the struggle of the working class against capitalist exploitation is "necessarily a political struggle" and "to turn this working class struggle into a conscious and unified one and to guide it to its necessary conclusion is the task of the Social Democratic Party". This programme shows the SPD, having just emerged strengthened from the period of the emergency laws, bursting with self-confidence. The theoretical section explains the need for a complete social revolution, based on the socialization of the means of production. The protracted economic recession seemed to confirm the expectation that capitalism would perish in a manner as swift as it was inevitable. In contrast, the practical, day-to-day demands put forward in the second part of the programme – from the introduction of universal, equal, direct and secret suffrage, the repeal of all laws limiting freedom of opinion, assembly and association and the equality of man and woman, to the declaration that "religion is a private

---

11 Reprinted in Dowe and Klotzbach (eds), Programmatische Dokumente, p. 187 ff.; these quotations, pp. 189 and 191 f.

matter" and the call to "secularize school" – showed the SPD with its feet firmly on the ground of the status quo. This applied even more to the demands listed "for the protection of the working class", which included the introduction of the eight-hour day, a ban on the employment of children under fourteen, a ban on the truck system, the reinforcement of the factory inspectorate, "granting agricultural workers and servants equality in law with industrial workers", "securing the right of association" and "the take-over of all workers' insurance schemes by the state with strong worker participation in their management".

The trade unions were certainly able to subscribe to this list of demands. Given their critical position in the early 1890s, they probably saw little alternative to accepting their allotted role as a recruiting school for the political labour movement. They modestly stepped back, ceding centre-stage to the political party that "seeks a total reform of the present social system", whereas the trade union movement, "because of the limits imposed on it by the law, stands on the ground of present-day bourgeois society in its efforts"[12]. A little later Carl Legien admitted: "We know full well that a lasting improvement in the lot of the working class, the elimination of wage labour, the appropriation of the full profits of labour can only be achieved politically. On the other hand, however," he said, in justification of trade union work, "the mass of workers must be won over to this idea, won over by the economic struggle in present-day bourgeois society."[13] Union work was thus "the means to an end"; it was to create the conditions enabling the "mass of workers to solve [. . .] the historical task that is the lot of the working class"[14]. According to Legien at the Cologne party congress of 1893, the unions were the "nursery of the political movement", the "best educational institution for our comrades"[15].

The unions, weakened by the industrial defeats and membership losses that occurred in the early 1890s, was confronted by a SPD leadership abrim with self-confidence and delighted with the electoral successes of 1890 and 1893. With the backing of 1.4 m voters, later increased to 1.7 m,

---

12 Carl Legien, An die Mitglieder der Gewerkschaften, in Correspondenzblatt der Generalkommission der Gewerkschaften Deutschlands (= Correspondenzblatt), no. 3 of 7. 2. 1891, p. 9
13 Zur Organisationsfrage, in: Correspondenzblatt No. 13 of 23.5.1891, pp. 51–3; this quot. p. 52
14 Quot. Helga Grebing, Geschichte der deutschen Arbeiterbewegung. Ein Überblick (Munich, 1970), p. 101
15 Carl Legien, Die Gewerkschaftsbewegung und ihre Unterstützung durch die Parteigenossen, in Protokoll über die Verhandlungen des Parteitages der Sozialdemokratischen Partei Deutschlands, abgehalten zu Köln a. Rh. vom 22. bis 28. Oktober 1893 (Berlin, 1893), pp. 181–88; this quot. p. 183 f.

the SPD leaders obviously thought that they could face the problems of the unions with equanimity. At any rate, they failed to give the unions the help they so desperately needed in the circumstances. The different positions of the SPD and the unions were evident in a press feud of 1892–93 and, particularly, at the 1893 party congress in Cologne. August Bebel, the chairman of the SPD, repeatedly warned members not to overestimate the trade unions' chances of success; what is more, he also feared that they might have a harmful influence on the revolutionary nature of SPD policy. In view of the inevitable collapse of capitalism, the unions' modest demands for reform could not appear as anything but deluded daydreaming on their part. The trade union leaders, on the other hand, were quite prepared to concede their work's subordinate importance for the final liberation of the working class, but requested the party's support in the acute crisis in which the unions found themselves. When, in this situation, Legien sought to make SPD members join the unions by decision of congress, after a defeat in 1892 he was brushed off at the 1893 Cologne congress with a non-committal statement in which congress "expressed its sympathies for the trade union movement" and, for the rest, declared once again that it was "the duty of party comrades to work tirelessly for recognition of the importance of the trade union organizations and to do everything in their power to strengthen them"[16].

When things improved for the trade unions and particularly when they succeeded in scoring a number of successes in the field of social welfare, the harmonious subordination of the trade unions to the party became more problematic. Trade unionists became more self-confident and started questioning the most important Social Democratic prediction, on which so much hinged – the inevitability of capitalism's collapse. "We, the organized workers, do not want the so-called crash to come, forcing us to create institutions on the ruins of society, regardless of whether they are better or worse than the present ones," said Legien at the 1889 trade union congress in Frankfurt, "We want peaceful development."[17]

The SPD leadership cautiously took these new attitudes into account; after all, they were ideas that were making headway within the party, too, leading to the revisionism debate. In a policy paper on "Trade Unionism and Political Parties" published in 1900, Bebel abandoned his earlier view that the unions were the "recruiting school" of the party[18]. The import-

16 ibid. p. 180 f.
17 Protokoll der Verhandlungen des 3. Kongresses der Gewerkschaften Deutschlands, abgehalten zu Frankfurt a.M.-Bockenheim vom 8. bis 13. Mai 1899 (Hamburg, 1899), p. 103
18 August Bebel, Gewerkschaftsbewegung und politische Parteien (Stuttgart, 1900)

ance of reformist work had to be scrutinized, if – or since – the "crash" of capitalism was taking such a long time. Furthermore, as the strength of the unions increased, so too did the SPD's interest in securing the votes of the masses who made up this movement. And, by the same token, the unions needed the SPD to champion their social demands in parliament.

Soon after the turn of the century, the realization that the SPD and the unions needed each other caught on in the SPD, too. Karl Kautsky, the leading party theoretician prior to the First World War, wrote with regard to the success of the trade unions: "The political organizations of the proletariat will always only embrace a small elite; only the trade unions are capable of forming mass organizations. A Social Democratic party without the unions as its core is therefore built on sand." The special role of the trade unions was also acknowledged: "The trade unions must stay outside the party; it is not merely the laws on association that demand it, but consideration for the special tasks of these organizations." Kautsky may have been thinking not only of the economic struggle but also of the problems caused by competition from the Christian trade unions, which derived their raison d'etre (indeed, perhaps even their necessity) precisely from the close links between the Free Trade Unions and the SPD. "But," Kautsky continued, "social democracy must constantly seek to ensure that the members of the trade union organizations are filled with the socialist spirit. Socialist propaganda among the trade unions must go hand in hand with trade union propaganda in the party's agitation work."[19] The fact that it was presented as the party's duty to ensure the socialist orientation of the unions indicated, however, that it was still considered the spearhead of the labour movement – and that the party leadership was not entirely sure of this socialist orientation. No wonder, for in the arguments about social democracy's conception of its role and objective, in the struggles between the reformists led by Georg von Vollmar and the revisionists loquaciously represented by Eduard Bernstein, between the party centre grouped around August Bebel and the Left, equipped with the theories of Rosa Luxemburg, the majority of trade unionists sympathized with the reform course advocated by a minority in the party.

The debate on the general strike led to a (temporary) resolution of the relationship between the SPD and the Free Trade Unions. The attainment of universal suffrage by means of the general strike in Belgium and Sweden lent plausibility to the idea of an active policy to force through socialist demands. But the trade unions, which, not without justification, consi-

---

19 Karl Kautsky, Zum Parteitag, in Die Neue Zeit 1902/3, vol. 2, pp. 729–39; this quot.
    p. 738

dered that a general strike would have to be organized by them, saw their position jeopardized thereby. "It cost us tremendous sacrifices," Theodor Bömelburg, the chairman of the Bricklayers' Union, reminded the assembled delegates at the Cologne trade union congress from 22 to 27 May 1905, "to reach the present stage of organization." He continued: "But in order to build up our organization, we in the labour movement need peace."[20] It was in keeping with this basic attitude that the Cologne congress – with only five "nays" – "deplored all attempts to establish a particular set of tactics by propagating the political general strike". Instead it recommended "organized labour to vigorously oppose such attempts" – and to see that the organization was strengthened.[21]

The differing opinions of the SPD and the unions on this point, which Theodor Bömelburg tried to gloss over at the Cologne congress with the phrase "Unions and Party are one"[22], were fully apparent a few months later at the SPD party conference in Jena from 17 to 23 September 1905. By 287 votes to 14, it adopted a motion tabled by Bebel, acknowledging the political general strike not as an offensive weapon but as a defence against any attempts to tamper with the electoral law and the law on association.[23] The union leaders firmly rejected the wording of the Jena party conference decision, which could be seen as basically a compromise between supporters of an offensive use of the general strike and the opponents of any use of the general strike at all. It speaks volumes for the union leaders' recent gain in self-assurance that – according to Adolf von Elm at the conference of union executives in February 1906 – they believed they were safe in assuming that the supporters of a general strike could "be simply swept away at a single party conference" – "if only trade union members would concern themselves more with the party".[24]

In February 1906 the trade union and party leaders entered into secret negotiations in order to settle the general strike issue. The outcome of

20 Theodor Bömelburg, Die Stellung der Gewerkschaften zum Generalstreik, in Protokoll der Verhandlungnen des Fünften Kongresses der Gewerkschaften Deutschlands, abgehalten in Köln a. Rh. vom 22. bis 27. Mai 1905 (Berlin, 1905), pp. 215–22; this quot. p. 221
21 Protokoll der Verhandlungen des 5. Kongresses, p. 30
22 Bömelburg's closing words in Protokoll der Verhandlungen des 4. Kongresses der Gewerkschaften Deutschlands, abgehalten zu Stuttgart 1902 (Berlin, 1902), p. 274; see also Protokoll der Verhandlungen des 5. Kongresses, p. 266
23 Protokoll über die Verhandlungen des Parteitages der Sozialdemokratischen Partei Deutschlands, abgehalten zu Jena vom 17 bis 23 September 1905 (Berlin, 1905), p. 142 f.
24 Quot. Eduard David, Die Bedeutung von Mannheim, in Sozialistische Monatshefte 1906, vol. 2, pp. 907–14; this quot. p. 908 f.

these talks was the "Mannheim Agreement" adopted by the next party conference, which met in Mannheim on 23–29 September 1906. Now that Bebel had sounded the retreat, it was "unthinkable to carry out a general strike unless the overall mood among the broad masses is favourable"; and after Legien had declared it nonsensical to commit oneself to rejecting the general strike, it appeared – according to Legien – simply to be a matter of "documenting unity to the outside world".[25] The agreement stipulated that the executives of the trade unions and the SPD were "to ensure that a uniform approach was adopted in matters equally affecting the interests of the trade unions and the party".[26] This document, spelling out the equal status of the party and union leaderships within the Social Democratic labour movement, reflected the actual position – in reality, neither an offensive nor a defensive general strike could be fought without the trade unions. At the same time, it amounted to a recognition of the real power of the trade unions, which intended to exert political influence commensurate with their strength – in 1906 there were roughly 1.7 m trade unionists compared with 384,000 Social Democrats. While in the early 1890s the trade unions had been content to accept the role assigned to them by the party, the SPD now feared that the unions were after supremacy. It seemed to many Social Democrats that the trade union movement was unequivocal in "recognizing [. . .] the necessity of collaboration between the unions and social democracy. But there were also moods and impulses best described as trade union illusions that must be flatly rejected".[27]

In the years following the Mannheim Agreement, SPD theoreticians repeatedly attempted to decide the importance of trade union work – partly in order to resist the influence of the unions, which the growing number of trade union officials among the party conference delegates were in a position to exert. The fact that the proportion of trade union officials in the SPD parliamentary party rose from 11.6 per cent in 1893 to 32.7 per cent in 1912 says it all. The most scathing criticism came from Rosa Luxemburg. Having previously viewed trade union policy as an indispensable but Sisyphean task that was doomed to failure in the long run[28], she shrewdly put her finger on one of the basic problems of trade

25 Protokoll über die Verhandlungen des Parteitages der Sozialdemokratischen Partei Deutschlands, abgehalten zu Mannheim vom 23. bis 29. September 1906 (Berlin, 1906), p. 231 ff. and 245 ff.

26 ibid. p. 305

27 Parvus, Die Bedeutung der Gewerkschaften und der Hamburger Kongress, in Die Neue Zeit 1907/8, vol. 2, pp. 509–14; this quot. p. 514

28 Rosa Luxemburg, Sozialreform oder Revolution (Leipzig, 1899), p. 36

union centralization, though in exclusively negative terms: by the "businesslike, bureaucratically regulated leadership of the trade union official" the working class was "degraded to an undiscriminating mass, for whom the virtue of 'discipline', that is passive obedience, is elevated to a duty".[29] Karl Kautsky also considered it necessary to allude to the limitations of union policy; in 1909, in view of the fact that real wages had ceased to rise, he believed that the social advancement of the proletariat had to be considered at an end.[30] The unions interpreted this not simply as a critique of the development of capitalism but also as a reproach addressed to them. Significantly, the General Commission's reply bore the title "Sisyphean task or positive successes? Contributions to an appraisal of the activity of the German trade unions".[31]

When, as a result of Rosa Luxemburg's demands, the SPD party conference debated the general strike issue once again in Jena in 1913, the battle-lines no longer ran between the trade unions and the SPD, but right through the middle of the SPD, between the party executive and the left wing. After Philip Scheidemann, for the party leadership, had repudiated the view that "you can prepare for a general strike by relaxing union discipline, by playing off the masses against their leaders, by glorifying the unorganized mass", Gustav Bauer, vice-chairman of the General Commission was able to adopt the stance that the unions "saw no need to engage in this discussion".[32] No wonder, then, that Rosa Luxemburg's resolution that a general strike could not "be artifically manufactured at the behest of party and trade unions bodies" but "could only spring from the aggravation of the economic and political situation, as the escalation of a mass action that is already in progress" was defeated by 333 votes to 142. Instead, conference adopted a resolution stating that the political general strike was dependent on the expansion of the movement's political and trade union organizations. It would be hard to find a clearer expression of the changes in the relationship between the SPD and trade unions, and in the policies of the party itself.

---

29 Rosa Luxemburg, Massenstreik, Partei und Gewerkschaft (Hamburg, 1906)
30 Karl Kautsky, Der Weg zur Macht. Politische Betrachtungen über das Hineinwachsen in der Revolution (Berlin, 1909)
31 Sisyphusarbeit oder positive Erfolge? Beiträge zur Wertschätzung der Tätigkeit der deutschen Gewerkschaften, hrsg. von der Generalkommission der Gewerkschaften Deutschlands (Berlin, 1910)
32 Protokoll über die Verhandlungen des Parteitages der Sozialdemokratischen Partei Deutschlands, abgehalten in Jena vom 14. bis 20. September 1913 (Berlin, 1913), pp. 231 ff. and 294 ff; motions and resolutions, p. 192 ff.

The Christian unions, the Catholic Church and the Centre Party: interdenominationalism and party political neutrality put to the test

In the Christian trade unions, too, organizational consolidation and the resulting self-assurance among the union leaders grouped around Adam Stegerwald led to a far-reaching conflict with their allies in the Catholic Church and its political party, the Centre. The Christian unions had emerged strengthened from the dispute over "joint" trade unions (that is, the possibility of a future merger with "genuinely neutral" Free Trade Unions), just as it had from the tariff dispute, when it had been left to the individual unions to deal with the aspects of the tariff question that directly affected them "professionally". But the "trade union dispute" (*Gewerkschaftsstreit*) represented a threat to their very existence. Admittedly, the tariff dispute of 1902 had led to the temporary expulsion of Franz Wieber and the Christian Social Engineering Workers' Union and thus – until unification in 1903 – weakened the organization. But the clash over the question of interdenominationalism and the right of the Catholic clergy to have a say strengthened internal forces within the union movement that threatened to smash the whole organization.

The thing that triggered the dispute was the question of whether the Christian unions, because of their interdenominational character, would put their Catholic members' faith at risk and lead them into "religious routine" or even push them into the arms of the Social Democrats. Catholics who adhered to "integralism"* saw their fears confirmed by the unions' refusal to submit to clerical leadership or participation, even admitting that for them "Christian" really only meant "non-Social Democratic". Consequently, they did not make a "positive" stand for a specific denomination but merely promised that, unlike the Free Trade Unions, in defending the "purely economic" interests of the workers they would not take any steps that might offend the religious sensibilities of their Catholic or Protestant members. Religious and moral education were, they claimed, the responsibility of the denominational workers' associations. It was more than anything the announcement that, if necessary, they intended to merge with the Free Trade Unions in the foreseeable future – if the latter adopted a neutral stance on party politics and ideology – that provoked the opposition of the Integralists. This opposition took hold in the Catholic workers' associations (based in Berlin) with the publication

---

* Translator's note. "Integralism": former totalitarian tendency in the Catholic Church that sought to impose the precepts of the Church on all areas of life.

of Franz von Savigny's pamphlet, "Workers' Associations and Trade Union Organizations in the Light of the Encyclical Rerum novarum"[33]. These workers' associations, which with their clergy-led trade sections sought to offer a non-militant substitute for the unions, received the backing of Cardinal Georg Kopp, Prince-Bishop of Breslau, and Michael Felix Korum, Bishop of Trier. These two clerics insisted on the Church's right to lead the Catholic labour movement; in their opinion, there was no separating economic from religious questions. They did not, of course, take the same line with farmers' and manufacturers' organizations, with the paternalistic justification that the workers needed special schooling and assistance.

It was mainly Kopp's doing that the German episcopate threw away the first chance to halt the looming conflict in the Fulda Pastoral Letter, which, while praising the Catholic workers' associations, did not deign to mention the trade unions. This threw open all sorts of interpretations of the intentions of the bishops' conference. The subsequent statements by the German episcopate and by Pope Pius X, who soon became involved in the disagreement, were notable for their scarcely veiled efforts to avoid taking a clear position. This is all the more surprising in that the majority of the German episcopate were favourably disposed towards the Christian trade unions; but time after time, in the desire to maintain a united front, they allowed themselves to be pressured by Kopp and Korum. Even when the Pope at last officially intervened in the conflict in 1912, with the encyclical "Singulari quadam" – partly at the request of some Centre politicians and representatives of the Prussian Government – his remarks about "so-called Christian trade unions', which "could be tolerated", were thoroughly ambiguous.[34] The outspoken resolution of the extraordinary trade union congress of 1912[35] and Kopp's implacable opposition were also partly to blame for the fact that the dispute persisted after the publication of the encyclical. Not until Kopp's death on 4 March 1914 and the outbreak of the First World War did this issue cease to be so important. In 1919 a measure of agreement, albeit superficial, was reached; the Christian unions finally received official approval from Pope Pius XI with the encyclical "Quadragesimo anno" (1931).

---

33 Franz von Savigny, Arbeitervereine und Gewerkschaftsorganisationen im Lichte der Enzyklika „Rerum novarum" (Berlin, 1900)
34 Quot. Texte zur katholischen Soziallehre. Die sozialen Rundschreiben der Päpste und andere kirchliche Dokumente, ed. Bundesverband der Katholischen Arbeiternehmer-Bewegung (KAB) Deutschlands (1975), p. 84
35 Protokoll der Verhandlungen des ausserordentlichen Kongresses der christlichen Gewerkschaften Deutschlands, abgehalten am 26 November 1912 in Essen/Ruhr (Cologne, 1912), p. 63 f.

The success of the Christian trade unions in fending off the leadership claims of parts of the Catholic Church was significant from several points of view. Their interdenominational character, and the recognition of this by the Catholic Church, were necessary to repudiate the Social Democrats' charge that the Christian trade unions were "lackeys of the Church" and to prove that they were a genuine, independent trade union movement. The principles of interdenominationalism and party political neutrality were mutually dependent, even though they were not achieved on any significant scale in reality. Firstly, only 10–20 per cent of members were Protestants; secondly, the Centre Party was obviously the unions' principal party political associate.

While the Free Trade Unions were quite clearly affiliated to the SPD – and in the pre-war period this relationship was relatively free of problems – the position was far more complicated for the Christian unions and their members. There was general agreement in rejecting social democracy, so that for this reason alone their claim to "party political neutrality" was based on a narrowed-down field. The main focus of the Christian unionists' party political commitment was undoubtedly the Centre, the party to which Johannes Giesberts, who in 1905 became the first Christian trade unionist to enter parliament, belonged. In 1907 the number of Christian trade unionist deputies rose to six – five sitting with the Centre and one with the Economic Association. In 1912, five of the seven Christian trade unionists in the Reichstag belonged to the Centre, one to the Christian Social Party (which succeeded the Economic Association) and one to the National Liberal Party. The conflicts resulting from the differing party political allegiances of the leaders and the members of the Christian trade unions only became fully apparent during the Weimar period. But one problem was in evidence already: the Christian trade unions were constantly discovering that in the parties closest to it their members' interests ranked alongside, or lower than, those of other groups, such as industry and agriculture.

With their political ties with the bourgeois parties, the Christian trade unions became the core of a Christian-nationalist coalition movement, whose most conspicuous manifestation was the German workers' congresses. The unifying factor of these congresses, first held in 1903, was the deliberate anti-Social Democratic programme, the other side of which was an overt nationalism, which now became at least as prominent as the social and religious elements of the programme. The importance of this coalition of non-Social Democratic labour organizations is illustrated by the number of members represented by their delegates at these congresses: 620,000 in 1903, 1 million in 1907, 1.4 m in 1913 and 1.5 m in 1917 (their own figures). The "German Workers' Congresses" symbolized the party political receptiveness of the Christian unions to all non-Social Democratic parties at a broad trade union level and from this point of view can be seen as the forerunner of the German (Democratic) Trade Union Federation, founded in 1919.

4. Industrial struggle, collective-agreements and social reform: trade union work under the Empire

Concentrating our attention exclusively on feuds at congress and in the press, on the umbrella organizations' desire to assert themselves vis-à-vis political parties and the Catholic Church, paints a false picture. For this was by no means the unions' main field of activity; in fact, they often regarded them as irksome distractions from their "real" duties. Trade union work under the Empire was the daily struggle against social and economic ills, discrimination against the working class and its organizations in law and its social marginalization.

*

Looking at the foundation phase of the trade unions, we saw the tremendous importance of industrial struggle as a driving force behind the organizations. This never fundamentally changed later on. There was often a dramatic increase in membership shortly before expected industrial action. And even though some of these new members would again turn their backs on the unions once the conflict was over, there was usually a lasting increase in membership as a result. It was clear to the unions that successful industrial action not only depended on the economic situation in the trade concerned; a crucial part was played by the strength of both sides, and hence the unions' degree of organization and financial resources. This is clearly shown by the figures: in the years of economic crisis and poor trade union organization from 1890 to 1894, of 544 strikes only 32.9 per cent were successful, a trade union figure which may even be an exaggeration; in contrast, during a period of economic expansion and growing union strength from 1895 to 1899, 57.8 per cent of 3,226 strikes conducted turned out to be a success for the wage earners.[36] This is the

---

36 See Die Streiks im Jahre 1894, in Correspondenzblatt No. 36 of 23. 9. 1895, pp. 161–64; Die Streiks im Jahre 1900, in Correspondenzblatt No. 29 of 22. 7. 1901, pp. 449–61

reason why calls were heard in the trade union press for the organization to be strengthened – and, further, for more common sense to be shown in "wage bargaining tactics". After the *Sturm und Drang* period of spontaneous protest strikes the trade unions should now – in 1897 – "systematize their warfare".[37] The strike regulations transferring the decision on industrial action to regional bodies accompanied and reinforced this trend, which on the one hand increased the clout of the organization through rational use of resources, but on the other frequently bolstered the impression of executive remoteness from the grassroots.

Without a doubt, there was a decline in the number and scale of local spontaneous strikes, though they persisted in breaking out: suffice it to mention the strike of 1896 that started in the Berlin garment industry, the strike of the Hamburg dockers in 1896–7 and the 1905 Ruhr miners' strike. These strikes were started either against the wishes of the union or without union backing, though some of them were subsequently taken over by the unions. The trend, however, was clearly towards well-organized industrial action, pitting trade unions and employers' federations against each other.

But strikes, especially if met by large-scale lockouts, were a double-edged weapon. Certainly, they helped enhance the workers' class consciousness and solidarity; but they not infrequently jeopardized the very existence of the trade union organizations if they encountered stubborn resistance from the employers. Moreover, strikes prompted the employers to develop organized forms of joint defence in turn. A few examples of the dual role played by industrial action must suffice. The printers' strike of October 1891 – January 1892 for the implementation of the nine-hour day mobilized 10,000 trade unionists and consumed the – by the standards of the day – enormous sum of 1,250,000 Marks. This financial drain was enough to cripple the printers' trade union activities for years to come; defeat in the strike itself only made matters worse and aggravated the mood of crisis that gripped the trade unions in the early 1890s.

Furthermore, the wave of strikes in 1889–90 mentioned above and the industrial struggles of the turn of the century gave a boost to the employers' efforts to organize. The (relatively) poor economic situation of 1901–3 led to greater intransigence on the part of the employers, which manifested itself in the month-long lockout of 6,000 Hamburg dockworkers and again in the industrial struggle of 1903 in the Crimmitschau textile industry. The strike at Crimmitschau – the first in which women

---

37 Zur Taktik bei Lohnbewegungen, in Correspondenzblatt No. 9 of 1.3.1897, pp. 45–47; this quot. p. 45

Women during the dispute in the textile industry at Crimmitschau, 1903-4

The army move in during the 1905 Ruhr miners' strike.

took a major part – was carefully prepared by the unions, but it occurred at an unfavourable point in the business cycle, that is, during a slump in the market. The main aim of the dispute was a reduction in working hours to ten hours a day. The workers received money from unions and wage earners all over Germany, but had no reply to the lockout imposed by the employers. Furthermore, the Saxony textile manufacturers were supported by the Central Federation of German Industrialists. The outcome was a crushing defeat for the strikers and those locked out. As we have seen, the Crimmitschau dispute also speeded up the process of organization amongst the employers. From now on, blacklists containing the names of "undesirable elements", the setting up of "sweetheart" unions and the aggressive use of large-scale lockouts were among the weapons most frequently used by the employers to hamper and hamstring the unions, if not destroy them. The fact that all workers were locked out and not just trade unionists was probably intended to ensure that in future the company concerned stayed "non-unionized".

The scope and magnitude of trade disputes increased in tandem with the degree of organization on both sides of industry. This was true of strikes such as the Ruhr miners' strike of 1905, involving some 220,000 of the 280,000 miners, which ended in a partial victory with the creation of workers' committees in the amendment to the Mining Law of 14 June 1905. But it also applied to lockouts: after the punitive lockouts for celebrating May Day in 1890 and 1891, and peaks in 1903 and 1905–6, they began affecting ever larger numbers of wage earners, as demonstrated by the lockout of 190,000 building workers in 1910.

But that was not the last major industrial dispute before the Great War. Let us recall the strike by some 190,000 Ruhr miners in 1912, which offered a textbook example of the collaboration between the authorities, the army, the judiciary and the employers. It also illustrates the effects of the split in the trade union movement: in 1912 the union of Christian miners, which had joined the strike of 1905, were not prepared to co-operate with the Free Trade Unions. This was probably due to fear of the threatening papal rejection of the Christian trade unions – obviously no-one wanted to provide an easy excuse for such a step. The schism within the movement indubitably undermined the position of the strikers, who suffered a heavy defeat.

If industrial struggle had a secure place in the "world view" of the Free Trade Unions, it was a bitter blow to the Christian unions that the employers refused to go along with their notions of an alliance of employers and workers. Petitions were ignored, negotiating offers rejected, and no distinction was made between the Christian trade union movement and the others – on the contrary, it was seen as a particularly sophisticated variant of the labour movement, which would anyway lead the workers into the arms of the Social Democrats. So, even in the early years, the Christian unions were involved in numerous industrial disputes, the employers' intention being to bring the young organizations to their knees. The Christian unions often took part in strikes in order to give the lie to their reputation as non-militant "bosses' lackeys" or "Church lackeys". In relation to the (low) level of benefits – dues were kept low to attract new members more easily – the proportion of money they spent on industrial disputes exceeded that of the Free Trade Unions. Only after 1905–6 – during the period of consolidation – did dues, benefits and expenditure on industrial disputes settle down at roughly the same level as the Free Trade Unions', although the proportion of Christian trade unionists taking part in industrial disputes remained a good bit behind the Free Trade Unions. In the period 1903–13, benefits to strikers and others involved in industrial disputes amounted to an average of 51.5 per cent of the Christian trade unions' total expenditure on benefits, exceeding the Free Trade Unions' 47.2 per cent; but the proportion of members taking part in industrial action averaged only 9.2 per cent, compared with 12.9 per cent in the Free Trade Unions.

Let us take a brief look at a form of industrial struggle that was rapidly becoming less important: the boycott. In the 1890s, above all, boycotts were often organized to support a strike by, say, bakers' or butchers' journeymen and to fight restrictions on the right of association in the breweries. Such action was, however, difficult to organize, since it required an enormous amount of publicity work; secondly, it could only be taken against the producers or purveyors of certain consumer goods – and the purchase of some items of food could not be postponed for very long. As in the case of strikes, the trade unions leaders pressed for national co-ordination of local boycotts. The Hamburg trade union congress took the decisive step in 1908, when it laid down that a boycott "could only be decided on at the request of the national leadership of the trade union engaged in the wage struggle, the area representatives of organized labour, the local union coalition (Kartell) and the local union associations'.[38] By now the heyday of the boycott was over. Collective bargaining, with or without an industrial dispute – more commonly the latter – was gaining ground.

*

38 Protokoll der Verhandlungen des sechsten Kongresses der Gewerkschaften Deutschlands, abgehalten zu Hamburg vom 22. bis 27. Juni 1908 (Berlin, 1908), p. 43 ff.

The growing scale of industrial disputes was both a symptom of and a spur to organization on both sides; this was particularly true of the institution of the collective agreement. The more peaceful collective bargaining became the norm, the more significance organizational power acquired as a means of applying pressure. But there was a long way to go yet. Not all unions saw the collective agreement as a sensible way of settling industrial relations since it impaired the workers' will to fight. In view of the high esteem in which strikes were held – "undoubtedly the most appropriate way" of "making the workers class conscious"[39] – it is scarcely surprising that the collective agreement was seen as "betrayal of the class struggle" and an expression of unforgivable collaborationist daydreaming. Not until 1899 did the Third Congress of the Free Trade Unions come out clearly in favour of the collective agreement "as evidence of the employers' recognition of the workers' equal right to determine working conditions".[40]

In the years that followed, the trade union leaders encouraged the conclusion of collective agreements, as they constituted "recognition of the workers' right to co-determination"[41] and were thus not "alliances of friendship with the entrepreneurial class but merely 'ceasefire treaties'".[42] These articles and speeches testify to lingering reservations about the collective agreement which obviously had to be dispelled. The fact that the Gutenberg League, the Hirsch-Duncker associations and the Christian unions all supported collective agreements in their day did not make matters any easier, especially as there were few prospective takers on the employers' side for a policy of peaceful negotiation. As late as 1905, the Central Federation of German Industrialists still considered collective agreements "thoroughly dangerous to German industry and its prosperous development", as they not only deprived the employer of the "necessary freedom to decide on the use of his labour and to fix wages' but also resulted in "the inevitable subjection of the workers to the organizations of labour".[43] However, it may have been precisely the employers' resist-

---

39 Zur Lage, in Correspondenzblatt No. 11 of 29. 5. 1893, p. 41 f.; this quot. p. 41
40 Protokoll der Verhandlungen des dritten Kongresses der Gewerkschaften Deutschlands, abgehalten zu Frankfurt a.M.-Bockenheim vom 8. bis 13. Mai 1899 (Hamburg, 1899), p. 150
41 Carl Legien, Tarifgemeinschaften und gemeinsame Verbände von Arbeitern und Unternehmern, in Sozialistische Monatshefte 1902, vol. 1, pp. 27–35; this quot. p. 29
42 Theodor Leipart, Die gewerkschaftliche Praxis und der Klassenkampfgedanke, in Sozialistische Monatshefte 1906, vol. 2, pp. 642–48; this quot. p. 647
43 Quot. Werktage werden besser. Der Kampf um den Lohnrahmentarifvertrag II in Nordwürttemberg/Nordbaden (Köln and Frankfurt, 1977), p. 10

ance that won over many of those who regarded collective agreements as a betrayal of the class struggle; often it was necessary to take industrial action to secure acceptance of the concept of the collective agreement.

The building workers did not get a collective agreement until 1899; the engineering workers, not until 1906. From then on, however, the number of collective agreements rose sharply – from 3,000 in 1906 to about 13,500 in 1913, covering 218,000 firms employing some two million people. Consequently, by 1913, 16.5 per cent of all industrial workers and 36.4 per cent of the members of the Free Trade Unions had their conditions of work regulated by collective agreement; 79.5 per cent of these agreements had been reached without a strike.

They were a motley assortment: company agreements as well as national ones, some covering small trades, some covering huge numbers of unskilled workers. Generally speaking, the collective agreements covered one to three years, with one to three months' notice required; most agreements were limited to quite small groups of companies and employees; they were easiest to push through in industries or trades in which the employers were relatively weak and isolated and the workers well-organized. Where employers were strong and well-organized, for instance in heavy industry, the unions did not manage to gain a foothold in terms of organization and collective agreements before 1914, though it was precisely in such areas that lockouts to weaken the unions were the order of the day. All in all, collective agreements were instrumental in promoting and securing an improvement in working class conditions; at the same time, however, they reflected the dominance of skilled workers within the unions and helped consolidate it further.

It was clear to unions of all tendencies that in the face of legal and political discrimination against the working class neither industrial militancy nor collective agreements could achieve any lasting improvement in the situation. Owing to the restrictions on the right of association, the inequities of the suffrage and the urgency of the social issues, the unions were virtually forced to deal with problems of policy. Matters were made easier for the General Commission by the abolition of the ban on links between political associations in 1899; the agenda of the Frankfurt trade union congress of that year was heavily weighted towards matters of social policy, the list of which lengthened in the following years. Prime concerns were the extension and protection of the right to carry out union work, that is, the guaranteeing and reform of the rights of association and assembly. It was also the undisputed task of the unions to put forward proposals for improving industrial safety: accident protection, industrial disease, special measures to protect women, young people and home workers, a ban on child labour, the fixing of working hours, a ban on unnecessary night work and holiday working and the improvement of the factory inspectorate. Decisions were taken and bills proposed on all these issues. Another problem concerned improvements to the existing national insurance law and the transfer of unemployment insurance and labour exchanges to the state. Lastly, there were demands that employees or unions be given a greater say in their industries; the idea was to set up company workers' committees and to create trades' councils as a counterpart to the chambers of commerce and trade corporations. With increasing frequency the trade unions also made clear their views on tariff and fiscal policy. They either focused on the interests of a particular trade, when special taxes on certain products – such as cigars or brandy – threatened to lead to reduced sales and hence job losses; or they were concerned to prevent increases in duties or taxes that were bound to affect the workers as consumers. The aim of all these initiatives – planned and co-ordinated, from 1910 on, by the General Commission's Social Policy Department – was to ensure a decent life for the working class.

Though there was no overlooking the occasionally physical confrontations between the trade union federations, there were clear signs of a rapprochement on specific points, ideological and party political differences notwithstanding. All the unions concentrated on legal improvements, attainable in the existing circumstances. The co-determination arrangements sought by the wage-earner organizations, whether in the shape of the "pure" trades' councils demanded by the Free Trade Unions or bipartite trades councils consisting equally of employer and employee representatives on the lines envisages by the Christian trade unions, revealed differences of degree, not of principle. It was of little importance for day-to-day union work whether policy prescribed the ten-hour or eight-hour day, so long as there was agreement on the need for a cut in working hours – and, anyway, up to 1914 the issue at the heart of the struggle was still the introduction of the ten-hour day. The list of areas in which the federations, separately, made similar demands extended from A to Z. Moreover, even before the World War I, there were the first signs of joint action and co-operation between the federations, for example over the German Home Workers' Day in January 1911.

5. *Trade union reform policy under the authoritarian state: a balance sheet*

Let us now sum up. The end of the Socialist Law ushered in a period of trade union consolidation within the economic and political status quo, which was widely accepted as a working basis. These years saw the emergence of the trade unions basically as we know them today, though the organizations which merged to set up the General Commission of the German Trade Unions were mainly trade associations, and it was their structure that continued to dominate well into the Weimar era, despite efforts to form industrial unions. Only towards the end of the nineteenth century was it possible to bring trade union organizational structures into line with the state of industrial and political development, with regard to the centralization of decision-making. Just as the local self help organizations of the skilled workers of a particular trade corresponded to the situation around the middle of the century – when demands for better working conditions were properly addressed to the company management – the unions' tendency to group skilled and unskilled together in national unions was in keeping with the growing concentration of the production process.

It actually proved easier to combine the individual unions into ideologically distinct umbrella organizations than it was to introduce the principle of the large industrial union. The first Christian unions appeared on the scene at a comparatively late stage, considering that by this time unions – Social Democratic and liberal – were already in existence catering for the major occupational groups. While the unions' organizational development ran largely parallel with the development of the economy during the nineteenth century – with the unions a few steps behind – the establishment of the Christian trade unions represents an exception to the general trend, though they were quick to catch up by forming an umbrella organization with unusual rapidity (1899–1903).

The establishment of umbrella organizations followed the emergence of centralized political decision-making structures. This, however, reinforced the growing gap between the union leaderships and the rank and file, which was to become a problem, particularly in times of crisis. The most conspicuous illustration of how much the unions were influenced by the centralism of the political system was perhaps provided by the relocation to Berlin of the General Commission and the Federation of Christian Trade Unions from Hamburg and Cologne respectively.

Even though the period 1890–1914 is a fairly short one in relation to union history as a whole, let us try to draw up a kind of "interim report" on trade union policy. The most striking feature was the unions' success in their "original" sphere of activity: the industrial struggle and collective agreements regulating working hours and wage levels.

The increase in wages and the cut in working hours achieved since the 1890s would hardly have been possible without the unions. The fact that the economic trend was generally favourable from the mid-1890s to 1912 not only aided the unions' organizational efforts but also – particularly in the boom years of 1902–6 and 1910–12 – improved the chances of success in industrial disputes. The development of wages and working hours (Tables 3a and 4a) was thus part of a general trend towards the improvement of the lot of the working class, which in times of economic prosperity offered more scope for wage rises and more opportunities for industrial action.

While government policy did not directly affect wage levels, it refrained from intervening to any large extent in the question of working hours, despite constant appeals from the trade unions. The modest legal moves to protect children, young people and women in particular were a result of increasing pressure from the labour movement, which also had indirect consequences. Fears that the SPD and trade unions might continue to grow won supporters for the idea of social reform outside the ranks of the working class; they hoped that by proving the Empire's willingness and ability to implement reform it would be possible to stem the "red peril".

Modest though the unions' successes over the legal regulation of working hours were, their achievements in other key areas of social reform were even more meagre. They failed to get the right of association extended or the Prussian three-class voting system abolished; the introduction of parliamentary democracy was as far away as ever; even the problems of public unemployment insurance and employment exchange remained unsolved. The trade unions never exerted any influence on economic, financial or trade policy. Nor was there any prospect of political reforms designed to democratize the Empire.

Nevertheless, mass membership and real successes in the industrial struggle and in tariff policy helped trade unions of all tendencies develop a sense of their own power and independence, enhancing their importance in their various political camps, as the general strike debate and union dispute demonstrated. Even before the First World War it was clear that the trade unions had become an important factor of economic, social and domestic politics which it would be difficult to resist politically. In view of this fact, the state and the employers would soon have no choice but to strengthen trade union pragmatism by making concessions and giving them a place in society. And this is exactly what happened: the Empire's willingness to carry out reforms, though limited to the social sphere, seemed to confirm the correctness of the policy, shared by trade unions of all persuasions, of gradual social reform on the basis of the status quo, thus increasingly depriving radical tendencies of support. The First World War was to provide the acid test of this policy.

Mobilization in 1914: heading for the front

V. Upheaval: the trade unions in the First World War 1914–1918

The outbreak of the First World War did not come like a bolt out of the blue to the Social Democratic labour movement – but it was caught unprepared none the less. For years it had been warning of the growing danger of war that imperialism entailed. Though the need to defend the country was not questioned, the resolutions of the congresses of the Second International in Stuttgart (1907), Copenhagen (1910) and Basel (1912) raised expectations that the Social Democratic movement would do all in its power to prevent a war, or at least to end it swiftly. The Stuttgart congress had adopted Bebel's draft resolution to the effect that, at the threat of war, "the working classes and their parliamentary representatives in the countries involved [shall be] committed to do their utmost to prevent the outbreak of war by the methods they deem most effective". It went on: "Should war nevertheless break out, it is our duty to work for its rapid termination and direct all our efforts to exploiting the resulting economic and political crisis to rouse the people and thus accelerate the elimination of capitalist class rule."[1] True, there were no similar decisions by the International Trade Union Federation, and the Free Trade Unions had not exactly been fervent champions of the political general strike. But might one not expect the Social Democratic labour movement – party and unions together – to try to prevent any war?

1. Beginnings of the political truce: for defence of the realm, peace through victory and social reform

The assassination of the heir to the throne of the Austro-Hungarian dual monarchy in Sarajevo on 28 June 1914 merely provided the immediate pretext for the imperialist powers of Europe to put into effect the bellicose "solution" to their economic and political clashes of interest for which they had long planning. Within a few weeks war had broken out between the German Reich and Austro-Hungary on the one side, and Tsarist Rus-

---

1 Kongress-Protokolle der Zweiten Internationale, vol. 2: Stuttgart 1907 – Basel 1912; reprinted Glashütten im Taunus 1976, p. 66

sia, France and Great Britain on the other. The entry of the United States into the war in April 1917 made it a world war.

It soon became clear that the plans of the German general staff were not working. According to the Schlieffen Plan, a swift victory over France would enable Germany to avoid the threat of a war on two fronts and turn the entire might of the German Army against Tsarist Russia. Russia did, indeed, suffer a crushing defeat at Tannenberg at the end of August 1914. But in the west, the planned mobile war became bogged down at the Battle of the Marne in early September 1914 and turned into trench warfare, with immense casualties on both sides in the battles around Verdun and on the Somme in 1916.

∗

As members of the great *Volksgemeinschaft* (national community) evoked by Kaiser Wilhelm II on 1 August, when he said that he "no longer knew any parties"[2], many Social Democrats forgot the decisions of the Second International, some succumbing to the general enthusiasm for war and confidence in victory, others responding with resignation. Although the General Commission issued another call for peace on 1 August 1914, the day Germany mobilized[3], the executive conference the following day stated despondently, "All the efforts of organized labour to preserve peace and stop this murderous war have been in vain."[4] And what was the position within the SPD? As late as 25 July 1914, "Vorwärts" had published an appeal by the party executive concluding with the call, "Down with the war! Long live international brotherhood!" But on 31 July, signalling an about-turn, the same paper stated: "Our solemn protests and our repeated efforts have failed; the circumstances in which we live have again become stronger than our will and that of our comrades in labour; we must now resolutely face whatever the future may hold."[5]

---

2 Quot. Schulthess' Europäischer Geschichtskalender, Neue Folge, 30th edition, 1914, vol. 1 (Munich, 1917), p. 371
3 Die Kriegsgefahr, in Correspondenzblatt No. 3 of 1. 8. 1914, p. 469 f.
4 Protokoll der Konferenz der Verbandsvorstände of 2.8.1914, in Quellen zur Geschichte der deutschen Gewerkschaftsbewegung im 20. Jahrhundert, vol. 1: Die Gewerkschaften in Weltkreig und Revolution 1914–1919, compiled by Klaus Schönhoven (Cologne, 1985), hereafter referred to as "Quellen vol. 1", pp. 74–85; this quot. p. 83
5 Party executive appeal of 25.7.1914, in Vorwärts No. 200 a (special edition) of 25. 7. 1914; Parteigenossen! Party executive appeal of 31. 7. 1914, in Vorwärts No. 207 of 1. 8. 1914

By August 1914 it was evident that both the Free Trade Unions and the SPD had become constituent parts of the Wilhelminian Empire. Both looked with pride at the organizational and political successes they had scored on the basis of the status quo. Both identified with the German Reich, its thriving economy and its pioneering social welfare policy. Both saw willingness to take part in the war effort not only as proof of their own patriotism but as a sort of "advance payment" for the long-overdue social and democratic development of the country. The unions may also have been influenced by the belief that their indirect decision to observe a political truce on 2 August, reinforced by the "official" abandoning of all wage struggles on 17 August, might help to preserve their organization through the war.

The unions' readiness to show their "allegiance" for the duration of the war, indirectly announced on 2 August, also had implications for the political deliberations of the SPD parliamentary party on 3 August. Yet it is hardly likely that their decision to vote the necessary war credits would have gone differently even if the unions had not announced their intention to refrain from striking. At most, the policy of the unions may have strengthened the majority of the SPD group in the stance which it had already adopted.

By deciding on a policy of political truce (*Burgfrieden*), the Free Trade Unions led the way for the other federations, too. Certainly, incorporation into the "national united front" presented no problems for the Christian-national trade unions. To them the war was a test of the nation's mettle: it would bring about "moral regeneration of the country"; it was "the furnace that will purge humanity of impurities and errors"[6]. War might have "threatened man's outward culture and happiness; but it has ennobled and uplifted the inner man"[7]. It was not by chance that in 1915 Theodor Brauer, the Christian unions' leading theoretician, praised the war "and its attendant phenomena" as "a grand confirmation, overwhelming in its nature, of the principles" of this section of the labour movement[8].

The liberal-national Gewerkvereine were also happy to fall in line with the "national united front" in August 1914[9]. They saw the Free Trade

6 Ursachen und Zusammenhänge des Weltkrieges, in Jahrbuch der christlichen Gewerkschaften für 1915, ed. by the General Secretariat of the Federation of Christian Trade Unions of Germany (Cologne, 1915), pp. 24–35; this quot. p. 24

7 Weltkrieg und sittliche Volkserneuerung, ibid. pp. 36–45; this quot. p. 36

8 Theodor Brauer, Der Krieg und die christlichen Gewerkschaften (M.-Gladbach, 1915), p. 5

9 Cf. Erklärung von Zentralrat und Geschäftsführendem Ausschuss des Verbandes Deutscher Gewerkvereine zum Kriegsausbruch, in Gewerkschaft No. 62 of 5. 8. 1914, p. 237

Unions' political truce policy as an "outright acknowledgement of our principles". They, too, expected the "national community" born of wartime to become a lasting social compact and lead to a policy of social reform.[10]

Such patriotic declarations of loyalty were part of a wave of nationalism that swept through the German media in the early stages of the war. Many people – including the trade union federations – believed that the German Reich was involved in a war of defence that had been forced upon it. The "counter-attack" breaching Belgian neutrality therefore seemed justified. Much as they regretted it, they could not escape "the observation that the German army command was in a predicament, and that by taking the action it did it was only anticipating a breach of neutrality already planned by the enemy."[11] Furthermore, in the months that followed, the Free Trade Unions professed their belief in war aims – modest though they may seem compared with those of industry. Firstly, it was a matter of economic advantages for the German Reich, in which the working class would also share; secondly, a "reward" was expected for the sacrifices made by the German working class. After the "peace through victory" (*Siegfrieden*), the Prussian three-class voting system would undoubtedly be scrapped and the right of association would be extended to all wage earners.[12] But there were more overtly military and political war aims, too: at the beginning of 1916 the Correpondenzblatt was still describing the "assumption" that occupied areas would be evacuated "without any compensation for the sacrifices incurred since then [as] so absurd that no German will engage in such discussions".[13] And as late as May 1917 – after the American entry into the war – Adam Stegerwald of the Christian unions presumed to state: "If a 'power peace' (*Machtfrieden*) is attainable, then let us have a power peace at all costs."[14] The differences of substance

---

10 Quot. Hans-Georg Fleck, Soziale Gerechtigkeit durch Organisationsmacht und Interessenausgleich. Ausgewählte Aspekte zur Geschichte der sozialliberalen Gewerkschaftsbewegung in Deutschland (1868 bis 1933), in E. Matthias and K. Schönhoven (eds), Solidarität und Menschenwürde, pp. 83–106; this quot. p. 104 f.

11 Die italienischen Gewerkschaften und wir, in Correspondenzblatt No. 47 of 21. 11. 1914, p. 617 f.; this quot. p. 618

12 Wilhelm Jansson (ed.), Arbeiterinteressen und Kriegsergebnis. Ein gewerkschaftliches Kriegsbuch (Berlin, 1915); similarly, Die deutsche Arbeiterklasse und der Weltmarkt, in Metallarbeiter-Zeitung No. 22 of 27. 5. 1916

13 Rückblick auf das Jahr 1915, in Correspondenzblatt No. 1 of 1. 1. 1916, pp. 1–4; this quot. p. 1

14 Arbeiterinteresse und Friedensziele. Vortrag, gehalten von Generalsekretär Adam Stegerwald auf der Konferenz der Vertrauensleute der christlich-nationalen Arbeiterbewegung am 6. Mai in Essen (Cologne, 1917), p. 9

between the federations on this point were rather small. The tone adopted by the Christian unions was, however, decidedly cruder; for example, in October 1917, Stegerwald called for the "ruthless continuation of the war"[15]; yet to hope for a victorious outcome could not, at this juncture, be anything more than whistling in the dark.

*

All these announcements brimming with reformist confidence and bellicose self-assertion cannot disguise the fact that union organization and policies were badly hit by the war. Even in 1913 the slowdown in the economy had an adverse effect on union membership; although spring 1914 seemed to bring the first signs of an improvement in the economic situation, the beginning of the First World War was gravely detrimental to the economic life of the country. The switch from peacetime to wartime production was by no means a smooth one. The proportion of unemployed trade unionists soared from 2.9 per cent in 1913 to 7.2 per cent in 1914, before declining to 3.2 per cent in 1915, 2.2 per cent in 1916, 1 per cent in 1917 and 0.8 per cent in January–October 1918.

Conscription and the expansion of arms production caused a major shift in the composition of the working class. Whereas the number of adult males in industrial enterprises employing more than ten people decreased by one quarter during the war, the number of women rose by 50 per cent. In 1914, twice as many men as women belonged to a sickness insurance scheme; by 1917 numbers were equal. Moreover, the working population grew younger owing to the increase in workers under sixteen. The consequences of this shift in the working population were exacerbated, for the unions, by the enormous turnover in manpower. For example, from the outbreak of war until mid-1917, Siemens-Schuckert had a staff turnover equivalent to eight times its workforce. The war had the effect of speeding up earlier, pre-war trends: the increased number of working women, the increase in unskilled and semi-skilled workers, and the rise in employment in the chemical and metal-working industries and in electrical and mechanical engineering.

All the federations suffered from the effects of conscription, unemployment and changes in the working population. The self-imposed curbs on the unions' freedom of action under the political truce policy may also

---

15 Adam Stegerwald, Arbeiterschaft und Kriegsentscheidung. Vortrag, gehalten auf der 4. Deutschen Arbeiterkongress, 28.–30. Oktober 1917 in Berlin (Cologne, 1917), p. 17

have contributed to the fact that many workers did not consider it important to belong to a union. Between 1913 and 1916, trade union membership fell from almost 3 m to 1.2 m; the Free Trade Unions alone lost more than 1.5 m members.

This fall in membership was accompanied by a collapse in internal union work. The conscription of officials and shop stewards brought union activity in many smaller areas to a halt; the trade union press was censored; declining revenue and the rising cost of benefits emptied union coffers. For these and other (political) reasons, trade union congresses were cancelled for the duration of the war – it even became rare for individual unions to hold conferences – and discussion of war policy was banned at local union meetings.

As early as 2 August 1914, Carl Legien had announced at the executive conference: "As things are today, democracy is a dead letter in the trade unions; now the executives have to make decisions on their own responsibility – for which they must answer to their own consciences."[16] The question is whether Legien – and other union chiefs with him – were perhaps rather too eager to submit to the "force of circumstances": were the curbs on internal union democracy imposed by the war used to push the executive's line through unopposed? Both the substance of the policies pursued and the shift of decision-making upwards, away from the discontent developing among the working class and the membership, contributed to the growing alienation of the grassroots from the leadership of the unions.

2. *Towards political integration*

All the trade union federations saw the First World War as a war of defence that had been forced upon the German Reich. They supported the war effort from the very outset, for example through appeals for help with the harvest, which unemployed factory workers were initially obliged to undertake, replacing farm labourers who had been called up. They all switched their expenditure from the industrial struggle to welfare benefits, particularly for the unemployed and soldiers' families, which incidentally helped to take the pressure off public funds. All the trade union federations hoped for "peace through victory" in order – more or less openly – to achieve economic and social war aims. The political peace pledge, whereby they themselves had renounced all militant defence of their memb-

---

16 Konferenz der Verbandsvorstände am 2.8.1914, in Quellen, vol. 1, pp. 74–85; this quot. p. 84

ers' interests, was regarded by them as voluntary proof of their sense of national responsibility. They believed it entitled them to seek acceptance for some long-standing demands of theirs.

The Reich, stressed the Correspondenzblatt in 1915, could not be defended "against a world full of enemies by a handful of capitalists". Precisely because the working class had done its duty, because it was needed, because it was bearing the main burden of the war, the "days of factory feudalism" were gone for good.[17] And in the exuberance of the first months of the war, the Metallarbeiter-Zeitung, the engineering workers' paper, claimed to discern not just the "solid co-operation" of all sections of society but "socialism wherever we look".[18]

But the unions were far too optimistic in their assessment of developments. The oft-evoked "spirit of the trenches" soon proved to be an illusion. War profits and war aims, food profiteering and the black market soon created quite a different picture of the German "national community". And the desired concessions by the employers, particularly in the arms industry and other large-scale industries, were not forthcoming. In industries dominated by small and medium-sized companies, which were prepared to conclude collective agreements even before the war and now found themselves overshadowed by the effects of rearmament on the economy, the unions were able to achieve increased recognition. This was partly because the manufacturers hoped in this way to win the support of trade unionists as champions of their particular industry in relations with the civil service and the military commanders. Patriarchal attitudes lingered on well into the war, at least in heavy industry and mining: "The colonel cannot engage in negotiations with the soldiers in the trenches -nor must the workers be given the power to make decisions on fundamental company matters." With this much-used comparison between military and industrial obedience, the trenches or barracks and the company, the head of the Association of Iron and Steel Manufacturers, Jakob Wilhelm Reichert, confirmed the entrepreneurs' claim to lead and rule at a meeting of the association's executive on 16 November 1916.[19]

This attitude of harsh dismissal of union demands for recognition and co-determination was, however, hard to keep up in practice. Ever since autumn 1914 there had been a shortage of skilled workers in various

---

17 Nichts gelernt und nichts vergessen, in Correspondenzblatt No. 17 of 24. 4. 1915, pp. 189–191; this quot. p. 191
18 Der Krieg und die sozialen Aufgaben, in MetallarbeiterZeitung No. 45 of 7. 11. 1914
19 Quot. Gerald D. Feldman, Armee, Industrie und Arbeiterschaft (Berlin and Bonn, 1985), p. 77

branches of the arms industry. Competition for staff aggravated the already serious problem of high turnover. In this situation the employers called on the state to help. Ernst von Borsig, chairman of the Association of Berlin Engineering Manufacturers, called for the introduction of forced labour. The War Ministry rejected this proposal on the grounds that forced labour would "have a paralysing and destructive effect on the co-operativeness of the unions".[20] When in January 1915 the Berlin Munitions Board prohibited workers from changing jobs for the sake of better pay, the unions – with Adolf Cohen, chairman of the Berlin engineering workers at the forefront – protested, declaring that in that case they could no longer guarantee the survival of the domestic political truce. At this, the Munitions Board took over Borsig's idea of making a change of jobs conditional on the issue of a "leaving certificate". Clearly it was necessary to end the argument and reach agreement with the unions to avoid endangering arms production. The engineering industry and the engineering unions set up the "War Committee for the Engineering Works of Greater Berlin", a body composed of representatives of both sides charged with adjudicating in disputes that could not be settled at company level.

The creation of committees of this type did not meet with the approval of the leading manufacturers' associations, who probably feared the gradual undermining of the employers' claim to be the sole legitimate decision-makers. The fact that in spite of this several such committees were set up at the instigation of the military authorities – for example, by the engineering industry in Hanover and Frankfurt – shows the concern of the High Command to ensure that arms production should proceed as smoothly as possible, which it believed could best be done by involving the trade unions. For their part, the unions saw any form of institutional co-operation with the employers and any backing given to them by the "decrees of the military authorities, framed with such refreshing clarity"[21] as evidence of the success of their political truce policy. It was a way of consoling themselves and the workers in their disappointment at the fact that by autumn 1916 no far-reaching social reform was in prospect. The concessions by the employers, the military authorities and the government went no further than was necessary to persuade the unions to continue observing the political truce, which served to maintain discipline among the workers, without carrying out the social reforms demanded in return.

20 Ibid. p. 77
21 Der Krieg und die sozialen Aufgaben, op. cit.

When their hopes remained unfulfilled, and the swift victory in which all believed failed to materialize, the trade unions adopted a more strident and urgent tone. It was no longer a matter of positive goals such as social reform; any departure from the political truce policy was unthinkable because of the feared outcome. In early 1916 the view was that support for the war effort was in keeping with "the unions' most vital interests, holding off any foreign invasion, protecting us from the dismemberment of German territory and the destruction of flourishing German industries, and preserving us from the fate of a disastrous end to the war, which would burden us with war reparations for decades to come."[22]

*

As the war dragged on there was a growing need for emotive appeals of this kind to justify the political truce policy to the working class when the dividend in terms of social reform was not forthcoming, or was at best double-edged. This also applied to the Auxiliary Service Law (Hilfsdienstgesetz), which the unions greeted as the greatest success of their policy. In the summer of 1916, the Third Supreme Command under Paul von Hindenburg and Erich Ludendorff, in collaboration with the representatives of heavy industry, put forward a programme to boost arms production, designed to mobilize all available manpower. As they also wanted to exploit demonstrable public readiness to perform "patriotic auxiliary service" as a weapon of war, the programme had to receive the broadest possible support from the population, documented by a parliamentary resolution. This was partly why, in the government's deliberations and in co-ordinating talks with the parties, Wilhelm Groener's view that the war "could not be won against the workers" gradually gained ground; it was clear to him, as head of the Prussian War Office, that "without the trade unions we cannot make the thing [the Auxiliary Service Law] work".[23]

The trade union federations, making the most of the fact that they were indispensable to the success of the auxiliary service scheme, made a concerted effort to push through improvements to the bill, for which they made sure they had the support of the parties to the left of the Conservatives. As a result of the co-operation between the federations they managed to put together a majority in the Reichstag stretching from the SPD to the left wing of the National Liberals, which made a number of

22 Quot. H. Grebing, op. cit., p. 144
23 Quot. Vaterländischer Hilfsdienst, in Zentralblatt der christlichen Gewerkschaften Deutschlands (hereafter referred to as Zentralblatt) No. 25 of 4. 12. 1916, p. 202

amendments to the bill in favour of the unions, without changing its general tendency, however. Owing, in part, to the bill's dual character, opinions were divided within the SPD parliamentary party: in an internal vote, 21 out of 49 members of the SPD group rejected the bill, and in the Reichstag vote one third of the SPD deputies defied the party whip. Neither were the Free Trade Unions so well disposed to the bill as a glance at the General Commission's publications would lead us to believe. In particular, there were massive protests at a shop stewards' meeting of the Greater Berlin engineering workers, and also at the general assemblies of the shoemakers' and woodworkers' unions.

Perhaps the protests would have been even more forceful, had there been more opportunity to voice them. For the Auxiliary Service Law as adopted on 2 December 1916 was a rather daunting measure. It introduced compulsory service for every male German between 17 and 60, conscripts excepted. In connection with this, freedom of movement and contracts of employment were largely abolished; a change of job was henceforth only possible with the approval of a bipartite mediation committee. The compensation for these restrictions on the wage earners' basic rights was the compulsory setting-up of worker committees in companies vital to the war with more than 50 employees; where there were more than 50 white-collar staff, a staff committee also had to be set up. The above mediation committees were also created. Long-awaited recognition of the unions as the legitimate representatives of the workers was granted by allowing union representatives on to all the official concilition and arbitration bodies right up to the War Office level.

Although the unions had to grapple over the coming months with the implementation regulations and the interpretation of individual passages – setting up the worker and staff committees proved particularly awkward – approval of the law remained more or less intact. They all put it down as a success for their policy – some Free Trade Unions even saw it as a "piece of state socialism".[24] The vehement rejection of the law by many employers may also have encouraged trade unionists to take a positive view of it. Some employers in heavy industry labelled it the Trade Union Auxiliary Law[25], and in a March 1918 memorandum of the Federation of German Employers' Associations the Auxiliary Service Law was said to be "an emergency law born of the constraints of war [. . .] which there will

---

24 Der militärische Zukunftsstaat, in Metallarbeiter-Zeitung No. 48 of 25. 11. 1916
25 Quot. Hans-Joachim Bieber, Gewerkschaften in Krieg und Revolution. Arbeiterbewegung, Industrie, Staat und Militär in Deutschland 1914–1920 (Hamburg, 1981), vol. 1, p. 301

obviously be no reason to retain once the war is over". It was therefore pointless to discuss whether the law "has really achieved the aim it was intended to achieve, viz. to step up arms production by increasing man-power and reducing job changes."[26] In fact, the effect of the law on the wartime economy was rather modest. Because reserves were so low the shortage of skilled workers remained a persistent problem, and high turn-over was only stemmed for a limited time.

But what did the balance sheet look like from the unions' point of view? Recognition by the state and the formation of workers' and arbitration committees were registered as clear successes. These seemed to be the pre-conditions for the rapid rise in their membership and, above all, the entry of the unions into the big companies that had hitherto remained closed to them. After the low of 1.18 m in 1916, combined union membership climbed to 1.65 m the following year and reached 3.51 m in 1918, thus exceeding the pre-war figure by more than half a million (Table 1a).

But for the trade unions the Auxiliary Service Law also had its draw-backs. The newly formed workers' committees often evolved narrow objectives of their own, selfishly seeking to further the interests of the company. In fact, many employers preferred the workers' committees to the trade unions as a negotiating partner and probably tended to make concessions over pay to the workers' committees quite deliberately, in order to make the unions in general seem superfluous. Finally, the work-ers' committees were often politicized in ways that were not congenial to the union executives. They were, after all, much closer to workers and their problems – a hectic work rate, longer working hours, and the disas-trous food situation – than the union leaderships. To make matters worse, the union leaders – and this also contributed to the emergence of a broad-based protest movement – were engaging in close co-operation with state and military administrative bodies and the employers over the imple-mentation of the Auxiliary Service Law.

Precisely by virtue of its dual character, the Auxiliary Service Law brings out with full clarity the fundamental problem of union policy during the First World War. Recognition of the unions, often deemed a success, could only be achieved at the cost of progressive integration into the ruling system of the Wilhelminian *Kaiserreich,* for whose policies the unions

---

26 Quot. Roswitha Leckebusch, Entstehung und Wandlungen der Zielsetzungen, der Struktur und der Wirkungen von Arbeitgeberverbänden (Berlin, 1966), p. 216

assumed a measure of responsibility and – in the eyes of a growing number of workers – some of the blame, too. Unions of all political hues accepted some political responsibility without being able to influence the broad lines of policy, though they did try to mitigate its worst social consequences. It was largely because this policy was such a limited success that the gap between the trade union leaders and sections of the membership grew ever wider.

The clearest illustration of this is the question of food supplies. The longer the war lasted, the more disastrous the food situation became. Lack of manpower and fertilizer (saltpetre was used for munitions) caused farm production to decline, and with the encirclement of Germany no food imports were coming into the country. Food shortages and price increases were the result. As early as January 1915 bread rationing was introduced, followed soon afterwards by fat, meat and milk. The black market began to prosper. "The unequal distribution of scarce goods", a police report stated, appeared to be "more conspicuous and provocative than the scarcity itself".[27]

To coordinate measures to ensure food supplies (and to demonstrate the government's willingness to take action) the Wartime Food Office was set up in May 1916, its board including August Müller, a Social Democrat, and Adam Stegerwald, the Christian trade union leader, who were thus rendered partly responsible for the unsatisfactory food situation. As a result, the hunger riots of the latter half of the war and the growing protest movement were also directed against the trade unions, who during the First World War not only acted as the champions of the working class on social matters but at the same time sought to channel its anxiety and protests.

There is no denying that by accepting posts on committees and in offices dealing with civilian and military supplies, thus assuming part of the political responsibility, all the trade union federations allowed themselves to become implicated in the war policy of the German state. Moreover, Stegerwald entered the Prussian Upper House as the first worker deputy, and Johannes Giesberts was appointed to a post at the Imperial Office for Economic Affairs as expert adviser to the secretary of state on social matters. Both Stegerwald and Max Schippel were given places on the Imperial Treasury's twenty-four man strong financial advisory council to examine the economic consequences of future tax proposals. Every new duty that gave the unions a say in decisions was seen by

---

27 Quot. Jürgen Kocka, Klassengesellschaft im Krieg. Deutsche Sozialgeschichte 1914–1918 (Göttingen, 1973), p. 34

them as another success for their political truce policy, and as a sign of a change of heart by the leading representatives of the state, the armed forces and the employers. In fact, the unions appeared to consider the growing intervention of the state in the economy – from the management of raw materials to the regulation of employment and supply policy – as a manifestation of "state" or "war socialism"[28]. From the vantage point of the present, this was a staggering misjudgement, but they were chiefly concerned with ensuring the smooth running of the arms-based economy and this required limited and double-edged concessions, designed to secure the loyalty of the masses to the unions' political truce policy.

∗

In view of the restrictions on pay that the unions accepted as part of the political truce, it is not surprising that the question of social reform assumed increasing importance the longer the war lasted. The Christian-national unions presented their demands in programme form in 1916, as did the Free Trade Unions in 1917–18, setting out what they expected of state policy and also the points on which they differed from it.

As early as September 1916, the committee of the German Workers' Congress published a basic programme, which was not finally put to the vote until after the war to give the members of the Christian-national labour organization who had been conscripted into the forces the opportunity to participate. The affiliated unions professed their unqualified allegiance to the "common culture and destiny of the German people', to the "maintenance of a strong defence force", to the "national necessity" of a global economic and colonial policy, to private property and to the monarchy. It then went on to detail measures giving equal rights to the workers, and other measures covering industrial safety, insurance, food supplies, housing reform and fiscal policy.[29]

As Franz Behrens made quite plain in his commentary on the programme, it was intended to give a clear statement of the Christian-national position for their own benefit and hence also to distinguish it from that of the Social Democrats. For when its supporters had "marched off to battle like everyone else and stood their ground as well as the next man", the question of the raison d'etre of the Christian-national labour movement had come under scrutiny. Certainly, the Christian-national and the Social

28 Der militärische Zukunftsstaat, op. cit.
29 Die christlich-nationale Arbeiterbewegung im neuen Deutschland, hrsg. vom Ausschuss der christlich-nationalen Arbeiterbewegung (Cologne, 1917), p. 14 ff.

Democratic labour movements could work together from case to case, but the fundamental differences between them – on Christianity, "national cohesion" and private property – should not be forgotten.[30]

Shortly afterwards, in November 1917 and January 1918, the Free Trade Unions followed suit. They, too, put forward a social programme, the eighteen points of which presented a lengthy list of demands, not only in the sphere of social policy proper but covering all the issues of social reform. It set out their proposals on such matters as employment exchanges, insurance and the law on collective agreements as well as industrial safety, popular education and housing.[31] However far-reaching these reform plans were, they were all quite clearly rooted in existing conditions. At any rate, this programme certainly did not strain the "common work" of the trade union federations that developed in wartime.

*

On a number of political questions – from the certificate of employment and the protection of home workers, to the Auxiliary Service Law and the deletion of paragraph 153 of the trade regulations – opportunities for co-operation across federation boundaries regularly presented themselves. The white-collar organizations also sought to pool their strength under the pressure of the war. In 1915 the Association of Technical Unions and the Association for a Standard Salaried Employees Law, from which emerged the General Free Union of Salaried Staff (the Afa-Bund), were set up. In October 1916, the bourgeois nationalist organizations merged to form the Association of Commercial Unions. In view of the poor employment position, falling salaries and the food crisis, in mid-1917 the three white-collar associations began to work together more closely. The clearest manifestation of the federations' readiness to co-operate politically was the joint founding of the "Popular League for Freedom and Fatherland" (Volksbund für Freiheit und Vaterland). Moreover, the broad trade union and party political co-operation tested in the auxiliary service discussions became the jumping-off point for cross-party co-operation in the Reichstag between the Majority Social Democrats, the Centre and the Progressive Party, which jointly tabled the peace resolution of 19 July 1917, calling for a peace without any territorial demands or claims for reparations.

30 Franz Behrens, Das neue Programm der christlich-nationalen Arbeiterbewegung (Leipzig, 1918), pp. 18 f. and 21 f.
31 Reprinted in Paul Umbreit, Sozialpolitische Arbeiterforderungen der deutschen Gewerkschaften. Ein sozial-politisches Arbeiterprogramm der Gewerkschaften Deutschlands (Berlin, 1918), pp. 102–12

3. *The trade union mass movement and non-union mass protest*

Neither for the Hirsch-Duncker associations nor for the Christian unions did the war entail a challenge to their political programmes, as they had both seen themselves as nationalist movements ever since the turn of the century. Not so, the Social Democrats. Since the beginning of the war and the debate on the war credits and the political truce policy, there had been growing internal opposition within the SPD. This included not only the radical Left, whose spokesmen were Karl Liebknecht and Rosa Luxemburg, but also a number of Social Democrats of the "centre", including Karl Kautsky, Eduard Bernstein and Hugo Haase. The leadership of the Free Trade Unions, itself a party to the political truce policy, resolutely supported the line of the group majority. Partly to avoid the split in the SPD spreading to the unions it advocated the consistent exclusion of those opposed to the political truce policy, which it believed was jeopardized by the internal opposition. As early as February 1915, Legien demanded the expulsion of Karl Liebknecht from the SPD parliamentary party for a breach of group discipline: he had, after all, openly voted against the granting of further war credits in December 1914. When an appeal was published in the Leipzig "Volkszeitung" in June 1915 – also signed by 150 trade union officials – calling on the SPD leadership to break with the "policy of 4 August", the General Commission responded with a sharp condemnation of any "sectarianism" within the SPD. The union executives backed this stance and reaffirmed their support for the policy pursued "by the great majority of the Social Democratic group, the party committee and the party executive". It went on to say: "The views represented by the sectarians in the party are in contradiction with the very nature and work of the unions; to implement them would be to put at risk all that the unions have created and achieved."[32] Furthermore, if the established political line was not consistently pursued, the General Commission threatened to set up its own trade union party. So the General Commission's actions further reduced the scope for compromise between the party leadership and the internal opposition, thus aiding the policy of marginalization. In spring 1916, the dissident deputies were expelled from the parliamentary party and set up the "Social Democratic Association". After meeting for a special conference in January 1917, which resulted in their expulsion from the party, they founded the Independent Social Democratic Party (USPD) at Easter 1917.

---

32 Protokoll der Konferenz der Verbandsvorstände vom 5.–7. 7. 1915, in Quellen, vol 1, pp. 181–219; this quot. p. 216

In March 1916 the General Commission expressly welcomed the split in the SPD group, since it meant a clarification of the situation. At the conference of union executives on 20–22 November 1916, the majority – with only three votes against – came out in favour of the Majority Social Democrats (MSPD), thus rejecting neutrality in the current party dispute.[33] But if the union leaders, particularly the General Commission, thought that that was the end of the problem, they were very much mistaken. Opposition was afoot in the unions, too. Its centres were Berlin and the industrial areas of central Germany and Rhenish Westphalia. The opposition was particularly strong where trade union and party groupings provided mutual assistance, especially in Berlin, Brunswick, Bremen, Hamburg and Leipzig. Furthermore, oppositional groups achieved considerable strength in some individual unions. At the Cologne conference of the German Engineering Workers' Union in June 1917, the executive line was approved by only 64 votes to 53; and in 1919 the opposition even took over the leadership. Even during the war the shoemakers' and textile workers' unions took the USPD line, and there were strong oppositional wings in the bakers', glass workers', shop assistants' and furriers' unions.

*

Although the Free Trade Unions, with their "marginalization policy", did not manage to prevent the internal struggles between the different wings of the SPD from affecting their own organizations, it did not lead to a split in the movement. The internal opposition within the unions – unlike their Social Democratic counterparts – continued to accept the political truce, for all their criticism. As a result, the protest movements of the latter half of the war developed without the participation of the unions, which believed that if they took the opposition line they would be jeopardizing the achievements which they ascribed to the political truce, or the rewards which they expected to obtain later. It was precisely what the union leadership counted a success that was partly responsible for large sections of the working class mounting a protest movement without, indeed even partly against, the trade unions.

The reduction in the bread ration announced in April 1915 had already led to protest strikes, which resulted in the decision being rescinded. The longer the war lasted, the more dissatisfaction and the urge to protest

---

33 Protokoll der Konferenz der Verbandsvorstände vom 20.–22. 11. 1916 in Quellen, vol. 1. pp. 252–58; see p. 255

grew, triggered more than anything by the inadequate and unfair supplies of food and directed against the war, as was the case with the strike by 50,000 Berlin engineering workers on 28 June 1916. From 1915–16 on there were continual hunger disturbances, chiefly involving women and young people, who suffered particularly badly from the disastrous situation and were not threatened by conscription. The "turnip winter" of 1916–17, in particular, caused the protest movement to spread and gave rise to numerous spontaneous strikes. War fatigue and the desire for peace, falling incomes and the catastrophic food shortages led to a number of strikes from January 1917 on, often without any union involvement. Even the incomplete figures of the Imperial Statistical Office reflect the increase in strikes: in 1915, 141 strikes involving 15,238 workers were recorded; in 1916, 240 strikes, involving 128,881; in 1917 the number of strikes soared to 562, and the number of strikers to 668,032 (Table 2c). The strike movement reached its first peak – probably in the wake of the February Revolution in Russia – in April 1917, when some 300,000 munitions workers in Berlin, Brunswick and Leipzig took to the streets in protest at the food shortage and for political reasons. After more strikes in the summer of 1917, about a million armament workers downed tools in January 1918. Under the slogan "Peace, freedom and bread" they demonstrated for an immediate halt to the war with no territorial claims, for a thorough democratization of the whole of society and improved food supplies. In Berlin alone, 400,000 workers came out on strike. The strikers elected 414 workplace delegates, who formed the Greater Berlin Workers' Council, headed by an action committee of 11 members, of whom three belonged to the MSPD and three to the USPD – but none to the trade union leaderships.

As a result of these strikes a new form of organization developed at company level, seen for the first time during the strike of April 1917. Under pressure from radicalized company workforces, a new group called the "revolutionary representatives" (Revolutionäre Obleute) emerged from the ranks of the shop stewards. Politically they were close to the USPD. Under the leadership of Emil Barth and Richard Müller they represented a new concept in the organized expression of opinion, the idea of councils. Whereas those who took part in the mass actions of 1917–18 were chiefly women, youngsters and unskilled workers, who were all outside the trade unions, these strikes were frequently organized by skilled artisans with trade union training who had joined the revolutionary representatives out of disgust at the political truce policy. In some cases strike movements were headed by the workers' committees set up under the Auxiliary Service Law.

The strikes did not meet with much direct practical success, nor did they seem to have much effect on the basic line of trade union policy. The mass protest did influence events indirectly, however, bringing home as it did to those at the head of the state and the armed forces the necessity of conceding at least the moderate demands of the trade unions, in order to strengthen their position. The unions themselves made use of the mass movements – which they otherwise tended to dismiss – with the very same argument.

Though the Free Trade Unions were able to prevent a split in their organization, they still had to keep a careful eye on the radical workers' protest movement, since it had clearly emerged from among their own supporters, or at least from those sections of the working class that were most easily mobilized by the unions. Of course, the strikes and protest movements of 1917–18 which finally culminated in the revolution must not be allowed to disguise the fact that some workers thought that trade union policy represented their interests well. While the anti-war strikes bypassed the unions, the *Durchhalteappelle* (the appeal to hold out), which all the trade union federations addressed to the workers in 1917–18, met with a good response. Both mass mobilization outside the unions and trade union recruitment of members were most successful in the big cities and large companies, so that it is not possible simply to talk about a "crisis of confidence" in the unions. The high level of political mobilization, taking in large sections of the working class who had previously not been politicized, thus occurred both inside and outside the unions. But the trade unions, which continued to feel committed to the political truce, forfeited the leadership of the rapidly expanding protest movement, which saw them as one of the chief buttresses of the *Durchhaltepolitik,* the policy of "holding out" until final victory.

Despite the political truce policy and the "common work" in individual cases, the balance sheet of trade union policy in the second half of the war was, on the whole, no more impressive than before. On 5 June 1916, against the votes of the Conservatives and the Social Democratic Association (which had split away from the SDP group), an amendment to the Law on Association was passed, finally limiting the possibility of declaring the trade unions to be "political associations" and hence subject to a special law. Under the Auxiliary Service Law, the unions were recognized as the representatives of the workers. And, finally, in May 1918, paragraph 153 of the trade regulations, which laid down specific penalties for forcing anyone to join a closed shop, but did not apply to employers who sought to interfere with freedom of association, was dropped without any replacement. But the abolition of the Prussian three-class voting system was deferred in the Kaiser's Easter message on 7 April 1917 until after the war.

Were the recognition of the trade unions, the establishment of workers' committees and the abolition of paragraph 153 really successes for the unions' political truce policy? Or was it not rather the indirect influence of mass protest that was at work, against which the union "dam" had to be strengthened? If one considers the point in time at which the triumphs blazoned on the union banners were achieved, much of the credit must be attributed to the strike and protest movement.

After the war in the east was terminated by the dictated peace of Brest-Litovsk in March 1918, which the Russian leadership was forced to accept in order to safeguard the revolution, the Supreme Command of the army

The reality of war

tried to force a conclusion in the west by launching a "great offensive" in spring 1918. This attempt failed, but the Supreme Command did not admit defeat until 29 September 1918, calling on the government to start ceasefire negotiations immediately. In early October Prince Max of Baden took over the government, which for the first time was in the hands of the majority parties in the Reichstag. And once again the unions were prepared to accept a share in the responsibility for the consequences of the policy of August 1914, for Gustav Bauer of the General Commission and Johannes Giesberts of the Christian unions joined the government that was faced with the difficult task of setting the final seal on the country's defeat.

The reforms "from above" up to and including the introduction of parliamentary democracy, had two basic aims. First, the representatives of democratic and social reform, from the trade unions to the parties allied to them, were to be made to share the responsibility for war policy, in order to divert attention from those who were really to blame – the Supreme Command and the nation's leaders. Second, something had to be done to take the wind out of the sails of the newly radicalized masses in order to prevent the overthrow of the state – the dreaded revolution.

VI. The struggle for a new political order: the trade unions in the early years of the Weimar Republic

With the armistice concluded at Compiègne on 11 November 1918 the First World War came to an end. On 29 June the Versailles peace treaty was signed. The annexations of German territory, the loss of colonies, reparations, and above all the war guilt clause, holding Germany solely to blame for the war, gave bourgeois, nationalist circles in Germany every opportunity to condemn the "shameful *Diktat*" and to insult those who signed this "ignominious peace". Death, suffering and misery – a total of 7.5 m dead and 20 m wounded – did not lead to the general proscription of war; rather, large sections of the German public believed that the defeat that so took them by surprise had been caused by their half-hearted homeland's "stab in the back" of the "undefeated army at the front", by the "November criminals". In a double distortion of the facts, blame for the outcome of the war and the consequences of defeat were laid at the door of the revolution and the revolutionary government, headed by the Social Democrats. Yet the revolution was not the cause of the German defeat, nor did the Social Democrats and the Free Trade Unions "make" the revolution.

1. *The trade unions in the revolution of 1918–19*

The trades unions of all tendencies had been advocating social and political reform – ever more insistently, the longer the war dragged on. Reforms were to be their reward, as it were, for the union policy of observing a political truce throughout the war. But although the partial success of this policy resulted in a increase in membership in the second half of the war, it could not prevent a fast-growing mass protest movement from springing up alongside the unions. The experience of years of oppression and browbeating, along with the poverty, misery and injustice of wartime and fear of the consequences of imminent defeat, had noticeably radicalized large sections of the working class, resulting not only in the split within social democracy but also in the spread of "new" grassroots movements, which even penetrated deep into the army. The very size of the protest movement demonstrated that union policy did not satisfy the political needs of large numbers of workers.

Berlin on 9 November 1918: the barracks of the Ulan Guard are handed over to members of the Workers' and Soldiers' Council

Car of the Workers' and Soldiers' Council at the Brandenburg Gate

The tension suddenly exploded with the mutiny of the Kiel sailors. On 29–30 October 1918, the crews of the German High Seas Fleet refused to leave harbour for certain death and several hundred sailors were arrested for mutiny. Protest at this step grew into the revolution that reached all the big cities within a few days and brought about the fall of the monarchy.

Although the Majority Social Democrats and the Free Trade Unions – not to mention the other trade union organizations – had neither planned nor carried out the revolution, on the abdication of the Kaiser on 10 November 1918 power fell into the hands of the Social Democrats. The MSPD and the USPD, with three representatives each – Friederich Ebert, Philipp Scheidemann and Otto Landsberg; Hugo Haase, Wilhelm Dittmann and Emil Barth – formed the revolutionary government, called the Council of Popular Delegates (Rat der Volksbeauftragten).

The government was faced with insuperable problems; the ceasefire and demobilization, the conversion and stimulation of industrial and agricultural production, supplying the masses with work, food and fuel – these were the acute problems that large sections of the population were expecting the government to solve. The hopes of the masses behind the revolution were pitched even higher: the establishment of the republic should not only lead to a considerable improvement in the conditions of the working class but also to a fundamental reorganization of society.

True, in its appeal of 12 November 1918[1] the Council of Popular Delegates pledged itself to a "socialist" governmental programme; but all it announced was a number of individual measures such as the lifting of legal restrictions on workers' organizations, the reform of the electoral law and improvements in social policy – especially the introduction of the eight-hour day. In addition, the government undertook to maintain "regulated production" and to "safeguard property against interference and to guarantee the freedom and safety of the individual". This was the sort of compromise between the established powers and structures on the one hand and the notions of a new order on the other that characterized the policies of the Majority Social Democrats and the Free Trade Unions at the end of 1918. It is also true of the relations between the revolutionary government and the armed forces: after all, having been told by Wilhelm Groener by telephone on 10 November of the Supreme Command's readiness to recognize the new government, Friedrich Ebert gave an assurance that the government would support the Supreme Command in maintaining order within the army. And it is also true of relations between the revolutionary government and business leaders, though future developments

---

1 Reichs-Gesetzblatt, 1918, p. 153

had already been shaped by the talks between the trade unions and employer representatives, which were virtually concluded when the "governmental programme" of 12 November 1918 was announced.

*

Only the realization that the war could no longer be won, and the consequent fears (exacerbated by the unrest) that it might lead to social revolution, prompted the employers to announce that they were willing to engage in lasting co-operation with the trade unions. The decisive factor in reaching this decision, according to Jakob Wilhelm Reichert, the leader of the Association of German Iron and Steel Manufacturers, was concern to "save manufacturers from socialization and nationalization, affecting all industries, and from approaching revolution".[2]

But the trade unions also saw their policies, and probably their very existence threatened by the radicalization of much of the working class. In addition, many trade unionists believed, according to Adolf Cohen of the German Engineering Workers' Union (DMV) at the trade union congress of June 1920, that the unions could "not solve the economic problems on their own, without the entrepreneurs".[3]

Against this background the willingness to co-operate, sealed by agreement on 15 November 1918, is explicable.[4] Paragraph 1 of this agreement laid down that "the trade unions are recognized as the appointed representatives of the workers"; paragraph 2, anticipating the constitution, guaranteed workers the right of association. The recognition of collective agreements (paragraph 6), the establishment of bipartite employment exchanges (paragraph 5) and workers' committees in companies with more than 50 employees (paragraph 7) tended to confirm the unions' assumption that with the November agreement democratization of the economy had come a good deal closer. Furthermore, in paragraph 3 the employers undertook not to support, directly or indirectly, "sweetheart unions", works associations committed to industrial peace. But this point, along with paragraph 9, reducing the working day to eight hours with guaranteed retention of wages, was soon to give rise to the first disputes. This may well have been largely because the quid pro quo for the employers' concessions was – taking into account the political possibilities of the day

---

2 Jakob Wilhelm Reichert, Entstehung, Bedeutung und Ziel der „Arbeitsgemeinschaft" (Berlin, 1919), p. 6
3 Quot. Helga Grebing, op. cit. p. 177
4 Published in Correspondenzblatt No. 47 of 23. 11. 1918, p. 425 f.

– a comprehensive though tacit renunciation by the unions of any property reforms, and thus of economic power.

In accordance with union policy, which was aimed at power-sharing, not the seizure of power, it was agreed under paragraph 10 of the November accord to set up a bipartite central committee with an underlying structure organized on occupational lines to handle the implementation of the arrangements agreed in November, oversee demobilization, ensure the continuation of economic activity and guarantee the livelihood of the workers, particularly war invalids. Pursuant to this paragraph, the "Central Association of the Industrial and Commercial Employers and Employees of Germany" (Zentralarbeitsgemeinschaft der industriellen und gewerblichen Arbeitgeber und Arbeitnehmer Deutschlands – ZAG) was set up. From the outset its work suffered as a result of the inequality in the real powers of the interest groups represented.

The Free Trade Unions nevertheless greeted the establishment of the ZAG as a "trade union victory of uncommon magnitude".[5] The Hirsch-Duncker associations and Christian unions also celebrated the November agreement and the ZAG as confirmation of their long-standing principles and hence a step in the right direction – towards co-operation in trust and partnership by both sides involved in production, capital and labour. "Democracy came to the big companies of Germany" was the effusive verdict of the Christian trade unions.[6]

Of course, not all trade unionists shared this optimism. There was considerable opposition to the policy of collaboration, particularly in the German Engineering Workers' Union, which left the ZAG at the end of October 1919. The other Free Trade Unions were also soon forced to recognize that the desired co-operation with the employers through the ZAG was foundering on the inequality of the parties' real power and that, in addition, it was being deprived of its role by the economic and political powers of other bodies, from the parliaments to the temporary National Economic Council (Reichswirtschaftsrat).

The employers rapidly consolidated their position. The National Federation of German Industry (Reichsverband der Deutschen Industrie –

5 Die Vereinbarung mit den Unternehmerverbänden, in Correspondenzblatt No. 47 of 23. 11. 1918, p. 425
6 Vereinbarung zwischen Arbeitgeber- und Arbeitnehmerverbänden, in Zentralblatt No. 25 of 2. 12. 1918, p. 202 f.; this quot. p. 202

RDI) was set up on 12 April 1919 and before long some 70–80 per cent of German companies belonged to its affiliated associations. On the workers' side, however, it was apparent even during the months of the revolution that there were almost irreconcilable differences of political position. Concerted action was hampered by the three-way split in the trade union movement, and even more by the conflicts within the socialist camp – the split into the MSDP, the USPD and (since 1 January 1919) the KPD (Communist Party).

First of all, there was disagreement over the role of the councils that had spontaneously sprung up as a new form of labour organization in the army and the factories. These workers' and soldiers' councils were at first frequently entrusted with the exercise of state power. They ensured order and managed supplies, liaising between the administration and the population and seeing themselves generally more as a supervisory body than as a replacement for the "old" rulers.

The local and regional leaders of the Free Trade Unions also took leading positions on the workers' and soldiers' councils in many places. At the Berlin congress of councils in mid-December 1918, for example, 87 of the 289 MSPD delegates (30 per cent) were full-time trade union officials. But the vast majority of the councils were formed without union representation. Neither the Christian trade unions, who sought to transform the councils into citizens' committees, nor the Free Trade Unions made any secret of their dislike of the councils. The councils were regarded as being in competition with the workers' committees, which had been set up under the Auxiliary Service Law or pursuant to the decree of 23 December 1918. The Free Trade Unions also disliked the fact that the councils born of the revolution were not content with worker participation in company and social matters, but also demanded political co-determination. So in accordance with their basic decision in favour of a parliamentary republic, the unions rejected any claim by the councils to political absolutism.

In the councils themselves this view enjoyed a broad majority, since the delegates at the congress of workers' and soldiers' councils that met in Berlin from 16 to 19 December 1918 decided to participate in the elections for the national assembly by about 400 votes to 50. Thus, to a certain extent they were relinquishing the political mandate given to them by the revolution. Certainly, the delegates at the council congress, like the supporters of the MSPD and the USPD in general, probably expected the elections to result in a clear socialist majority. All the greater was the shock, then, on 19 January 1919 when the votes had been counted: the MSPD and USPD failed to win an absolute majority, even taken together. But co-operation between the two was almost unthinkable anyway, as the

USPD representatives had already walked out of the Council of Popular Delegates in December 1918, after Ebert had sought the old army's help during the mutiny of the marine division in Berlin on 24 December 1918. Gustav Noske and Rudolf Wissell – both MSPD – took over the posts of the USPD. It was Noske who subsequently used the Freikorps to crush the January revolt of 10–11 January 1919. The disturbances instigated by radical council supporters in early 1919, for instance in the Ruhr district, Bremen, Central Germany and Munich, were also put down by military force.

To the radical concept of councils the Free Trade Unions opposed – after a long debate – their own plan for workers' councils (probably also intended as a compromise) at their executive conference of 25 April 1919. Paragraph 9 of the "Guidelines for the future activity of the trade unions" stated that after primary elections workers' councils organized according to occupation should be set up in each local area; the social, economic and local political tasks of the trade union "cartel" would be transferred to them. Under paragraph 10, the workers' councils were to form chambers of commerce together with employer representatives at regional and then national level, to propose and scrutinize draft legislation and to participate in socialization. What concerned the unions most is evident from the fact that these "guidelines" were completed by highly detailed "Regulations governing the tasks of the works councils".[7]

Both of these policy statements were submitted to the first congress of the Free Trade Unions to be held after the war, from 30 June to 5 July 1919 in Nuremberg. The internal union opposition presented its own draft proposal on the councils, introduced by Richard Müller: without even mentioning the unions, he outlined a model for council organization based on region and trade, headed by a Central Council and the National Economic Council. But the line advocated by Theodor Leipart and Adolf Cohen, in accordance with the decisions of the executive conference of 25 April, carried the day by 407 votes to 192.[8] This paved the way for the Works Councils Law (Betriebsrätegesetz); even the planning for it was based on the assumption that there would be no overthrow of the property system leading to a shift in economic power. This was entirely in keeping with trade union policy on the socialization issue.

---

7 Reprinted in Klaus Schönhoven (1985) op. cit. pp. 751–54
8 See Protokoll der Verhandlungen des 10. Kongresses der Gewerkschaften Deutschlands, abgehalten zu Nürnberg vom 30. Juni bis 5. Juli 1919 (Berlin, undated), p. 426 ff.

On 12 November 1918 the Council of People's Delegates had announced that it wished to carry out the "socialist programme". On 18 November it decided "that those industries which in terms of their development are ripe for socialization shall be socialized immediately". Whether this announcement really would be put into effect was open to doubt, especially as not even the Free Trade Unions – let alone the Hirsch-Duncker associations and the Christian unions – were convinced of the correctness or importance of socialization. Indeed, on 10 December 1918, Carl Legien, the chairman of the General Commission, had stated, "Socialization of an economy shaken and disorganized by wartime is not possible."[9]

The first socialization commission started work before the end of the year. The demand for socialization was emphasized by a large number of strikes – particularly in the Ruhr – as well as by the delegates to the council congress in Berlin. The government sought to relieve some of the pressure on it by making verbal concessions. On 1 March 1919 placards went up proclaiming, "Socialization is on the march". But the Coal Industry Law passed on 23 March 1919 failed to live up to the expectations of the supporters of socialization, or the fears of its opponents, by not decreeing any changes in ownership.

The goal of most Majority Social Democrats was not socialization in the true sense of the word, but the construction of a system of economic self-management, a planned economy – even though talk was always of "socialization". This is clearest in the idea of the "co-operative economy" (*Gemeinwirtschaft*), whose keenest proponent was Rudolf Wissell, formerly the vice-chairman of the General Commission, now Minister for the Economy. According to the the memorandum submitted by the National Ministry for the Economy in May 1919, the co-operative economy was supposed to be "the national economy, managed on a planned basis and under social control for the benefit of the national community". The idea of creating an economic order designed to benefit all, while retaining private ownership of the means of production, was greeted with great scepticism by the MSPD (not to mention the USPD and the KPD). But it accorded with the ideas of the Free Trade Unions and, in particular, the Christian unions, and left its stamp on the "council articles" of the Weimar constitution (especially Article 165.3). In the situation obtaining in spring 1919, Wissell's policy foundered on the resistance of the advocates of socialization, who, however – confused over their aims and riven

---

9 Quot. H.-J. Bieber, op. cit. p. 629 f.

by dissent – were unable to prevail over the continued opposition of the MSPD and the bourgeois parties.

Thus the plans for socialization and the co-operative economy blocked each other – with the result that neither was put into practice. What is more, under the impact of events in Russia both the MSPD and the unions misjudged the role of the councils and by fighting against these organizations relinquished part of their own power base. Fears that if plans for socialization and the setting up of councils went through, the inevitable consequences would be economic chaos, the dictatorship of a minority or civil war were – it may now be said – at least partly imaginary and were one of the reasons why options that were perfectly feasible were not fully exploited. Consequently, the undemocratic (not to say anti-democratic) top echelons of the Kaiserreich in the administration, education, the judiciary, the armed forces and in large-scale industry and agriculture retained their leading positions, which they soon began to use to undermine the young republic.

But we should not lose sight of the successes of the revolution and the republic. On the basis of the Council of Popular Delegates' "governmental programme" of 12 November 1918 some key union demands were met. By an order of the popular delegates of 23 December 1918, for example, collective agreements were declared legally and generally binding; from 1919 to 1922 the number of wage earners covered by collective agreements had more than doubled. Furthermore, a succession of decrees was issued, finally consolidated on 12 February 1920, governing the employment and dismissal of wage earners. Dismissals were made difficult for employers and it was laid down that soldiers returning from the war should be given their old jobs back. This was made easier by the fact that women who had worked during the war went back to their homes and families, or failing that were forced back (which was perfectly in keeping with trade union thinking). Together with the cuts in working hours and the inflationary state of the economy, these measures played a large part in holding down unemployment, which from a high of 5.1 per cent (of union members) in December 1918 steadily fell in the following years to 3.7 per cent in 1919, 3.8 per cent in 1920, 2.8 per cent in 1921 to 0.8 per cent in March-October 1922.[10]

---

10 Statistics from Dietmar Petzina, Werner Abelshauser and Anselm Faust, Sozialgeschichtliches Arbeitsbuch III. Materialien zur Statistik des Deutschen Reiches 1914–1945 (Munich, 1978), p. 119

Through the interim demobilization decrees of 23 November 1918 and 18 March 1919 the eight-hour day was introduced for workers and salaried staff. The fact that the unions, in a rider to the November agreement, had conceded that cuts in working hours could "only be made permanent [. . .] when the eight-hour day is laid down for all civilized countries by national agreement" meant that this was merely a postponement of, not a solution to, the question of working hours. True, the introduction of the eight-hour day and the 48-hour week was agreed at the first International Labour Conference, held in Washington from 29 October to 29 November 1919 (with no delegates from Germany or Austria). But the industrial states did not exactly fall over themselves to ratify the "Washington agreement", so that the unions were soon back on the defensive over the question of working hours – all the more so as the trade union federations were divided on the issue.

The underlying principles of the November agreement finally found their way into the Weimar constitution of 11 August 1919. This is true, for instance, of the legal basis for trade union work: Article 159 states, "Freedom of association to preserve and promote the conditions of labour and the economy is guaranteed for everyone and all trades. All agreements and measures limiting or seeking to obstruct this freedom are unlawful." The right to strike was, however, deliberately excluded from the constitution, as the lawmakers feared that they would not then be able to limit it for certain specific groups – farmworkers, railwaymen, and so on. Article 165 declared collective agreements legally binding; in addition, it confirmed that workers and salaried staff were "called upon to regulate wages and working conditions and to participate on an equal basis in the overall economic development of the productive forces". This article also pledged that "legal representation" would be established on "works councils, regional workers' councils and a national workers' council", which were supposed to take part in efforts to implement a "co-operative economic order" and socialization under Article 156. The constitution thus granted the trade unions the right to co-determination and influence not only in the field of social policy, but also in shaping the entire economic life of the country, which was to be organized in conformity with the principles of justice, with the aim of ensuring a decent life for all (Article 152). For this reason, the possibility of expropriations and the social obligations of property were expressly set out (in Article 153). Articles 157 and 163 should not be overlooked, either: they placed "labour" under the "special protection of the nation" and guaranteed the right to work or – if this was not feasible – the right to maintenance.

But the difficulty of holding on to the achievements of the revolutionary period and the guarantees set out in the constitution soon became apparent. The form taken by the workers' right to co-determination in economic matters completely failed to come up to the expectations of the revolutionary period. The National Economic Council set up pursuant to Article 165 never got past the provisional stage, for lack of any organizational base. Neither was it able at any time during the Weimar Republic to acquire the decisive powers necessary to influence economic policy and the economic system.

Only at company level did the unions succeed to any extent in giving any legal form to the regulations governing the tasks of the works councils adopted at the Nuremberg trade union congress of 1919. The Works Councils Law of 4 February 1920[11], adopted after serious disturbances and against the votes of the USPD and the rightwing bourgeois deputies revived the workers' committee regulation of the Kaiser's era and provided for the election of a shop steward in companies employing five people or more and, where there were 20 employees or more, the election of a works council consisting of several people. Paragraph 1, however, imposed twin duties on this works council: on the one hand, it was to "defend the common interests of the employees (workers and salaried staff) vis-à-vis the employer"; on the other, it was to "support the employer in achieving company objectives". Although the works council had the right to inspect the company books, the dual loyalty demanded by paragraph 1 prevented it from ever properly representing the interests of the workers. But compared with earlier rules, the right to a say in matters of social welfare and in dismissals had been greatly improved. While the Christian trade unions and the Hirsch-Duncker associations welcomed the law, voices critical of the Works Councils Law were heard coming from the Free Trade Unions, particularly the DMV.

The social reforms laid down in the constitution and in legislation had little time to prove their worth, though; furthermore, they were soon firmly rejected by the employers.

2. *Policy changes and union reorganization, 1919–20*

The end of the war, revolution and the foundation of the Weimar Republic confronted the unions with tasks they were ill-equipped to cope with. Only when important fundamental decisions affecting the construction of

---

11 Reichs-Gesetzblatt No. 26, 1920, vol. 1, pp. 147–174

the state and the social order had already been taken did the trade unions (still split along ideological lines) attempt to adapt their programmes and organizations to the new situation, that is to say, working in a parliamentary republic.

The Free trade unions

The key factor in the reorganization of much the largest branch of the trade union movement was the tenth congress of the Free Trade Unions, which was held in Nuremberg from 30 June to 5 July 1919. Apart from the acute social ills of the day, the congress concentrated on such issues as the political truce, collaboration with the employers, workers' councils, socialization and party political orientation. Furthermore, an attempt was made, in the shape of the above mentioned "guidelines", to adopt something resembling a trade union programme.

After a heated debate, congress passed a vote of confidence in the General Commission by 445 votes to 179, thus lending its approval to the fundamentals of its wartime and post-war policy. It was no surprise, then, that the formation of the Central Association was also approved (by 420 votes to 181). By a large majority, the Mannheim Agreement between the SPD and the Free Trade Unions dating back to 1906 was scrapped. The Free Unions proclaimed their neutrality with regard to the political parties, particularly as, in view of the split in the socialist labour movement, there was no longer any single party with a claim to representing the interests of all workers. It was also a sign of political self-awareness that the Free Trade Unions did not consider that they had to limit themselves to "the narrow representation of members' occupational interests"; instead – in the words of the resolution on the relations between trade unions and parties – they must "become the focus of the proletariat's class endeavours, so as to help lead the struggle for socialism to victory".[12]

Judging by the votes taken at the congress, there was consistently strong opposition to the line taken by the executive. Some 420–440 delegates approved executive policy, while there were about 180 who took a different view on crucial issues. The internal union opposition received its strongest backing from the engineering workers, shoemakers and textile workers. There were strong dissident minorities in the railwaymen's and garment workers' unions. Probably about one third of the miners' dele-

---

12 Protokoll der Verhandlungen des 10. Kongresses der Gewerkschaften Deutschlands, p. 56

gates could be regarded as belonging to the opposition; the proportion would doubtless have been higher but for the orchestrated resignations of the second quarter of 1919 and the establishment of the General Miners' Union, which later gave rise to the General Workers' Union. On the other hand, the opposition was very weak in the unions of the woodworkers, building workers, factory workers and book printers. Its regional centres were Berlin, Saxony and Thuringia, Hamburg and Bremen – generally speaking urban rather than rural industrial areas. There were hardly any other sociological or organizational common denominators: the opposition embraced both female and male-dominated unions, unions chiefly consisting of both skilled and unskilled workers, and both large and small organizations.

The importance of party political allegiance in all this should not be overestimated, for the formation of "wings" within the unions followed the split in social democracy, and when the USPD split, that was reflected, too. Although the chief party political loyalties of the Free Trade Unions were again clearly seen to lie with the MSPD and the rump of the USPD in 1922, the conflict with the KPD and the Communist trade unionists, who were accused of forming cells inside the unions, became a perennial problem, resulting in union expulsions and attempts by Communist trade unionists to set up their own organizations.[13] Communist trade union policy of the 1920s largely conformed to "guiding principles" laid down at the Second World Congress of the Communist International in Moscow in July–August 1920. Communists of all countries were instructed to seize political control of the trade unions, to subordinate the unions to the party leadership and finally – if a social revolutionary realignment of the trade unions proved impossible – to create their own unions. It should also be remembered that the socialist workers' critical attitude towards the unions was also articulated in their own syndicalist unions, though after the revolution petered out they lingered on in obscurity for a while, until their members drifted back to the Free Trade Unions – or, from 1929–30 on, went over to the RGO, the Revolutionary Trade Union Opposition (or Organization).

*

While the friction resulting from the formation of political wings within the Free Trade Unions caused certain losses that impaired their effective-

---

13 According to Werner Müller, Lohnkampf, Massenstreik, Sowjetmacht. Ziele und Grenzen der „Revolutionären Gewerkschafts-Opposition"(RGO) in Deutschland 1928 bis 1933 (Cologne, 1988), p. 26 ff.

ness, the reorganization of the unions was intended to strengthen it. The tenth congress of the Free Trade Unions held in Nuremberg in 1919, the first post-war congress, established an umbrella organization, the General German Trade Union Federation (Allgemeiner Deutscher Gewerk-schaftsbund – ADGB). The General Commission, set up in 1890, was now replaced by a fifteen-man federal executive consisting of a chairman, two vice-chairmen, a treasurer, an editor, two secretaries and eight unpaid committee members. The unions' supreme body was the federal congress, which – every three years – also determined the composition of the executive. The work of the executive was overseen by the federal committee, on which each union executive had one vote or, in the case of unions with over 500,000 members, two votes. Thus whereas the federal committee stressed the unions' equal standing, the number of delegates at the trade union congress was roughly in proportion to membership. Regionally, the ADGB was divided into local committees (the former local "cartels"), in which the local payment offices of the ADGB unions were amalgamated under a self-elected executive, and, from 1922 on, regional committees whose secretaries were appointed by the federal executive. The local ADGB organizations were expressly forbidden to encroach on the powers of the individual unions, which retained the right to decide on policy matters relating to the industrial struggle.

New ideas on the structure of the individual unions, whose construction was similar to that of the ADGB, were also aimed at tightening up trade union organization. After a great deal of controversy, the ADGB's Leipzig congress of June 1922 recommended the setting up of industrial unions – one company, one union.[14] The DMV, in particular, had come out strongly in favour of organization by industry so as to be in a better position to square up to the employers, who had closed ranks against the unions. This idea was opposed by men such as Fritz Tarnow, the chairman of the Woodworkers' Union, who in a resolution adhered to the principle of occupational solidarity as a "valuable method of trade union organi-zation, schooling and discipline". So matters went no further than a rec-ommendation, which was only tentatively carried out anyway. But things were nevertheless (slowly) moving in that direction: the number of indivi-dual unions fell from 52 in 1919–20 to 44 in 1923.

Admittedly, the tendency in the white-collar and civil service unions was different. In November 1920 the Association of Free Unions of Sala-

---

14 See Protokoll der Verhandlungen des 11. Kongresses der Gewerkschaften Deutsch-lands (1. Bundestag des Allgemeinen Deutschen Gewerkschaftsbundes), abgehalten zu Leipzig vom 19. bis 24. Juni 1922 (Berlin, 1922), p. 35 f.

ried Staff became the General Free Union of Salaried Staff (Allgemeiner freier Angestelltenbund, or AfA-Bund), which concluded a co-operation agreement with the ADGB in April 1921 and under Siegfried Aufhäuser pursued a policy of social reform. When the German Civil Service Union (Deutscher Beamtenbund – DBB) was formed in late 1918 as the top organization for all civil servants' unions, the Free Trade Unions initially refrained from setting up a civil servants' union of their own. Then in 1920 the federation of senior officials left the DBB, forming the core of the National Federation of Senior Civil Servants, with approximately 60,000 members. And in 1922 the union-oriented civil servants left the DBB over its refusal to support the first strike by German civil servants (the railwaymen's strike of 1922). They set up the General German Federation of Civil Servants (Allgemeiner Deutscher Beamtenbund – ADB), which in March 1923 also concluded a co-operation agreement with the ADGB.

By 1922–23 these amalgamations were largely over. The trade union organizations – the smaller ones included – had evidently stabilized. It is worth noting, however, that by 1922 the five largest unions alone (the engineering, factory, textile, transport and agricultural workers) accounted for more than 50 per cent of all the Free Trade Unions' members.

*

The unions' growing membership and greater chances of influencing the economy and the state confronted them with a host of new tasks. Let us first look at their efforts to target specific groups of workers. When the restrictions contained in the Law of Association were lifted, the proportion of young people (14–18) and women in the unions increased. Under the leadership of a youth leader or representative (usually 18–25 years old) young people were organized in local youth sections, for which the ADGB's Youth Secretariat published the monthly paper "Jugend-Führer" (Youth Leader). The women's side of trade union work was also strengthened. In 1916 the Free Unions had started a trade union newspaper for women, the "Gewerkschaftliche Frauenzeitung", edited by Gertrud Hanna, which was intended to counteract the oppositional line of another paper, "Gleichheit" (Equality). It was also Gertrud Hanna who spoke on the "organization of female workers" at the Nuremberg congress of 1919 and demanded special efforts to reach and recruit women. The resolution adopted by congress was in line with her comments. Educational work among women was to be stepped up, organized women activated and every effort made to ensure that the demand for "equal pay for equal work" was met. Moreover, congress recognized the right of women to

Carl Legien in 1908. Until 1920 chairman of the General Commission of the German Trade Unions and the General Federation of German Trade Unions

Theodor Leipart, chairman of the General Federation of German Trade Unions 1920-33

Siegfried Aufhäuser, chairman of the General Free Union of Salaried Staff until 1933

Anton Erkelenz, one of the most prominent trade unionists in the leadership of the Federation of German Trade Associations (H-D)

Adam Stegerwald, until 1929
chairman of the General Association of German Christian
Trade Unions, and the (Christian-National) German Trade
Union Federation

Bernhard Otte, chairman of
the General Association of German Christian Trade Unions,
1929-33

Heinrich Imbusch, chairman
of the (Christian-National)
German Trade Union Feder-
ation 1929-33

"workplaces that are in accord with their nature, strength and abilities. It makes it incumbent on the unions to ensure that misogynist views are not permitted to play any part in the recruitment and dismissal of employees."[15]

But the reality was often quite different. Although the wording of the demobilization regulations was not "gender-specific", the criteria on which redundancies were enforced placed women at an overwhelming disadvantage: it was permitted to dismiss anyone who was not forced to take paid employment and who was not in paid employment at the outbreak of war. The participation of women also had the backing of the Works Councils Law (paragraph 22); but from 1919 on it was above all women who – as Gertrud Hanna said – showed understanding for the "exigencies of the hour" and relinquished their jobs. Moreover, women's wages continued to lag behind men's throughout the 1920s (Table 3e). When, at the eleventh trade union congress in 1922, four of the seven female delegates (out of a total of 690) made yet another attempt to put their demands across, they were thwarted by the men's lack of interest. The problem of "women and the unions" ceased to be a matter of topical concern for the time being.

The "major task" which the trade union congress of 1919 set itself in paving the way for socialism was the "socialization of education". And in actual fact trade unionists needed more knowledge in order to make full use of co-determination. As early as 1919 the Free Trade Unions set up the Tinz Heimvolkshochschule (Home Folk High School), near Gera. This was followed in 1930 by the ADGB's first federal college of its own in Bernau. In collaboration with the universities, the "Free Trade Union College" was established in Cologne and – together with the Christian trade unions – the Academy of Labour in Frankfurt; in 1922 the colleges of economics and administration in Berlin and Düsseldorf, in which the trade unions were involved, opened their doors.

Looking at the realignment and reorganization of the Free Trade Unions, one is left with an ambivalent impression. The successful centralization and expansion of the organization must be seen alongside the political strife within the unions. Despite the powerful internal opposition the majority nevertheless managed to get their political ideas enshrined in the

---

15 Protokoll der Verhandlungen des 10. Kongresses der Gewerkschaften Deutschlands, p. 412 f.

"programme" almost unchallenged, from the political truce policy to the Works Councils Law. This was partly due to the unassailable personal position of Carl Legien, to whom the opposition could provide no alternative, nor even an adequate challenger.

On Legien's death on 26 December 1920, the Free Trade Unions quickly installed a successor who had established a profile at the turn of the century and in the war years and also in his role as main speaker at the Nuremberg congress, as a representative of the "old" executive line. On 19 January 1921 Theodor Leipart was appointed chairman of the ADGB. This was no change of generation: Leipart, born the son of a tailor in Neubrandenburg on 17 May 1867, was only six years younger than Legien. From 1881 to 1890 he worked as a turner. In 1886 he was elected on to the executive of the German Turners' Union; and in 1890 he assumed editorial responsibility for the "Fachzeitung für Drechsler" (Turners' Journal). In 1901 Leipart became chairman of the Turners' Union and, when the turners joined the German Woodworkers' Union, vice-chairman of this national union. As a member of the MSPD, Leipart was the Württemberg Labour Minister in 1919–20 – until his move to the top of the ADGB. The continuity of executive policy was ensured; but whether Leipart would attain the stature of a Legien depended on the outcome of the disputes that were to mark the months and years to come.

The Christian-national unions

While the Free Trade Unions did little to actively promote the revolution, the Christian unions saw it as their duty to prevent any social upheaval. Even at the autumn committee meeting of 29–30 October 1918, the federation of Christian unions was still proclaiming its loyalty to the throne.[16] But a few days later, after the Kaiser's abdication, the Christian unions were pressing for the convening of a "constitutive German national assembly". The readiness of the Christian unions to play a part in building up the new state was, of course, chiefly motivated by the desire to prevent "something worse" – that is, a socialist revolution.

This hostility towards the revolution facilitated efforts to forge a united front of non-socialist unions. On 20 November 1918, the German Democratic Trade Union Federation (Deutsch-Demokratischer Gewerkschaftsbund – DDGB) was founded by the organizations affiliated to the

---

16 See Sitzung des Ausschusses des Gesamtverbandes, in Zentralblatt No. 23 of 4. 11. 1918, p. 190–92

German Workers' Congress and the Congress of Libertarian-national Workers' and Salaried Employees' Unions, headed by the Hirsch-Duncker associations.

As the revolution petered out and it became clear who commanded a majority and where the power lay in the working class and the labour movement, the differences between the liberal and the Christian-national organizations once again became more apparent. After the federation's name had been changed on 19 March 1919 to the German Trade Union Federation (Deutscher Gewerkschaftsbund – DGB), to avoid being identified too closely with the German Democratic Party (DDP), on 14 November the Federation of German Trade Associations (Hirsch-Duncker) left the DGB. On 22 November 1919, the German Trade Union Federation was set up as an amalgamation of the Christian-national unions, consisting of three pillars: the General Association of German Christian Unions (the "workers' pillar"); the General Association of German Salaried Staffs' Unions (Gedag), which also included the German Nationalist Union of Clerical Assistants' (DHV); and the General Association of German Civil Service Unions, which was, however, disbanded in 1926.

*

The Christian-national trade unions of the DGB considered themselves to be professional organizations (*Standesorganisationen*); the term *Stand** was not merely a functional definition of their status in the "popular community", which was based on "solidarity between the classes" (*Stände*), but above all a criterion incorporating a value judgement. They saw the 'popular community' (*Volksgemeinschaft*) as an historical community of destiny and culture, which thus bridged the classes and was essentially national in character. In this the Christian-national unions were clearly differentiated from the class struggle ideology and internationalism of the Free Trade Unions, who were accused of toeing the Social Democratic line in their policy commitments.

The Christian-national trade unionists, on the other hand, were spread over the entire spectrum of the bourgeois parties. Whereas the overwhelmingly Catholic Christian unions' closest political ally was still the

---

* Translator's note: The German word "Stand" has no one-to-one equivalent in English. Historically, it corresponds to English "estate (of the realm)", though in a more modern context this is not a satisfactory rendering. It may be variously translated, depending on the context, as profession; class or rank; status or station.

Centre Party, with only a few representatives in the German People's Party (Deutsche Volkspartei – DVP) and the German National People's Party (Deutschnationale Volkspartei – DNVP), the protestant-dominated unions were allied with the bourgeois nationalist parties. As a result of the radicalization of large sections of white-collar workers, which particularly benefited the German Nationalist Union of Clerical Assistants (DHV), around 1930 the National Socialist German Workers' (Nazi) Party (NSDAP) was also to join the ranks of the DGB unions' political interlocutors. In all these parties, however, the Christian-national trade unionists were lobbying alongside, if not among, other organizations. The Centre included, in addition to the workers' wing, strong agricultural and industrial groups; in the DVP and DNVP the trade unionists were not only in the company of landowners and industrialists but also of "sweetheart unions", that is, representatives of labour associations committed to industrial peace. The latter had amalgamated in October 1919 to form the "National Federation of German Trade Unions", whose name was changed in 1921 to the "National Federation of German Occupational Associations" (Nationalverband Deutscher Berufsvereine).

It is against this background that one must consider Stegerwald's policy speech at the Essen congress of the Christian trade unions, in which he expounded the idea – not without a certain measure of political ambition of his own – of founding a trade union-oriented party of the centre. Its fundamental principles would be: German, Christian, democratic and social.[17] Despite the assent with which the idea was greeted, the plan came to grief over people's reservations about Stegerwald personally (he always wanted to be both things simultaneously, a politician and a trade unionist) and over the Catholic workers' traditional links with the Centre. The time to establish an explicitly Christian, though non-denominational party was not yet ripe.

Much more specific than the steps to set up a "People's Party" were the discussions at the Essen congress on the matter of organizational structure, which were basically similar to the ADGB's. There were other similarities, too, in the expansion of work among youth and women, and in the construction of a broad-based trade union education system. The launching of the DGB's own newspaper – "Der Deutsche" (The German) – in April 1921 was in keeping with its ambitious political plans to create a Christian-national coalition movement.

---

17 See Adam Stegerwald, Die christlich-nationale Arbeiterschaft und die Lebensfragen des deutschen Volkes, in Niederschrift der Verhandlungen des 10. Kongresses der christlichen Gewerkschaften Deutschlands, abgehalten vom 20. bis 23. November 1920 in Essen (Cologne, 1920), p. 183 ff.

The Hirsch-Duncker associations

After leaving the DGB in November 1919, the following year the Hirsch-Duncker associations set up an umbrella organization of their own, the "Trade Union League of Workers', Salaried Staff's and Civil Servants' Associations". Though the H-D associations had great reservations about the revolution, they positively welcomed the November agreement and the ZAG, and supported both the elections to the national assembly and the "construction of the republican state", which they ultimately helped defend against the Kapp *putsch*. The "doctrine of class struggle" was firmly rejected, "because it is un-trade union and also undemocratic", to quote the words of Gustav Schneider, of the Trade Union Federation of Salaried Staff at the fourth congress of the Trade Union League in November 1930.[18] They continued to profess party political independence and religious neutrality, and wished to offer no more (and no less) than a purely economic and social reform movement representing its members' interests. The strike was endorsed as the ultimate means of asserting one's interests, but in practice the negotiated settlement was preferred to a much greater extent than in the Free Trade Unions. Ideologically, the H-D associations and the Trade Union Federation of Salaried Staff (Gewerkschaftsbund der Angestellten – GdA) and their affiliated unions had their roots in socially oriented liberalism, so that they found "their" party political ally in the DPP, the leading leftwing liberal party of the Weimar period. This also entailed a decisive acceptance of the Weimar republic, which was convincingly championed by Gustav Hartmann and especially Anton Erkelenz in the leadership of the Trade Union League. When the DDP was almost entirely wiped out at the end of the Weimar republic, the H-D associations moved closer to the SPD and the ADGB.

International trade union confederations

Almost as fast as they fell apart on the outbreak of war, the international organizations of labour were reconstituted after it. As early as 28 July–2 August 1919, 90 delegates from 14 countries, representing almost 18 million trade unionists, met in Amsterdam to reconstitute the International

---

18 4. Freiheitlich-nationaler Kongress des Gewerkschaftsrings deutscher Arbeiter-, Angestellten- und Beamtenverbände am 15. bis 17. November 1930 in Berlin (Berlin, undated), p. 67

Trade Union Federation, to which the ADGB also belonged. The German trade unionists had to accept the loss of their leading position in the Federation because of their war policy. The establishment of other international union federations showed that the schism and conflict in the German trade union movement were symptomatic of more universal tensions. The Communist and syndicalist unions, and also the oppositional groups in the "reformist" unions, got together to form the Red Trade Union International. Its inaugural congress in Moscow in July 1921 was attended by 380 delegates from 42 countries, representing some 17 million members. After disagreements about the role played by the German Christian trade unions in the war, the Christian trade unions also reconstituted the International Federation of Christian Trade Unions (IFCTU), with its seat in Utrecht. This was also the headquarters of the International Federation of Neutral Trade Unions, set up by the liberal unions in 1928.

Membership trends

Looking solely at the rise in total union membership, one cannot say that the unions had no backing for their policies. Membership of the Free Trade Unions exceeded 8 million in 1920, the Christian unions had 1.1 m members and the H-D unions a good 225,000. In addition to these, there were the Free and Christian-national federations of salaried staffs with 690,000 and 463,000 members respectively. This amounted to a tripling of the pre-war (1913) membership figures. In 1920 a total of 12.5 m workers, salaried employees and civil servants belonged to trade unions or similar organizations. Using the results of the 1925 occupational survey as a basis, one arrives at a level of organization of 40 per cent – or indeed as high as 68 per cent, taking the workers' unions on their own.[19] Thus the politicization of the working class by no means bypassed the trade unions; but it did not lead to a stable membership, owing to the swift onset of disappointment with the course and results of the revolution, and, in particular, the social and economic crisis of the inflationary years.

The increase in union membership 1919–20 was probably influenced crucially by legal and political developments. The recognition of the unions by employers and the constitution, the extension of freedom of association to all occupations, the fundamental politicization of broad

---

19 Heinrich Potthoff, Freie Gewerkschaften 1918–1933. Der Allgemeine Deutsche Gewerkschaftsbund in der Weimarer Republik (Düsseldorf, 1987), p. 43

sections of society, especially the workers, during the war and the period that followed – all these factors made it easier for the unions to make progress in occupations, companies and regions that had previously been closed to them.

At first the new members tended to come from occupations that had scarcely (if at all) been organized before – government workers, railwaymen, farmworkers and white collar workers – though union success in organizing farmworkers, home workers and white collar workers should not be overstated. "New" regions were conquered. The Free and Christian trade unions penetrated into areas where they had previously found it hard to get a foothold because of the political or religious situation. The Free Trade Unions spread to eastern Germany and the Saar region, the Christian unions to central and eastern Germany and, again, the Saar – especially as the end of the "trade union dispute" promised episcopal sufferance, if not support. Though the overall membership of the Christian unions always lagged a good way behind the Free Trade Unions', it should be borne in mind that their regional concentration – as late as 1929, one half of their members were in the Rhineland and Westphalia – made them stronger than the Free Unions in the small and medium-sized towns in this region. Only now were the unions managing to work their way into the large concerns, aided by the provisions of the Auxiliary Service Law and, from 1920, the Works Councils Law. It was above all the number of women, young people and unskilled workers that was on the increase. For the reasons mentioned above, however, the proportion of organized women continued to lag far behind the proportion of women employed in all industries or trades.

Another structural characteristic of trade union development in 1918–19 was the growing distance between the membership and the officials. Many posts in the unions leaderships had to be filled, because some executive members had switched to politics or administration; but there was no change of generations. Instead, it was "second rank" officials who advanced into the key positions. So the "old guard", chiefly consisting of long-serving trade unionists, stayed at the top. Trained as artisans, they were used to discipline and firm believers in the long, slow path of reform. By contrast, the new members had often simply taken a job in a factory, with no apprenticeship behind them, and first felt the impact of politics during the war or immediately after. This difference in experience between the generations contributed in no small measure to the tensions between the leadership and the rank and file, resulting in growing opposition, particularly in the Free Trade Unions.

The extent and speed of the rise in membership raised a number of problems for the machinery of all the federations. Simply issuing hundreds of thousands of membership cards, not to mention the opening of new payment offices, placed a tremendous strain on officials and increased the need for more full-time and part-time staff. Yet conditions of work were far from attractive. An eight-hour day was out of the question and pay was poor; the demands of the job had, however, increased with the growth in the unions' organization and functions. "Union officials" gradually emerged as a breed to whom critics of Right and Left would insultingly refer as "big shots" and "bureaucrats", blaming them for many, if not all, the problems of the Weimar republic.

3. *Back on the defensive: from the Kapp Putsch to inflation*

The November agreement and the Weimar constitution changed the whole basis of trade union work. The unions pinned all their hopes on an expansion of social reform under the Weimar republic. The Free Trade Unions and the H-D associations identified unreservedly with the new parliamentary system. As stated above, they exerted considerable influence on the social system in the early years of the republic and were thus able to record what were, by their own lights, quite a few successes. But this was exactly what provoked much of the criticism of the young republic.

*

The disappointment and resentment of large sections of the political Left at the limited success of the revolution were probably exceeded by the contempt and hatred of the "nationalist Right" for the "November criminals" and "fulfilment politicians" (so-called for their readiness to "fulfil" the Treaty of Versailles), the *Diktat* of Versailles and the entire "Weimar system". The first obvious sign of this war on the republic was the Kapp Putsch. When the "Ehrhardt Brigade" marched into Berlin on 13 March 1920, proclaiming the former East Prussian civil servant Wolfgang Kapp Chancellor and the legitimate government – left in the lurch by the *Reichswehr* – fled Berlin, large numbers of workers and civil servants proved their loyalty to the endangered government. On the very same day, 13 March, the ADGB and the AfA-Bund called a general strike; the call was supported by the Communist KPD on the 14th, the Christian trade unions on the 15th and the German Civil Service Union on the 16th. After

153

The Kapp Putsch on 13 March 1920: the insurgents gather at the Brandenburg Gate

a general strike lasting five days, on 17 March the authors of the coup gave up.

The Free Trade Unions now considered that they were entitled to ask the government to meet a number of their demands as thanks for their help. In their statement of 18 March, they demanded not only that "all public and corporate administrations be thoroughly purged of all reactionary elements"; they also called for "a decisive say [. . .] in the shaping of the national and provincial governments" and the "overhaul of economic and social legislation".[20]

Although the unions of all political tendencies had stuck together through the general strike, this unity soon collapsed. The Christian unions saw the demands of the Free Unions as an attempt at political blackmail, in which they would have no part. They observed with suspicion the nego-

---

20 Der Generalstreik gegen den Monarchistenputsch, in Korrespondenzblatt No. 12/13 of 27. 3. 1920, p. 152 f.

tiations to form a pure workers' government, headed by the ADGB chairman, Carl Legien. But such plans anyway came to naught because of the schism between the USPD and the MSPD – and Legien's refusal to assume the office of Chancellor. Instead, a coalition government consisting of the SPD, Centre and DDP was formed. And the pledges given to the Free Trade Unions when the general strike was called off went largely unfulfilled, for example, with regard to union influence on the formation of the Cabinet, and socialization policy. Many trade unionists were also, no doubt, enraged at the way the armed disturbances on the Ruhr, which were to a certain extent to demand the concession of the revolutionary demands (though not supported by the unions), were bloodily crushed. The situation changed entirely to the detriment of the (Free) trade unions after the elections of 6 June 1920, when the MSPD share of the vote almost halved, leading to the formation of a bourgeois coalition government by the Centre, DDP and DVP.

The unions had proved strong enough to ward off the Kapp Putsch; but they were too weak to give practical political effect to their claims to power, which were not asserted with much cohesion. That discredited them with the Left; but on the political Right, the union claim to exercise decisive political influence was sufficient in itself to taint them with the slander of seeking to establish a "trade union state". This slogan concealed the fact that nothing could be further from the truth. What were the actual facts of the matter? Social policy was stagnating under the pressure of devaluation; there had been no thorough democratization of the administration or judiciary; and the question of economic power – specifically, the issue of socialization – had never been reopened.

Soon afterwards the unions were dragged into the Ruhr struggle and soaring inflation, which combined with the Hitler Putsch made 1923 the most crisis-ridden year of the 1920s. Unions of all tendencies allowed themselves – more or less willingly – to be drawn into the government's policy of "passive resistance" to the occupation of the Ruhr, which was ruining the national finances and fuelling inflation. Partly against their better judgement the Free Trade Unions were also infected by the nationalist slogans of this "spontaneous defensive struggle" – perhaps also hoping to reap some reward, in the shape of concessions in the sphere of social policy, for demonstrating yet again their readiness to "do their patriotic duty". But this was not to be. On the contrary, in the wake of inflation the unions were forced back on to the defensive even on their own ground – pay policy.

*

While the unions' main concern in 1918–19 had been to make up for the loss of purchasing power during the war, in 1920 the race against devaluation began. Wages were unable to keep pace with the soaring cost of living. Though pay varied according to industry, occupation, qualifications and locality, there can be no doubt about the general drop in living standards. Inflation attacked the unions' very existence. Their finances worsened rapidly as a result of the fall in dues and the devaluation of their assets. Officials had to be dismissed, newspapers closed, benefits reduced or stopped entirely. And the remaining full-time officials were faced with the need to conduct constant wage negotiations that strained the machinery to breaking point.

At the beginning of 1920, the Free Trade Unions had rejected a sliding wage scale; from the end of 1922 pay talks took place every week; on 4 July 1923 the ADGB's federal committee recommended the individual unions to include a wage adjustment clause in their collective agreements. Pay was to be calculated on pay day on the basis of an official yardstick equivalent to the weekly rise in the cost of living, and from the summer of 1923 this cost of living index was, in fact, adopted.

The unions were also on the defensive over the question of working hours, not only in the field of industrial struggle – for example, in the south German engineering industry – but also in law. After long arguments which culminated in the SPD leaving the ruling coalition, a new decree on working hours was promulgated on 21 December 1923, which retained the principle of the eight-hour day but permitted a whole range of exceptions. The consequences were soon apparent: while until 1923 the unions were able to fend off all onslaughts on the eight-hour day and 48 hour week, in 1924 the working week increased to 50.4 hours following the relaxation of the rules, and then slowly decreased once more (Table 4b).

The trade union commitment to questions of pay and working hours led to a great number of industrial disputes in the years 1920–22, despite the decline in purchasing power (Table 2c). Of course, willingness to strike is clearly dependent on the ups and downs of the economic cycle. But the sudden leap in strikes and the high level maintained from 1919 to 1922 demonstrated more than anything the expectations of the workers, who were determined to bring about some improvement in their social and economic position. As early as 1923 – during the surge of inflation – these hopes gave way to bitterness and resignation. The fact that industrial action did not reach its "old" level in 1924 was no doubt partly due to the weakness of the unions, but chiefly to the introduction of the arbitration service.

*

In view of the high level of industrial action, it was in the interests of the employers and the state to push through peaceful ways of settling disputes, which the weakened unions were initially prepared to accept, believing they would not be able to assert themselves on their own. After several arbitration decrees, the arbitration service was given its definitive form by the decree of 30 October 1923. If the parties could not agree, the authorities – bipartite arbitration committees, mediators and the national Labour Ministry – would propose a settlement. If this was rejected, the chairman of the arbitration committee or the mediator had to form an arbitration tribunal and summon employer and employee representatives in equal numbers. "If this still did not result in consensus, the tribunal had to put forward a proposal as a basis for an agreement (arbitration award). If both parties accepted the award, it had the effect of an agreement."[21] If they were unable to agree on an arbitration award, the chairman had the casting vote. After a new round of talks the award could be declared binding by the mediator for that district or by the Labour Minister. The award thereupon acquired the status of a collective agreement, even against the will of one of the parties.

The way the arbitration process was constructed, particularly the instrument of compulsory arbitration, involved the state in industrial relations. The consequence was that the unions and employers were no longer absolutely constrained to reach agreement; they were able to shift the responsibility for, say, wages on to the state. The consistently high number of cases referred to arbitration and particularly the high proportion of one-man awards and declarations making them binding indicate a tendency for both sides to dodge the responsibility and "pass the buck" on to the state.

A survey of union policy in the early years of the Weimar republic does not present us with a consistent picture. It must be counted a success for the unions that they managed to expand in the way they did, itself a result of the improvements gained in their legal and political position with the wind of revolution in their backs. But the contribution of the revolution was exactly the element which the unions were inclined to play down; their policy was sustained by the illusion that the achievements of

21 Hans-Hermann Hartwich, Arbeitsmarkt, Verbände und Staat 1918–1933. Die öffentliche Bindung unternehmerischer Funktionen in der Weimarer Republik (Berlin, 1967), p. 29

November 1918 had also ensured parliamentary democracy. But as the works councils and socialization campaigns petered out, the traditional power structure was consolidated and its beneficiaries remaining in place. This was also a consequence of trade union policy. The policy of the *Arbeitsgemeinschaft* ("working union") undoubtedly brought the unions and employees clear social and political improvements; but at the same time it provided the employers with a jumping-off point for a fresh rise to political power – as was already becoming apparent in the early 1920s. The "era of the working union" came to an end – largely owing to the ruthless policy pursued by heavy industry – in profound disillusion. The Free Trade Unions left the ZAG in January 1924, though the Christian unions clung on to the idea of the working union – even though there were hardly any employers willing to co-operate.

VII. The trade unions' role in constructing the social state 1924–1930

After 1924 there was a clear improvement in the economic situation, accompanied by a degree of political stabilization. The succession of bourgeois Cabinets – generally under Centre leadership – and, in particular, the policy of Gustav Stresemann (DVP) gave the republic a spell of peace, the conservative nature of which was symbolized by the election of Paul von Hindenburg as president in 1925. All in all, the mid-1920s was when the "normality" of the Weimar republic evolved, that is, a system containing elements of both the "social state" and private capitalism, not yet consolidated but capable of development. We must be careful, however, to distinguish the concept of the "social state" from the welfare state, precisely because of the democratic measures it implies.

1. Heading for the "social state"? The middle years of the Weimar Republic

In 1924 the end of inflation, the settlement of the reparations issue through the Dawes Plan and the flood of foreign credit brought an economic revival, the clearest sign of which was the doubling of industrial output between 1923 and 1928–29. Without attaining pre-war proportions, the chemical, electrical engineering and optics industries, partly also textiles and mechanical engineering, managed to win back their positions in the world economy, with positive effects on German exports and the foreign trade balance.

The economic upturn was certainly given a considerable fillip by the increases in productivity arising from more rapid rationalization. In the German engineering industry, for example, labour productivity rose by 45 per cent between 1924 and 1927; in the iron industry by 41 per cent between 1925 and 1927. The German economy tried to assert itself against international competition by means of concentration and cartels on the one hand, and improved productivity through the scientific planning of work processes and through new technology on the other.

The dark side of these efforts and successes was the intensification of work and high unemployment even in comparatively prosperous times. From 10 per cent in 1924 it receded to 7–8 per cent in 1925, soared to 15 per cent in the recession of 1926, and was back to 8–9 per cent in 1927–28. In 1929 – with the worldwide depression in the offing – it rose to 13–14 per cent (Table 5a).

∗

It was thanks to union policy that wage earners shared in the benefits of economic recovery. Though the unions had emerged weakened from the inflationary crisis, their attitude to the industrial struggle in 1924 was conspicuous for its militancy. The restabilization of the currency and the December 1923 decree on working hours made new collective agreements necessary; 1924 became the "year of struggle", as a glance at the industrial dispute statistics will show. The numerical relation between offensive and defensive strikes also reveals that the unions were on the defensive, from which they did not emerge until 1925, as the organizations started to gain strength. One cannot fail to note, however, that after the period of inflation industrial militancy was well below the immediate post-war level, owing to the weakness of the unions and to state arbitration (Table 2c).

∗

Wages were the central concern of union policy. From 1924 to 1929 wages rose faster than the cost of living, so that by 1928–29 real weekly wages had reached or exceeded their pre-war level (1913–14) (Table 3b). Wage trends varied considerably throughout the 1920s according to occupation and industry. It is indicative of union policy that women's wages were unable to sustain the level reached after the war; the gap between women's and men's pay widened again (Table 3e).

True, the "wage ratio", that is, wages and employers' social insurance contributions as a proportion of national income, rose steeply from 46.4 per cent in 1913, to 57.6 per cent in 1927 and 59.8 per cent in 1929. But population trends must be taken into account here and also, more importantly, the impoverishment of the middle class by inflation: "unearned income" declined as a share of the total and the number of wage earners rose.

In the public debates of those years pay levels were a controversial issue. While the unions believed that by improving workers' incomes, and hence overall purchasing power, they were stimulating economic activity[1], the employers persisted in taking the view that the high level of wages

---

1 See especially Fritz Tarnow, Warum arm sein? (Berlin, 1928)

160

was making investment decisions very difficult, leading to paralysis of the economy and a worsening of unemployment. The trade unions were blamed for pay levels – but also state arbitration, whose aid the unions admitted, despite being critical of the curbs on the right to strike, they would find it hard to do without.

The controversy over wages and arbitration has resurfaced again recently, and many historical observers also see wage levels as one of the causes of the "sickness" of the German economy in the 1920s which, in a long-term comparison, revealed itself in relatively poor economic growth, low rate of investment and high unemployment. Taking this argument to its logical conclusion, trade union policy and compulsory state arbitration are regarded as major causes of economic adversity as far back as the 1920s.[2] There is no need to go into the debate on this question here, but it should be pointed out that wages did not burst the framework imposed by the development of productivity, nor were wages the only factor governing costs by any means – others, such as interest rates, were equally important. Lastly, it could be argued that, in view of the worldwide trend towards protectionist policies, it was not possible to stimulate demand by increasing exports, so it was necessary to boost mass purchasing power in order to revitalize the economy and bring down unemployment. Without the wage rises of the 1920s the economic situation would undoubtedly have been even worse.

Another major bone of contention between the unions and the employers was – of course – the issue of working hours. In the summer of 1924 the employers presented a memorandum on working hours that stated, "The German economy has been brought to the verge of collapse by the Versailles *Diktat,* inflation and the anti-production social policies of the post-war period" – especially the "routine eight-hour day".[3] On the basis of this statement and with the backing of the December 1923 decree on working hours, employers in virtually every industry seized the opportunity and

---

2 See, for example, Knut Borchardt, Wirtschaftliche Ursachen des Scheiterns der Weimarer Republik, in Hagen Schulze (ed.), Weimar. Selbstpreisgabe einer Demokratie. Eine Bilanz heute (Düsseldorf, 1980), pp. 211–49, especially p. 217 ff. Cf. the controversy involving Claus-Dieter Krohn (Geschichte und Gesellschaft 1982, pp. 415–26 and 1983, pp. 124–137) and Carl Ludwig Holtfrerich (Historische Zeitschrift 1982, pp. 605–31 and 1983, pp. 67–83, and Geschichte und Gesellschaft 1984, pp. 122–41)
3 Die Arbeitszeitfrage in Deutschland. Eine Denkschrift, verfasst von der VDA (Berlin, 1924), p. 5

imposed longer working hours. Despite considerable militant activity in 1924 (considering how weak the unions were), more than 50 per cent of full-time workers had their 48-hour week taken away that year. The trade unions only partially withstood the pressure to increase working hours. The collective agreements that came into force on 1 January 1925 permitted a working week in excess of 48 hours for 10.9 per cent of wage earners, and the proportion rose to 13.4 per cent over the next two years.

When it came to holidays, union policy was more successful. In 1920, 65.7 per cent of collective agreements contained provisions governing the number of days' holiday; by 1 January 1925 this had risen to 86.6 per cent. After one year's employment, a worker was generally entitled to 3–4 days' paid holiday per year; holiday entitlement grew with length of "service" to reach a maximum of 12–14 days. For white-collar workers, many of whom had enjoyed holidays even before the war, a holiday entitlement of 2–3 weeks became common during the Weimar period.

But in view of increasing rationalization and the high rate of unemployment, the Free Trade Unions came out repeatedly in favour of a return to the eight-hour day, and before long were seeking cuts in working hours that went even further. In a public statement supporting this demand on 28 October 1926, the link between unemployment and rationalization was stressed: "The prevailing unemployment has its roots in present-day economic developments. Positive measures are therefore required to bring about a significant fall in unemployment, which is an inevitable result of the continuing advances in technology and company organization."[4] The resulting demand for the immediate enactment of an emergency law on working hours restoring the eight-hour day was not unexpectedly turned down flat by the employers.

Forced into a corner by an SPD bill and with the Christian trade unions applying pressure on the Centre Party, in March 1927 the government introduced its own bill, which was passed by the Reichstag on 8 April 1927. This "emergency law on working hours" rendered those who accepted voluntary overtime liable to prosecution; it made it necessary to obtain official approval to exceed ten working hours per day. Overtime, measured on the basis of the eight-hour day, was to be paid at 25 per cent above the going rate.[5]

4 Ein Notgesetz über den Achtstundentag, in Gewerkschafts-Zeitung No. 45 of 6. 11. 1926, p. 625
5 Gesetz zur Abänderung der Arbeitszeitverordnung vom 14. 4. 1927, in Reichsgesetzblatt, Part I, No. 18 of 16. 4. 1927, p. 109 f.

Although representatives of the employers' organizations had worked on the wording of the law, voices were heard criticizing the fact that basically the eight-hour day remained in force; it was especially galling to the employers that overtime was also calculated on that basis. The Free Trade Unions, however, rejected the law for making a "mockery of the eight-hour day"[6] and, in view of rationalization, unemployment and the world-wide economic crisis, soon set about campaigning for the 40-hour week.

*

For all the short-lived changes in economic, social and political development under the Weimar republic, there is no denying that the 1920s were an integral part of an accelerated process of social change that had commenced in Wilhelminian and wartime Germany and changed the conditions of trade union action.[7] One indication of this transformation is the restructuring of the economy. Looking at the number of persons employed by individual sectors of the economy as a proportion of the whole in 1907, 1925 and 1933, one is struck by the decline of agriculture and forestry (from 35.2 to 28.9 per cent) and the expansion of the tertiary (service) sector (from 24.7 to 30.7 per cent), especially in the area of trade and transport (Table 6a). Though these statistics conceal counter-trends in some areas of the economy, these facts may suffice to illustrate the dominant trend: the beginning, in the 1920s, of Germany's transition from an industrial to a service society.

In tandem with the growth of the service sector and the increasing importance of industry's research and distribution sectors, the number of white-collar workers increased; the expansion of the public sector also made a significant difference. While the number of workers rose in absolute terms, their relative share of the total working population went down from 55 per cent (1907) to 50 per cent (1920). The number of salaried employees and civil servants, on the other hand, rose over the same period from 10.3 to 17.4 per cent, an increase of 70 per cent (Table 6b). This trend was also evident in trade and industry, where the number of salaried employees rose from 5.73 per cent in 1907 to over 9.22 per cent in 1922 and to 9.43 per cent in 1933. The peculiarities of the white-collar mental-

---

6 Kritik am Arbeitsschutzgesetz-Entwurf, in Gewerkschafts-Zeitung No. 9 of 26. 2. 1927, pp. 117–19; this quot. p. 118

7 The following figures are taken from Walther G. Hoffmann, Das Wachstum der deutschen Wirtschaft seit der Mitte des 19. Jahrhunderts (Berlin, Heidelberg and New York, 1965), p. 194 ff.

ity caused the unions a great many problems: there was a hidden explosiveness about it that was generally underrated by the (Social Democratic) labour movement. This was to become increasingly apparent as the world depression neared.

This also applied to women's work. The proportion of women in the total working population changed little, except for a rise (not documented here) during the Great War. In 1907 the figure was 33.8 per cent, in 1925 35.8, and 1933 35.5 per cent. As a proportion of all women, the number of working women rose from 30.4 to 35.6 to 34.2 per cent over the same period.

It should also be mentioned that large-scale industry was continuing to expand. While in trade and industry the proportion of employees working for small firms employing 1–5 workers fell from 31.2 to 25.4 per cent, the proportion of those working for large companies in general rose, notably concerns with over a thousand employees – from 4.9 to 6.8 per cent. This trend affected the unions in two different ways. Firstly, it changed the experiences and occupational structure of the working class, which entailed problems in recruiting members. Secondly, the rise of the large-scale concern reflected the process of concentration which, together with the formation of cartels, led to the takeover of entire industries by small numbers of companies. In 1926, 98 per cent of potash mining, 97 per cent of mining, 96 per cent of the paint industry, 86 per cent of the electrical engineering industry, 80 per cent of shipping and 73 per cent of banks were grouped into large concerns or cartels.[8] Large concerns such as IG-Farben and Vereinigte Stahlwerke (United Steelworks) date back to this period. Trade unions of all tendencies believed they could overcome the adverse effects of this process by means of draft legislation designed to control the cartels and monopolies and put a stop to price-fixing.

∗

One of the trade unions' key fields of political activity was still social policy, and it was a tremendous advantage for trade unionists of all hues that in the years of a bourgeois government majority the Minister for Labour was Heinrich Brauns of the Centre Party, a politician with a keen interest in social affairs. It was his doing that, after the years of inflation, the virtually bankrupt social insurance scheme was rebuilt and indeed enlarged. The fact that for Brauns, too, social policy took second place to

---

8 Statistics from Manfred Clemenz, Gesellschaftliche Ursprünge des Faschismus (Frankfurt/M., 1972), p. 197

economic policy was not so noticeable since the relative economic upturn of the mid-1920s produced more wealth to distribute.

The pinnacle of the Weimar social legislation was undoubtedly the Law on Employment Exchanges and Unemployment Insurance (AVAVG), which came into force on 1 October 1927. The AVAVG bill had been drawn up by the ADGB in collaboration with the Christian unions, revised by the Ministry of Labour under Brauns and finally placed before the Reichstag by the Centre Party. It handed over responsibility for the two areas mentioned in the title of the law to a central institution – the National Institute for Employment Exchanges and Unemployment Insurance. This new institute pointed the way ahead in several respects: responsibility was divided (equally between employers, employees and the state); contributions were shared (employer and employee paying half each); benefit consisted of a main payment and a family supplement, and was payable for a limited time only. But the scheme was also flawed, particularly (with more than half a million unemployed) as far as meeting its commitments was concerned, and this would shortly become apparent.

There was a marked rise in overall public spending compared with the *Kaiserreich*. It rose to an annual average of 13.7 billion Marks (in 1913 prices) for the period 1919–1929, as opposed to 6.8 bn Marks for 1909–13. While economic performance as a whole declined, government expenditure as a proportion of GNP doubled in nineteen years under the impact of the new social insurance scheme, rising from 17.7 per cent in 1913 to 25 per cent in 1925, 30.6 per cent in 1929 to 36.6 per cent in 1932.[9] This expansion was first and foremost a consequence of "social interventionism", the chief manifestation of which, apart from house building and job creation measures during the crisis of 1925–26, was the extension of social insurance. This readiness to intervene in social and economic policy was evident in the Works Councils Law, the rules on working hours and the arbitration system, and it was this extension of state involvement, especially the expansion of public enterprises, that was one of the most controversial domestic political issues of the 1920s. The entrepreneurs' organizations, in particular, thought that it smacked of "creeping socialization" .

If the unions tried to leave the narrow area of social policy, however, they did not meet with much success. This proved to be the case over fiscal policy. The trade unions repeatedly advocated raising property taxes, thus taking some of the burden off wage earners: with no success. Neither were

---

9 Statistics from D. Petzina et al., Sozialgeschichtliches Arbeitsbuch III, pp. 139 f. and 150

the Free Trade Unions able to get their way in the question of protective tariffs. In fact, there was seldom agreement between the federations on such matters.

*

While the unions' broad party political ties offered opportunities – as co-operation over the AVAVG had demonstrated – the limits of their influence within the parties became clearly apparent towards the end of the 1920s. In 1925 the Free Trade Unions withdrew to their original sphere. At the Breslau congress Leipart stated that from the start from unions had been "pushed into tasks" which were "really not their concern"; the plan for the future was to devote more effort to "proper trade union business".[10] And he insisted on the independence of the unions vis-à-vis the Grand Coalition government formed in 1928 under Social Democratic leadership; at the Hamburg congress he expressed the hope that the government would pursue a "socialist policy" but declared that the unions would criticize the government "without mercy" when they considered it "necessary in the interests of the workers".[11] With decisions like this the Free Trade Unions drew the conclusions from its experiences since the Kapp *Putsch,* which had taught them that trade union positions are frequently sacrificed to political considerations when a coalition is involved.

The Christian unions also had expectations of their party political allies – in terms of political representation in key positions – and they were not fulfilled, either. Stegerwald was voted on to the Centre Party executive in 1920, yet neither he nor Joseph Joos, the editor-in-chief of the journal of the West German Catholic Workers' Associations, the "Westdeutsche Arbeiter-Zeitung" (West German Workers' Newspaper), managed to obtain the chairmanship at the 1928 party conference, which elected the prelate Ludwig Kaas, professor of ecclesiastical law at the University of Trier, instead. With the election of Alfred Hugenberg to the post of party chairman, the DNVP also fell into the hands of a man who cannot be said to have maintained close links with the unions. As a result many Protestant workers left the DNVP in 1929 for the "Christian-Social People's Ser-

10 Protokoll der Verhandlungen des 12. Kongresses der Gewerkschaften Deutschlands (= 2. Bundestag des Allgemeinen Deutschen Gewerkschaftsbundes), abgehalten in Breslau vom 31. August bis 4. September 1925 (Berlin, 1925), p. 112
11 Leipart, in Protokoll der Verhandlungen des 13. Kongresses der Gewerkschaften Deutschlands (3. Bundestag des ADGB), abgehalten in Hamburg vom 3. bis 7. September 1928 (Berlin, 1928), p. 80

vice" (Christlich-sozialer Volksdienst). Walther Lambach, the leader of the shop assistants' union, the DHV, had already taken this step in 1928, though the majority of DHV members drifted over to the NSDAP (the Nazis). Of the 107 National Socialist deputies elected to the Reichstag in 1930, 16 belonged to the DHV; or, put another way, almost one third of the 47 Christian-National trade unionists in parliament were NSDAP members. The white-collar workers' reaction to the risk of *declassement* and loss of status was to move to the nationalist, conservative Right.

When Stegerwald became leader of the Centre Party group in the Reichstag and Minister of Transport, he resigned his union offices. The fact that Bernhard Otto was elected chairman of the national federatioon of Christian unions in 1929 and Heinrich Imbusch advanced to the top of the DGB was proof of the "self-reflection" within the Christian-National unions, which led them to rethink their trade union tasks and withdraw from politics – experimentally, at least.

As for the Hirsch-Duncker associations, the end of the 1920s saw their political plans in tatters. Although their political ally, the DDP, had obtained some 18.5 per cent of the vote in 1919, it was soon reduced to a splinter party. In September 1930 it could only muster 3.7 per cent of the vote. After the DDP re-formed in 1930 as the German State Party (Deutsche Staatspartei), in collaboration with the Young German Order, many leftwing, liberal members, including Anton Erkelenz, one of the leaders of the Trade Union League, switched to the SPD.

*

To sum up, one might say that the 1920s witnessed the development of a volatile interplay between social protectionist measures and measures to promote the stabilization of advanced private capitalism. In the process, state intervention underwent a major transformation, both qualitatively and quantitatively: it was no longer limited to the field of social policy proper but extended to the awarding of public contracts (job creation) and industrial relations (working hours, arbitration) – and even to customs tariffs and fiscal policy. But the government often intervened only indirectly in the social and economic system, leaving it initially to the two sides of industry to find common ground. Only when no compromise emerged was the arbitration procedure enforced. Although trade union work was faced with severe tests both at the start and the end of the 1920s, for a number of years a certain measure of co-operation – constantly endangered though it was – had nevertheless developed between the unions, employers and state. Unfortunately this "Weimar pluralism", which can hardly be described as a balance of power in view of the domination of the entrepreneurs, was not given the time to develop solid traditions and resilient structures.

2. *The unions' organizational consolidation*

While the long-term trends described above – for instance, the problems of recruitment among women and white-collar workers – only affected trade union organization indirectly, the unions' economic successes and economic improvement in general had a more direct effect on membership. Overall, the membership figures of the federations picked up after 1924–25, but did not reach their old post-war peak again by 1929, which saw the beginning of the Depression. The Free Trade Unions maintained their leading position, with a membership that grew from 4 m in 1924 to nearly 5 m in 1929. The Christian unions were next with almost 613,000 (1924) rising to 673,000 (1929) – a long way ahead of the Hirsch-Duncker associations, which had 147,000 members in 1924 and 168,000 in 1929 (Table 1a).

While the Free Trade Unions remained the strongest workers' organization by far, the Afa-Bund was overtaken as the largest union of salaried staff by the Christian-national white-collar unions amid the surge of radical nationalist conservatism that swept through the middle classes. While the membership of the Afa-Bund fell from 447,000 (1924) to just under 400,000 (1927) and then rose again to 450,000 in 1929, the membership of the Christian-national Gedag increased steadily from 393,000 (1924) to 557,000 (1929); even the liberal GdA recorded an increase from 260,000 to 320,000 members (Table 1b).

*

As their membership increased, the unions were able to rebuild their internal organizational structure, which had been badly hit during the years of inflation. Of the 13 regional offices of the Free Trade Unions closed down in 1923, eight were reopened in 1924 and another three in 1925. The ranks of the union employees were also replenished. In the 1920s, one full-time union official for every 700–800 members became the norm, so that in the early 1930s the Free Trade Unions had roughly 6,000 officials, 4,000 of whom were employed in local administration, just over 1,100 at national level and a mere 43 by the ADGB executive.

This also illustrates how weak the ADGB was as an umbrella organization, and this was particularly true at regional level.

At the congress in Breslau in 1925 and the 1928 congress in Hamburg the voluntary nature of the 1922 decision to go ahead with industrial unions was emphasized again. The number of ADGB-affiliated unions did go down from 40 to 33 between 1924 and 1929, but there was still a long way to go until the industrial union was established. Resistance to a thorough-going industrial union system led to more emphasis being given to the "trade" aspect of trade unions in the mid-1920s, by the Free Trade Unions as well as the others.

There continued to be differences of interest between the large and the small unions, between the individual unions and the ADGB executive. At the 1928 Hamburg congress the rules governing the make-up of the federal committee were changed. The unions would no longer send one representative each – two for those with more than 500,000 members – to the federal committee; a greater measure of differentiation was introduced. Henceforward a further member was to be appointed for 300,000, 600,000 and 900,000 members. The DMV, which had previously been the only union with two members, was now given four seats, and five more unions two each.

The small unions generally pressed for the expansion of the federation institutions, in order to cut their own organization costs, while the large unions regularly voted against any increase in central expenditure – and hence greater powers – for the ADGB. This was the case with the ADGB's educational work, which in 1927 it employed an education officer to co-ordinate, and its press. The "Gewerkschafts-Zeitung" was expanded, the theoretical monthly "Die Arbeit" was founded, and in 1928 the industrial law supplement of the "Gewerkschafts-Zeitung" was turned into an independent publication called "Arbeitsvermittlung und Arbeitslosenversicherung" (Employment Exchange and Unemployment Insurance) with Clemens Nörpel as editor. In addition, the Free Trade Unions got together in 1925 with the SPD and the co-operative movement to set up the Research Centre for Economic Policy (Forschungsstelle für Wirtschaftspolitik), headed by Fritz Naphtali, to supply the unions with expert advice on economic and social policy.

*

This phase of comparative economic and political stabilization was also the heyday of the co-operative enterprises. Achievements in this area were to change the face of the trade unions in the 1920s. The consumer co-operatives and insurance enterprises were founded back in the pre-war years, but these and many other freshly established undertakings experienced a tremendous upswing in the Weimar period; trade unionists and trade unions of every persuasion became "entrepreneurs". Being economically active within the overall framework of the capitalist economy was bound to alter the Free Trade Unions' perception of themselves and their role; they realized – in the words of Bernhard Meyer of the Workers' Bank – that "in their way of conducting business they could not infringe the laws and methods of capitalism as long as it occupied a dominant position".[12]

First, then, the Free Trade Unions. In 1923–24 the "Bank der Arbeiter, Angestellten und Beamten AG" (Bank of the Workers, Salaried Staffs and Civil Servants) was established, and until 1929–30 it was a great success. The enterprises who combined to form the federation of social housing companies also prospered, as did the Deutsche Wohnungsfürsorge AG, the Volksfürsorge insurance company, the consumer co-operatives and the ADGB publishing house. The same was true of the enterprises run by the Christian trade unions: the "Christian Trade Union Publishing House" and the publishing house "Der Deutsche" were able to consolidate; and the "Deutsche Volksbank AG" (based in Essen), the "Deutsche Lebensversicherungs-AG" insurance company and the "Deutsche Heimbau Gemeinnützige AG" housing company also flourished. The Christian unions were also involved in the "Grosseinkaufs- und Produktions-AG" (Bulk Buying and Production Company), known as Gepag, and the building society "Bausparkasse der Gemeinschaft der Freunde Wüstenrot GmbH". In addition, the Christian unions supported the activities of the national federation of the consumer (co-operative) societies and the construction co-operatives.

There was frequent co-operation between the national union federations over the co-operative movement. The co-operative idea occupied a central place in their programmes, making co-operative self help a possible starting point for a policy rapprochement between them.

3. *The beginnings and limits of a joint programme of all the national union federations*

Compared with the bitter controversies of the pre-war years, the 1920s were a time of rapprochement between the different national trade union

---

12 Quot. Otto de la Chevallerie, Die Gewerkschaften als Unternehmer (Berlin-Zehlendorf, 1930), p. 35

tendencies. This was the result of a number of things: collaboration in the wartime economy and the ZAG, the common sense of threat inspired by the revolutionary movements of 1918 and 1919, the workings of the collective agreement and arbitration systems, work together on the works councils and, not least, renewed pressure from the employers – all these factors virtually compelled them to grow closer. Collective bargaining and industrial disputes were for the most part conducted jointly, and the demands for improved welfare benefits, the establishment of unemployment insurance and a new, uniform industrial law were so alike as to be almost identical. Finally, the nationalist component also played a part, demonstrated by the unions' willingness to back the policy of opposition to the occupation of the Ruhr.

∗

While joint positions and statements, as well as their pay policies, showed that the federations were ready to grant mutual recognition, the Christian unions continued to insist as emphatically as ever on their independence of outlook. The Christian idea of community versus the mechanistic socialism of the class struggle and the materialism of Mammon – this was the Christian unions' motto, designed partly to legitimize their own existence. They were also concerned to maintain the unity of the Christian trade union movement, for its heterogeneous denominational and party political make-up produced centrifugal forces that needed to be tamed by evoking the bogeyman of "socialism" and appealing to the sense of identity engendered by a common faith. A tangible expression of this appeared in the 1923 programme, which developed "the spiritual foundations of the Christian-national labour movement". As if invoking this spirit, it proclaimed, "We must feel inside us that we are different human beings. We think differently, we feel differently." For this reason – said the 1923 yearbook – there might be working alliances from case to case with "movements of different persuasions", "but never a meeting of minds, an alliance based on a common outlook".[13]

These hints were obviously required in order to remind consciously Christian workers of the continued need for unions of their own, especially as during the war and under the republic social democracy had scarcely proved to be the consistent champion of socialist ideas that the

---

13 Gewerkschaften und Arbeitervereine, in Jahrbuch der christlichen Gewerkschaften für 1923, hrsg. vom Gesamtverband der christlichen Gewerkschaften Deutschlands (Berlin, undated), pp. 44–49; this quot. p. 45 ff.

Christian unions had made them out to be. The Free Trade Unions' claims of party political neutrality – adopted by the Nuremberg congress in 1919 as a result of the split in the SPD – were considered a tactical trick; and the drop in anti-Church comments in the Social Democratic party and trade union press was denounced as a smoke-screen. But it was generally admitted that the Social Democrats' affirmation of the state, their programme for economic democracy and their attempts to recruit Catholic workers made the Christian unions' propaganda work more difficult and thus required a stepping-up of the ideological confrontation.

For the Hirsch-Duncker associations the position became increasingly difficult. They had no "identity" like Christianity to fall back on and their stagnation and political homelessness reflected the decline of the liberal parties.

*

There was no mistaking the first signs of common ground in the debates on the economic system during the revolutionary period and in the discussion on economic democracy: all the trade unions – Christian, Hirsch-Duncker and Free – believed that with the setting-up of the ZAG and the enshrining of freedom of association and far-reaching rights of economic co-determination in the constitution they had attained their goal of workers' participation as equals in shaping the economy and the state. But all three federations were soon forced to realize that the rights codified in 1918–19 did not entail a redistribution of real power. This realization was the basis of the various economic democracy programmes that were discussed by the national federations in the mid-1920s.

Ideas of economic democracy, or to put it another way, the demand for participation and co-determination, were also firmly supported by the Hirsch-Duncker associations, since such plans were capable of giving wage earners equal rights in the economy and the state by creating "co-operation bodies". "The trade union movement has always been and will always remain a force for democracy," said Anton Erkelenz at the third congress of the Trade Union League in 1926.[14] Support for political and economic democracy – with the latter being extended via the works councils – were a key point in the programme of the H-D associations.

According to their speaker on economic policy, Friedrich Baltrusch, the Christian unions were also in favour of co-ownership and co-deter-

---

14 Anton Erkelenz, Neue Aufgaben der Gewerkschaftspolitik (Berlin-Zehlendorf, 1926), p. 40 ff.

mination as preconditions of a democratization of the economy.[15] This demand assumed tangible form with the speech of the textile workers' leader, Heinrich Fahrenbrach, at the Dortmund congress of the Christian unions in April 1926[16]; it was his ideas that dominated the programmatic resolution adopted by the congress.[17]

It was ideas like this that revealed the common ground with the Free Trade Unions' demand for economic democracy, though of course the Christian and Hirsch-Duncker unions distanced themselves from the goal of socialism, to which the Free Trade Unions expressly committed themselves at their 1928 Hamburg congress. At this congress the Free Trade Unions – against a background of relative economic consolidation and the SPD's electoral success of May 1928 – set out once again to give a more precise shape to their ideas about the democratization of the economy.

The issue had already been addressed at the Breslau congress of 1925, when Herman Jäckel, chairman of the German Textile Workers' Union, had rejected the illusion of harmonious co-operation between employers and workers, stressing that the democratization of the economy was "itself a phase of capitalist economy", though characteristic of a "transitional period leading to higher forms of economic order". Jäckel's key demands were for an end to the educational privileges of the property-owning classes; the strengthening of trade union influence in politics and public enterprises; and increased union participation in the bodies of economic self-management. It was necessary to push these through if "unionized labour" was to become "a factor in the economy with equal rights".[18]

These ideas only matured into a programme as a result of the work of a commission set up by the ADGB. The commission's most eminent members were probably Fritz Baade, Rudolf Hilferding, Erik Nölting and Hugo Sinzheimer. Fritz Naphtali, head of the Research Centre for Economic Policy, presented the results of the commission's deliberations at the

15 Friedrich Baltrusch, Konsumgenossenschaften und Arbeitnehmerbewegung (Cologne, 1929), p. 10
16 Heinrich Fahrenbrach, Mitbestimmungsrecht und Mitbesitz der Arbeitnehmer in der Wirtschaft. Vortrag, gehalten auf dem 11. Kongress der christlichen Gewerkschaften in Dortmund (Berlin, 1926)
17 Niederschrift der Verhandlungen des 11. Kongresses der christlichen Gewerkschaften Deutschlands, abgehalten vom 17. bis 20. April 1926 in Dortmund (Berlin, 1926), p. 524
18 Herbert Jäckel, Die Wirtschaftsdemokratie, in Protokoll der Verhandlungen des 12. Kongresses der Gewerkschaften Deutschlands (2. Bundestag des Allgemeinen Deutschen Gewerkschaftsbundes), abgehalten in Breslau vom 31. August bis 4. September 1925 (Berlin, 1925), pp. 202–16

ADGB congress in Hamburg in 1928.[19] The speech on "the realization of economic democracy" which he gave in Hamburg[20] was based on the tenet that the political democracy gained in 1918 needed completing and safeguarding through the democratization of the economy; a democratic economy was indissolubly linked with the final goal of socialism. The gradual democratization of the economy could and should begin at once; all the more so, as capitalism could "be bent before it breaks".

The resolution passed in Hamburg[21] specified a package of measures with the common aim of intervening in central economic decisions; the company level, on the other hand, remained neglected. Furthermore, the consequences of failing to discuss measures to force economic democracy through against the predictable opposition of the employers were soon to become apparent.

Some delegates did criticize Naphtali's statements (probably still influenced by the SPD's electoral victory) for being far too optimistic in their assessment of the state's role in putting the unions' democratization ideas into practice; but the vast majority professed support for the "Hamburg model" of economic democracy. The response was not slow in coming. The employers made economic democracy the focus of a massive media showdown with the unions. The speeches and decisions made at the ninth assembly of the RDI (Federation of German Industry) held in Düsseldorf on 20–21 September 1929 were published in book form under the title "The Problem of Economic Democracy". The demand for economic democracy was denounced as a manifestation of the trade unions' bid for supreme power. Collectivism, socialism and now economic democracy completed the "demise of German-ness" to summarize Emil Kirdorf.[22]

The ferocity of the employers' reaction to the Free Trade Unions' demands, whose socialist rhetoric was taken literally, regardless of their reformist practice, may have given trade unionists the feeling that they had already gone as far as they possibly could. The Free Trade Unions used the employers' stance as evidence of their own political radicalism,

---

19 Fritz Naphtali, Wirtschaftsdemokratie. Ihr Wesen, Weg und Ziel (Berlin 1928; reprinted Frankfurt/M., 1966)
20 Fritz Naphtali, Die Verwirklichung der Wirtschaftsdemokratie, in Protokoll der Verhandlungen des 13. Kongresses der Gewerkschaften Deutschlands (3. Bundestag des Allgemeinen Deutschen Gewerkschaftsbundes), abgehalten in Hamburg vom 3. September bis 7. September 1928 (Berlin, 1928), pp. 170–90
21 ibid. p. 20 ff.
22 Das Problem der Wirtschaftsdemokratie. Zur Düsseldorfer Tagung des RDI, hrsg. von der Deutschen Bergwerks-Zeitung (Düsseldorf, 1929), p. 73

thus winning back part of the internal opposition.[23] The criticism of the KPD, which warned of "illusions of economic democracy"[24], could not be stemmed; nor could the Communist trade unionists be thereby prevented from setting up their own, independent organization, the Revolutionary Trade Union Opposition, or Organization (RGO).

While the Free Trade Unions regarded democratization of the economy as a step on the road to socialism, the Christian unions saw their plan as a contribution to the "social elevation of the working class", an essential precondition for the formation of an "organic popular community" (*Volksgemeinschaft*). The differing objectives of the two plans for economic democracy were, however, scarcely mentioned by those who took part in the discussion at the time. The *rapprochement* was never reflected in a joint trade union programme. In fact, after a lull in the inter-union arguments in the mid-1920s as the federations drew closer in their views, the polemics were resumed with renewed intensity. Like the Christian unions' reaction to the Hamburg congress of 1928, the following year the Free Trade Unions in their response to the Frankfurt congress ascertained that their demands were virtually the same. But the Christian unions saw this as all the more reason to insist on the need to keep up the spiritual confrontation. It was no coincidence that Elfriede Nebgen's pamphlet on the "Spiritual Foundations of the Christian-National Labour Movement" that first appeared in 1923 appeared in a revised version in 1928. Theodor Brauer's work, "Modern German Socialism", extracts from which were reprinted in the "Zentralblatt" in 1929, served to clarify the continuing ideological differences and was intended to counteract the pressure for unity that obviously existed within the Christian trade unions.

*

But the trend towards *rapprochement* between the major trade union federations in day-to-day union work not only had ideological barriers to overcome; there were fundamental differences between the Free Trade Unions and the Hirsch-Duncker associations on the one hand, and the Christian unions on the other, in their relations with the Weimar-style parliamentary republic. Certainly, the Free Trade Unions' attitude to the republic was by no means unproblematic. They often gave their assent to parlia-

---

23 See Fritz Naphtali, Debatten zur Wirtschaftsdemokratie, in Die Gesellschaft I (1929), pp. 210–19
24 See Walter Ulbricht, Wirtschaftsdemokratie oder Wohin steuert der ADGB (Berlin, 1928)

mentary democracy "merely" as an arena for maintaining their own interests, the one that seemed to offer the best conditions for building up a social democracy and/or socialism. What distinguished them from the Christian unions was the fact that the latter were by no means agreed that the republic was the most appropriate form of government for achieving the social *Volksstaat* (popular state) they wished to establish.

It was this issue that the speech and resolution by Adam Stegerwald, chairman of the national federation and the DGB, at the 1926 Dortmund congress of the Christian unions were supposed to clarify. The desired "popular state" might – according to Stegerwald[25] – take the form of a monarchy or a republic. The state itself was more important to the Christian unions than the form it took. By lifting this abstraction out of the contemporary debate, he was able to claim that it was possible to be "a monarchist in principle and none the less a good servant of the republic"; Hindenburg was given as an example. Stegerwald also emphasized his dislike of the existing republic, but with the express reservation that the Christian unions were fully aware "that there is no question of changing the form of government by violent means".

Reservations about the republic were also evident in the resolution, which the republicans around Karl Arnold tried in vain to amend. In 1926 the Christian unions expressed their commitment to the "state and its Christian-national foundations", rejecting "all efforts to bring about a change in the form of government by illegal means". This refusal initially to express fundamental support for the Weimar democracy, and the rejection only of "illegal" means of changing the form of government gave added weight to the congress resolution's criticism of the "present German parliamentary system of government", which could not "be regarded as perfect"[26]. This did not put a stop to the arguments about their attitude to the republic, however; it flared up again just a few years later, during the Depression.

4. *Into the crisis: the Ruhr iron dispute 1928*

In 1928, even before the Depression made itself felt in Germany, there was a marked increase in industrial disputes, culminating in the Ruhr iron

---

25 Adam Stegerwald, Die christlichen Gewerkschaften und die Gestaltung des deutschen Volkslebens, in Niederschrift der Verhandlungen des 11. Kongresses der christlichen Gewerkschaften Deutschlands, abgehalten vom 17. bis 20. April 1926 in Dortmund (Berlin, 1926), pp. 218–250; this quot. p. 243 ff.
26 Ibid., p. 515 ff.

Auch die Schiffahrt muß ruhen
Stillgelegte Schlepper im Duisburger Hafen

»Den Abkehrschein bitte«...
Diese Maßnahme mußte getroffen werden, um aus den Versammlungen berufsfremde Agitatoren fernzuhalten

Die Lohnbureaus sind geschlossen
zahlen sonst die Hamborner Thyssenwerke aus

Hütten- und Metallarbeiter!
Ein Aufruf der Gewerkschaft

Hier darf nicht gearbeitet werden
Ein verschlossenes Tor in den Essener Kruppwerken

Links:
Ausgesperrte Arbeiter
vor dem Volkshause

Rechts:
Die tägliche Kontrolle
Jedes Verbandsmitglied muß den Unterstützungsausweis im Kontrolllokal abstempeln lassen

Rechts:
Das Essener Gewerkschaftshaus

Links:
Was wird werden?
Diskutierende Ausgesperrte vor einem Versammlungslokal

Der Gewaltstreich der Ruhrmagnaten

Pictures of the 1928 Ruhr iron dispute from "Volk und Zeit" dispute. It was triggered off on 28 October 1928 by the engineering unions giving the Rhenish-Westphalian iron industry due notice that they intended to terminate the collective agreement. This was linked with a demand for a pay rise of 15 Pfennigs per hour for all workers over 21. The employers, however, considered that wages – a skilled worker earned about 80 Pf. and an unskilled worker about 60 Pf. an hour – had already risen to a level that ruled out further rises. The employers' association of the north-west group of the Federation of German Iron and Steel Manufacturers refused to grant any pay rise at all and on 13 October 1928 gave notice of a lockout of all workers commencing on 1 November.

At this, the trade unions applied for arbitration and, when the Düsseldorf arbitration tribunal could not reach agreement, the case was judged on 27 October by the special mediator Wilhelm Joetten, whose ruling was declared binding by Wissell, the Labour Minister. It laid down a compromise of 6 Pf. per hour, the trade unions having meanwhile reduced their claim to 12 Pf. per hour. The unions submitted to the mediator's ruling; but the employers rejected it. The lockout of over 220,000 wage earners began. Not until 30 November was it agreed in separate talks between union and employer representatives and government officials to embark on a new arbitration procedure, to be headed by the Social Democratic Home Secretary, Carl Severing. The employers and the unions recognized in advance the mediator's ruling as a collective agreement, and the employers lifted the lockout.

Severing found himself in an awkward situation. He had to seek a middle way between disowning his party comrades and his ministerial colleague, Wissell, and the concessions to the employers' camp that were obviously necessary; moreover, the solution had to be acceptable to the workers concerned. After informing himself in detail of the economic and social position in the Ruhr district, Severing announced his ruling on 21 December. Not unexpectedly, he did not match Joetten's decision but allowed it to stand until 31 December 1928; from 1 January 1929 wages were to be increased by 1–6 Pf. per hour.

Whereas the Free Trade Unions' reaction – probably because Severing was a Social Democrat – ranged from cool to favourable, the mediator's decision provoked harsh criticism from the employers that was out of all proportion to the substance of the ruling; it revealed a tendency towards extremism on the part of the industrial magnates that was to be characteristic of the closing stages of the Weimar Republic. The fact that talks on the interpretation of individual provisions of the new collective agreement dragged on until October 1929 and the perceptible increase in one-man rulings from 1929 on showed that, with the economy going into a dive, the two sides of industry were not really willing or able to reach acceptable compromises by means of independent negotiation.

The employers had criticized the provisions enabling the state to declare a mediator's decision binding ever since they were introduced in 1923. So why did they go on to the offensive in October 1928? The answer may have something to do with the state of the economy, but the principal reason – though they denied it – was probably political. It was a good opportunity to bring home to the trade unions and the SPD, which had been included in the government since the elections of May 1928, the limits of their political influence on the private economy. The employers may have been all the more convinced that it was in their interests to do so since they feared that an SPD-led government would give the unions a better chance of achieving their demands for economic democracy. Undoubtedly, the employers' policy in the Ruhr iron dispute could also be seen as an indication of their disaffection with Weimar democracy, which – given the polemical option of "rise or fall"[27] – finally culminated in rejection of the entire "system".

---

27 See Aufstieg oder Niedergang. Denkschrift des RDI (Berlin, 1929)

VIII. In the shadow of the Depression: the dissolution of the trade unions 1930–1933

After a few short years of comparative political and economic stability, the trade unions ran into a new, serious crisis which finally threatened to sweep away the very basis of their existence. The trade unions were rapidly caught between the front lines of political radicalization, which restricted their scope for integration and action even further. Moreover, with the concentration of decision-making over economic policy and collective agreements to the political executive under the emergency decree policy (*Notverordnungspolitik*), they were once again obliged to shift the main emphasis of their work into the political sphere, though this strategy was not destined to be a success. The unions could do nothing to prevent the slump, with its disastrous social consequences for the working population, nor the Nazis' seizure of power – nor even their own break-up. Even though the Weimar democracy did not fail owing to objective economic difficulties but was deliberately wrecked, the Great Depression formed the background against which the irresolute conduct of the labour movement and the success of their opponents must be viewed.

1. *The Depression and the weakening of the trade union organizations*

Ever since 1928 there had been signs in Germany of a downturn in the economy – a decline in the profits of German industry and a corresponding fall in investment. The downward trend became even more noticeable in 1929, the turning point coming in 1930, when there was a sharp drop in both output and employment.[1] This process of economic contraction was evident in the rapid decline in national per capita income : from 1413 Marks in 1927, it rose to 1453 Marks in 1928 but then declined steadily to 1436 (1929), 1372 (1930), 1201 (1931) and 1094 Marks (1932).

Socially and politically, the unemployment figures are one of the most important indicators of economic crisis. After reaching its lowest point under the Weimar Republic in 1927, the number of those out of work was

---

1 The following figures are from Karlheinz Dederke, Reich und Republik. Deutschland 1917–1933 (Stuttgart, 1969), pp. 278 and 193

Mass unemployment in 1933: applicants for one vacancy as a shorthand typist

Unemployed engineering workers collecting the dole in Leipzig, 1932-33

averaging 1,892,000 by 1929, rose to 3,076,000 in 1930, reached 4,520,000 in 1931 and continued rising to reach an average for the year of 5,575,000 in 1932; it peaked in February 1932, with 6,128,000 registered jobless (Table 5a). This meant that by 1931 one tenth of the population had experienced unemployment at first hand – those on short time not included. This proportion was, however, much higher in the highly industrialized areas, where it could reach one in four, for example in the cities of the Ruhr district, which was particularly hard hit by the crisis.

The cold facts of the economic situation in the early 1930s cannot give an idea of the misery and despair caused by the Depression, the extent of resignation, on the one hand, and radicalization on the other. As the 1931–32 yearbook of the Engineering Workers' Union said: "The sufferings of the unemployed are immense. The loss of outward happiness, the struggle against economic distress are perhaps not even the worst part of it. The destruction of physical, spiritual and moral labour power, and thus the inner happiness of the unemployed and their dependants is appalling. The longer unemployment lasts, the more depression and passivity increase, and criminality assumes menacing proportions."[2] Käthe Kollwitz expressed this feeling in her diary (Easter 1932): "Then there's the unspeakably dreadful general situation. The distress. People sinking into the darkest distress. The repellent political incitement."[3]

The deterioration in the conditions for union action caused by the Depression hit the development of the organizations particularly hard.[4] In 1929 the trade unions once again registered an overall increase in membership. But the trend reversed in 1930 and 1931. Compared with the end of 1929, the Free Trade Unions lost 16.5 per cent of their members, the Christian unions 14.2 per cent and the Hirsch-Duncker associations 11.2 per cent. Membership continued to fall in 1932; the ADGB unions alone (the only ones for which figures are available) lost 600,000 members, that is, more than 14 per cent (Table 1a).

---

2 Der Deutsche Metallarbeiter-Verband im Jahre 1931. Jahr- und Handbuch für Verbandsmitglieder, hrsg. vom Vorstand des Deutschen Metallarbeiter-Verbandes (Berlin, 1932), p. 56

3 Käthe Kollwitz, Aus meinem Leben, hrsg. von H. Kollwitz (Munich, 1957), p. 126

4 See Klaus Schönhoven, Innerorganisatorische Probleme der Gewerkschaften in der Endphase der Weimarer Republik, in Gewerkschaften in der Krise. Anhang zum Reprint: Gewerkschafts-Zeitung, 1933 (Berlin and Bonn, 1983), pp. 73–104

The white-collar unions had a different story to tell. The three largest amalgamations were still able to record an increase in membership in 1930 – the Christian-national Gedag even managed it in 1931, too, when the Afa-Bund and the liberal GdA were already losing members. During the Depression the nationalist white-collar unions continued to gather support, while the Christian-national worker trade unions suffered almost as many losses as the Free Trade Unions (Table 1b).

These overall figures – even if one simply looks at the Free Trade Unions – conceal a number of quite different processes, though in most cases members of the same union were equally affected by the general pattern of unemployment. By 1929 the hat makers, shoemakers, tobacco workers, leather workers and textile workers were all losing members, with average unemployment levels ranging from 29.3 to 10.3 per cent. In other unions, such as the building workers' union, the initial sign of the onset of the Depression was a slowdown in the rate of increase compared with the previous year. By 1930 the Depression had affected virtually all industries and trades; 23 per cent of Free Trade Union members were out of work and 13.4 on short time. Particularly high losses – 10 per cent or more – were, however, the result of unemployment that was well above average; examples illustrating this are the stonemasons, roofers and saddlers, with unemployment rates of 47.7, 48.3 and 35.9 per cent respectively.

If one takes turnover into account, that is, the total number of members joining and leaving each year, one finds that the drop in membership in 1930 was not (yet) mainly due to resignations, but to the fall in new members, which obviously reflects the unions' dwindling popularity. Not until 1931 did the unions actually start to lose members. Crucially, not only were a disproportionate number of these semi-skilled and unskilled workers, but the skilled unions also found that their "core membership" was being eroded.

Another factor of major importance from the union viewpoint – and this can be demonstrated using the engineering union as an example – was the change in the age structure of union members. Between 1919 and 1931, the proportion of members under 20 years old went down from 22.7 to 12 per cent; the DMV, however, continued to derive its main support from the 20–40 year-old age group (56.6 per cent in 1931, compared with 54 per cent in 1919). This trend reflected the surge of new members in the revolutionary post-war period, and the fall in the birth-rate during the First World War, which reduced the pool of potential new recruits to the unions. Finally, youth suffered disproportionately from mass unemployment in the early 1930s, so that many of them never found their way into a union. No matter how much the unions deplored this and stepped up their agitation, there was little they could do about the Depression's deleterious effects on solidarity.

The proportion of women members also fell during the Depression. Whereas in 1919 21.8 per cent of ADGB members had been women, this had dropped to 14 per cent by 1931. Nevertheless, at 617,968 the number of unionized women in 1931 was almost three times what it had been in 1913 (230,347). The fact that women found it hard to feel "at home" in the unions may have accounted for their poor representation on trade union bodies, as well as other factors, such as their role in the socialization of children, gender stereotyping and workplace conditions. There were hardly any women delegates at trade union congresses, and there were no female members at all on the federal executive. The exclusion and absence of women from posts of responsibility certainly encouraged the "estrangement" between female wage earners and the unions that contributed to the continuous decline in the proportion of women from 1919 to 1931.

From 1930 on, the efficiency of the unions was undermined. The fall in membership, unemployment, short time and wage cuts for the remaining members brought a drop in the number and size of membership dues coming in. In 1930, over half the ADGB members paid more than 52 Marks per year; by 1931 only a third of members were still in this contribution category. In 1931, the Free Trade Unions' revenue fell by more than one fifth, but spending could only be cut by about 10 per cent. The number of claimants increased, so the unions were forced to reduce the duration and level of their benefits to make the money go round. In 1931, spending on benefit payments was down 11 per cent on the previous year; administrative and staff costs were also cut, by 12.2 per cent. Part of the financial burden of the crisis could be met by money saved on industrial disputes. Despite mass unemployment strikes were still organized to fight wage cuts and so on; but the number of actions fell by a third between 1929 and 1931, while the number of strikers in 1931 was just over a quarter of the figure for 1929 (Table 2c).

Of course, the Depression did not leave union enterprises intact. Their banks and insurance companies, building and consumer co-operatives all had to face cuts in turnover and profits from 1931 on – not only restricting the financial scope for union action but also heightening the sense of crisis and reinforcing the growing feeling of resignation.

2. Powerless in the crisis

The unions did not view the economic developments of 1929–30 as the start of an unprecedented slump. Throughout this period the republic was too dogged by crises to make a fresh rise in unemployment seem anything "extraordinary". Of course, there was no overlooking the fact that at the first hints of economic stagnation confrontations with the employers – heavy industry, in particular – had intensified. But the unions underestimated the interplay between economic forces on the one hand and the employers' economic and political crisis strategies on the other, which as the slump worsened became more and more clearly aimed at dismantling the Weimar republic's social legislation, and eventually the democratic foundations of the state itself.

The deterioration of the overall economic situation confronted the unions with a host of new tasks: attempts to stabilize wage levels, to safeguard insurance benefits and to reduce prices went hand in hand with demands for the "equitable" distribution of the burden of the Depression; efforts to achieve shorter working hours and create new jobs were accompanied by the demand for the phasing-out of reparations. Union work "at grass-roots level" often included local employment and cultural programmes designed to consolidate the organization. But the wide variety of these activities cannot disguise the fact that – as the crisis deepened, the emergency decree policy was implemented and state intervention in the economy increased – the focus of conflict shifted from clashes between individual unions and employers' federations to confrontation (or cooperation) between the union leaders and central government.

The collapse of the Grand Coalition in March 1930

The limits of trade union influence on policy had been apparent at the time of the Grand Coalition under Chancellor Hermann Müller of the SPD. The succession of conflicts in which the Free Trade Unions saw their claims ignored in order to save the coalition government culminated in the dispute over the funding of unemployment insurance. Like the eight-hour day, this was an issue of great symbolic importance to the labour movement, especially as it interfered in the laws of capitalist economics not only by mitigating the social consequences of unemployment but also by relieving the downward pressure on wages. When the deficit in the unemployment insurance scheme again became acute in March 1930, the Free Trade Unions advocated a rise in contributions from 3.5 to 4 per cent to prevent benefits from being cut. But the DVP was not prepared to accept this solution, claiming it would lead to increased costs for an economy already under strain, thus ruining its export capability. With an eye to saving the governing coalition, the majority of the SPD ministers accepted a proposal put forward by Heinrich Brüning (Centre), though it was only designed to provide temporary cover for the deficit, so that before long benefits would have to be cut anyway. In the SPD group in the Reichstag, however, the trade unionists prevailed: the SPD rejected Brüning's compromise. The Müller Cabinet, the Weimar republic's last parliamentary government, resigned on 27 March 1930.

This conflict was really about far more than safeguarding unemployment insurance. The issue was basically: who should bear the brunt of the crisis? Bearing in mind earlier setbacks over social policy and competition from the KPD, the Social Democrats and the Free Trade Unions had their backs to the wall. This situation was not respected by the DVP – on the contrary, they exploited it to force the SPD out of the coalition through its own intransigence. The end of the Müller government demonstrated that the (Free) unions were strong enough to bring the SPD into line; but they could not swing policy round in their favour. In addition, the first clear signs had emerged of the conflict between the SPD as a popular party prepared to enter a coalition and the unions as the traditional champions of workers' interests.

The "Brüning Era": fruitless tolerance and loyalty

Union expectation of Heinrich Brüning's government, the first "presidential Cabinet", varied from one federation to the other. In the early 1920s Brüning had been secretary of the Christian-national DGB, and Stegerwald, the Christian trade unionist with the highest profile, now became Minister for Labour. The Christian unions hailed Brüning's Cabinet as a "turning point in German politics".[5] But the ADGB did not have such optimistic expectations. The new government called itself a "bourgeois united front", but according to the union newspaper, it was a "business-like commercial company with limited liability", which was not based on

---

5 See Wende in der deutschen Politik! Rettung der staatlichen Grundlagen gesunden sozialen Lebens, in Zentralblatt No. 8 of 15. 4. 1930, p. 113 f.

a parliamentary majority "that is able to summon up a unified, long-term, political will".[6]

*

Like the Müller Cabinet before it, the Brüning government pressed for a balanced budget. In response to the steady decline in state revenue -- from 20.1 bn Marks (1929/30) to 13.8 bn (1932/33)[7] – Brüning implemented a rigorous programmme of economies, which actually helped to make the crisis worse by reducing state investment and cutting social benefits and wages.

This soon put the Christian unions in the awkward position of having to combine political loyalty to the government with the task of representing their members' interests. Despite all protests they eventually decided they would have to be silent in the face of the clearly "unsocial" emergency decree policy – not primarily because they had to choose the lesser of two evils, but because they did not wish to cause their "own" government even more difficulties than it already had. Furthermore, their very "proximity" to the Brüning government, whose assessment of the reparations question as the central problem of German domestic and foreign policy they shared, prevented the Christian unions from developing their own alternatives to the policy of deflation. They went no further than declarations opposing wage and price cuts, supporting an emergency levy on the highly paid and those in permanent jobs to stabilize unemployment insurance, and calling for joint action by employers and unions to create jobs.

While the tone adopted by the Free Trade Unions was certainly more aggressive, there were initially no major differences of substance between their demands and those of the Christian unions. The government pursued a policy that was largely in line with employers' demands to cut production costs (taxes, wages, social costs) as a preliminary to price cuts designed, so it was said, to ensure or restore the competitiveness of the German export industry in the world market. The Free Trade Unions, on the other hand, pointed out, as they had in the late 1920s, that the way out of the crisis lay not in an increase in exports but in stimulating demand at home.

---

6 Die neuen Steuern und der neue Kurs, in Gewerkschafts-Zeitung No. 17 of 26. 4. 1930, p. 261 f.
7 Horst Sanmann, Daten und Alternativen der deutschen Wirtschafts- und Finanzpolitik in der Ära Brüning, in Hamburger Jahrbuch für Wirtschafts- und Gesellschaftspolitik 10 (1965), pp. 109–40; see p. 113

Considering the measure of agreement on the question of price reductions, there did seem to be a chance of a co-ordinated crisis policy. In May–June 1930, the employers and unions met to draw up a joint declaration on economic policy which also explored the chances of a parliamentary coalition. At first a compromise seemed to be on the cards, at least over wage and price cuts. But the talks failed. The (Free) trade unions considered that their position as a party to collective agreements had been called in question; the employers attempted to shift the burdens of the crisis on to the workers by means of pay cuts, the relaxation of collective agreements and the dismantling of social provisions. The first clear signal was the Bad Oeynhausen mediator's decision of May 1930, declared binding on 10 June, cutting all wages and salaries in the north-west German iron industry that exceeded the going rate by 7.5 per cent. The wage struggle of August 1930 in the Mansfeld copper mining industry illustrated the same process: though the employers did not obtain the reductions of 15 per cent which they had demanded, pay was nevertheless cut by 9.5 per cent.

Despite the incalculable consequences of government and employer policy, the Free Trade Unions considered it necessary to hold back; they did not wish to jeopardize the policy of toleration vis-à-vis the Brüning government it had decided upon after the elections of September 1930. The shock of these elections – in which the NSDAP had leapt from 12 seats to 107 – affected the ADGB's attitude to the Brüning government, whose programme was deemed as inadequate as it was unjust as far as measures to tackle the crisis were concerned. In line with the policy of the SPD parliamentary party, the ADGB also saw no alternative to tolerating "Brüning's quiet dictatorship" in order to prevent the "lurch into overt dictatorship".[8] For the end of toleration, so it was feared, would lead to a Hitler-Hugenberg government, that is, an NSDAP/DNVP coalition, which would not only result in the isolation of Germany abroad but in grave social conflict at home. So in view of the threat of National Socialism, disputes about social and economic policy had to take second place to the struggle to save parliamentary democracy and basic civil rights, which it was the unions' duty to safeguard – even if it demanded sacrifices.[9]

8 See Das Jahr 1930, in Gewerkschafts-Zeitung No. 1 of 3. 1. 1931, pp. 1–4; this quot. p. 3
9 See Jahrbuch 1930 des Allgemeinen Deutschen Gewerkschaftsbundes, pp. 47 f. and 91 f.

Particularly the Hirsch-Duncker unions under the leadership of Anton Erkelenz were constant advocates of "the loyalty of the wage earners to the state, the republic and democracy". But with the setting-up of the German State Party to succeed the DDP in July 1930, which led to Erkelenz's defection to the SPD, the H-D unions increasingly lost their political importance. They continued to see themselves as representatives of a "sensible" middle way, as much opposed to the Communist doctrine of class struggle as to the National Socialists' racial theories.

Unions of all hues were agreed in rejecting national socialism, whatever differences may have emerged in their public arguments. Whereas the Christian unions – linked with the DHV under the umbrella of the DGB – found it hard to form a convincing defensive front, the H-D unions and the Free Trade Unions were united in their approach. All the unions were perfectly well aware that the impetus of national socialism could not be halted by "somebody proving the irrationality or factitiousness of any of the National Socialist theories".[10] It was partly for this reason that union policy was directed above all at achieving a swift economic upturn which would lessen "social tension" automatically, as it were.

*

One of the key demands of union policy was the safeguarding and, at the same time, the "equitable" distribution of such jobs as still remained. So when the ADGB demanded the introduction of the 40-hour week in a federal committee resolution of 12–13 October 1930, it was chiefly to combat unemployment. This put the Christian unions on the spot, as their own discussions were not yet concluded. Theirs was a "wait-and-see" attitude, according to Bernhard Otte, "not a dismissive one".[11]

In autumn 1930 the introduction of the 40-hour week was still intended purely as a temporary measure. This reservation was probably a way of taking heed of misgivings in the unions' own ranks. Even the supporters of this demand did not really expect a cut in working hours to have a major effect on the labour market: at most, half a million jobless might be able to find work as a result.[12] And doubt was cast even on this modest

---

10 Walter Dirks, Katholizismus und Nationalsozialismus, in Die Arbeit No. 3, March 1931, pp. 201–9; this quot. p. 205 f.
11 See Rundschreiben des Gesamtverbandes der christlichen Gewerkschaften an die angeschlossenen Verbände of 16. 10. 1930 (Bundesarchiv Koblenz, Kleine Erwerbungen 461–2, No. 126 f.)
12 See Theodor Leipart, Gewerkschaften und Wirtschaftskrise, in Gewerkschafts-Zeitung No. 48 of 29. 11. 1930, pp. 756–59

success. Because there was little chance of a shorter working week being introduced with no loss of wages, it was often rejected within the trade union movement on the grounds that it was merely a "redistribution of misery".

As average hours worked in industry fell from 49.9 in 1927 to 41.5 in 1932, a legal cut in hours would only have had a marked effect on the labour market in 1930 (Table 4a). Nevertheless, the trade unions clung to the demand for a 40-hour week: from spring 1931 they wanted it introduced as a permanent measure. In August 1931 they presented a detailed survey entitled "Labour market, Wages and Working Hours"[13] in support of their campaign on working hours. It was emphasized that "it is not enough simply to make the demand. The demand is followed by the struggle. The struggle will be hard." However, with mass unemployment, membership that had been declining ever since 1930/31, strike pay that was constantly being cut and, above all, the dissension among the different federations, the Free Trade Unions' militancy seemed somewhat contrived. The demand for a 40-hour week was regarded more as "an appeal to workers in work to show solidarity with the unemployed and also [as] a demand addressed to the employers and the legislature, to the powers that dominate politics and the economy".

The question of working hours was the biggest stumbling block in contacts with the employers. No sooner had the top-level talks between the unions and employers failed in the summer of 1930, than a fresh attempt was made a few months later to reach agreement on the urgent economic and social questions. While the two sides had come together on their own in June, in November 1930 they met at the invitation of Stegerwald. Agreement was close on the issue of price cuts, but the parties differed over their extent, and especially over the importance of wage cuts in bringing prices down. There was no *rapprochement* in sight on the issue of reductions in working hours, where anyway the unions themselves did not agree. But while the executives of the DGB and the H-D associations gave their negotiating teams approval for a draft agreement drawn up on 9 December, the ADGB's federal committee referred the decision to the union executives, who predictably voted almost unanimously for rejection. At the end of January 1931 the Free Trade Unions declared that they could not accept the December draft.

---

13 See Die 40-Stunden-Woche. Untersuchungen über Arbeitsmarkt, Arbeitsertrag und Arbeitszeit, hrsg. im Auftrage des ADGB von Theodor Leipart (Berlin, 1931); quotations from pp. 5 and 203

The Christian unions regretted the decision of the ADGB unions and after the latter's departure continued to pursue a policy of institutionalized contacts with the employers. But the attempts of the Christian unions in particular to give the Brüning government what help it could by reaching a compromise with the employers on economic and social matters were a failure. The wrangling continued unabated between the employers' federations and the unions over the problem of collective agreements, the issue of state intervention in the economy, and pay and social policy; indeed, it grew visibly worse. Soon it was no longer a question of wage cuts but of the very existence of collective bargaining. The employers' attempts to force through the adjustment of wages to suit the needs of individual companies, entailing a wage cut on a broad front, and to amend the law accordingly, under the slogan "Relax the collective bargaining system", were a manifest threat to the collective agreement.

The employers' position also had its impact on arbitration, for example, in the Berlin engineering industry. In October 1930, 85 per cent of the organized engineering workers of that city voted to reject a mediator's decision decreeing a wage cut of 8 per cent in some cases and 6 per cent in others. On 15 October some 130,000 workers came out on strike. The unions, however, broke off the strike, against the will of the workers involved, and agreed to a fresh arbitration procedure. The outcome was fairly predictable: the mediator's "new" ruling only softened the cuts slightly.

The Brüning government did little to help the unions strengthen their position. It made no attempt to be accommodating. On the contrary, the emergency decrees of 1931, with their continual cuts in pay, eventually started interfering with existing wage agreements. Union statistics for 1931 showed wage cuts affecting 7.3 million employees; at the beginning of 1932, agreed hourly rates were 17 per cent below the 1930 level; real weekly wages were 15–20 per cent lower than in 1929 (Table 3b). Even worse, price cuts failed to keep pace with wage cuts.[14] The trade unions protested, but persisted in their powerless and hopeless policy of "keeping quiet", the main aim of which was to keep the National Socialists out of power.

The Communists took this policy, which they condemned as "opportunist" and "social fascist", as a pretext for stepping up their struggle against the leadership of the Free Trade Unions. Since about 1925–26 the KPD had tried to organize dissident trade unionists – not in unions of their own, but within the Free Trade Unions, as decided at the first

---

14 See Schönhoven, Innerorganisatorische Probleme, p. 81

national congress of the RGO on 30 November–1 December 1929. The setting-up of cells within the Free Trade Unions, designed to facilitate the independent preparation and conduct of industrial disputes, was particularly controversial. However, at the fifth congress of the RGO in August 1930, the view prevailed – true to the theory of social fascism – that autonomous "revolutionary fighting trade unions" should be established. The KPD continued to support dissident groups within the Free Trade Unions in the years that followed, but it also carried out the RGO decision. Autumn 1930 saw the formation of the "United Union of Berlin Engineering Workers" and the "United Union of German Miners"; and at the second national congress on 15–16 November 1930 the RGO set itself up as a trade union organization in its own right. But these unions did not experience a mass influx of members; by spring 1932 the RGO had "only" some 260–300,000 members, three-quarters of whom belonged to no party.[15]

With increasing bitterness the Free Trade Unions saw themselves caught "between the fronts". The annual reports of trade union officials repeatedly complained of systematic "subversive activities by the Nazis and Kozis" – meaning both the National Socialist company cell organization (NSBO) and the RGO. These were often blamed by union officials for the difficulties they encountered in their own organizational work: the KPD was accused of waging "war on our movement" in combination with the Nazis.[16]

The NSBO and RGO won support from the unskilled and unemployed in particular, and especially from the young. The 1931 works councils elections give a rough idea of the relative strength of the different factions: the H-D unions won 1,560 seats, the RGO 4,664, the Christian unions 10,956 and the Free Trade Unions 115,671.[17] In some industries, though, the proportion of "oppositional" unions was very high. Thus the Free Miners' Union's share of the vote dropped in 1931 from 52.5 (in 1930) to 45.1 per cent, while the RGO increased its share from 19.4 to 24.7 per cent, and the non-striking groups went up from 3.2 to 5.7 per cent; the NSBO list managed 2.4 per cent. In the Ruhr district the Free Trade

---

15 See Frank Deppe and Witich Rossmann, Kommunistische Gewerkschaftspolitik in der Weimarer Republik, in E. Matthias and K. Schönhoven (eds.), Solidarität und Menschenwürde, pp. 209–31, especially p. 226
16 See Jahrbuch 1930, hrsg. vom Vorstand des Verbandes der Bergbauindustriearbeiter Deutschlands (Bochum 1931), p. 246; quot. K. Schönhoven, Innerorganisatorische Probleme, p. 92 f.
17 See Deppe and Rossmann, op. cit., p. 226

Unions obtained 36.4 per cent of the vote, the RGO 29 per cent, and the National Socialists 4.1 per cent.[18]

*

On the other hand, the economic and political situation brought the "established" unions closer together. After several internal moves, there was eventually a public exchange of views on the topic of trade union unification, under growing pressure from the crisis.[19] In the autumn of 1931 the DMV had proposed "a strengthening through unification" in the engineering workers' newspaper, the "Metallarbeiterzeitung": in view of the political and economic crisis, it claimed a merger of the front-line unions was the only way of acquiring more influence. The Hirsch-Duncker engineers responded in their newspaper, the "Regulator", with "three questions". Desirable as the elimination of trade union division might be, it must be clarified whether party political neutrality, freedom of religious opinion and the struggle against "Communist-Bolshevik revolutionizing", against a militant, reactionary entrepreneurial class and for improved living standards for workers could be accepted as common basic principles. The "Metallarbeiterzeitung" answered these questions in the affirmative. The importance which the ADGB attributed to this discussion is probably best illustrated by the fact that Leipart himself wrote an article on the subject in the "Gewerkschafts-Zeitung". On behalf of the ADGB, Leipart accepted the demands for party political and religious neutrality, and posed a question of his own: did not politics and religion lack any significance as trade union problems if they were omitted from propaganda work? The final question in the "Regulator" was also answered in the affirmative by Leipart, to the effect that "in his opinion what unites us far outweighs what separates us". At least between the ADGB and the H-D associations there were "no contradictions that might justify maintaining the separation". In addition, Leipart expected "that a unification of the trade unions would open up entirely new perspectives for the consolidation of the republican state through the formation of a comprehensive social and political power bloc".

Even before the appearance of Leipart's article, the Christian engineering workers' union had also entered the discussion. It saw the stance of the

---

18 See Deppe and Rossmann, Kommunistische Gewerkschaftspolitik, p. 226
19 See documents 42a–e, in Ulrich Borsdorf, Hans O. Hemmer and Martin Martiny (eds), Grundlagen der Einheitsgewerkschaft. Historische Dokumente und Materialien (Cologne and Frankfurt, 1977), p. 196 ff.

"Regulator" as proof of the critical position within the H-D associations, which had been prompted by the "demise of the liberal idea" and the financial crisis of their benefit funds. The DMV's appeal was also seen as a sign of the weakness of the Free Trade Unions, who were feeling the loss of the thrust that Marxist ideas had provided. Unification with the Free Trade Unions was impossible, it claimed, as short-term common interests could not bridge fundamental differences in outlook.

*

While all the unions agreed on the demand for the creation of jobs, it was the ADGB that presented a practical programme based on the idea of a policy to counter the effects of the economic cycle. In the summer of 1931, Wladimir Woytinsky, the head of the ADGB's statistical bureau, published an action plan for boosting the economy.[20] This led to a fierce debate within the Social Democratic labour movement. The critics' spokesman was Fritz Naphtali, who objected to Woytinsky's proposals on the grounds that they would be undeniably inflationist and thus entail "a misdirection of the energies" of social democracy.[21] Bearing in mind the experience of runaway inflation, these fears are understandable; but they were based on a false assessment of the economic situation, as demonstrated by the prevailing policy of deflation, which contributed to a process of progressive contraction. As for the attitude of the Social Democratic parliamentary party, which largely supported the reservations expressed by Naphtali, their chief concern might have been the decision to tolerate the Brüning government, who would have been opposed to the idea of pursuing an active economic policy by extending credit. Fundamental reservations about the independence of the Free Trade Unions, which had been growing ever since the turn of the century, and about the use to which they put it, may have played some part in the SPD leadership's delaying tactics. For the Woytinsky plan could, in fact, be seen as offering socially motivated survival aid to the system of private capitalism, which seemed to be in a "terminal crisis", thus robbing the programme to overcome capitalism of all credibility. This was exactly the same problem that Fritz Tarnow addressed in his speech at the SPD party conference (31 May – 5 June 1931), "Capitalist economic anarchy and the working class", where he put

20 Wladimir Woytinsky, Aktive Weltwirtschaftspolitik, in Die Arbeit No. 6, June 1931, pp. 413–40; this quot. p. 439
21 Fritz Naphtali, Neuer Angelpunkt der Konjunkturpolitik oder Fehlleitung von Energien? in Die Arbeit No. 7, July 1931, pp. 485–97

forward the controversial idea that the economic crisis might well turn the SPD and the Free Trade Unions into doctor and heir at the sickbed of capitalism, whether they liked it or not.[22] The delegates approved the resolution arising from the speech, but these ideas were never spelt out in practical terms in the discussion within the SPD about its programme.

On the other hand, the job creation ideas of Wladimir Woytinsky, Fritz Tarnow and Fritz Baade, leader of the national research centre for agricultural marketing and member of the SPD parliamentary party, were taken further. At the end of 1931 and beginning of 1932 they presented the WTB Plan, so called after its authors, urging public works to a tune of 2 billion Marks, putting one million unemployed back into production for a year, to a certain extent as pump-priming.

The crisis congress of 13 April 1932 rounded off the internal trade union discussion and was to be a "signal", around which all those who supported an immediate end to the crisis should gather. The resolution passed by congress summarized the ADGB demands and also attempted to link them with the programme for "rebuilding the economy".[23]

The ADGB was not the only trade union organization to discuss a plan for actively combating the economic crisis. The Christian unions, too, repeatedly called for action to create jobs; but no practical definition of tasks nor any financial models were ever forthcoming, so that the demand for job creation was really more declamatory by nature. Nor should we forget the economic programme of the AfA-Bund[24]; the traditional Social Democratic ideas on a planned economy were undoubtedly more conspicuous in this scheme than in the WTB Plan. On this point the Afa-Bund programme was obviously largely in accord with the intentions of the Social Democrats' Reichstag group. In particular, the articles on the subject of job creation starting in the January/February 1932 issue of "Vorwärts", and then the SPD's parliamentary bills of late the same summer, followed various planned economy models, to which the ADGB gave its backing, albeit very cautiously, in the paragraph on "rebuilding the economy" subsequently added to its job creation programme.

---

22 See Sozialdemokratischer Parteitag in Leipzig 1931 vom 31. Mai bis 5. Juni im Volkshaus, Protokoll (Leipzig, 1931), pp. 32–52; this speech p. 45
23 Protokoll der Verhandlungen des ausserordentlichen (15.) Kongresses der Gewerkschaften Deutschlands (5. Bundestags des ADGB), abgehalten im Plenarsaal des Reichstages in Berlin am 13 April 1932 (Berlin, 1932), p. 18 f.
24 See Fritz Croner, Kurs auf Sozialismus! in Marxistische Tribüne für Politik und Wirtschaft No. 7 of 1. 4. 1932, pp. 201–4; Otto Suhr, Mobilisierung der Wirtschaft, in Marxistische Tribüne No. 8 of 15. 4. 1932, pp. 250–52

Then, in June 1932, the ADGB published detailed "Guidelines for rebuilding the economy".[25] Linking up with the AfA-Bund's proposals, this presented a whole list of demands, bundling the Free Trade Unions' goals of nationalization and a planned economy, and combining them with demands on economic, social and financial policy. Admittedly, these guidelines did not offer by and large any fundamentally new demands, but in summary they acquired a programmatic quality that promised to appeal above all to the "Left" – though without leading to mass mobilization.

Thus the programme for "rebuilding the economy" overlooked the shift in the balance of power in the summer and autumn of 1932, just as the job creation plan had. Although one should not be over-optimistic in assessing the chances of the job creation programme and its impact on the employment situation, one must ask oneself whether a policy of this kind, had it been introduced in the early spring of 1932, might not have been able to boost confidence in the government's readiness and ability to take action, and perhaps that of the Weimar Republic as a whole, or at least to stem the loss of confidence.

Though from autumn 1931 on the unions resisted Brüning's policies with increasing vehemence, they were forced further and further on to the defensive. This impression remains, even if one takes into account the fact that the Free Trade Unions organized company branches into *Hammerschaften* (Hammer Squads) and set up the "Iron Front" with the SPD in December 1931, and that the Christian unions formed a "Popular Front", a militant organization to fend off attacks by the National Socialists. How to stop the National Socialists seizing power using parliamentary, legal means – that was the dilemma. This was also the intention in supporting the re-election of Hindenburg as President, which was accepted by the Free Trade Unions as a "necessary evil", though unreservedly advocated by the Christian unions. It was this same Hindenburg who then withdrew his confidence from Brüning and by appointing Franz von Papen Reichskanzler hastened the destruction of the Weimar republic.

---

25 Gewerkschafts-Zeitung No. 27 of 2. 7. 1932, p. 418 ff.

Against the Papen Cabinet: powerless opposition

From the outset, the Papen Cabinet was fiercely criticized by all the unions. The unions saw their fears confirmed by the emergency decree of 14 June 1932, which scarcely managed to disguise the continuing run-down of the welfare system with a job creation programme costing 135 m Marks. Although the ADGB came out against the emergency decree together with the other union federations, a united front with the KPD was rejected.[26] The goal and path of the new government seemed clear, in view of the new burdens placed on the workers by emergency decrees, the dissolution of the Reichstag and the lifting of the ban on the S.A. and the wearing of uniforms. It is noticeable, however, that only two "pillars" of the DGB – the Christian unions and the Federation of German Transport and State Employees – signed the joint protest statement issued by the union federations; a united DGB reaction to Papen was probably thwarted by the opposition of the DHV.

The days of the republic were numbered. Another step towards the destruction of democracy was the "Prussian coup", whereby the Social Democrat-led Prussian Government was deposed on 20 July 1932. Trade unions of all political tendencies responded with a declaration of protest, culminating in an appeal to observe discipline.[27]

In view of the big gulfs between the Social Democrats and the Free Trade Unions on the one hand, and the Communists on the other; in view of the Communists' theory of "social fascism", which the Social Democrats countered with the charge that the KPD was the pawn of Moscow; in view of the differences in the assessment of the Weimar Republic; and, finally, in view of the radically different policies of the ADGB and the RGO – hopes of setting up a "united front" for the defence of the republic were certainly illusionary.[28]

Among the rank and file, on the shop floor and in the course of day-to-day political work at grassroots level there may have been instances of obvious common ground, especially where the brutality of Nazi gangs had to be confronted; but at a higher level hostilities had grown to such an extent that it blighted ideas of unity for years after 1933. The unions' reactions to Papen's "Prussian coup" show that the national federations were

---

26 Erklärung der Gewerkschaften zur Notverordnung, in Gewerkschafts-Zeitung No. 26 of 25. 6. 1932, p. 401
27 Gewerkschafts-Zeitung No. 30 of 23. 7. 1932, p. 465
28 See Zur Frage der Einheitsfront, in Gewerkschafts-Zeitung No. 26 of 25. 6. 1932, p. 412 f.; Nach der Reichsexekution gegen Preussen, ibid. No. 31 of 30. 7. 1932, p. 484 f.

closer to one another than to the RGO or KPD. The unions believed that Papen would be paid out for his policies not by means of the strike weapon but through the ballot box.

The most striking result of the elections of 31 July 1932 was a further rise in the NSDAP vote, which did not lead to a kind of union toleration of the Papen government, even though they were in overall agreement with it on the central question of job creation and supported its scheme to promote voluntary labour service, though with reservations. Instead, the Papen government's economic plan, first unveiled on 28 August 1932, was hailed as an "incomprehensible monstrosity" and after it was made the basis of an emergency decree to boost the economy on 4 September it was sharply rejected on account of its social-reactionary basic tendency, which ruled out any prospect of success.[29] Of course, some individual (notably Christian) trade unionists did acknowledge that the Papen programme signified a shift towards an "active economic policy"; but they emphasized that it was a policy for which the workers would have to pay and that consequently no thorough-going revival of the economy could be expected.[30] Alongside payments to employers for taking on more staff, the possibility of undercutting the agreed rates of pay came in for particularly fierce criticism, since, according to Leipart at a meeting of the ADGB federal committee on 9 September 1932, it rendered collective agreements worthless. Therefore, the rescission of the emergency decree was demanded in advance.[31] The basic tendency of trade union policy remained protest and fierce opposition to the Papen government.

∗

This was also evident at the September 1932 congress of the Christian trade unions, which professed allegiance to the Weimar republic more clearly than ever before. It was the position taken in the speech by executive member Jakob Kaiser on the "popular-political and national will of the Christian unions".[32] Many of the words and concepts used by Kaiser,

---

29 See Fritz Tarnow, Ankurbelung der Wirtschaft, in Gewerkschafts-Zeitung No. 36 of 3. 9. 1932, p. 561 ff.; Belebung der Wirtschaft durch Papen, ibid. No. 38 of 17. 9. 1932, p. 593 f.

30 See Wladimiar Woytinsky, Das Wirtschaftsprogramm der Reichsregierung, in Die Arbeit No. 10, October 1932, pp. 585–97

31 See Die Gewerkschaften und die Notverordnung, in Gewerkschafts-Zeitung No. 38 of 17. 9. 1932, p. 595

32 Jakob Kaiser, Der volkspolitische und nationale Wille der christlichen Gewerkschaften. Vortrag, gehalten auf dem 13. Kongress der christlichen Gewerkschaften Deutschlands in Düsseldorf am 19. September 1932 (Berlin, 1932)

ranging from *Volkstum, volklich, national* to *Blut und Eisen,* though current at the time, today seem dated and alien. Furthermore, Kaiser rejected "mechanical, westernizing democracy" and turned his back on "formal democracy"; he was willing to accept a further development of the constitution, provided the foundation of a "social *Volksstaat* is preserved". For him, this foundation rested on "the political and social equal rights and equal worth of all Germans, all strata and classes of society".

At the same time, however, there was an apparent return to ideas about professional classes (*Berufsstände*), for which the Christian unions' best known theoretician, Theodor Brauer, was seeking support, with Pope Pius XI's encyclical at his back. At the Düsseldorf congress Brauer expounded his ideas for social reform to favour the idea of professional groups.[33] More clearly than ever before he distanced himself from professional programmes, "behind which [. . .] lurks a marked antagonism to democracy". He also deemed it apt to give a more up-to-date interpretation of the "outmoded term *Berufstand*" (professional group or class); "in its modern sense" it could only mean "the totality of all those who work together in a branch of production and through this co-operation produce an overall result". If closely scrutinized this meant the abandonment of the traditional concept of a profession or trade, based on certain values as well as certain skills, in favour of accepting the various branches of trade and industry as the building blocks of the economy. It was only the husk of the term that was preserved, and it was to this husk the Christian unions clung – even at the risk of getting into social-reactionary and anti-democratic company, since the distinction between a society based on class or *Stände* ("estates") and a society based on professional groups or classes (*Berufsstände*) is a fluid one. But what mattered above all to the Christian unions was that the old "honourable" terms held a fascination capable of glossing over the lack of any actual substance – which was probably the intention. The idea of reconstructing the old professional classes was hailed as the universal panacea in the Depression years, though the absence of properly thought-out plans for reform was hard to conceal.

We must consider whether comments revealing an equivocal attitude to the parliamentary republic and the propagation of ideas of "professional class" did not contribute indirectly to a weakening of the Weimar democracy. True, the policies of the Christian unions showed that they underestimated the National Socialists' desire for power, though they did

---

33 Theodor Brauer, Der Kampf um die Sozialpolitik als gesellschaftliche Kraft, in Niederschrift der Verhandlungen des 13. Kongresses der christlichen Gewerkschaften Deutschland, Düsseldorf, 18.–20. September 1932 (Berlin, undated), p. 368–93

not greatly differ from the Free Trade Unions in this. But the Christian unions' efforts to steal the thunder of the National Socialists by flaunting their own nationalist sentiments or to "tame" them by letting them participate in government, may have helped give the NSDAP a certain aura of respectability.

*

The emergency decree of September 1932 was followed by a spate of strikes which in many cases successfully fended off or at least reduced the size of wage cuts. Although industrial action of this kind helped to strengthen the organizations, the unions were reluctant to become involved. This was also true of the strike of Berlin transport workers, the so-called BVG strike.[34] The national federation of workers in publicly owned industry and passenger and goods transport had negotiated an agreement that their wages would not – as the management had wanted – be reduced by 10–17 Pfennigs per hour from 1 November but "only" by 2 Pf. When balloted, 66 per cent of the workers, but not the required three-quarters majority, voted in favour of a strike. But as the votes cast were sufficient as a proportion of all those entitled to vote, the NSBO and RGO called a strike anyway. It ended in defeat on 8 November, after five days. Like the events of 20 July 1932, this demonstrated the basic pattern of trade union policy: the "old" Social Democratic trade unionists' experience and mentality made them sceptical with regard to industrial disputes – and suspicious if there was reason to fear that the strike might slip out of their hands politically. This paralysis was particularly noticeable when strong radical groups determined to take part in a strike to broaden their mass base – and in the case of the BVG strike two groups had done so at once.

The election campaign for 6 November 1932 was dominated by resistance to the NSDAP and the Papen government, which was branded "unsocial" and undemocratic. This verdict related to government plans for constitutional reform, which were not only designed to strength the hold of central government over the *Länder*, but also (and this was the primary objective) to strengthen the executive at the expense of Parliament. The election results, especially NSDAP's vote losses, was optimistically assessed by the ADGB: it claimed the NSDAP was breaking up, while the SPD was standing its ground – despite losing 700,000 votes.[35]

---

34 See the documents in Frank Deppe and Witich Rossmann, Wirtschaftskrise, Faschismus, Gewerkschaften. Dokumente zur Gewerkschaftspolitik 1929–1933 (Cologne, 1981), p. 212 ff.

35 Das Wahlergebnis, in Gewerkschafts-Zeitung No. 46 of 12. 11. 1932, pp. 721–23

The fact that the trade unions gauged the extent of the National Socialist threat largely by the yardstick of election results clearly shows the faith of the Social Democratic labour movement in the ability of the parliamentary system to function even in times of crisis. Yet their political adversaries – the NSDAP – had long before realized the importance of mass mobilization and made use of it. In any event, the balance of power had shifted "behind the scenes" in favour of the National Socialists, so that the Schleicher government was merely an interlude.

The Schleicher Cabinet: a last-minute attempt at stabilization

The government formed by Kurt von Schleicher on 2 December 1932 was regarded with a good deal of optimism by the trade unions. Their hopes seemed entirely justified. In putting the Cabinet together, Schleicher had already been in touch with the unions, giving top priority to job creation and on 14 December it finally repealed the particularly objectionable sections of Papen's emergency decree of September that year. The chief factor behind this policy was no doubt Schleicher's efforts to forge a parliamentary base for his government by creating a "trade union axis", grouping together all deputies with trade union ties, irrespective of their party political allegiances. Instead of wrenching 60 deputies, headed by Gregor Strasser, away from the NSDAP group as intended, the attempt failed and Strasser himself was stripped of power. Nor did the Christian trade unions show any inclination to drop their co-operation with the Centre. The ADGB – probably under pressure from the SPD leadership – adopted a wait-and-see attitude to the Schleicher Plan. Leipart's end-of-year appeal, however, showed a readiness to co-operate with the government, in spite of reservations, though he believed time was needed to prepare for this, to allay the misgivings of the SPD and union members.[36]

But the period for such preparations had already expired a few days later: on 28 January the Schleicher government resigned. Once again the unions tried to influence the formation of the government; on the same day, the union federations appealed to President Hindenburg not to permit a Cabinet consisting of "social reactionaries". But as far as the chancellorship was concerned, the die had been cast on 4 January 1933 when, at a meeting at the house of the Cologne banker Kurt von Schröder, Papen

---

36 Theodor Leipart, An die deutsche Arbeiterschaft, in Gewerkschafts-Zeitung No. 53 of 31. 12. 1932, p. 833

and Hitler had struck a deal. On 30 January 1933 Hitler was appointed Reichskanzler.

3. The trade unions in the Weimar Republic: a balance sheet

The balance sheet of trade union policy during the Weimar Republic is confused. Certainly, the workers' achievements during the Weimar Republic are notable compared with the situation under the Empire (not to mention the Nazi dictatorship). Equal suffrage and parliamentary democracy, freedom of association and social and economic co-determination, the eight-hour day and works councils, the extension of the welfare system and the creation of an unemployment benefit scheme – the list of improvements introduced under the revolution and the republic could be made longer still. It should not be forgotten that more and more trade unionists entered parliaments at all levels and moved into leading administrative and governmental posts, spearheading the drive towards democratization as a "political reserve elite".

Of course, the achievements with which unions of all tendencies credited themselves – with greater or lesser justification – had a number of weak spots. The eight-hour day could not be retained. Co-determination rights at company level and on social and economic policy-making bodies were severely limited or existed on paper only (as was the case with the National Economic Council). Social policy never freed itself from dependence on the economic situation, on which the unions had no influence at all. In addition, social policy and wage levels provided the starting points for employer campaigns that not only shifted the blame for the critical state of the economy on to the unions but were soon also denying the unions' very right to exist, eventually culminating in a fundamental rejection of parliamentary democracy.

But do the successes of union policy justify the conclusion that the Weimar Republic was a "trade union state"? Without a doubt, the position of the unions in the state and society had been radically transformed with the establishment of parliamentary democracy. This opened up quite new opportunities to exert political pressure on the basis of their members', and hence to some extent the public's, approval. And the unions were, indeed, taken seriously by some parties as instruments for influencing and mobilizing the electorate. But the integration of the unions into the political system does not entitle one to draw the conclusion that they exerted a decisive influence. All too often the limits of their power were brought home to them: the series of defeats ranges from the consequences of the Kapp Putsch to the legal regulation of working hours, from fiscal and economic policy to the question of job creation – and finally to the demise of the parliamentary system and the dissolution of the trade unions themselves.

In view of the limited extent to which the unions succeeded in defending their interests and the way in which the state made use of them – for instance, in the Ruhr struggle – the Weimar Republic certainly cannot be regarded as a "trade union state". It is not even possible to speak of a tendency to seek absolute power; the unions' aim was power-sharing within the framework of a pluralist society. They were probably not even aware that in the 1920s they had made a vital contribution, in extremely difficult economic and political conditions, to an initial attempt to bring about a social and democratic social order, to construct a modern "social state". And although the unions may have proved too weak to "save" the Weimar Republic, the waning popularity of which was a constant source of new opponents, the unions were certainly not among those who deliberately took advantage of the crisis to destroy it.

IX. Under the National Socialist dictatorship: persecution, resistance and exile 1933–1945

The "transfer of power" to Hitler and the NSDAP marked the beginning of a new chapter in the history of the trade unions. After a few months when the unions hoped to safeguard the survival of their organization with a policy that wavered between protest and compliance, they were smashed. The break-up of the unions and the construction of a authoritarian social order, termed a *Volksgemeinschaft* by the Nazis, were the logical outcome of National Socialist ideology, which was resisted by trade unionists of all persuasions both at home and abroad.

1. *Between protest and compliance: the end of the trade unions under the National Socialists*

"Organization – not demonstration: that is the slogan for today," was how Theodor Leipart outlined trade union policy for the weeks and months ahead to the ADGB's federal committee on 31 January 1933.[1] Like the ADGB leadership, the Christian unions' executive also regretted Hindenburg's "fateful decision" to confirm the "Cabinet of the Harzburg Front" headed by Hitler.[2] In a joint declaration, the trade unions expressed the fear that the "parties and groups that have hitherto openly advocated that manual and white-collar workers be deprived of their social rights, that democracy be destroyed and parliament cast aside" might now – in government – "seek to put their plans into effect". Thus the vital interests of all working people were at stake. "To fight off attacks on the constitution and law effectively in an emergency requires a cool head and self-possession. Do not be misled into rash and therefore harmful individual actions."[3]

Anyone waiting for an appeal for organized mass action was to be disappointed. These calls for discipline scotched the KPD's appeals for a gen-

---

1 See Die Gewerkschaften und der Regierungswechsel. 13. Bundesausschußsitzung des. ADGB am 31.1.1933, in Gewerkschafts-Zeitung No. 5 of 4.2.1933, p. 67 f. ; on this point, see p. 67
2 See An die christliche Arbeiterschaft, in Zentralblatt No. 4 of 15.2.1933, p. 37
3 An die Mitglieder der Gewerkschaften, in Gewerkschafts-Zeitung No. 5 of 4. 2. 1933, p. 65

eral strike, though even without the non-cooperation of the unions they would probably not have been heeded more than sporadically. At any rate, the trade unions clearly dissociated themselves from the "tireless theoreticians of the general strike". This point was emphasized by the deputy chairman of the ADGB, Peter Grassmann, at the leaders' meeting of the Iron Front on 13 February 1933: "The general strike is a terrible weapon, not only for the adversary; one can only instigate one and be answerable for it if there is no other course open, if it is a matter of life and death for the working class."[4]

Who could deny, looking back, that the very situation he dreaded had actually come about? But the insidious undermining of the social and political achievements of the revolution and republic, the weakening of the trade unions in the years of political and economic crisis, and probably resignation in the face of an opponent who seemed invincible and was attracting the masses in droves – all these factors contributed to the unions' capitulation without a fight. Moreover, the labour movement was not capable of acting as one man: in addition to the split between Communists and Social Democrats, there were also tendencies towards polarization within the trade union movement. The joint statement by the trade union federations on Hitler's take-over of the government was signed by the ADGB and the AfA-Bund, the liberal Trade Union League of German Workers', Salaried Staffs' and Civil Servants' Associations and the General Association of Christian Trade Unions, but not by the DGB. In its telegram of congratulation to Hitler on 1 February 1933, the DHV pointed out that it had not been able to sign a trade union statement – and this was why the DGB had broken ranks – in which the new Cabinet was rejected as a government of "social reaction".[5] A few weeks later the DHV was voluntarily disbanded; thus by April 1933 the DGB was broken as a united organization.

Even though they continually warned of the consequences of a National Socialist government for the workers, it was obvious that the Free Trade Unions did not really expect the unions to be destroyed, either. Instead, they hoped that by stressing in the media the importance of the trade unions in providing "schooling in responsibility" for a people that was growing aware of its "right to national self-determination", the movement would be spared as a sort of reward. To this end, Theodor Leipart

---

4 Peter Grassmann, Kampf dem Marxismus!? Rede anlässlich des Führerappells der Eisernen Front am 13. 2. 1933 (Berlin, 1933), p. 21
5 See the DHV to Hitler on 1. 2. 1933 (Bundesarchiv Koblenz, R 43 II, 531, No. 2)

recalled the "trade unions' achievements for people and state".[6] And Lothar Erdmann, editor of "Arbeit" and Leipart's confidant, was at pains to contribute to the ideological reconciliation of "nation, trade unions and socialism"[7] by rejecting any internationalist tendencies.

The unions stuck grimly to their policy of keeping a "cool head", as it was called, even after the Reichstag fire on 27 February 1933, which the Free Trade Unions branded "an attack on the whole parliamentary system".[8] True, there was much talk in union announcements at this time of "struggle" (*Kampf*) and "readiness for the struggle" (*Kampfbereitschaft*) – but this was an allusion to the electoral campaign (*Wahlkampf*) more than anything; once again, the unions – including the Christian unions – were pinning all their hopes on the electorate.

After the elections of 5 March 1933, in which the NSDAP gained an absolute majority, the unions began to adjust to the fact that Hitler's government was not going to be just a brief interlude. But even in the Free Trade Unions the hope obviously prevailed that things would not be that "bad" – in any event, no worse than under the Socialist Law.

In March 1933 the bloody terror against the trade unions reached an initial climax. On 13 March alone, the ADGB executive received alarming reports from more than twenty places.[9] But the attacks and acts of violence failed to bring about any fundamental change in union policy. It is not possible to view the protests against these violent attacks, which were largely the work of the SA, as acts of resistance. The unions' complaints to Hindenburg, for example, were more in the nature of reproachful protestations of innocence, accompanied by assurances of their readiness to cooperate with the government, if only it would keep the "rank and file" of its movement under control.

The unions' willingness to fall into line went to the very brink of surrender. A statement by the ADGB executive of 21 March 1933 finally recognized the "right of the state to intervene in conflicts between organized labour and the employers if the common good required it". "State supervision" of the "common work of the free organization of the economy

---

6 Theodor Leipart, Leistungen der Gewerkschaften für Volk und Staat, in Soziale Praxis No. 8 of 23. 2. 1933, columns 225–231

7 Lothar Erdmann, Nation, Gewerkschaften und Sozialismus, in Die Arbeit No. 3, March 1933, pp. 129–61

8 See Brand im Reichstag, Bundesausschußsitzung des Allgemeinen Gewerkschaftsbundes, in Gewerkschafts-Zeitung No. 9 of 4. 3. 1933, p. 129

9 Henryk Skrzypczak, Die Ausschaltung der Freien Gewerkschaften im Jahre 1933, in Matthias and Schönhoven (eds.), Solidarität und Menschenwürde, pp. 255–70; this information p. 261

might actually be beneficial, enhance its value and facilitate its execution". Even the form of organization was left open, as "championing the interests of labour takes precedence over the form of organization".[10]

While there is no mistaking the Free Trade Unions' attempts to adapt to the situation, the Christian-national unions appear to have succumbed to the emotionalism of the "revolution": "That which was rotten is gone. And a wave of young strength has swept over Germany." That was how they hailed this "revolution". At the executive and committee meetings of 16 and 17 March 1933, the Christian unions proclaimed their readiness to co-operate with the "new state"; and in adopting the "Essen Programme"[11] for the construction of a social order based on professional groups it was placing itself – according to Otte – "consciously in the service of the great cause".[12]

Saving their own organization was their guiding principle. Accordingly, the Christian unions dissociated themselves from the Free Trade Unions, and both federations distanced themselves from their former political allies, so as not to share the fate of parties that the regime obviously disliked. So the ADGB federal executive soon copied the step taken by the Christian unions at the Essen conference and brought its policy into line. On 9 April it declared its willingness "to place the autonomous organization of labour, created by the trade unions over the decades, in the service of the new state". The ADGB recommended that the trade union movement should be placed under a *Reichskommissar*. And on 13 April Leipart, Grassmann and Wilhelm Leuschner discussed the future organizational form of the union movement with representatives of the NSBO. Only when the NSBO men opined, by way of an ultimatum, that Leipart should hand over his post to a National Socialist, was the limit of union compliance finally reached: Leipart insisted that the leadership of the trade unions should be decided by the delegates.[13]

The result of the Reichstag elections, the terror of March 1933 and the vote on the "Enabling Act" (Ermächtigungsgesetz), whereby the German parliament – against the votes of the SPD – gave up its powers, had worn

10 Erklärung des Allgemeinen Deutschen Gewerkschaftsbundes, in Gewerkschafts-Zeitung No. 12 of 25. 3. 1933, p. 177
11 See Richtlinien der christlich-nationalen Gewerkschaften, in Zentralblatt No. 7 of 1. 4. 1933, p. 87 ff.
12 Quot. Tagungen der Christlichen Gewerkschaften, in Gewerkschafts-Zeitung No. 12 of 25. 3. 1933, p. 178
13 See Manfred Scharrer, Anpassung bis zum bitteren Ende. Die freien Gewerkschaften 1933, in Scharrer (ed.), Kampflose Kapitulation. Arbeiterbewegung 1933 (Reinbek bei Hamburg, 1984), pp. 73–120; on this point p. 107 ff.

May Day 1933: celebrating "National Labour Day" in Berlin

down trade unionists. Only the spring works council elections brought a faint ray of hope, but the National Socialist regime broke off the elections as they were not producing the desired results. After the election of a good 9,000 works councils it was apparent that at the end of April there was still a great deal of loyalty to the trade unions, hard pressed though they were. The Free Trade Unions received 73.4 per cent of the vote, the Christian unions 7.6, the Hirsch-Duncker unions 0.6 and the RGO 4.9 per cent; the NSBO "only" managed 11.7 per cent.[14] On the other hand, the National Socialist leadership may have concluded from this result that in order to put into effect their plan for a new social order they would have to smash the unions once and for all.

At the same time as the unions were declaring their readiness to adapt and negotiating on *Gleichschaltung* (falling into line) with the NSBO, they were making last-minute efforts to unite the trade union movement. The fact that talks between the representatives of the federations were supposed to lead to a "*Gleichschaltung* from below", to prevent reorgani-

---

14 Figures from Neuwahl der Betriebsräte 1933, in Gewerkschafts-Zeitung No. 17 of 29. 4. 1933, p. 270

208

2 May 1933: the SA occupies the trade union building in Berlin on the Engelufer

zation as a compulsory state-run trade union,[15] shows how little scope for action the union leaders now saw. At the end of April 1933 the "United Trade Union Leaders' Group" was set up – certainly no alliance for action; instead, the talks were an effort to ensure at least the survival of the organizations, albeit in a new, non-political form. The programme of this merger between the Free, Christian and Hirsch-Duncker unions worked out at the end of April was characterized by readiness to take an active part in the reorganization of economic and social life.[16] For the rest, this draft programme was more of a makeshift roof than a solid foundation for a united union movement. To forge a true union it was first necessary to endure the shared experience of dissolution and annihilation, persecution and resistance.

The unions' policy of compliance reached its climax and its finale with their appeals on May Day 1933, which the government – hijacking the tra-

---

15 See Erkelenz to Stegerwald on 1. 4. 1933 (Stegerwald-Archiv, Nachtragsband, No. 19)

16 Reprinted in Gerhard Beier, Zur Entwicklung des Führerkreises der Vereinigten Gewerkschaften Ende April 1933, in Archiv für Sozialgeschichte XV (1975), p. 389 ff.

dition of the international labour movement – had declared "National Labour Day". The ADGB's federal executive welcomed the May Day arrangements on 15 April, recalling that on May Day "the declared belief of the German worker, filled with a passionate desire for culture, flared up, seeking to snatch the working man away from a dull life of toil and give him a place in the community of the people as a free, confident personality".[17] Whereas the federal executive left participation in the state May Day celebrations up to members, on 19 April the ADGB's federal committee finally called on workers to take part.[18] May Day was even welcomed by the executive of the Christian trade unions, (which had not exactly shown much enthusiasm for May Day before) as a sign "that the Hitler government professes its faith in the social German heritage (*Volkstum*)".[19]

Many trade unionists deluded themselves that their organizations had a newly defined but firm place in the "national popular community". A day later, the trade unions were brought up sharp by reality. On the morning of 2 May all the important buildings of the ADGB and the individual unions were occupied by SA and SS troops. The Nazis vented their hatred of the Free Trade Unions in a spree of arrests, torture and murder. On 3 May the other federations meekly submitted to the "Action Committee for the Protection of German Labour". That was the end of the trade union movement. The policy of appeasing the new dictators to the very limits of self-respect, even the trade unions' political suicide, had not been able to prevent their break-up – though they may have made it easier.

2. The social order of the "Führer state"

Anyone who had imagined that, given their anti-union propaganda, the National Socialists might certainly obstruct the trade unions but stop short of destroying them was deceived. The assumption that an industrialized country could not do without trade unions to represent and integrate working people proved an illusion. Very quickly the National Socialist rulers were trying to construct a social order in tune with their ideology, and in this order there was no room for the independent, self-determined representation of workers' interests. Does it need emphasizing that the NSDAP was anything but a socialist party?

*

---

17 Gewerkschafts-Zeitung No. 16 of 22. 4. 1933, p. 241
18 ibid.
19 An die christliche Arbeiterschaft, in Zentralblatt No. 9 of 1. 5. 1933, p. 105

In April 1933 the rights of the works councils were cut back with the Law on Company Representation. After the dissolution or "bringing into line" of the trade unions, free collective bargaining was abolished in May 1933 by the Law on the Trustees of Labour. In the same year a general wage freeze was decreed, with a resulting boost to company profits in the economic upturn that got off to a hesitant start but picked up speed as rearmament got underway. In May 1934 farmworkers were forbidden to change jobs without official permission. In February 1935 the "work book" for manual and white-collar workers was introduced, regulating the labour market but, most importantly, keeping a check on job changes, too.

The cornerstones of National Socialist labour legislation were the "Law on the Organization of National Labour", passed on 20 January 1934, and the "Law in Preparation for the Organic Construction of the German Economy" of 27 February 1934. These laws were based on the underlying idea of a harmony of interests between employers and wage earners, expressed in the notion of the popular and corporate community as a "productive community". Thus, Article 1 of the Law on the Organization of National Labour stated: "Within the company the entrepreneur, as the leader of the company, and the staff and workers, as the workforce*, shall work together to promote company objectives and for the common benefit of people and state.' The "leader of the company" was required – in Article 2 – to "ensure the welfare of the workforce. The latter must observe the loyalty to him that is founded in the corporate community". Industrial peace was characterized as the workforce's natural "duty of loyalty" to the leader. Both employers and employees had to bow to the aims of the National Socialist state, which were, however, clearly in line with the ideas of many employers, when it came to crushing the labour movement. This may have consoled them for the loss of their own federations, which fell victim to the "class-based construction" (*ständischer Aufbau*) of the German economy. This meant that the entire economy and labour market were subjected to state regimentation, but the system of private property and opportunities for profits were retained.

By stressing the community principle – from the works community to the popular community – the abstractions of Nazi ideology only superficially concealed the actual consolidation of capitalist power structures, which were reinforced by giving the "leader principle" legal status in the economy and crushing the labour movement. The arguments over collective agreements were replaced by state decrees by the trustees of labour;

---

* Translator's note: The German word used here is *Gefolgschaft* (retinue, entourage, followers), a deliberate archaism that formed part of National Socialist jargon.

the place of the works councils was taken by "representative councils", which were "elected" by the staff from a list put forward by the employer and whose chairman was the "company leader". Presumably because of these peculiar regulations, the turn-out by the workers in the first elections for these new councils in March 1934 was not as good as the regime had hoped, so that no extensive list of results was ever published. Only for mining were there any faintly reliable figures, showing that in the pits about two-thirds to three-quarters of the valid votes had been cast for the official lists.

The place of the trade unions was to be taken by the German Labour Front (Deutsche Arbeitsfront – DAF), though it initially saw its position threatened by the National Socialist Company Cell Organization (NSBO). Formed on the model of the Communist RGO, since 1928 the NSBO had spread from Berlin throughout the large industrial regions of Germany; by 1932 the National Socialist company cells had roughly 170,000 members. NSBO members often remained in the trade unions too, so as to be covered financially in the event of a strike. Following the National Socialist seizure of power the number of NSBO members soared to some 700,000 by May 1933. This encouraged the NSBO leadership to believe that it would become the heir of the trade unions; for this reason, the NSBO, as a populist grass-roots movement with plenty of mass support, was at first a serious rival to the DAF. But soon the DAF took over the NSBO's major tasks. Not all NSBO officials were content to act simply as "recruiting officers" for the DAF and some repeatedly tried to formulate their own wage earner policy. Consequently, after an initial "general purge" in autumn 1933, the NSBO was politically brought to heel in the summer of 1934.

According to the announcements of May 1933, the DAF was supposed to act as a substitute union, but in its November 1933 form it organized all those who were gainfully employed, irrespective of their economic or social position (both workers and employers), clearly bearing the stamp of the *Volksgemeinschaft* ideology. In addition, the DAF was a National Socialist organization, which meant – to quote Robert Ley, the DAF chairman – that it was "solely dependent on the will and leadership of the NSDAP".[20] The DAF was an organization with considerable financial resources: not only did it take over the trade unions' capital, but wage earners (for whom membership was compulsory) also had to pay 1.5 per

20 According to Hans-Gerd Schumann, Nationalsozialismus und Gewerkschaftsbewegung. Die Vernichtung der deutschen Gewerkschaften und der Aufbau der "Deutschen Arbeitsfront" (Frankfurt, 1958), p. 101

cent of their wages in dues. With roughly 30 million members in 1939 – some 10 per cent of employees were able to avoid membership – the DAF amassed a considerable sum, and having no negotiating functions to fulfil, it was able to spend the money on its company social policy and the leisure organization, *Kraft durch Freude (Strength through joy)*. Robert Ley repeatedly tried to extend the DAF's sphere of influence, for example by putting forward proposals for the reorganization of social insurance and by intervening in internal company disputes; but the DAF remained principally a source of publicity for the National Socialist state, which could thus advertise its high regard for the "workers of brain and muscle".

Seldom has a regime fostered such a cult of labour and the working people – and at the same time deprived the working class so completely of political power. The National Socialist state intimidated the workers, deprived them of political and trade union representation – but surrounded them with an almost mythological enhancement of the picture of the worker in art and political propaganda. There could be no doubt about the ends to which this was all devoted. Under the programmatic title "We are all helping the Führer", Robert Ley made it quite clear in 1937: "What is good for Germany is right; what is harmful to Germany is wrong." A year later the wage earners were confirmed in the role as "soldiers of labour": "When you are asleep, it is your private business, but as soon as you wake up and come into contact with another person, you must bear in mind that you are one of Adolf Hitler's soldiers and you must live and conduct yourself in accordance with a set of rules."[21]

The militarization of work, giving the "work effort" of the "soldier of labour" a place in the "battle of labour" was not just so much rhetorical verbiage; with the progressive "taming of the working class",[22] from deprivation of political rights to the introduction of compulsory labour (1938), propaganda was simultaneously preparing for war, which was Hitler's main aim from the outset.

*

While large numbers of workers may have been sceptical about the fine phrases of Hitler's propaganda, the improved standard of living that accompanied the economic upturn may have been some consolation for

---

21 According to H. Grebing, op. cit., p. 212
22 See Tim Mason, Die Bändigung der Arbeiterklasse im nationalsozialistischen Deutschland, in Carola Sachse et al., Angst, Belohnung, Zucht und Ordnung. Herrschaftsmechanismen im Nationalsozialismus (Opladen, 1982), pp. 11–53

their loss of political rights. Was it not thanks to National Socialist policies, many people may have asked themselves, that the number of unemployed fell from 5.6 m in 1932 to 4.8 m in 1933? Who could see through the way in which propaganda dressed up the unemployment statistics? The extension of voluntary labour service, which was soon made compulsory, and the accumulation of emergency work led to a further drop in the unemployment figures, although the number of persons in gainful employment did not rise, but actually fell from 18.7 m (1932) to 18.5 m (1933). The situation eased as the war generation, which was relatively small, came on to the labour market. On the other hand, the job creation programme, which was proclaimed with a great deal of propaganda, was not particularly successful. Moreover, it should be borne in mind that the creation of jobs, which aroused the admiration of many observers (and not only contemporary ones) was clearly designed to further the goal of "restoring the German people's fighting capability", to quote Hitler's words in February 1933.[23] And we should recollect that only with the rearmament programmes from 1934–35 onwards was unemployment cured. In 1936 arms spending was twice as high as investment for civilian purposes. It was not only the large concerns like the Hermann-Göring-Werke that profited, but also a multitude of small suppliers. The consumer goods industry also benefited from the higher demand resulting from greater purchasing power.

From 1937 on, there was a lack of skilled workers in crucial areas of the arms industry, particularly in engineering; about this time it is probably accurate to speak of full employment. This resulted in a sharp increase in the number of working women, who were pilloried in National Socialist propaganda. "Moral" pressure, but also social and economic measures, had caused a drop in the proportion of women in the working population, but when rearmament pushed the economy into an upward trend and manpower became scarce as a result, state and industry called up the "reserve army" of women, as has repeatedly happened throughout history.

The late 1930s brought an improvement in the material standard of living for large sections of wage earners. Despite the wage freeze decreed in 1933, full employment was a major factor in enabling wage earners to

23 Dietmar Petzina, Hauptprobleme der deutschen Wirtschaftspolitik 1932/33, in Vierteljahrhefte für Zeitgeschichte 15 (1967), pp. 18–55; this quot. p. 43

achieve individual wage rises through a "wage policy off their own bat".[24] In 1937 real wages again reached the pre-war level (Table 3b).

The other side of this accelerated run-up to war was an extension of working hours. Because of the Depression, working hours had fallen to an average 40 hours per week in 1932; in the period prior to the war they went up to 48 hours (1939), and during the war they rose again, to 60 hours per week (Table 4b), thus pushing to the very limits the rules on working hours laid down in 1938. According to these rules, which are still in force today, regular working hours must not exceed eight hours per day or 48 hours per week. But this may be extended to up to ten hours per day by collective agreement, with a set overtime bonus of time and a quarter.

A few months later – on 1 September 1939 – the legal provisons governing industrial safety and limits on working hours were suspended by the "Decree modifying and complementing regulations in the field of industrial law" for the duration of the war. But then, immediately before the attack on France, they were brought back into force, except for bonuses for the nineth and tenth hours worked, to avert any resentment that might have jeopardized arms production.

$$*$$

On the outbreak of war, living conditions changed astonishingly little, apart from conscription and the ever-growing number of casualties. The experience of the First World War had shown that the successful waging of war largely depended (or so its seemed) on social peace on the "home front". One of the aims of war policy was therefore to ensure a high standard of living for the civilian population. Providing for the families of soldiers at the front and productivity incentives in the form of bonuses and leisure activities were intended to guarantee the smooth running of war production. This calculation was based on the assumption that the "Blitzkrieg" strategy would permit the immediate plundering of the countries subjugated.

At first things seem to be working out as planned. After the victories of 1940–41, the occupied countries were not only forced to provide raw materials for German armaments but also food supplies for the population. In order to maintain German output without drastically increasing

---

24 See Detlef J. K. Peukert, Die Lage der Arbeiter und der gewerkschaftliche Widerstand im Dritten Reich, in Ulrich Borsdorf unter Mitarbeit von Gabriele Weiden (ed.), Geschichte der deutschen Gewerkschaften von den Anfängen bis 1945 (Cologne, 1987), pp. 447–98; this quot. p. 470

the number of working women, civilians were deported to Germany, where they, along with prisoners of war and the inmates of concentration camps, were put to work for the large German concerns. Owing to the high proportion of foreigners in production, German workers were often able to leave the "shitty jobs" to them and, as members of the *Herrenvolk*, step into supervisory ("leadership") roles.

It was only with the retreat of the German troops on all fronts after the Battle of Stalingrad in January 1943, that the effects of the war began to be felt with increasing harshness in Germany. Although nominal wages continued to rise, supplies became scarce, and food and fuel rationing became part of everyday life, as did hours spent chasing goods in short supply. But this still did not give rise to the explosive atmosphere caused by the First World War food shortages. Both the ubiquitous informer and the sense of helplessness in the face of the catastrophe signalled by the nightly bombing raids fostered a climate of passivity, characterized by hope and fear, grumbling and subjection. Of course, a number of actions by young people did stand out, though the markedly maladjusted behaviour of groups of tearaways such as the "Edelweiss pirates" cannot be considered political resistance as such. And even during the war itself, go-slows, absenteeism for sickness and the insolence of many workers cannot, despite the growing risks of such conduct, be considered opposition, or resistance, although it should be borne in mind that these were the only ways of putting a dissident political attitude into practice. And these forms of individual protests certainly were risky – from telling political jokes and "belly-aching" to minor misdemeanours at work, which counted as sabotage.

3. *Trade unionists in the resistance and in exile*

By smashing the labour movement, the regime deprived the workers of their only chance of putting up any organized resistance. And with the machinery of the police and persecution pervading every area of life, every germ of collective resistance was destroyed. The only way of gathering oppositional elements together, if at all, was in the strictest secrecy – illegally, of course. For the unions, accustomed to mass support and operating in public, this posed problems with which their structure was not able to cope. The majority of trade union leaders were scarcely in a position to start indulging in conspiratorial methods of struggle, especially as they themselves, when not under arrest, were subject to special police surveillance. In the conditions of terror and persecution, surveillance and denunciation, there was simply no question of building up a trade union mass organization under ground.

∗

What form did trade union resistance take in practice? Despite the complete power of the National Socialist state to subjugate and punish its subjects, not every form of maladjusted behaviour can be classified as resistance. Reserving the term resistance for practical action to harrass or destroy key areas of the National Socialist dictatorship, the mere refusal to knuckle down and co-operate with the regime, or criticism of individual measures – however brave and whatever sacrifices they may have entailed – cannot be labelled resistance. Nor can the concept of trade union resistance be applied to the continuation of traditional union work, as the unions had been suppressed, along with the political role they had played. Certainly, in the conditions described, attempts to organize trade union activities, even to the point of striking, command respect. What is meant by trade union resistance, however, is the attempt by individual trade unionists to engage in political work directed against the National Socialist regime itself.

Trade union resistance was, firstly, trying to maintain personal solidarity between oppositional trade unionists. It was trying to illegally gather and pass on information on the situation in industry. It was trying to counter the propaganda tirades with political education. It was trying to maintain contact between resistance groups at home and in exile, and between German and foreign trade unionists. And it was trying to make preparations for "afterwards".

With these perhaps rather modest-sounding tasks and objectives the trade union resistance groups reacted to the situation in which they found themselves. Any large-scale resistance operations were out of the question in view of the terror immediately imposed and the indulgent, "wait-and-see" attitude evinced by growing sections of the population towards the regime. Even the attempt to build up a broadly based illegal organization was doomed to failure. This was demonstrated by the KPD's attempts to cling on to the RGO's cell plan, which led to mass arrests in 1933–4. The beginnings of underground trade union work within the DAF, employing "Trojan horse" tactics, were also fruitless; and because of the – alleged – collaboration of the Communists in the DAF it confused the working class.

The first precondition for mounting trade union resistance was to keep in touch, so as to strengthen one's own political convictions against the growing pressure of National Socialist propaganda and to exchange information. Thanks to skilful camouflage, some well-known trade union leaders even managed to carry out this task, for example, Alwin Brandes of the engineering workers, Fritz Husemann of the miners and Jakob Kaiser of the Christian trade unions. Kaiser had taken on the job of championing the pension and benefit claims of the Christian-national trade unionists dismissed in 1933, which enabled him to pay many "legal" visits to former union officials. The profession of commercial traveller also provided good opportunities for secret contacts – Bernhard Göring travelled in cigars, Hans Gottfurcht as an insurance agent. Any job to do with transport was also a good cover, so it is not surprising that the railway workers under Hans Jahn and transport workers under Adolph Kummernuss played a large part in the resistance work of the 1930s, especially as they had the backing of the International Transport Workers' Federation under Edo Fimmen. According to Jahn, in March 1936 his organization had 137 area centres, with 284 area centre leaders and 1,320 officials. The engineering workers also had a good network of contacts, with organizers such as Alwin Brandes, Heinrich Schliestedt, Max Urich, Richard Teichgräber, Hans Böckler and Walter Freitag.

Such contacts and groups may be regarded as resistance if they carried out operations against the regime – such as the transport and exchange of secret articles and information bulletins and – of course – the printing and distribution of leaflets. But neither meetings disguised as visits by commercial travellers (when communication was by word of mouth only) nor the groups that sprang up as a result were safe from the Gestapo. Heinrich Schliestedt and Hans Gottfurcht had to flee abroad, and Hermann Schlimme was arrested in 1937. The network of railwaymen's centres built up by Hans Jahn was almost entirely smashed by mass arrests in 1937, and the illegal circle around Alfred Fitz of the Federation of Food and Beverage Workers suffered the same fate.

It should be pointed out that there were also sporadic joint actions by Social Democratic and Communist trade unionists. The best known were the groups of textile and engineering workers formed at company level in the Wuppertal area, which had several hundred members in autumn 1934. They printed and distributed leaflets and ran their own newspapers. In January 1935 the groups were smashed by mass arrests. The accused in the "Wuppertal trials", which were the subject of a tremendous propaganda campaign, received a great deal of support from abroad, particularly the Dutch "Wuppertal Committee".

At about the same time, the SPD and KPD resistance groups were broken up, so that by 1936–7 there was scarcely any organized resistance by the labour movement at all. Only the leftwing splinter groups that had prepared for illegality were partially able to survive and carry on their work under ground. In the years that followed, trade union resistance was basically limited to the "Illegal National Leadership of the German Trade Unions", that is to say, the contact groups of former top officials, who met to discuss plans for "afterwards".[25] The union leaders cannot have had any contact with the masses but they did have a secret information network that made them particularly valuable as contacts for those colleagues who had fled abroad.

*

In view of the persecution and threats to which trade unionists were subjected, attempts were made at an early stage to set up emergency reception centres in neighbouring countries. Until it was annexed by Germany in 1935, the Saar district offered a refuge to exiled trade unionists. Then Czechoslovakia (until 1938) and the border regions of Holland, Belgium, France and Denmark assumed this function, until they, too, were overrun. But it was not simply a matter of setting up reception centres for trade unionists forced to leave Germany; the main task was to co-ordinate work from these regional centres.

In autumn 1934 the German trade unions' foreign legation was founded in Czechoslovakia at a conference in Reichenberg. After Schliestedt's death in 1938 it moved its seat to Copenhagen, where Fritz Tarnow was in charge, though not all foreign representatives recognized him as leader. The foreign legation received financial assistance from the International Trade Union Federation – by no means a matter of course, in view of the dismay engendered by the ADGB's policy of "compliance" in spring 1933 and particularly its withdrawal from the ITUF on 22 April 1933.

Abroad, too, there were sporadic instances of co-operation between Social Democratic and Communist trade unionists. But in the final analysis the United Front slogan launched by the Communist International in 1935 did not have much of an impact. Although the "Co-ordinating Committee of German Trade Unionists' was set up in France, as a parallel to Heinrich Mann's Popular Front initiative, the failure of the Popular Front experiment and, above all, the Moscow purges had killed off the co-ordinating committee by 1937–8. Mention should also be made of the working

---

25 Gerhard Beier, Die illegale Reichsleitung der Gewerkschaften 1933–1945 (Cologne 1981)

party of Free Trade Union Miners, which was set up at a meeting of the executive committee of the Miners' International in Paris. This saw, among others, Franz Vogt, Richard Kirn and Hans Mugrauer of the (Social Democratic) Old Union working alongside the Communist Wilhelm Knöchel. Vogt committed suicide following the German invasion of the Netherlands; Knöchel, who played a leading role in the reorganization of the Communist resistance in Germany in the years that followed, was arrested in 1943.

*

At the outbreak of the Second World War, many of the trade unionists who had fled Germany had to find a new home, Sweden, England and Switzerland being the major host countries.

In Sweden and England, groups of German trade unionists were set up with the primary aims of helping refugees secure the basic necessities and aiding the resistance in Germany by collecting and disseminating information. They also sought to influence the Allies' policy towards Germany, particularly by working with the unions of their adopted countries, through their own publicity work and by working with the Allied information services. The last course frequently followed the realization that the National Socialist dictatorship could only be destroyed from outside. Finally, the national groups drew up plans and programmes for building up the trade unions and reconstructing the labour market and the entire political system of the "post-Hitler era".[26]

One of the principal instances of this was the programme submitted by Fritz Tarnow in December 1941 to the "Stockholm Association of German Social Democrats", which was based on the assumption that, in rebuilding the unions after the war, it would be possible to take over the organizational structure and principles of the DAF. This idea failed to secure strong backing in Stockholm or in London, so in 1944–5 the national group of German trade unions in Sweden put forward "proposals with regard to the problems of reconstruction in Germany", based on disbanding the DAF and setting up democratic and independent trade union organizations. In 1945, the national group of German trade unionists in London, which collaborated closely with the exiled leadership of the SPD in London, drew up a plan for "The new German trade union move-

---

26 Reprinted in Ulrich Borsdorf, Hans O. Hemmer and Martin Martiny (eds), Grundlagen der Einheitsgewerkschaft. Historische Dokumente und Materialien (Cologne and Frankfurt, 1977), p. 248 ff.

ment",[27] co-written by Walter Auerbach, Willi Eichler, Hans Gottfurcht, Wilhelm Heidorn (= Werner Hansen), Hans Jahn, Ludwig Rosenberg, Erwin Schöttle and others. It proposed the setting-up of industrial unions, based on the principles of voluntary membership and political independence. In Switzerland and France, too, emigrants discussed plans for the reconstruction of the unions, though those drawn up by the London group proved to be the most influential.

*

The work of the German trade unionists in England was important preparation for the re-establishment of the trade unions after the war. But there was nothing it could do to end the war or bring down the dictatorship. This was, however, the aim of individual trade unionists, such as Wilhelm Leuschner of the Free Trade Unions and Jakob Kaiser of the Christian unions, who were in contact with the resistance groups of 22 July 1944 inside Germany. Their involvement accorded with the interests of conservative resistance groups, which sought to include the (formerly) organized workers in the planned revolt, linking them with the new state apparatus from the start and preventing the development of any revolutionary or communist movements. On the other hand, the trade unionists were well aware that they would hardly be able to put an effective end to the National Socialist regime without the backing of the armed forces, and certainly not in the face of their opposition. Despite these misgivings and the intermittent distrust of political co-operation between such disparate groups as the aristocracy, the labour movement, industry, the Church and the armed forces, they were bound together by their common grounding in Christian morality and their belief in the rule of law and social reform. It enabled them to agree on a governmental alliance for the post-coup period. In addition to Ludwig Beck and Carl Friedrich Goerdeler, other names discussed were Wilhelm Leuschner and Julius Leber (SPD) as chancellor and vice-chancellor or interior minister respectively. According to a final draft of a list of ministers dated July 1944, the Christian labour movement was to be represented in the Cabinet by Bernhard Letterhaus.

Even though representatives of the old trade union federations – Leuschner of the Free Trade Unions, Kaiser of the Christian unions and Max Habermann of the German National Union of Clerical Assistants –

---

27 Die neue deutsche Gewerkschaftsbewegung. Programmvorschläge für einen einheitlichen deutschen Gewerkschaftsbund (London, 1945), especially p. 5 ff.

took part in the deliberations of resistance circles, this did not mean that they had succeeded in pushing through the plan for a united trade union agreed in spring 1933. Goerdeler's plan for constructing a "German Trade Union" was too closely based on the reality of the DAF, and the plans of the Kreisau circle envisaged the "works community" sort of industrial harmony.

The groups that planned the attempt on Hitler's life on 20 July 1944 were united not by a common programme but by the desire to end the violent rule of the National Socialists. The attempt failed, and the people behind it had to expect the most brutal persecution. Jakob Kaiser managed to go under ground and remain in hiding to the end of the war. But Wilhelm Leuschner was arrested and sentenced to death, bequeathing to posterity the much-quoted injunction, "Create unity!"[28]

Of course, we must always remember that the National Socialist dictatorship was not overthrown by the actions of any of the resistance groups. The Third Reich perished when Germany lost the war and was occupied by the Allied troops. But the fact that there had been some resistance was tremendously important when it came to making a fresh start. And the price of resistance had been high. Thousands of men and women had been sentenced to imprisonment and hard labour, deported to concentration camps, tortured, murdered and executed. In 1936 alone, 11,687 people were detained for illegal socialist activity. At the outbreak of war there were roughly 25,000 people interned in concentration camps for political reasons; by 1942 this had risen to almost 100,000. According to official statistics at least 25,000 people were sentenced to death as political dissidents, among them trade unionists of all tendencies.[29] These sacrifices lent some credibility to the fresh start in 1945, and the resistance put up by trade unionists and the labour movement, after the impotent policy combining protest and compliance in 1933, helped justify and underline their claim to political participation in post-war German politics.

---

28 According to G. Beier, op. cit., p. 83
29 Figures from Manfred Funke, Gewerkschaften und Widerstand. Zwischen Ausharren und Orientierung auf die Zukunft, in Widerstand und Exil 1933–1945 (Bonn, 1985), pp. 60–75; see especially p. 66

Wilhelm Leuschner before the "People's Court"

X. Between hopes of reconstruction and restoration: the re-establishment of the trade unions 1945–1949

When the Second World War ended with the German capitulation of 8 May 1945, Germany and Europe lay quite literally in ruins. Casualties ran into millions. Millions of deportees, prisoners of war and concentration camp survivors were drifting about Europe. Millions of demobilized soldiers, refugees and displaced persons were seeking new homes. The overwhelming priorities after the war were providing people with food, fuel, clothing and housing.

But was the end of the war really the "zero hour" of German history? Germany was undeniably a scene of devastation, but the political and economic reconstruction of the country fell back on traditions that had survived: property, the economic structure and basic political ideas had been shaken by the downfall of National Socialism and the end of the war, but not destroyed. In addition, the advocates of a fundamental reorganization of the economy and society had to contend with the occupying powers. Germany was occupied by the troops of the victorious Allies, in quite a different way from after the First World War. It was split up into zones of occupation, with military governors initially assuming the powers of government. It was the law of the occupying forces that determined the re-establishment of the unions and the form and pace of their reconstruction.

1. *From local beginnings to national organizations*

The ideas of the occupying powers on the economic and social reconstruction of Germany and hence the importance of the trade unions left a lasting mark on the overall conditions for trade union policy in the post-war period. An idea of the Americans' aim may be derived from a statement by General Dwight D. Eisenhower on 22 December 1944, announcing that the DAF would be dissolved and – "as soon as circumstances permit" – democratic trade unions would be set up. "All forms of free economic associations and combinations of workers" would be allowed, "provided they do not have or assume political or military tendencies". So the freedom of association and collective bargaining withdrawn by the National Socialists was to be restored. Strikes and lockouts "directly or indirectly endangering military security" would be prohibited. And the "German wage arrangements currently applicable" were to remain in force.[1]

In fact, the reconstruction of the trade unions in the western zones was based on the outline conditions laid down by Eisenhower as a representative of the occupying power in control there. A succession of individual provisions was introduced that did not exactly facilitate the unions' organizational development. In many western parts of Germany, the spontaneous re-establishment of the unions had begun immediately after the arrival of the Allied troops – partly even before the capitulation of 8 May 1945. Trade unions were set up in Aachen and Cologne in March 1945 and re-appeared in Stuttgart, Hamburg and Hanover in April and May. Officially, however, the establishment of trade unions was not permitted by the Allies until after the Potsdam Conference of July–August 1945, and they had to meet specific conditions.

For all the differences in actual occupation policy, the western Allies were agreed that only local organizations would be permitted. This restriction was probably not so much the result of fears that the newly founded organization might be subverted by Communists, who would then possess a centrally controlled instrument of power. Rather, the real reason for preferring the gradual development of trade unions was suspicion that National Socialist ideas lingered on under the surface – even among the working people of Germany, a notion that was confirmed for many by recent experiences. Undoubtedly, the western Allies' ideas on organization were greatly influenced by the example of the English and American trade unions – which, indeed, sought support for their own organizational models through frequent contacts with the German trade unions – and it was these ideas that pointed the way ahead.

The response to Allied permission to set up trade unions was impressive. In the British zone alone, more than 400 applications for authorization were received between October 1945 and March 1946. The organizational principles to which the new unions adhered were as many and various as they were controversial; there was not only disagreement about division into trade associations or industrial unions but also about whether to create a unified national or general trade union or a trade union federation. But the trade union founders were agreed on one thing: distinct trade union federations divided on philosophical and party political lines were a thing of the past. Their joint failure in 1932–33, the persecution endured together and resistance mounted jointly by trade

---

1 According to Borsdorf et al., op. cit., p. 269

Hans Böckler, chairman of the German Trade Union Federation, on 11 March 1950, delivering a speech to 4,000 workers opposing the dismantling of plant

unionists of formerly separate federations virtually ruled out any alternative to the idea of a united federation after 1945. It may have been easier to push through as a result of the experience of the all-pervading organizational approach adopted by the DAF. The men behind the re-establishment of the unions – from Hans Böckler in the Rhineland and Westphalia and Willi Richter in Hessen to Erhard Kupfer and Lorenz Hagen in Bavaria – were in agreement in learning a lesson from German trade union history and opting for the unified trade union.

Hans Böckler was a particularly important figure in German trade unionism, albeit only for a few years. From his background it would have been difficult to predict Böckler's rise to the head of the DGB in 1949. Born in 1875 in Trautskirchen, the son of a coachman, he learnt the trade of a gold and silver-beater and joined the DMV (and the SPD) in 1894. In 1903 he became DMV secretary for the Saar district, then in Frankfurt, and in 1910 he was appointed area head for Silesia. Wounded out of the army in 1916, he returned to the DMV and became secretary of the ZAG in Berlin. When the DMV left the ZAG, he went to Cologne as a authorized representative of the DMV and in 1927 he became ADGB area chairman in Düsseldorf. In May 1928 he was elected into the Reichstag. In 1933 he was several times put into "protective custody" but managed to survive the war relatively unharmed, despite his contacts with the resistance. His finest hour came in the post-war period during the re-establishment of the trade unions.

*

While the western Allies were agreed on the fundamentals of their trade union policy, there were marked differences in the development of trade union organization from zone to zone, as a result of the differing policies of the occupying powers.

The establishment of trade unions was permitted in the British zone from 6 August 1945. But the further development of the unions was subject to a three-phase plan – as finally laid down in Industrial Relations Directive No. 10 – whereby the trade unions would initially draft programmes and projects and hold their first meetings at local level only. In the second phase, that of "provisional development", rooms could be rented and members recruited. Lastly, the growth phase would allow officials to be elected and trade union work resumed. Transition from one phase to the next had to be supervised and approved by the military government. The British thus ensured that they would be able to keep a check on developments and object if necessary.

This frustrated trade union efforts to achieve centralization as rapidly as possible, completely blocking the central or general trade unions that had sprung up in Saxony and were preferred by Hans Böckler. The occupying power and the English trade unions made it clear to the union leaders in the British zone that they were not amenable to the plan for a central united trade union, only to the principle of a federation of industrial unions. The fact that there was a basis for this idea in German trade union history certainly facilitated its implementation. So, for the time being at least, it was independent individual trade unions that finally set up the German Trade Union Federation for the British zone in Bielefeld on 22–25 April 1947; Hans Böckler was elected its head.

While centralization in the British zone culminated in a federation covering the whole zone, things turned out rather differently in the American zone. Here, too, progress was made in steps but led, in late August 1946 and late March 1947, to the setting-up of provincial federations based on the Länder: the Free Trade Union Federation of Hessen (24–25 August 1946), the Trade Union Federation of Baden-Württemberg (30 August–1 September 1946) and the Bavarian Trade Union Federation (27–29 March 1947). The unions did not press for a body covering the whole zone to avoid granting formal recognition to the zone boundaries. The position was similar in the French zone, where provincial trade union federations were set up in South Württemberg and Hohenzollern (15–16 February 1947), Baden (1–2 March 1947) and the Rhineland-Palatinate (2–3 May 1947)

In the Soviet zone, in contrast, the construction of trade unions proceeded quite rapidly. On 10 June 1945, the Soviet military administration's Order No. 2 granted the right to form trade unions (and political parties). This was followed in February 1946 by the establishment of the Free German Trade Union Federation (FDGB). We cannot, however, trace the history of this national organization here, owing to the quite separate conception of trade unions and differing overall conditions for union work in the Soviet zone, later the German Democratic Republic (GDR).

*

Restricting ourselves to the western occupation zones, we find that recruitment of new members varied greatly from one zone to another. The strongest union federation was the one in the British zone, where almost 2.8 m workers were organized by 1948, that is, 42 per cent of the working population. In the same year the American zone had 1.6 m trade unionists, and the French zone only 385,000 – 38 per cent and 30 per cent unionization respectively.

The trade unions embarked on a wide variety of organizational activities remarkably early, long before the creation of a union federation embracing all the western zones. As early as 1946, the Institute of Economic Science was created, at the instigation of Hans Böckler; its task was to provide the unions with expert advice and provide scientific support for its arguments. 1947 saw the launch of the Gutenberg Book Guild and the trade union-run Bund-Verlag publishing house. The same year saw the foundation of the Social Academy, sponsored jointly by the state of North Rhine-Westphalia, the city of Dortmund and the trade unions, and the Ruhr Festival in Recklinghausen took place for the first time. In 1948 the Hamburg Academy for Co-operative Economy, which later gave rise to the College of Economics and Politics, was set up by the city of Hamburg, the co-operatives and the DGB. The next year, the trade unions and the folk high schools decided to create a joint system for education and training, "Arbeit und Leben" (Work and Life), initially in Lower Saxony. In 1949–50, in collaboration with the co-operative movement, the unions established the co-operative banks at provincial (state) level; these later merged to become the Bank für Gemeinwirtschaft (Bank for Co-operative Economy).

*

Despite the restrictions imposed by the occupying powers, trade unionists persisted in trying to organize co-operation across zone boundaries. On 6 November 1947, the Economic Council for the American and British Zones was formed, joined on 20 December 1948 by the Trade Union Council of the French zone.

Efforts to form a trade union merger were at their most evident in the inter-zone conferences of the trade unions of all four zones. From mid-1946 to mid-1948 unionists met at nine conferences (not counting the first inter-zone meeting in Frankfurt am Main on 13–14 July 1946) to ensure the cohesion of the organization, to discuss fundamental policy matters and prevent the partition of Germany. These inter-zone conferences were encouraged by the World Federation of Trade Unions (WFTU), which had demanded that a nationwide German trade union organization be set up as a condition of membership. On the key issues of post-war politics, the trade unions of all zones were able to reach a large measure of agreement.[2]

---

2 The texts of the resolutions are reprinted in Versprochen – Gebrochen. Die Interzonenkonferenzen der deutschen Gewerkschaften von 1946–1948, hrsg. vom Bundesvorstand des DGB (Düsseldorf, undated) p. 163 ff.

The resolutions contain declarations on works councils, consistent denazification, the standardization of social insurance, wages and the expected peace treaty. Agreement was also reached in February 1947 on fundamental principles for the "development of the German trade unions" – industrial unions, party political neutrality and religious tolerance. This resolution was completed by detailed consideration of the problems of organizing women and white-collar workers.

The main focus of these discussions was, however, on matters relating to the "reorganization of the economy". In May 1947 the trade unions agreed on the following demands: restoration of the economic and political unity of Germany; socialization of the key industries, banks and insurance companies; the development of a planned and directed economy, with a central planning authority and self-management bodies with trade union participation; the raising of output and a stop to the dismantling of plant; the drafting of an import and export plan; land reform and the presentation of an agricultural plan; and a single currency and financial reform for all Germany.

These reorganization plans thus comprised the essentials of a nationwide trade union programme. Like the justification given for the trade unions' demand for co-determination, these plans for reshaping the economy laid particular emphasis on the prevailing distress and the experiences of the recent past. The unions' concern "that the reactionary and military forces that were chiefly responsible for the Hitler regime and the war, with their deep roots in monopoly capitalism and the administration, are in part holding on to their positions or trying to win them back" seemed to give more force to their demands.

Like the "resolution on the political position of the trade unions and their relations with the political parties", the principles underlying the "reorganization of the economy" gave a good idea of the trade unions' self-image – anti-Fascist and anti-militarist. "It is the duty of the new German trade unions to give an economic and political lead in restoring a united Germany by rebuilding the economy, social legislation and a new cultural life," stated the final, unanimously adopted resolution of the inter-zonal conference of February 1948.

With the disagreements over assistance under the Marshall Plan and the drifting apart of the blocs, the borders between which bisected Germany, the burgeoning East-West conflict affected the trade union movement. At the eighth inter-zonal conference in May 1948, the representatives of the FDGB rejected the Marshall Plan, which the west German trade union federations supported. Though there was a final inter-zonal conference in August 1948 – after the June 1948 currency reform in the western zones and after the blockade of Berlin had started – the trade unions were not able or willing to resist the pressure of the blocs to which they were attached. The ninth inter-zonal conference on 17–18 August 1948 came to grief – to outward appearances – over the issue of the participation of the Berlin opposition, which had split off from the FDGB that June and set itself up as the Independent Trade Union Organization (UGO) on 14 August. But this was only the pretext for the breach, which had already emerged in protracted debates about decisions of principle on trade union policy in the shadow of the Cold War. The ultimate cause was, however, the differing concepts of social order in East and West, the incompatibility of which was felt, above all, by the (West) Berlin trade unions, which had clearly opted for the model of western, parliamentary democracy.

The Cold War also had an impact on efforts to rebuild the international trade union movement. The World Federation of Trade Unions, founded in Paris in October 1945, was joined in 1949 – owing to the domination of the Communists in the latter – by the rival International Confederation of Free Trade Unions (ICFTU), to which the unions of 52 countries, including the Federal Republic of Germany, belonged.

2. *Trade union work under occupation law*

Anyone who expected to see the prompt rebirth of the trade unions as democratic mass organizations was disappointed. Once again – just as under the Kaiser – the unions were forced into the role of local and regional organizations as a way of curbing their development. Along with other problems such as travel restrictions, poor postal, telephone and transport services and the lack of newspapers, this was a major obstacle to union work, which combined action to relieve acute distress with ambitious reorganization objectives.

The main concerns of union work in the immediate post-war period were determined by the dismal situation, of which unemployment, a housing shortage and hunger were the chief features. The unions sought to prevent the dismantling of plant, to contribute to economic reconstruction and provide the people with food, clothing, fuel and housing. Many entrepreneurs, compromised by their activities as "leaders of the economy" in the National Socialist state, had gone under ground or were interned, so that in a number of companies unions and works councils took the job of restarting production into their own hands. They led clearance work, organized repairs and arranged supplies of raw materials and orders.

The west German economy had been badly damaged by the war, by remorseless war production and bombing, but its core survived. In view of the difficult conditions of the post-war period, however, production was slow to get going. Plant had been destroyed or worn out, raw materials were lacking, and the productivity of the workforce was low, exhausted as it was by the war and war production. Matters were made worse by the fact that conversion from wartime to peacetime production ran into considerable difficulties, especially lack of purchasing power to sustain demand.

In addition, Allied objectives had to be taken into account. Chief among them was the endeavour to curb the German economy to prevent it competing on the world market and, in particular, to prevent it from re-emerging as a military threat.

In the Potsdam Agreement of August 1945, the Allies had agreed on the "elimination of the present over-concentration in the economy" of Germany[3]; this resulted in the confiscation of the major economic enterprises, which were to be "unbundled" and re-formed as smaller economic units. Further, certain areas of the economy such as iron and steel were placed under Allied control. Finally, the occupying powers were to be entitled to compensation for war damage by dismantling German industrial plant and also in the form of goods taken out of current production.

The first industrial plan drawn up by the Allied Control Council in March 1946 limited German industrial output to 55 per cent of the 1938 figure; 1,800 companies were to be dismantled. After tough negotiations in which the unions teamed up with the owners in opposing the policy of dismantlement, as it destroyed jobs and production alike, the number of firms destined for dismantling was cut to 682. In the years that followed, the trade unions continued to press for an end to dismantling and for the formation of viable enterprises when large concerns such as IG Farben were dismembered.

But the Allies not only proceeded to put their economic objectives into practice; in 1945–46 a number of directives were issued exerting a decisive influence on industrial relations and hence the narrower sphere of trade union policy. Freedom of association, labour courts, the arbitration service, works councils and the standard eight-hour day were all restored. But wages were frozen at the level of 8 May 1945, thus depriving the trade unions of one of its prime fields of action.

---

3 Official Journal of the Control Council for Germany, ed. by the Allied Secretariat (undated), Supplement No. 1, German section, p. 13 ff.

Trümmerfrauen (women of the ruins) came to symbolize the desire for re-construction after the war

The wage freeze policy was partly to blame for the decline in real wages as the value of money fell steadily. Wage earners had nothing to offer on the black market, whether buying or bartering. They had to rely on the food ration, which was often below subsistence level. By the end of 1945, the official ration gave 1,200 – 1,500 calories per day; United Nations experts, however, calculated that the minimum requirement was 2,650 calories. Allied restrictions on trade union work and the general poverty led many people to seek individual solutions: hoarding trips, vegetable gardening and the quest for better-paid jobs (with wages partly in kind) were some of the ways of improving the situation. Competition between wage earners and those seeking work certainly did little to promote the development of the unions. In the minds of large sections of the population, trade unions played a minor role, all the more so as the traditional conflict between capital and labour had been obscured by the clash of interest with the occupying power. In attempting to find solutions to problems such as the wage freeze, food shortages and the mass unemployment that lasted until 1949–50, it was not the employers but the occupying powers, presently followed by the German authorities, who were considered the proper quarter to address.

*

But the trade unions of the post-war period did not suffocate in the daily grind of union work, which placed an enormous strain on them, with the reconstruction of the organizations on the one hand, and the relief of acute social distress on the other. In fact, trade union demands aimed at a fundamentally new order of things: the denazification of state and economy, the transfer of key industries into public ownership, co-determination and economic planning – it was with these objectives in mind that the unions advocated the re-shaping of society in 1945. The fact that this list of demands did not contain any potentially explosive issues as far as the emergent "unified unions" (*Einheitsgewerkschaften*) were concerned was partly because these goals were common to most of the major political groupings – the SPD, KPD, and also sections of the CDU. In its Ahlen programme of February 1947, the CDU of the British zone considered the "age of the unrestricted rule of capitalism" over and conceded the need to "socialize the primary industries, iron and coal".[4]

---

4 Reprinted in Dokumente zur parteipolitischen Entwicklung in Deutschland seit 1945, Vol. 2, Part 1 (Berlin, 1963), p. 52 f.

The lesson of the past seemed obvious. At the first trade union conference in the British zone in March 1946, Hans Böckler declared, "What happened to the German workers in 1920–21 shall not occur again – that in spite of their honest efforts they ultimately end up being deceived once again." And he drew the conclusion, "We must be represented on a completely equal footing in the economy; not only on the individual bodies of the economy, not in the chambers of the economy alone, but in the economy as a whole. So our plan is: seats on the managing and supervisory boards of the companies."[5] Accordingly, the introduction of co-determination at concern level and the improvement of the old Works Councils Law of 1920 were demanded.

Erich Potthoff, head of the DGB's Institute for Economic Science from 1946 to 1949 and from 1952 to 1956, doubtless spoke for many of his contemporaries when he observed at the British zone trade union conference in Bielefeld in August 1946, "The collapse of the National Socialist regime signified the collapse of the capitalist economy as a whole."[6] In 1945–46 there was a widespread belief that basically there was no need any longer to fight for the trade unions' ambitious goals – it would suffice to give them legal form and then have them passed by the parliaments.

Co-determination and socialization were the key concepts in the unions' demands for the "reorganization of the economy", and the issue of co-determination had two levels: corporate and supra-corporate.

Post-war ideas on co-determination showed a greater concern with the company level than had been the case in the 1920s. This was at least partly the result of experience in the Weimar period, when the trade unions, despite programme declarations to the contrary, rarely entrenched their policies in the companies. But after 1945 the situation was different. Although works councils had proved their worth in reconstruction, in getting production going again and in questions of supply, the structural tensions between workplace representation and trade union policy grew worse for many wage earners, not least because of heavy Communist representation. Moreover, the western occupying powers, who through the Allied Control Council had provided a legal basis for the activities of the works councils formed immediately after the war, regarded an active works council policy with suspicion precisely because they feared a growth in Communist influence.

5 Die Gewerkschaftsbewegung in der britischen Besatzungszone, Geschäftsbericht des Deutschen Gewerkschaftsbundes (britische Besatzungszone), 1947–1949 (Cologne, 1949), p. 79
6 Erich Potthoff in Protokoll der Gewerkschaftskonferenz der britischen Zone vom 21. bis 23. 8. 1946 in Bielefeld (Bielefeld, undated), p. 10

The union demand for democratization of the economy could certainly be traced back to the ideas of the Weimar period. But alongside the goal of a supra-corporate co-determination arrangement, from 1947–48 on attention increasingly focused on the idea of co-determination at company level. The legal introduction of co-determination was considered a matter of urgency, as it was assumed that it would not be possible to push through socialization (the unions' real aim) immediately after the war. The chance to secure rights of co-determination came along with the first positive action by the British military government to break up the cartels. The unions believed that with the introduction of bipartite co-determination in the iron and steel industry the first step had been taken towards the democratization of the economy. They failed to see that the offers put forward by the employers in early 1947 to grant bipartite co-determination were also – and primarily – designed to secure trade union support for opposition to the Allies' plans for dismantling plant and breaking up the large corporations. Concessions over co-determination were also intended to avert worker discontent, thus leaving calls for socialization to peter out.

In fact, for a while it did look as though demands for socialization, for example, might be met. In 1946–47 the possibility of expropriations by the state was written into several of the regional constitutions. But it soon turned out that the unions did not have the expected backing of the political parties nor, crucially, of the occupying powers. The Truman doctrine of March 1947 and the failure of the foreign ministers' London conference in December 1947 clearly showed that Germany was split in two by the boundary between two different and mutually hostile social systems. The western zones and the Soviet zone thereby took their allotted places in the military and political blocs.

It was a natural consequence of American thinking on the economy, in particular, that socialization plans and laws were doomed to fail. For instance, the law passed by the regional parliament of North Rhine-Westphalia, implementing the socialization article of the regional constitution, to bring the mining industry into public ownership was suspended by the military governor of the "Bi-zone" in September 1948. The occupying powers (and many German politicians with them) maintained that socialization was a matter for federal law that could only be settled after the establishment of a west German state.

*

As early as autumn 1946, the miners had refused to work special shifts. Widespread worker discontent with the food situation, and also with the delays in meeting demands for the reorganization of the economy, erupted in April–May 1947 into demonstrations and strikes in the Ruhr district. Tens of thousands of workers underlined their demand for better food supplies and immediate socialization. With their 24-hour strike on 3 April 1947, the miners also marked their support for the "just control and distribution of available food supplies" under trade union supervision, for "backyard controls", for severe punishments for black marketeers and spivs and for socialization – particularly of the mines.[7]

Protests of this kind were condemned not only by the military administration but also by the trade unions. On 10 April 1947 the conference of trade unions of the American zone unanimously adopted a declaration protesting against further cuts in food rations and expressing fears that "in the event of further cuts the peace and discipline that have hitherto prevailed among the workers cannot be guaranteed", though they did not see "taking strike action" as "an appropriate means of improving the present food situation".[8] True to this view, the trade unions refused to give their backing to the wave of strikes in the winter and spring of 1948. A single pay rise of 15 per cent in April 1948, sanctioned by the Allied Control Council, was intended to take the wind out of the strikers' sails.

The trade unions were neither willing nor able to resist the trend towards the stabilization of economic conditions. Although they must have realized that Marshall Aid was designed to strengthen private capitalism and would exacerbate the economic and political divisions in Germany, the German representatives at the international trade union conference of March 1948 approved the European Recovery Program – that is, the Marshall Plan. After heated debate, the extraordinary congress of the trade union federation of the British zone, which met in Recklinghausen from 16 to 18 June 1948, adopted the same position. The intimate link between American economic aid and the stabilization of private capitalism was evidently underestimated – or accepted – by the trade unions.

The collapse of the socialization plans and disappointment at the consequences of the currency reform caused the trade unions to change course for a while. By the currency reform of 20 June 1948 liquid assets and debts

7 Quot. Anne Weiss-Hartmann and Wolfgang Hecker, Die Entwicklung der Gewerkschaftsbewegung 1945–1949, in F. Deppe, G. Fülberth and J. Harrer (eds), Geschichte der deutschen Gewerkschaftsbewegung (Cologne, 1977), pp. 272–319; this quot. p. 295 f.
8 Quot. ibid., p. 297 f.

were devalued at the rate of 100 to 6.5 and 100 to 10 respectively; individuals were paid 40 Marks each, followed by another 20 Marks later; firms received a business grant of 60 Marks per employee. This procedure alone clearly discriminated in favour of those who owned material assets. On top of this, on 25 June 1948 price controls on most goods were abolished, though the wage freeze in the Bi-zone was maintained until 3 November 1948 – another redistribution of wealth detrimental to wage earners. The cost of living rose by 17 per cent in the second half of 1948; unemployment doubled, reaching a million. The shops filled with goods after the currency reform, demonstrating that the disastrous shortages of yesterday had not always been due to a genuine scarcity of goods but often to hoarding and production cuts with a view to the imminent reform.

Calls by the trade unions and the SPD for some of the burden to be lifted from the wage earners went unheeded. Principally out of resentment at this situation, the trade union council of the Bi-zone decided in October 1948 to prepare for a general strike. The aims of the strike were, firstly, the repeal of the provisions of the currency reform that were felt to discriminate unfairly in favour of holders of material assets and the introduction of a system of financial compensation that benefited wage earners, and secondly, the implementation of economic democracy. Internal union dissension, in combination with the intervention of the military governors, restricted the strike on 12 November 1948 to a symbolic 24-hour walkout in the American and British zones, with 9.25 m workers taking part out of a total of 11.7 m. A strike ban was enforced in the French zone.

*

Political differences in the leading trade union bodies and Allied restrictions prevented the unions from asserting their organizational strength in 1947–48. Economic unity in the western zones, the currency reform and the Marshall Plan were all implemented without trade union involvement. When dismantling was finally stopped in 1950 it was due more to efforts to integrate the Federal Republic into the West against the background of the Cold War than to trade union pressure. The calls for reorganization of the economy also went unheeded – apart from passages to that effect in some of the regional constitutions of 1946–47 – after the US Government had thrown its weight behind the view that radical changes in social policy should only be tackled after the formation of a German central government.

Certainly, there was such a thing as a socialist mood in 1946–47. Even the CDU policies of those years had a strong social tinge – for instance, the call for a "true Christian socialism" in the Cologne principles of June 1945, the call for the transfer of large-scale industry and the major banks into public ownership in the Frankfurt principles of September 1945 and, lastly, the above-mentioned Ahlen programme of February 1947, drawn up by the CDU in North Rhine-Westphalia. However, this phase of strong pressure for social reform was short-lived, and had passed by the time the Marshall Plan was implemented. Misgivings about Communist experimentation and any form of state control or "dirigisme" were reinforced by the picture of the economic and social reorganization measures taken in the Soviet zone. These reservations were subsequently confirmed by the economic upturn that followed the currency reform, which was seen as a success for the market economy. The idea of the "social market economy" advocated by Ludwig Erhard (CDU) was based on the following neo-liberal principles: private ownership of the means of production and entrepreneurial initiative were to be retained and encouraged; the "social component" was to be ensured, firstly, by the law of the market (supply and demand regulating prices) and, secondly, by means of "market-oriented" state control measures, from the company statute and controls on monopolies to social policy.

＊

Discussions on the Basic Law (Grundgesetz) were also affected by the political *Zeitgeist* of the late 1940s. On the basis of the "London recommendations" of December 1947, the west German regional parliaments set up a parliamentary council to draw up the constitution. Vital decisions of principle had already been taken by the Frankfurt Bi-zone economic council set up in June 1947, which consolidated the idea of the "social market economy" popularized by Ludwig Erhard with economic and financial action. Trade unionists were not represented. The SPD, which had not managed to secure its candidate a director's post, retreated into an oppositional role. The Social Democratic Party and the trade unions not only underestimated the influence of the Economic Council as a "quasi-parliament" but also the importance of constitutional deliberations; several times they shelved their demands in the social sphere and their ideas on reorganization, believing that the Basic Law was of a provisional character only.

For this reason, trade union views on the constitution (which were anyway limited) were not put in any emphatic way. It was chiefly Böckler, at the head of the Trade Union Federation of the British zone, who supported the establishment of the right of association and the principle of the social state in the form of a Basic Law. The 38-point declaration, "On the constitutional question", which initially summarized the DGB's demands in the British zone with regard to the regional constitution of North Rhine-Westphalia, was also the basis for its stance on the discussions on the Basic Law. This set of demands included formal recognition of the right to work, the right of association and right to strike, the transfer of primary industries to public ownership and a guaranteed minimum wage.[9] Böckler reiterated these constitutional demands in a letter to Konrad Adenauer, the president of the Parliamentary Council in Bonn. But it did not seem necessary to mobilize the workers behind these aims, simply because the unions and the SPD believed that the SPD would win a majority in the forthcoming *Bundestag* elections, enabling it to put the ideas of both organizations into effect by using the law.

Once again the expectations of the unions proved to be illusory, in more ways than one. The Basic Law adopted by the Parliamentary Council on 8 May 1949 did not turn out to be the constitution of a short-lived provisional set-up; it laid down the ground rules that determined the long-term framework of trade union activity. Article 9.3, for example, stated: "The right to form associations to protect and improve working and economic conditions is guaranteed for everyone and for all professions." Other provisions of particular importance to trade union work – apart from the overall provisions of the Basic Law – are the requirement to use property for the common good (Article 14.2), the permissibility of expropriation for the public good (Articles 14.3 and 15) and the definition of the Federal Republic as a democratic and social federal state under the rule of law (Articles 20.1 and 28.1). The implications of the emergency constitution and the jurisdiction of the Federal Labour Court for the law on industrial relations are dealt with below.

Hopes of an SPD victory in the Bundestag elections of 14 August 1949 were dashed. With 29.2 per cent of the vote, the SPD could not even attract one third of the electorate. A coalition government consisting of the CDU/CSU, Free Democratic Party (FDP) and the German Party (DP) was formed, with Konrad Adenauer as Chancellor and Ludwig Erhard as Economics Minister. It did not have a reputation for excessive friendliness towards the trade unions.

---

9 Die Gewerkschaftsbewegung in der britischen Besatzungszone, p. 343 ff.

3. *The foundation of the German Trade Union Federation*

The formation of the Trade Union Federation in the British zone, the regional unions in the American and French zones and the Trade Union Council for all three zones marked the end of the reconstruction of the unions during the years under occupation law. The principle of the unified union had carried the day – though only in the sense that the split into federations of different political tendencies had been superseded. Another principle that had gained acceptance was the principle rooted in the German tradition and encouraged by the Allies of the federate combination of independent industrial or trade unions, in which manual and white-collar workers and officials were organized together. If one regards centralization and organization as helping to strengthen union power, this was a major advance on the movement's earlier division into politically based federations and its fragmentation by trade and status during the Weimar period.

But as early as 1946–47 there were signs that these plans for unified unions might be frustrated, with efforts to set up separate unions for white-collar workers and civil servants instead of organizing them alongside the workers. This was undoubtedly partly due to the fact that the immediate post-war years saw a growth in influence of those white-collar workers within the German Salaried Employees' Union (DAG) who had formerly belonged to non-Social Democratic organizations. Though these groups did not dominate, they clearly expressed the special mentality of many white-collar workers. In April 1946, the "DAG-Post" answered the question of why a separate white-collar union was needed by referring to the wishes of the employees themselves, to the special law on salaried staff and the special interests of white-collar workers, who were demanding their own organizations.[10]

There were thus no party political or ideological considerations behind the fact that the DAG disengaged itself from the process of forming a unified nationwide umbrella organization. In fact, in subsequent years there were several instances of joint positions and actions by all the trade unions, including the DAG. In the talks on the unification of the trade union movement in the western zones, the unified unions offered the DAG a concession by proposing that white-collar workers in commerce, the banks, insurance companies, publishing houses etc. should be organized in a union of their own; but otherwise the principle of industrial

---

10 Warum Angestelltengewerkschaften, in DAG-Post No. 12 of 29 April 1946, p. 3

unions had to be respected. When this was rejected by the DAG, with an eye to the white-collar workers in other areas of the economy, the breach was complete. As some groups of civil servants were also insisting on separate organizations, the foundation of the German Trade Union Federation (DGB) in October 1949 did not unite all the unions set up after the war; although it eliminated the feud between federations of different tendencies, it did not quite succeed in overcoming differences of professional status.

∗

From 12 to 14 October 1949, the DGB held its constitutive congress in Munich. Sixteen industrial unions got together under a single umbrella organization: Construction, Stone and Earth; Mining and Power; Chemicals, Paper, Ceramics; Printing and Paper; Railwaymen; Education and Science; Horticulture, Agriculture and Forestry; Commerce, Banking and Insurance; Wood and Plastics; Art; Leather; Engineering; Food and Beverage; Public Services, Transport and Communications; Postal workers; Textiles and Clothing.

The DGB's organizational structure, as adopted in 1949, was supposed to be permanent. What did it look like? And how much has survived?

Since 1949-50 the DGB – like the individual unions – has covered the territory of the Federal Republic and West Berlin and is organized into three levels: the federal, regional and local levels.

Supreme authority is vested in the federal congress, for which the delegates of the affiliated unions assemble every three years. The number of delegates depends on the numerical strength of the unions. The highest ranking body between congresses is the federal committee, which meets quarterly and consists of the federal executive (25 members), the nine regional chairmen and 100 representatives of the unions. Each union received at least two (now three) seats for the first 300,000 of its members; after that, seats were allocated in accordance with each union's size – one delegate for every 300,000 members.

The federal executive, which meets once a month, consists of the chairmen of the individual unions and the nine-man federal management committee, which in turn consists of the federation's chairman, two vice-chairmen and six other members. The DGB's constitutive congress in 1949 elected Hans Böckler chairman by 397 votes out of 474.

Nine regions form the DGB's next level, structurally a theoretical parallel to the federal level; the regional bodies are the regional conferences and the regional executives. The former regional federations gave rise to the following regions: Baden-Württemberg, Bavaria, Hessen, Lower Saxony (including Bremen), Nordmark (Schleswig-Holstein and Hamburg), North Rhine-Westphalia and Rhineland-Palatinate; not until 1950 did the UGO join the DGB, as the Berlin region; the Saar region followed in 1957 after the Saarland was handed back to Germany. The unification of Germany in 1990/91 will bring more regions into the organization.

Just as the regions largely correspond to the *Länder,* the DGB areas are coterminous with the local authorities; at this level, trade union work is directed by meetings of area delegates and the area executive.

From the point of view of organizational uniformity it is certainly a cosmetic flaw that the industrial union concept was not consistently applied, particularly in the public service area, which in addition to the Public Service, Transport and Communications Union, is also covered by the Postal Workers, the Railwaymen and Education and Science, as well as the Police Union, which joined the DGB at a later stage. It should also be remembered that there are other, autonomous unions such as the DAG and the German Civil Servants' Union (DBB), which detract from the DGB's image as the sole, all-embracing trade union federation. Moreover, it was not long before Christian unions were set up once more (1955-56), a fact which illustrates the DGB's difficulties in persuading people of the credibility of its claim to be independent of political parties.

The DGB is thus a federation of 16 industrial trade unions seeking to put into effect the principle of "one company – one union". The individual unions are autonomous and independent, that is, they have their own rules, manage their own finances and formulate their own policy guidelines at their own congresses. The umbrella organization initially received 15 per cent of the individual member unions' dues (soon reduced to 12 per cent) to discharge its duties.

In 1949, the individual unions affiliated to the DGB had over 4.9 m members, though they were very unevenly distributed among the unions. There were huge industrial unions such as IG Metall, the engineering union, with 1.35 m members, alongside small organizations such as the Art Union with its 42,000 members.[11] There were unions with more than a thousand full-time officials and staff, such as IG Metall, alongside those with less than a hundred, such as the Leather Union. Together, the 16

---

11 Figures taken from Protokoll. Gründungskongress des DGB, München, 12–14 October 1949 (Cologne, 1950), p. 282

unions maintained a total of 1,073 administrative offices with a staff of 4,749 – 167 of whom worked for the DGB's federal executive.[12]

In view of the differences in size between the unions, it was not surprising that their financial resources also differed greatly. This not only affected the level of benefits they were able to offer but also their ability to engage in information and publicity work. For this reason, the smaller unions, in particular, welcomed the DGB's readiness to build up a strong union press, the main features of which were laid down in 1949-50. January 1950 saw the publication of the weekly "Welt der Arbeit", whose circulation quickly topped 100,000; the same month also saw the first issues of the officials' journal "Die Quelle" and the forum for theoretical discussion called "Gewerkschaftliche Monatshefte". For young people there was "Aufwärts"; for female wage earners, "Frauen und Arbeit"; for white-collar workers "Wirtschaft und Wissen" and for civil servants "Der Deutsche Beamte". These were followed in 1952 by "Soziale Sicherheit", a periodical on social policy, and "Arbeit und Recht", the periodical on industrial law.

*

It was of decisive significance for the policy statements adopted by the Munich congress in October 1949 that the essential decisions on the social foundations of the Federal Republic of Germany, established just a few months earlier, had already been taken. The balance of political power was also apparent following the *Bundestag* elections of August 1949, allowing the trade unions to relapse into their familiar role of petitioner, with no real chance to influence or shape developments. And yet the congress speeches and resolutions revealed an unmistakable confidence.

This was apparent in Hans Böckler's address on "The tasks of the German trade unions in the economy, state and society", in which he made a number of current demands: higher wages, shorter working hours, a cut in unemployment and the speeding-up of house-building – these were the "tasks" he assigned to the trade unions. Over and above this, he mapped out the unions' economic and socio-political principles, which were adopted in programme form by the congress. Rooted in the demand that political democracy had to be completed and protected by economic democracy, the "DGB Programme" on economic policy advocated co-de-

---

12 According to Geschäftsbericht des Bundesvorstandes des DGB 1950–1951 (Düsseldorf, undated), p. 55 ff.

termination, the transfer of key industries into public ownership and central economic planning.[13]

The principles put forward in Munich did not, it is true, constitute a comprehensive trade union programme by the standards of later "programmes of principle". Rather, they represented an attempt to point the way ahead in some major areas of trade union work, where it was necessary to impose a measure of social control on the newly established market economy. In view of the relative strengths of the parties in the Bundestag and the deterrent effect of developments in the GDR, it is scarcely surprising that the DGB's ideas on socialization and the planned economy were never achieved.

4. *The post-war period – a "wasted opportunity"?*

The years between the end of the Second World War and the creation of the Federal Republic brought a succession of decisions, the effects of which are still felt today: reconstruction on the basis of a private capitalist, market economy, the foundation of a parliamentary democracy and the partition of Germany with each of the resulting states tied to one of the power blocs. The trade unions did not manage to push through a reorganization of the economy and a guarantee for their own rights, especially the right to strike, before the Basic Law was passed. Because of the hopes they pinned on the SPD and a good showing by the party in the first elections for the *Bundestag,* the unions were rather too restrained in influencing the discussions on the Basic Law. They failed to realized that the crucial work in creating a new order had to be accomplished before the adoption of the constitution, that the Basic Law would only perpetuate the status quo and that their demands for a "social state" were destined to remain just that – demands. It should be borne in mind that the unions only became centralized (with the creation of the DGB) when the overall conditions governing their policies had already been established – even the formation of the Adenauer government. More than anything, it was the Cold War that reduced the chances of a policy of reform as desired by the unions and the SPD. For it not only entailed the rejection of the GDR but also discredited all socialist-influenced ideas on reconstruction in the internal arguments about social policy.

---

13 Protokoll. Gründungskongress des Deutschen Gewerkschaftsbundes, München, 12.–14. Oktober 1949 (Cologne, 1950), pp. 318–26

Can it be said, then, that in the post-war years the unions missed their opportunity to put their ideas on reorganization into effect? By the standards of the unions' own pretensions and the anti-capitalist mood of large sections of the population in 1945-46, one's initial instinct is to answer in the affirmative. But what real chances did the unions have of pushing through their plans under occupation law? They could not force their ideas for reorganization through against the wishes of the occupying powers. Though the British Labour Government may have shown understanding for the unions' plans, in view of their own financial dependence they were neither willing nor able to defy the Americans, to whom any moves in the direction of a "social state" were quite alien; and the French Government was chiefly concerned with safeguarding its own security interests.

And anyway how high should one rate the workers' readiness and stamina for large-scale industrial action, in view of the disastrous food situation? Putting the list of demands in order of priority, the acute problems were certainly more important, and the short duration of the strikes of 1947-48 speaks for itself. To make matters worse, strikes expressly directed against the measures of the occupying powers would have been very risky.

The final question which needs asking is this: will the balance-sheet of trade union policy in the post-war period not bear scrutiny if assessed against objectives such as safeguarding the working class against social risks and the construction of a democratic state? The answer to this question must be sought in the history of the Federal Republic.

XI. Social successes and political defeats: the trade unions in the years of the "economic miracle" 1950–1965

The currency reform and especially the effects of the "Korea boom" on the West German economy triggered an economic upturn of unexpected proportions. The integration of the Federal Republic into the West, the intensification of the Cold War and above all the "economic miracle" of the 1950s determined the social and political conditions for the policy of the trade unions, which at the start of this phase made yet another attempt to put into effect their ideas on democratizing the economy.

1. The disputes over the Law on Co-determination in the Coal and Steel Industry and the Company Statute Law

Ever since the economic democracy programme of the 1920s it had been one of the basic assumptions of trade union policy that the "democratization of political life" – to quote the "Economic Policy Principles" of 1949 – "must be complemented by the democratization of the economy". Repeated references were made to the fact "that in 1933 a surprise seizure of state power was able to succeed because the democratic constitutional form remained devoid of living substance, ossified into a bloodless formula, while the economic life of the country was able to imbue its very real power structure with new vigour daily". The experience of the destruction of political democracy in 1933 was considered the most important argument in favour of abolishing "unenlightened absolutism" in the economy.[1]

The employers in heavy industry – threatened by dismantling of plant, expropriation and break-up – had offered the unions participation in management early in 1947, and the British military government had introduced co-determination in the iron and steel industry in their zone in March 1947. Shortly after the foundation of the Federal Republic it turned out that these co-determination provisions would neither be secured nor extended "automatically", as it were. But in return for their

---

1 Viktor Agartz and Erich Potthoff, Die Mitbestimmung der Arbeitnehmer in der Wirtschaft (December 1949, duplicated)

assent to the Marshall Plan and their cautiously favourable position on rearmament (in contrast to the SPD under the chairmanship of Kurt Schumacher) the unions, led by Hans Böckler, basically expected concessions by the governing majority in shaping the economic and social systems.

∗

The unions assumed that the uniform national settlement of the Company Statute Law (Betriebsverfassungsgesetz) would be based on the regional laws passed in 1947–48. Particular importance was, naturally, attributed to the extent and status of the works councils' co-determination rights. On the lines of the Company Statute Law in South Baden and Hessen, the trade unions demanded that the works councils not only be given rights of information, consultation and proposal, but also equal powers of co-determination – in welfare, staff and economic matters. Secondly, the unions were hoping to push through bipartite representation on the boards of directors of all large companies, on the model of the coal and steel industry.

These goals can be found in the "Proposals for the reorganization of the German economy" adopted by the DGB's federal committee on 14 April 1950. A little later, on 22 May 1950, the DGB submitted a draft bill, "On the reorganization of the economy and society"[2], laying down that in all undertakings with more than 300 employees or company assets of more than DM 3 m, the supervisory board or, in the case of unlimited companies, the advisory committee, should be occupied in equal proportions by representatives of the shareholders and the trade unions. They wanted the worker-director system practised in the coal and steel industry to be applied to other large undertakings. In companies employing 20–300 staff, economic committees with the same make-up should be created. In order to achieve economic co-determination, chambers of commerce, industry, trade and agriculture should have bipartite representation. Alongside the wage earner's rights of co-determination at company level and on economic self-management bodies, provision was made for the formation of an agricultural council and a federal economic council, on which the trade unions would also be represented, as advisory bodies for government and parliament.

---

2 See Geschäftsbericht des Bundesvorstandes des Deutschen Gewerkschaftsbundes 1950–1951 (Düsseldorf, undated), p. 182 ff.

These proposals went much further than the government draft of 17 May 1950. With the aim of bringing their positions somewhat closer, talks began in early summer 1950 between employers, unions and government representatives. While agreement was soon in sight on the question of the creation of a federal economic council, agricultural council and chambers of economics, the employers firmly rejected joint representation on chambers of commerce and industry and boards of directors, as well as rights of economic co-determination for works councils. As the discussions failed to lead to a result acceptable to the trade unions, the DGB federal executive and federal committee declared a deadlock on 18 July 1950 and announced their intention to take industrial action. The two sides were no closer together at the end of July, either, when the governing parties' draft Company Statute Bill was given its first reading; the SPD parliamentary party tabled its own bill, based on the proposals of the unions. The same was true of discussion in committee, which were broken off in autumn 1950 owing to the debate on co-determination in the coal and steel industry.

*

It very quickly became evident that the trade unions were coming up against determined resistance on the part of the employers. There was, they said, no place for the reorganization of the economy demanded by the unions within the framework of the German system of laws; moreover, co-determination provisions of the kind suggested would jeopardize the development of the economy, which was just taking off again.

The trade unions were caught unawares by the speed with which the employers' had once more become entrenched in their "old" positions and rebuilt their economic and industrial organizations.

As early as 1945–46, the chambers of commerce and industry in the British zone, for example, had resumed work with the agreement of the military government. The chambers in the British and American zones then amalgamated to form the Association of Chambers of Commerce and Industry of the United Economic Area, and in October 1949 they founded the German Industrial and Trade Association (Deutscher Industrie- und Handelstag – DIHT).

The employers' trade associations were also rapidly re-established in 1945–46, initially for the individual *Länder*. As early as 1946 they set up umbrella organizations such as the Employers' Committee for North-Rhine Westphalia. There followed in 1947 the Employers' Association for the British zone, and then the Central Secretariat of the Employers of the

United Economic Area. In 1950 the Federal Association of German Employers' Federations (Bundesvereinigung der Deutschen Arbeitgeberverbände – BDA) was founded.

The formation of business and commercial associations was also approved by the western occupying powers in autumn 1945. By April 1946, 24 business associations and 26 special trade associations had been set up in the British zone; undertakings throughout the zone were organized in six associations with 32 affiliated trade associations. The centralization of the employers' associations gradually went ahead; in October 1949 they merged to form the Industrial Associations' Committee on Economic Affairs, from which emerged in 1950 the Federal Association of German Industry (Bundesverband der Deutschen Industrie – BDI).

So by the summer of 1950, the trade unions were once again confronted by the full panoply of economic interest associations, which forged a united front against union demands. The employers, led by Fritz Berg, the president of the BDI, warned the government against giving any co-determination arrangements in the coal and steel industry the force of law, and rejected any such measures on behalf of all large-scale industry.

*

The employers' ideas had evidently not failed to have a political impact; at any rate, the trade unions found out in November 1950 that the Ministry for Economic Affairs headed by Ludwig Erhard was preparing an implementation decree on Control Council Law 27, whereby the supervisory boards of large concerns in the coal and steel industry would be made up "in accordance with German law" – that is, with no union participation. The issue at stake was thus not the extension of the co-determination measures demanded by the unions in May 1950, but the defence of the co-determination provisions decreed by the British military government in 1947.

The unions concluded that the move by the Ministry compelled them to take some action. The Engineering Union and the Mining and Power Union conducted ballots in November 1950 and January 1951 on the question of whether the workers were prepared to strike to secure or extend co-determination rights. The result was unambiguous: 96 per cent of trade unionists in the steel industry were in agreement with industrial action, and 92 per cent of the miners.

Chancellor Adenauer condemned the conduct of the unions as unconstitutional in a letter to Böckler on 4 December 1950: in a "democratic state [. . .] there could not be a strike against the constitutional organs of legislation".[3] The union militancy evinced by the ballots led, however, to fresh talks, which culminated on 25 January 1951 in the conclusion of an agreement on co-determination in the coal and steel industry. This compromise, whereby existing co-determination provisions were kept and extended to the coal industry – though not to other large undertakings – formed the basis of the Law on Co-determination in the Coal and Steel Industry passed by the Bundestag on 10 April 1951, with a few abstentions and about 50 votes against – for instance, from the ranks of the FDP (Free Democratic Party) and the 15 KPD deputies.

The Law on Co-determination in the Coal and Steel Industry[4] gave legal endorsement to co-determination for wage earners on the supervisory boards of all joint stock companies, limited companies and mining-law companies with more than a thousand employees and producing chiefly coal and iron-ore or iron and steel. In more detail, its provisions were as follows. The supervisory boards of these undertakings were to consist of equal numbers of shareholder and staff or union representatives; in addition, there was to be a "neutral" member, on whose appointment both sides had to agree. For the employee side this meant that, of a board with 11 members, the trade unions would nominate two representatives, and a third with no personal interest; the other two worker representatives were to be proposed by the works council of the company concerned. The supervisory board was to appoint the company's executive committee, including the worker-director, who could not be appointed or dismissed without the majority approval of the employee side.

Like the Stinnes-Legien agreement of 15 November 1918, the Law on Co-determination in the Coal and Steel Industry was applauded as a major union success: "These clauses constitute a revolutionary document, a milestone – on the third road to a new social order." Of course, it was obvious that it had only "kicked open the door to a new social order", which could only be achieved "when the social system throughout Germany is freed from the fetters of the rule of capital over labour".[5] Precisely because of these ambitious objectives, the trade unions' chief concern now had to be to extend co-determination to *all* large concerns. But they

---

3 According to Theo Pirker, Die blinde Macht. Gewerkschaftsbewegung in Westdeutschland, Vol. 1 (Munich, 1962), p. 192
4 Gesetz über die Mitbestimmung der Arbeitnehmer in den Aufsichtsräten und Vorständen der Unternehmen des Bergbaus und der Eisen und Stahl erzeugenden Industrie vom 21. Mai 1951, in Der Bundesminister für Arbeit und Sozialordnung (ed.), Mitbestimmung (Bonn, 1979), p. 123 ff.
5 Walther Pahl, Mitbestimmung in der Montanindustrie nach dem Gesetz vom 10. 4. 1951, in Gewerkschaftliche Monatshefte 1951, pp. 225–7; this quot. p. 226

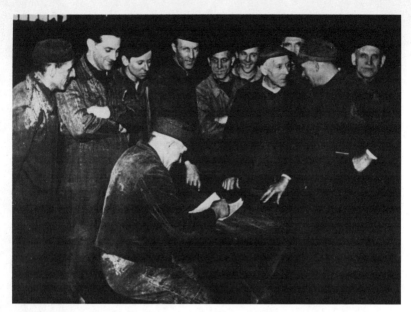

Co-determination strike ballot on 17-19 January 1951

Rally of 100,000 workers in Frankfurt on 20 May 1952 to protest against the Company Statute Law

were still a long way from realizing the ideas on socialization and the planned economy that had informed their 1949 "Economic Policy Programme" – so far, in fact, that these demands were soon eclipsed by the call for co-determination.

*

Having secured legal backing for co-determination in the coal and steel industry by threatening industrial action, the unions' main concern was now to extend this scheme to the economy as a whole. But when the consideration of the Company Statute Bill by the relevant parliamentary committee was completed in April 1952, it was plain that the bill hardly accorded with union ideas. Furthermore, on 22 February the Cabinet had announced a draft Staff Representation Bill for the public services, making it quite clear that the unions' demands for bipartite co-determination and equality of treatment for the public service and the private sector would not be met.

At this, the DGB's federal executive, now headed by Christian Fette, the chairman of the Printing and Paper Union, who was elected at an extraordinary federal congress in Essen in June 1951 following the death of Hans Böckler on 16 February, decided at an extraordinary meeting on 10 April 1952 to take action against the government proposals. They actually wanted a negotiated settlement, especially as the threat of strike action and the strike ballot in the co-determination dispute in the coal and steel industry had been much criticized for putting pressure on the democratically elected parliament. The demonstrations and protest strikes, probably involving some 350,000 people in all, were intended to force the government to the negotiating table. The protests culminated in the "newspaper strike" by the Printing and Paper Union from 27 to 29 May 1952. This particular strike, which was widely seen as an attack on the freedom of the press, cost the unions a good deal of sympathy, even among those who were favourably disposed towards trade unions demands.

No doubt swayed by the militancy demonstrated by the trade unions, Adenauer offered a new round of talks; in addition, the second reading of the company statute law was deferred. At this, the DGB federal executive called off all further protests on 4 July 1952 – an act that was criticized by many middle-ranking and junior union officials as a backdown and a sign of weakness.

In June 1952 talks were duly held between the Chancellor and representatives of the unions and the governing parties. They led to the formation of a commission that was instructed to draw up proposals for amending the Company Statute Bill. But things did not turn out as the unions had wished. They were unable to obtain a postponement of the governing parties' timetable and when it also came out that the Cabinet had already adopted the draft Staff Representation Bill, they broke off negotiations. There was no fresh call for organized protests.

On 16 and 17 July 1952, the *Bundestag* gave the Company Statute Bill its second reading, and eventually passed it on 19 July by 195 votes to 139 with 9 abstentions – that is, against the votes of the SPD and KPD.

What were the provisions of the Company Statute Law promulgated on 11 October 1952[6]? The rights of participation granted to the works councils to be set up in firms with at least five employees were severely limited. In staff matters they only had the right to object in questions of recruitment and dismissal, and in economic matters they were given a say only where company objectives were to be modified or in company closures. The economic committees to be set up in companies with at least 100 employees were granted a right to information only. The composition of the supervisory boards of joint-stock companies with more than 500 employees did not meet union demands, either: the employee representatives were given one third of the seats only, and there was no provision for a worker-director on the management board, as there was in the coal and steel industry.

On top of this, there were problems over a number of other provisions. The works councils were, on the one hand, supposed to be independent of the trade unions; on the other, pursuant to Paragraph 49, they were supposed to co-operate with the employer "within the framework of the prevailing collective agreements in a spirit of trust [. . .] for the benefit of the company and its employees, taking into account the common good". By making the works councils wear two hats – appointing them as representatives of the workforce while obliging them to collaborate with the employers – and by limiting their powers to a say in social and staff matters, the government made it quite clear that this law was pursuing the ideals of "social partnership" without intervening in the economic decision-making processes of the management. The Company Statute Law thus fell well short of works councils laws previously adopted by a number of the *Länder*. And whether rights of participation in a jointly appointed supervisory board could really be described as "co-determination" is very much open to question. In 1953 came the Staff Representation Law, with sep-

---

6 Betriebsverfassungsgesetz of 11 October 1952, in Der Bundesminister für Arbeit und Sozialordnung (ed.), Mitbestimmung, p. 145 ff.

arate arrangements for the public service, setting the seal on the defeat suffered by the unions over the Company Statute Law.

Though the trade unions accepted the decision of parliament, they could certainly not have been satisfied with this law. For them, the crucial factor was that it had prevented "the urgent reorganization and democratization of the economy". They criticized the fact that "the fundamental structure of the capitalist economy is not changed and the entrepreneur's sole right of decision-making is retained".[7] And Otto Brenner, the chairman of the Engineering Union, looking back, reached the bitter verdict: the Company Statute Law's "inherent ideology is that of an age which we thought we had overcome once and for all in 1945"; this was an overt allusion to the Law on the Organization of National Labour of 20 January 1934, with its notions of popular and corporate communities.[8]

The harshest criticism, because it was the most fundamental, came from Viktor Agartz of the DGB Institute of Economic Science. To his mind the Company Statute Law was reactionary and anti-union, since it drove a wedge between the staff of a company and the trade unions. For the rest, he repeatedly stressed that "co-determination rights for wage earners in companies, however far-reaching" were still no substitute for state planning, when it came to "clearing the way for socialism".[9] Before long nobody wanted to know about such radical plans as this, even within the union movement.

The employers, however, had good reason to be pleased. For them the "crucial" factor was that in the Company Statute Law "the basic elements of free enterprise are preserved: the freedom of the entrepreneur to make decisions on the economic management of his company and the freedom of entrepreneurial initiative".[10]

What were the reasons for the trade unions' lack of success in getting their policies implemented? The DGB's second federal congress in October 1952 did debate the failure of the unions' co-determination demands in some depth; but criticism focused on the men at the top. Christian Fette was voted out of office and replaced by Walter Freitag of the Engineering Union. But this very course of action prevented any

---

7 Machtpolitik, in Die Quelle 8, August 1952, p. 393 ff.; this quot. p. 394
8 Otto Brenner, Fortschrittliche Betriebsverfassung – Prüfstein der Demokratie in unserer Zeit (Frankfurt, 1966), pp. 121–32; this quot. p. 125
9 Viktor Agartz, Mitbestimmung als gesellschaftsformende Kraft, in Die Quelle 10 (1952), p. 509 f.
10 Der Arbeitgeber of 15. 7. 1952; quot. Wolfgang Hirsch–Weber, Gewerkschaften in der Politik. Von der Massenstreikdebatte zum Kampf um das Mitbestimmungsrecht (Cologne and Opladen, 1959), p. 110

genuine elucidation of the causes of defeat. For criticism of Fette only got at half the truth. Though Fette may not have acquired the stature of Böckler, he rather seems to have been made the scapegoat for a flawed union strategy. The provisions of the Company Statute Law giving the unions less than equal representation were already on the cards once a separate co-determination law had been accepted for the coal and steel industry. Furthermore, the conditions for industrial action had again shifted in 1951–2 to the disadvantage of the unions. While the issue of co-determination in coal and steel was basically about defending an arrangement that was already widespread, an extension of this model to all large undertakings would actually have been an innovative step for which the climate was not really favourable in 1952. The market economy had stabilized, as had the position of the employers. The passage of the Company Statute Law brought home to the unions with the utmost clarity the limits of their political influence. The unions were already on the political defensive in the dispute over co-determination in coal and steel; with the Company Statute Law it turned into defeat. The significance of this defeat was all the greater in that the arguments about co-determination also concerned the importance of the unions' role in the Federal Republic's democratic system.

*

The conflict over the Company Statute Law had far-reaching implications. Firstly, there were the direct consequences of union policy: the resultant strikes and other action were seen by many as an attempt to coerce Parliament. A fierce legal controversy flared up over the unions' right to strike for clearly political demands, that is, demands on the lawmakers. The opposing positions were championed by Joseph Kaiser, Erich Forsthoff and Hans Carl Nipperdey on one side, and Wolfgang Abendroth on the other. The former saw the political strike as an attack by the unions' minority interests or special interests on the common good, represented by the state; Abendroth depicted the unions as the *champions* of democracy, who without the weapon of the political strike would have to stand by helplessly and watch the state fall prey to the privileged classes under the monopoly capitalist economic system.[11] Abendroth also

---

11 See Joseph H. Kaiser, Der politische Streik (Berlin 1955); Hans Carl Nipperdey, Streikrecht, in Handwörterbuch der Sozialwissenschaften, vol. 10 (1959), pp. 226–31; Wolfgang Abendroth, Verfassungsrechtliche Grenzen des Sozialrechts, in Gewerkschaftliche Monatshefte (1951), pp. 57–61

appeared as an expert on behalf of the unions to substantiate the proposition that "a demonstration strike that is temporary – that is, limited in time – and has the sole aim of bringing the attitude of the wage earners firmly to the notice of the competent legislative bodies during the preparation of a law [could] not be considered unconstitutional".[12]

But in their rulings the labour courts and, from 1954 on, the Federal Labour Court took the view that the trade unions' right to strike had to be restricted. The judgment of 28 January 1955[13] established the principle that strikes were only permissible if they were over demands that the other party to a collective agreement, the employer or employers' federation, was in a position to meet. At the same time, it established the principle of "equality of weapons" – strike and lockout – as this was considered the only way of ensuring "parity" in the struggle between unions and employers. The lockout ban in the Hesse regional constitution was thus circumvented, as it had already been with the adoption of the Basic Law. Shortly afterwards the scope for trade union militancy was restricted even further. The evaluation of the strike ballot as a form of industrial action (1958) and the ban imposed in 1963 on participation in "wildcat strikes" (that is, strikes that had not been properly called by the unions on expiry of the obligation to desist from industrial action) showed the clear tendency of the judiciary to curb the right to strike.

The controversies about co-determination in the coal and steel industry and the Company Statute Law also had a major effect on the way the unions regarded themselves. With the market economy and the power of the employers firmly entrenched, union plans for reorganization concentrated on, or confined themselves to, the problem of co-determination. The unions thus dropped the links between socialization, the planned economy and co-determination established in the 1949 principles of economic policy. The crucial factor in this was no doubt an appraisal of the relative power of the two sides in 1950–51, which also suggested that it might be wise to concentrate on the issue on which the unions could count on the support of some sections of the Catholic Church. For co-determination offered an opportunity to consolidate the idea of the "unified union" in union programmes; after all, the 1949 Catholic assembly in

12 Wolfgang Abendroth, Die Berechtigung gewerkschaftlicher Demonstrationen für die Mitbestimmung der Arbeitnehmer in der Wirtschaft, in Antagonistische Gesellschaft und politische Demokratie (Neuwied and Berlin, 1967) p. 203 ff.; this quot. p. 229
13 Reprinted in Michael Schneider, Aussperrung. Ihre Geschichte und Funktion vom Kaiserreich bis heute (Frankfurt, 1980), p. 243 ff.

Bochum had supported this objective.[14] By detaching the demand for co-determination from their other plans for reorganization, the unions were granting express recognition to the goal of equal rights for capital and labour, which was firmly rooted in the tradition of all three of the major union federations of old.

It was apparent to the trade unions that with the current distribution of parliamentary seats they had no chance of pushing through even their limited ideas on reorganization. Since they did not want to take the course of mobilizing extraparliamentary support for fear of Communist subversion, but also because they had recognized the foundations of parliamentary democracy, they focused all their expectations on the outcome of the next Bundestag elections, when – once again – they were pinning their hopes on a good performance by the SPD. "For a better Bundestag" was the slogan with which the unions attempted indirectly to recruit electoral support for the SPD. Ironically, the DGB was heeding a suggestion of Adenauer's in doing this. During the arguments about the Company Statute Law, the latter had written to Fette that in the forthcoming elections the following year the DGB would have "the opportunity to put forward its views on a uniform and progressive company statute in the manner provided for in our constitution". But the DGB failed in its appeal to members to vote "only for such men and women who are either members of unions or by their attitude in the past have shown that in the new *Bundestag*" they will fulfil the "justified wishes and demands" of the wage earners. In the general elections of 6 September 1953, the CDU and CSU increased their share of the vote to 45 per cent. Furthermore, the appeal led to internal tensions, since – borrowing Adenauer's arguments – the Christian Democratic unionists, in particular, considered that the DGB's "obligation, under its rules, to observe party political neutrality" had been "breached in the gravest manner".[15] We shall have occasion to examine the consequences of this below.

2. The unions' share in the "economic miracle": policy on wages, working hours and social welfare

After the failure of the campaign "for a better *Bundestag*", the unions concentrated on their original field of action – pay policy and social policy;

---

14 See W. Hirsch-Weber, Gewerkschaften in der Politik, p. 83
15 Quot. Dieter Schuster, Die deutschen Gewerkschaften seit 1945 (Stuttgart, 1973), p. 42 f.

more far-reaching ideas about reorganization took the back seat. This is most clearly reflected by the DGB's First Action Programme for May Day 1955, unanimously adopted by its federal executive and federal committee. It presented demands for a pay rise, shorter working hours, improvements in social provision and industrial safety, and the consolidation and extension of co-determination. Unlike the debate on the economic system and the conflict over co-determination in 1951–52, in these areas the unions were to prove thoroughly successful. These successes, however, were only attained on the basis of an economic boom without parallel in German history.

The economic trend

Though the economic statistics were already indicating an upward trend after the currency reform of 1948, the upward forces were still weak. It was not until the "Korea boom" came along that the rates of increase in the gross national product reached the level characteristic of the 1950s.

From summer 1952, the German economy enjoyed a self-perpetuating upswing which brought average economic growth of 6.3 per cent annually from 1952 to 1966, though it showed a tendency to slow down around the mid-1950s that grew more pronounced in the early 1960s.[16]

Two features of the Federal German economic structure should be singled out for special mention. From the early 1950s the Federal Republic's balance of trade showed a growing export surplus; in the 1960s it became the second strongest trading nation after the United States, and later after Japan. The growth of the export side of the economy was given a lasting boost by membership of the European Economic Community, which was created in 1958. In addition, the concentration of the economy went ahead at a furious pace in the 1950s. Between 1954 and 1963, the turnover of the 50 largest industrial enterprises rose from DM 36.8 to 118 billion; their share of total turnover rose from 25.4 to 36.2 per cent over the same period.[17]

---

16 The growth rates of the GNP were as follows: 1951, 10.4%; 1952, 8.9%; 1953, 8.2%; 1954, 7.4%; 1955, 12.5%; 1956, 7.3%; 1957, 5.7%; 1958, 3.7%; 1959, 7.3%; 1960, 9%; 1961, 4.9%; 1961, 4.9%; 1962, 4.4%; 1963, 3%; 1964, 6.8%. Figures from Karl Theodor Schuon, Oekonomische und soziale Entwicklung der Bundesrepublik Deutschland 1945–1981, in Lern- und Arbeitsbuch deutsche Arbeiterbewegung, vol. 2, p. 733
17 Jörg Huffschmid, Die Politik des Kapitals. Konzentration und Wirtschaftspolitik in der Bundesrepublik Deutschland (Frankfurt 1969), p. 44

Hand in hand with economic growth there was a clear shift in the relative importance of the different sectors of the economy. Agriculture and forestry declined steadily, while manufacturing industry and the service sector grew. Whereas in 1950 23.7 per cent of the working population were still engaged in agriculture, this had fallen to 10.6 per cent by 1965. Those engaged in manufacturing industry increased as a proportion from 43.3 to 49 per cent over the same period, and those working in the service sector from 33 to 40.4 per cent (see Table 6a). Parallel with the steady expansion of the service sector and the increasing importance of administration and retailing in the manufacturing sector, white-collar workers increased as a proportion of all employed persons from 22.9 per cent (1950) to 32.1 per cent (1965); the proportion of civil servants also increased – from 6.1 to 8.2 per cent; but the proportion of manual workers fell from 70.9 per cent (1950) to 59.7 per cent (1965). If the changes within the wage-earning groups are also related to the total working population, the result is an illuminating picture of social change in the 1950s and 1960s (Table 6b).

The economic growth rate led to a rapid fall in unemployment, which had been as high as 11 per cent in 1950. From 5.6 per cent in 1955, it fell to 1.3 per cent in 1960 and 0.7 per cent in 1965 (Table 5b). Despite the influx of millions of refugees and the increased number of working women, towards the end of the 1950s there was virtually full employment – indeed even a labour shortage, so that when domestic manpower reserves started to dry up, industry began recruiting large numbers of workers from abroad.

Economic growth was on such a scale that it opened up opportunities for distributing profits, enabling the unions to score successes in wage policy and social policy without the need for a high level of industrial action. It was precisely the favourable economic trend that was crucial in convincing large sections of the public of the advantages of the market economy. And the majority of employers accepted the trade unions as a force for order – all the more easily as, in their day-to-day policies, the trade unions had given up their ideas of introducing radical changes in the system.

Pay policy: a fair wind

The Law on Collective Agreements of 9 April 1949 having laid the legal foundation for annual pay rounds, in the 1950s they became a matter of course. The cornerstone of the Federal Republic's collective bargaining system is the concept of *Tarifautonomie* ("pay autonomy"), meaning that the negotiating parties are independent and answerable only to themselves; the state has no powers to force them to go to arbitration. In view of the rate of growth and the resultant prospects for greater profits, the employers were more inclined than before to yield to the unions' demands for a share in the benefits of increased productivity. The employers probably also saw a possibility of forestalling more radical political demands by showing some financial flexibility. And the trade unions were quite prepared to take into account the figures for the national economy as a whole in their pay policy.

*

Not until the mid-1950s was an attempt made to use pay policy – theoretically – as an instrument of income redistribution. Viktor Agartz put forward his plan for an "expansive wages policy", designed to raise living standards and demand, ensure economic prosperity and full employment and, at the same time, a fairer distribution of the national product.[18] One of Agartz's chief supporters was Otto Brenner of the Engineering Union, who introduced the slightly more moderate concept of the "active wages policy" into the debate – and saw to it that Agartz delivered the main speech on economic policy at the DGB's 1954 congress. The concept of the active or expansive wages policy also amounted to a rejection of the government's plans to encourage "wealth formation" by employees, which it put into effect with such measures as the Encouragement of Savings Law (1959) and the introduction of "people's shares" (1961).

Agartz's ideas on pay policy led to a debate on principles inside the unions. The militant turn which Agartz wished to give to trade union policy displeased many Christian Democratic unionists. In contrast to Agartz, they advocated the wage earners' co-ownership of the wealth produced by business, since wealth creation plans – in accordance with the Christian-social tradition – were regarded as a step towards equal rights for wage earners in the economy. In view of the ferocity of the internal union arguments about the basic principles of wages policy, which contributed to the setting-up of the Christian trade union movement in 1955, Agartz resigned from the Institute of Economic Science at the end of 1955.

It would, however, be simplistic to view the controversy over the questions of pay policy and wealth creation simply as a quarrel between the

---

18 Viktor Agartz, Beiträge zur wirtschaftlichen Entwicklung 1953. Expansive Lohnpolitik, in WWI-Mitteilungen 12, 1953, p. 245 ff.

Otto Brenner, chairman of the Engineering Union, IG Metall

Georg Leber, chairman of the Construction Union, IG Bau, Steine, Erden

Christian-social and Social Democratic trade unionists. The dispute continued to rage within the DGB even after Agartz's resignation and the re-establishment of the Christian trade unions. It now focused on the differing views championed by Otto Brenner of the Engineering Union and Georg Leber of the Construction Union. Brenner was undoubtedly voicing the majority opinion in rejecting the sale of state shares in economic enterprises – even in the form of widely distributed "people's shares" – as a reckless waste of public property. The same is true of his fears that the shares would in any event soon be concentrated in a few hands once again, so that ultimately all that could be expected was a strengthening of big business. Moreover, this type of popular capitalism would inevitably lead to the workers' final acquiescence in the system of private capitalism, without any significant changes in its structure. At most, Brenner was prepared to accept the transfer of wage earner shares into union-administered funds.[19]

While Brenner took it for granted that a just distribution of income and wealth could never be achieved under the capitalist system, Leber held that the workers had to acquire, here and now, through the collective bargaining process, a share in the wealth produced by the economy.[20] The Construction Union consistently followed this path: on 31 December 1962 a collective agreement for the building industry was signed, according unionized building workers fringe benefits and in 1965 agreement was reached on wealth-creating benefits for the building trade. The differences on pay policy between Brenner and Leber (or between the Engineering Union and the Construction Union) were at bottom a manifestation of a deep-seated political conflict over attitudes to the West German state and divergent views of the union movement – as a counter-balancing power or as a regulatory force. Brenner and Leber stood for different political positions within the unions that were repeatedly in collision, in the debate on the emergency laws and again over the 1963 "programme of principle". Who were these two union leaders who helped shape the image of the unions in the 1950s and 1960s?

Born in Hanover in 1907, Otto Brenner had a typical trade union career behind him when, in 1952, he took over the leadership of IG Metall, the Engineering Union, which he headed with Hans Brümmer until 1956, and then alone until his death in 1972. He had worked his way up from general labourer to factory electrician and electrical engineer. At 15 he had joined the DMV and in 1926 the SPD, which, however, he left in

---

19 Otto Brenner, Die Zeit nutzen, in Die Quelle 10, 1955, p. 449 f.
20 Georg Leber, Vermögensbildung in Arbeitnehmerhand (Frankfurt, 1964)

1929 over the armoured cruiser affair, co-founding the SAPD in 1931. In 1933 Brenner was arrested by the Gestapo and sentenced to two years' imprisonment for preparation for high treason. He remained under police surveillance until the end of the war, scraping a living as a builder's labourer, fitter and newspaper roundsman. In 1945 he joined the SPD and the Engineering Union, becoming chairman of the Hanomag works council and, in 1947, head of the Hanover district of the union. From 1952 on, "Otto the Iron Man" – his nickname expressed admiration and respect – took a leading part in determining the policy of IG Metall.

His adversary within the union movement was the equally forceful Georg Leber. Born the son of a bricklayer and Christian trade unionist in 1920 in Obertiefenbach an der Lahn, he completed a business training and became a white-collar worker, and then after the Second World War, a bricklayer. In 1947 he joined the union and the SPD; from 1949 to 1952 he was local secretary of the Construction Union in Limburg. After becoming editor of the journal "Grundstein" in 1952, he advanced to vice-chairman of the union's executive committee in 1955, and took over the leadership two years later. The same year, Leber became a *Bundestag* deputy. From then on his career was notable for the fact that, unlike other trade union leaders, he simultaneously played an important part in the SPD. In the 1960s and 1970s he occupied leading positions both in the SPD and in the government, as Transport Minister (1966–69) and Defence Minister (1972–78). His energetic advocacy of the "social partnership" idea meant that he was always being cast in the role of Brenner's internal opponent within the movement; but at the same time it made him a useful mediator in awkward situations, for example, in the struggle for a reduction in working hours in 1984.

*

But back to the 1950s and 60s. The successes of union pay policy were nothing to be ashamed of: for all the differences between one industry and another, between men's and women's wages and between the agreed rates and actual rates, it is a fact that in the five year period 1956–1960 real wages rose by an average of 4.6 per cent a year, and in the following five years by even more, 5.3 per cent (Table 3c). The clear fall in the rate of increase to 2.5 per cent in 1963 reflected the beginning of economic difficulties, which led – as evidenced by the industrial dispute in the engineering industry in North Baden-North Württemberg – to an intensification of pay conflicts. The successes of union pay policy were all the more substantial in that from the second half of the 1950s pay rises were accompanied by the first cuts in working hours, the cost of which was added on to the rate of increase in wages in all collective agreements.

If one looks more closely at the development of wages, the remarkable thing is that – with a few exceptions – there was no year in which it outstripped the growth in productivity. Secondly, it appears to have been more than a minor blemish in union policy that the pay differences between men and women persisted. For it was precisely pay policy that had to be the acid test of the seriousness with which the unions took the decision announced at the founding congress in Munich to work for equal rights for men and women in social and economic matters.[21] True, the DGB's 1954 congress did instruct the trade unions "to set wage and salary brackets in collective agreements according to the nature of the work involved and no longer according to sex, and not to agree to any passages permitting lower payments to female employees";[22] but in practice the problem of female wage brackets was solved, from a legal point of view, by employing gender-neutral wording, while the effective differences in fact survived more or less unchanged thanks to the device of *Leichtlohngruppen* ("light wage groups", that is, groups of – usually female – workers paid less than other workers performing comparable tasks) (Table 3e).

Although the unions were able to take the credit for the annual increase in real wage rates during the years of full employment, the question is, thirdly, whether co-operation with the employers over pay policy really did bring in as much as it might have done. Payments above the agreed rate, quite substantial in some industries, would seem to indicate that a union policy less anxious to avoid industrial strife could have won workers in flourishing sectors of the economy wage awards higher than they actually received. This "wage drift" prompted proposals to formulate pay policy closer to the shopfloor – which might also have boosted worker participation in union work. But the trend towards centralization of collective bargaining (and disputes) could not be halted by the notion of a "shopfloor pay policy". The automatic nature of the annual pay rounds and wage rises may also have led large numbers of workers to regard union membership as unnecessary, since they received the wage rises negotiated by the unions anyway, without any effort on their part.

Fourthly, it should not be forgotten that while average income from paid employment more than doubled between 1950 and 1960, the income

---

21 Protokoll. Gründungskongress des Deutschen Gewerkschaftsbundes, München, 12.–14. Oktober 1949 (Cologne, 1950), p. 338

22 Protokoll. 3. Ordentlicher Bundeskongress, Frankfurt a.M., 4. bis 9. Oktober 1954 (Düsseldorf, undated), p. 701

of the self-employed increased threefold over the same period. Again, wages as a proportion of national income rose (on the face of it) from 58.4 per cent in 1950 to 59.4 (1955), 60.6 (1960) and up to 64.7 per cent in 1965. But if one takes into account the steady rise in the number of wage earners as a proportion of the working population as a whole, there is a drop in the adjusted figures from 58.4 (1950) to 54.1 (1955), and 53.6 (1960) to 54.8 per cent in 1965.[23]

Against this background, plans for "wage earner wealth formation" took on new importance. The path taken by the government in 1961 with the "312 Mark Law' and the issue of "people's shares" were regarded by most trade unionsts as "popular capitalism", to which they preferred the idea of wealth accumulation via large funds in which wage earners would receive share certificates.[24] The fact is that neither the Capital Formation Law of 1961 nor the raising of the exempt savings limit to DM 624 by the law of 30 June 1971 did anything to alter the distribution of the wealth produced by the national economy.

Heading for the 40-hour week

With the improvement in the economic situation in the early 1950s the average working week in industry returned to pre-war levels. From 1950 to 1956, it was somewhere between 47.5 and 48.6 hours (Table 4b). May Day 1952 was devoted to the union demand for the introduction of the 40-hour week. Point 1 of the action programme of 29–30 March 1955 set out the aim: "A five-day week, eight-hour day with no loss of wages". The intensification of work was the reason given: the reduction in working hours was necessary to "refresh exhausted powers" but also to protect the "social and moral foundations of family life".[25]

Ever since its programme of principle in 1953, the DAG had also supported the demand for the introduction of the 40-hour, five-day week. And in the action programme adopted at its party conference in Dortmund in 1952 and extended at the 1954 Berlin party conference, the SPD supported the union call for the "reduction of working hours without loss of wages" to 40 hours per week.

---

23 Frank Deppe, Autonomie und Integration. Materialien zur Gewerkschaftsanalyse (Marburg, 1979), p. 64

24 Bruno Gleitze, Sozialkapital und Sozialfonds als Mittel der Vermögenspolitik, 2nd ed. (Cologne, 1969)

25 According to Geschäftsbericht des Bundesvorstandes des DGB 1954–1955 (Düsseldorf, undated), p. 72 ff.

Agitation for the 40-hour week culminated in the mid-1950s. The most famous slogan was the DGB's 1956 May Day appeal, "On Saturday Daddy belongs to me!" The unions took the view that the reform should be introduced by law – failing which by collective agreement – with provision for a gradual reduction in working hours permitting adjustments to be made to production techniques. Since the prospect of full employment was just around the corner, there were only sporadic references to the effect on the employment, that is, that continuing rationalization was releasing wage earners, whom cuts in working hours would enable to secure new jobs. Otto Brenner warned even then of the danger of "technological unemployment".[26] But in the 1950s this seemed a distant prospect.

With the profits at their disposal, the employers were quite ready to compromise. The employers' associations presented their position on the question of working hours in a ten-point programme on 12 January 1956. The share of the productivity increase due to the employee should be divided up between pay rises and cuts in working hours, with the cuts following the development of productivity in stages.[27] This negotiating offer not only safeguarded "social peace" – from the employers' point of view – but held the unions to a cut in working hours that entailed no loss of output nor any relative increase in wages as a proportion of national income.

The success of union policy on working hours had an impact at the level of the individual trade unions. On 14 November 1956, for example, the Food, Beverage and Allied Workers' Union concluded a general agreement on conditions of employment for workers in the cigarette industry, reducing working hours to 42.5 hours per week from 1 January 1957 to 31 December 1958, and implementing the 40-hour week (Monday to Friday) from 1 January 1959. The major breakthrough in the widespread introduction of the 40-hour week was the work of the Engineering Union. In June–July 1956, IG Metall and the employers' association, Gesamtmetall, concluded the "Bremen Pact", recommending that from 1 October 1956 the working week should be cut from 48 to 45 hours with no loss of pay in all areas covered by collective agreements. Then, under the "Soden Pact" of 28 August 1958, working hours in the engineering industry were cut to 44 hours per week from 1 January 1959. Finally, under the terms of the Bad Homburg Pact of 8 July 1960 agreement was reached on the step-

26 Otto Brenner, Automation und Wirtschaftsmacht, in Gewerkschaftliche Monatshefte 1958, pp. 198–201
27 Vorschläge zur Frage Arbeitszeit und Lohn, hrsg. von der BDA (place and date of publication not given); Jahresbericht der BDA 1. 12. 1955 – 30. 11. 1956 (Bergisch-Gladbach, 1956), p. 126

by-step introduction of the 40-hour week. The Bad Homburg Pact served as a model for many of the settlements governing working hours in other industries. In detail, it was agreed that, "With effect from 1 January 1962, the regular contractual working time per week shall be reduced to 42½ hours; from 1 January 1964, to 41¼ hours; and from 1 July 1965, to 40 hours. On the controversial issue of "wage compensation" it was stated: "To compensate for the reduction in working hours [. . .] standard (basic) wages shall be increased as follows: by 3.5 per cent from 1 January 1962; by 3 per cent from 1 January 1964; and by 3.1 per cent from 1 July 1965." It went on to say, "The parties concur that the step-by-step plan agreed between them to reduce working hours is intended both to conserve the employees' labour power and to put the economy in a position to take the necessary steps in good time to cope with the production tasks incumbent upon it." For this reason, the parties agreed: "a) In the years in which a reduction in working hours coincides with new wage settlements, the material impact of the reduction in working hours is to be taken into account. b) The parties to the wage agreement shall, if one of them so wishes (from stage 2 on), engage in discussions, three months before the dates mentioned above, on the feasibility of implementing the reduction in working hours in the light of the current economic situation. Regardless of these discussions, the reductions in working hours shall come into force on the agreed dates, unless the parties to the wage agreement decide to amend the arrangements by a voluntary agreement."[28]

This problem was also at the heart of one of the biggest industrial disputes in the history of the Federal Republic, the dispute in the Baden-Württemberg engineering industry in spring 1963, which is described in more detail below. Suffice it to say that the employers did not attain their aim of deferring the reduction in working hours set for 1 January 1964 by resorting to a mass lockout, though they were able to slow down the increase in pay.

Some time later, however, use was made of the possibility of postponement provided for in the Bad Homburg Pact, in view of the recession in the engineering industry. Under the first and second Erbach pacts (of 13 July 1964 and 18 February 1966) the reductions in working hours set for 1 July 1965 and 1 July 1966 were postponed, so that the 40-hour week was finally introduced in the engineering industry on 1 January 1967. In addition, the first Erbach Pact contained provisions increasing the number of

---

28 Reprinted in Michael Schneider, Streit um Arbeitszeit. Geschichte des Kampfes um Arbeitszeitverkürzung in Deutschland (Cologne, 1984), p. 249 ff.

days' holiday from 1965 and 1967 and increasing holiday pay by 30 per cent.

But it was some time yet before the 40-hour week became the agreed norm for virtually all wage earners. In 1973 "only" 69 per cent of employees worked an agreed 40-hour week; not until 1978 did the proportion reach 92.6 per cent. The fact that reduced working hours were enshrined in collective agreements and not in law was undoubtedly an indication of the reluctance of governments since the days of Konrad Adenauer to take political action over working time.

The holiday question was the only one in which the situation reached through collective bargaining was given legal status – through the Federal Holiday Law of 1963. While holidays averaged about two weeks in the first half of the 1950s, by 1960 this had risen to three. The legally stipulated three weeks' annual holiday was, however, swiftly overtaken by negotiated improvements: by the end of the 1960s the average holiday was four weeks, and by 1975 it was pushing five.

It is a striking fact that the working week has been reduced since the 1950s without any significant reduction in daily working hours. The reduction in the working week is principally due to the abolition of Saturday working. Nor should the increase in part-time working be overlooked. Part-time workers as a proportion of all wage earners rose from 2.6 per cent in 1960 to 8.5 per cent in 1977. Part-time work was – and still is – largely the province of female workers; it was instrumental in boosting the number of married women who go out to work, which has risen continuously since the 1950s. Incidentally, another consequence of the cut in working hours was the increase in shift work during the 1960s.

The introduction of the 40-hour week was not without its impact on the employment situation. Employers' fears that the reduction in working hours would lead to a shortage of labour proved unjustified – but only because the demand for labour was, so it seemed, easily satisfied. Firstly, by recruiting foreign workers and, secondly, by increasing the number of working women. In actual fact, much of the effect of reduced working hours on the labour market was probably absorbed by rationalization measures, as a result of the gradual introduction of the 40-hour week.

Strike policy

The years of the "economic miracle" established the German trade unions' reputation for being particularly "peaceful" by international standards. This verdict was certainly justified if one compares the German unions with the Italian, French or English unions, in particular. It is also accurate if the 1950s and 60s are compared with earlier periods in German history. Never before were so few workers involved in industrial disputes and the number of days lost so small (Tables 2c and 2d). But this does not mean that the unions were dedicated to preserving industrial peace in these decades. Of course, their organizational strength and their potential threat to the employers on the one hand, and steady economic growth with production running at full capacity on the other, made it easier to secure demands without industrial strife. It may also have been of some significance that the Federal Labour Court restricted the right to strike in several judgments of principle. Out of respect for the rule of law, the unions recognized these judgments, which equated strikes and lockouts, banned spontaneous and political strikes and established the principle of "social adequacy" (that is, a strike must be directed against the party that is in a position to meet the demands made). Consequently, from the mid-1950s the strike weapon was employed only in highly controversial issues of principle.

Closer scrutiny shows that the first half of the 1950s was a time of relatively high industrial militancy, compared with the years that followed. From 1950 to 1955, 1.1 m employees took part in industrial action, with a loss of 6.3 m working days. In the following years – 1956–60 – it was "only" 332,000 employees and 3.6 m days lost. Then, between 1962 and 1967, the number of workers involved rose to 664,000, while the number of days lost fell to 2.8 m (Table 2d).

The strikes were very unevenly distributed across the different sectors of the economy. Looking at the number of strikers, we find that in the 1950s it was mining, metal working, the public services and the iron and steel industry that showed an above-average level of industrial action. The number of days lost reveal that workers in metal working and the iron and steel industry waged the longest industrial struggles by far.[29] Even this brief survey shows the importance of the part played by the Engineering Union, IG Metall, which was the bargaining agent in both industries.

What were these struggles about? After the threat and limited use of "political" strikes in 1951–52 in the confrontation over co-determination in the coal and steel industry and the Company Statute Law, the unions concentrated on their real strength, collective bargaining. In the first half of the 1950s, it was often a matter of pushing through the idea of regular

---

29 Walther Müller-Jentsch, Streiks und Streikbewegungen in der Bundesrepublik 1950–1978, in Joachim Bergmann (ed), Beiträge zur Soziologie der Gewerkschaften (Frankfurt, 1979), pp. 21–71; these figures p. 27

pay rounds. Since the employers and the Ministry for Economic Affairs took the view that improvements in productivity benefited the wage earner in the form of lower prices, pay rises did more harm than good, in their opinion, because their effect was to force prices up. A number of strikes right across the economy – from the construction industry (1950) and farming (1951), the graphical trade (1952) and the textile industry (1953 and 1958) to local authority enterprises (1954 and 1958) and the timber industry (1956) – were concerned with levels of pay. In the engineering industry alone, there were ten strikes between 1951 and 1954 over wages. The number of industrial disputes shows two things. Firstly, there was no union that was prepared to take on the job of outrider, taking the lead in collective bargaining. Secondly, there was no precise co-ordination between the major unions over which area they should start with. Not until the mid-1950s did IG Metall assume the role of "trailblazer" in matters of pay and working hours.

Few of these strikes are remembered today. But it is worth recalling the six-week strike which IG Metall conducted in Schleswig-Holstein in 1956–57 over the continued payment of wages in the event of sickness and for longer holidays. This strike effectively forced the *Bundestag* to grant legal recognition to the actual equality between manual workers and white-collar workers which the unions had secured. The Law on the Continued Payment of Wages in Cases of Sickness of 26 June 1957 laid down that workers should receive 90 per cent of their net wages from the third day of sickness; in 1961 this regulation was improved, so that the full net wage was paid out from the second day of sickness; on 1 January 1970 full equality between shopfloor and white-collar workers came into force.

Though in view of the above the strike may be considered to have been a success, it had adverse effects on the rules governing the right to strike. The employers sued IG Metall for damages, construing the conduct of a strike ballot during the arbitration talks as industrial action in breach of the obligation on both sides to refrain from industrial action during wage negotiations. The Federal Labour Court supported this interpretation on 31 October 1958 and sentenced IG Metall to damages. The employers did not insist on immediate compensation, hoping they would be able to browbeat IG Metall into behaving well for a few years by threatening to demand payment of the damages. At least as important was the fact that the Federal Labour Court assessed strike ballots as a form of industrial action in themselves; in consequence the unions had to take another legal obstacle into account in their strike policy if they wished to avoid incurring more damages.

As well as the longest industrial dispute of this period, mention should also be made of the most widespread: the dispute in the engineering industry of North Baden–North Württemberg, which brought the lockout – which had almost been "forgotten"[30] – back into the public eye. When the economic boom of the early 1960s started to run down, while the unions went on pressing for increases in real wages, the employers – Gesamtmetall – made the following demands, as early as October 1962: (1) a wage freeze; (2) postponement of reductions in working hours; (3) central negotiations and longer validity for collective agreements; and (4) the conclusion of an arbitration agreement. In talks with the unions in the winter of 1962–63 the employers tried hard to push their demands through. They threatened to declare the talks stalled if IG Metall – as planned – terminated the current collective agreements on 28 February without declaring its readiness to defer the reduction in working hours that had, in fact, already been agreed. Fresh talks were constantly held, dragging on into the spring of 1963. But only after a strike and a lockout, affecting more than 300,000 workers, was agreement reached on 7 May 1963 (backdated to 1 April) on a pay rise of 5 per cent, to be increased by a further 2 per cent on 1 April 1964. The agreed reduction in working hours was to come into force on 1 April 1964, while the collective agreement as a whole was to remain in effect until the end of September that year. The IG Metall executive accepted this outcome on 7 May, as did Gesamtmetall. Whereas 73 per cent were in favour of ending the strike in the ballot held in Baden-Württemberg, in North Rhine-Westphalia – where no lockout had been called – the proportion was only 55 per cent.

Decisions of principle on social policy

After their defeat over the Company Statute Law, the unions concentrated on pay and social policy. It was not until the mid-1950s that the problem of co-determination once again featured in the public discussion. When Hermann Reusch described the law on co-determination in the coal and steel industry as "the result of brutal extortion by the trade unions" at the general meeting of the Gutehoffnung mine, 800,000 workers responded with a protest strike on 24 January 1955. A little later the point at issue was the safeguarding of coal and steel co-determination in the concern's holding companies.

---

30 According to Rainer Kalbitz, Aussperrungen in der Bundesrepublik. Die vergessenen Konflikte (Cologne and Frankfurt, 1979)

As the concentration of undertakings proceeded, the employers tried to change the structure of the undertaking by setting up holding companies, so that the co-determination law for the coal and steel industry would no longer be applicable. This process was facilitated by the "old" coal and steel companies' move into chemicals and plastics. In order to prevent this attempt to undermine co-determination in the industry, the Supplementary Co-determination Law (Holding Amendment) was passed in August 1956, ensuring co-determination in the holding companies of the coal and steel concerns. But the process of dismantling co-determination in the coal and steel industry could not really be halted by law. In 1958, for example, Mannesmann AG incorporated six formerly independent and thus "co-determined" subsidiaries into the main company; not until the "Lüdenscheid Pact" between the unions and the company management in 1959 was bipartite co-determination protected in the coal and steel companies.

If one examines the social measures of the 1950s, it becomes clear that they were, and remained, subordinate to economic decisions. The importance attributed to the market economy is illustrated by the attempt to curb or control the process of concentration in the economy by means of legal measures. Because the market economy was being jeopardized by concentration, a law was introduced in 1957 to counter restrictions on competition, a cautious move towards the monitoring of monopolies. This was also the idea behind the "aligned society" programme advocated by Ludwig Erhard in the mid-1960s: to avoid endangering the market economy by stemming concentration and the influence of organized lobbies. The unions probably had a sharper eye for the problem of the concentration of economic power, because they saw it from a political angle. The law against restrictions on competition was considered far from adequate when it came to coping with the political consequences of the accumulation of economic power.[31] For the unions the concentration trend was not so much a threat to the market economy but a "danger to the democratic state", according to the resolution passed at the big rally held in November 1958, "The concentration of economic power – social asset stripping".[32]

The governing majority may have been dismissive about all the unions' more far-reaching plans for the reorganization of the economy,

31 Karl Kühne, Kartellgesetz und Wettbewerb, in Gewerkschaftliche Monatshefte 1957, pp. 529–36
32 Rudolf Quast, Konzentration und Mitbestimmung, in Gewerkschaftliche Monatshefte 1959, pp. 513–21; this quot. p. 513

but on issues of social policy some pioneering decisions were taken in the 1950s. The way was smoothed by the favourable development of the economy, which boosted state revenue as well as profits. But the expansion of the system of social welfare was also related to traditional Christian-social ideas. Acting upon these ideas put some social flesh on the market economy, gave it greater stability and, at the same time, made it acceptable in the eyes of large sections of the public.

Decisions of principle governing the "social state" were made in 1952 and 1953 with the law setting up the Federal Institute for Labour Exchanges and Unemployment Insurance, later the Federal Institute of Labour, and the laws on labour courts and social welfare tribunals. This was followed in 1954 by the introduction of a system of child benefit. On 22 January 1957, with the votes of the CDU/CSU and SPD (opposed by the FDP), the *Bundestag* passed a law reforming old age pensions, allowing for adjustment to keep pace with increases in earnings. The union demand for a standard national pension, or a minimum pension laid down by law, was not met. The same year – on 26 July 1957 – a law stipulating equal treatment of manual and white-collar workers in the event of sickness was enacted. In 1962 a nationwide social security scheme was set up and in 1963 a holiday law was introduced giving legal force to the three-week minimum annual holiday which had already been incorporated in collective agreements.

The unions assisted in the preparation of all these laws; in some cases – for example, the continued payment of wages in the event of sickness – it required weeks of industrial action to attain the goal of equal treatment for manual and white-collar workers in collective agreements, thus paving the way for legislation. It was also thanks to union pressure that welfare benefits as a proportion of GNP rose from 17.1 per cent in 1950 and 16.3 per cent in 1955 to 18.7 per cent in 1960 and 24 per cent in 1965.[33] Furthermore, it was, above all, the unions that attempted to influence the climate of the 1950s in their favour, with their ideas on the "social state" as formulated by Wolfgang Abendroth.[34] While the unions had some success as far as social policy was concerned, this did not result in fundamental recognition of the unions as an "integrating factor in democracy". And the political commitment that sprang from this view of themselves was continually rejected.

---

33 According to Bernhard Schäfers, Sozialstruktur und Wandel der Bundesrepublik Deutschland (Stuttgart, 1981), p. 190
34 For example, Wolfgang Abendroth, Zur Funktion der Gewerkschaften in der westdeutschen Demokratie, in Gewerkschaftliche Monatshefte 1952, pp. 641–8

3. The trade unions as a political opposition

It was by no means a universally accepted thing for the unions to express an opinion on political issues that went beyond wages, conditions and social policy. Particularly when making pronouncements on "general political" questions the cohesion of the unified trade unions was put to the test. In the debates on the economic system and the "expansive wage policy", the old dividing lines in the union movement had often taken the form of party political differences, leading in 1953 to the formation of the Christian-social group within the DGB. There was an even more violent collision of views over the justification for and content of trade union statements on other political issues.

In numerous debates in the early 1950s about the unions' view of themselves and their role, the possibilities and limitations of the unified union as a political factor were explored.[35] The two opposing viewpoints were represented by Goetz Briefs and Wolfgang Abendroth. Briefs thought that with the establishment of parliamentary democracy and the recognition of their rights by the state and by public opinion, the trade unions had become "entrenched". Henceforth – in line with the theoretical approach of the earlier Christian unions, in particular – the unions ought to see themselves as "organs of the national economy", that is, they had to place their power at the service of the "organic pluralism" of the democratic state, which would otherwise not be able to fulfil its task of ensuring the welfare of all. Where unions were not prepared to do this voluntarily, their freedom of action – for instance, the right to strike – should and must be legally curtailed. Briefs even saw the unions' calls for co-determination as steps on the road to a "trade union state".[36]

In contrast to this, Abendroth considered it the unions' duty to transform "formal" democracy into "substantive" (that is, social and economic) democracy. Society should be democratized by a consistent union policy. This meant that the unions could and must claim a general political mandate in order to gain a hearing for the will of the wage earners.[37]

This controversy had a profound impact on the unions, as shown by a large number of articles in "Gewerkschaftliche Monatshefte", the DGB's

---

35 See especially the articles in Gewerkschaftliche Monatshefte 1952 by Wolfgang Abendroth (p. 641 ff.), Viktor Agartz (p. 464 ff.), Eugen Kogon (p. 482 ff.) and Theo Pirker (1951: p. 481 ff.; 1952: p. 76 ff., p. 577 ff. and p. 708 ff.)
36 Goetz Briefs, Zwischen Kapitalismus und Syndikalismus. Die Gewerkschaften am Scheideweg (Munich, 1952)
37 Wolfgang Abendroth, Die deutschen Gewerkschaften. Weg demokratischer Integration, 2nd ed. (Heidelberg, 1955)

theoretical journal. The "European discussions" were also characterized by a struggle to find a position acceptable to all trade unionists. But a consensus of this kind could not be found theoretically; it had to be recaptured again and again in the arguments on single political issues, though, in contrast to 1951–52, there was no debate about an overall concept of the social order desired. The task was made more difficult, however, by the fact that controversies over political issues always involved party political loyalties as well.

Simply looking at the distribution of trade union members in the parliamentary parties and the party allegiances of the trade union leaders gives a false impression. Certainly, there can be no doubt about the large overlap between the unions and the SPD in terms of individuals. Of the 115 unionized deputies in the first German *Bundestag* (1949), 80 belonged to the SPD group and 22 to the CDU/CSU group. A 1953 survey revealed 142 SPD and 47 CDU/CSU deputies out of a total of 194 trade unionists. The number of unionists in the *Bundestag* carried on rising; the corresponding figures for 1957 were 202 unionists (154 SPD and 46 CDU/CSU) and for 1961, 223 (179 SPD and 41 CDU/CSU).[38]

So what about the party loyalties of the union leaders? Like the chairmen of several individual unions, Walter Freitag and Willi Richter, the DGB chairman from 1956 to 1962, were members of the SPD group in the *Bundestag*; most of the union leaders were members of the SPD, or sympathized with the party.

The question of party political neutrality was thus a constant stumbling block in the way of trade union unity. In the view of leading trade unionists, neutrality should mean being independent of political parties while adopting a firm stance on political issues. It is hardly surprising that this turned out in favour of the SPD, given the similarities in policy content and the party political commitment of most union leaders.

The discrepancy between claims to party political independence and the reality of the situation did not merely give rise to arguments with Christian-social and Christian-democratic trade unionists; in addition, there was the problem of confrontation with the Communists in the unions, aggravated by the partition of Germany. Their work on the works councils won the recognition of many, including trade unionists; but there were fears, too, that the unions might be turned into instruments of the Communist Party. Partly in view of developments in the GDR – for instance, the revolt on 17 June 1953 – the unions frequently reacted by

---

38 Kurt Hirche, Gewerkschafter im 5. Deutschen Bundestag, in Gewerkschaftliche Monatshefte 12, 1965, pp. 705–12; these figures p. 708

marginalizing and finally expelling Communists. At any rate, the ban imposed on the KPD in 1956 was not opposed by the unions, who sided with the government in their anti-communism. Of decisive importance to the trade unions' course in the early 1950s was not merely the rejection of communism, which it shared with the SPD, but above all their support for firm links between the Federal Republic and the West, symbolized by the May Day rallies in West Berlin.

Against rearmament and the issue of nuclear equipment to the Bundeswehr

There is no question, then, of total political unanimity between the SPD and the unions. Whereas the DGB consented to the 1949 Petersberg Agreement and hence the entry of the Federal Republic into the international Ruhr authority, the SPD under Kurt Schumacher was – for all the internal party criticism – on the whole against it. Nor could the differences be overlooked in the debate on rearmament. Both under Böckler's leadership and under Fette the DGB accepted rearmament, which the SPD rejected in the circumstances as cementing the partition of Germany. For the same reason, the SPD rejected the Schuman plan for setting up the Coal and Steel Union, which the unions supported as a contribution to economic reconstruction. The same thing applied to the idea of European integration; the unions came out in favour of it at any early stage – Otto Brenner and Ludwig Rosenberg were their spokesmen – calling for a European policy with a strong emphasis on social reform.[39]

There had already been criticism of the preparations for German rearmament at the second DGB congress, held in Berlin in October 1952. After the defeat over the Company Statute Law this criticism grew more vocal and the critics increased in number. The third DGB congress in October 1954 firmly rejected a German defence contribution, though without any action being taken to mobilize the membership. This was no doubt due to the threatened split in the movement.

Many former Christian trade unionists, such as Jakob Kaiser and Karl Arnold, had felt the DGB's 1953 election appeal to be a breach of the obligation to observe party political neutrality. Then, from 1952, the

---

39 See, for example, Ludwig Rosenberg, Eine Idee beschäftigt die Welt, in Gewerkschaftliche Monatshefte 6, 1950, pp. 241–4; and Europa ohne Konzeption, in ibid. 4, 1951, p. 169 ff.; Otto Brenner, Die Gewerkschaften und die europäischen Institutionen, in Die Neue Gesellschaft 5, 1957

DGB rejected the first move towards German rearmament, the German defence contribution, which it had initially accepted, as jeopardizing international detente and the reunification of Germany. It underlined this vote at its 1954 congress by 387 votes to 4. Moreover, it failed firmly to reject Viktor Agartz's ideas on economic policy. This eventually led to the establishment of a new Christian union movement. After the return of the Saarland in 1957, this union movement could boast some 200,000 members and in 1959 it renamed itself the Christian Trade Union Federation (CGB). It was supported by the leadership of the German Catholic Wage Earners' Movement (KAB), especially by Johannes Even and Bernhard Winkelheide; but there were also prominent Christian Democratic trade unionists such as Jakob Kaiser, Karl Arnold and Anton Storch who steered clear of the CGB.

After the predictable failure of the trade union protest against rearmament, the unions were more reluctant to tackle politically sensitive issues. Leading trade unionists and SPD politicians took part in the Paulskirchen movement, formed in January 1955, against the Paris treaties of May 1955; and the DGB's 1956 congress in Hamburg expressed support for those who were attempting by democratic means to halt rearmament, which was formalized with the introduction of compulsory military service in July 1956.

Finally, the unions had to interpret the results of the elections for the third *Bundestag* on 15 September 1957, which still reflected the feeling of shock at the crushing of the 1956 Hungarian uprising, as broad approval for the policy of integration in the West. The CDU/CSU gained 50.2 per cent of the vote and 270 out of 497 seats, giving it an absolute majority; Konrad Adenauer was re-elected for his third term as Chancellor. The SPD could only raise its share of the vote from 28.8 per cent (in 1953) to a modest 31.8 per cent and remained in opposition – now alongside the FDP.

＊

The second major domestic political controversy flared up in 1957–8 over the deployment of nuclear arms in the Federal Republic and the equipping of the *Bundeswehr* with tactical nuclear weapons, that is, in fact, over whether the *Bundeswehr* should be equipped with delivery systems, the nuclear warheads for which would remain under American control. An emergent extraparliamentary opposition, consisting of trade unionists and professors in particular, was more strongly in evidence now than during the rearmament debate. After the DGB congress of 1956 had stated its opposition to atomic and hydrogen bomb tests[40], in April 1957 the DGB federal executive rejected the storage and manufacture of atomic weapons and training in the use of such weapons on German soil. And on 12 April 1957 eighteen scientists warned of the consequences of nuclear armament in the "Göttingen declaration"; another 44 university and college professors expressed their opposition to nuclear weapons on 26 February 1958. The oppositional movement merged on 10 March 1958, setting up the action committee "Fight against nuclear death", in which Willi Richter took part on behalf of the DGB.

The parliamentary conflict over this issue culminated in the *Bundestag* debates of 20 and 25 March 1958, in which the SPD speakers – albeit for different reasons – came out against nuclear armament and the construction and deployment of nuclear weapons on German soil. Adenauer stressed, however, that it was necessary to equip the *Bundeswehr* with nuclear arms, as it was an important part of NATO; but NATO itself had to be strengthened in order to open the way for successful talks with the Soviet Union. A declaration to this effect was passed by the *Bundestag* with the CDU/CSU (plus one FDP vote) outvoting the SPD (and one FDP vote), and most of the FDP abstaining.

Concurrently with the *Bundestag* debate, the "Fight against nuclear death" action committee organized a series of events and meetings, calling on parliament and the government to break off the arms race, at least in nuclear arms. They also wanted efforts to set up a nuclear-free zone in central Europe to be supported, as a contribution to detente between East and West.

On 24 March 1958 the DGB federal executive's management committee had also decided to support the campaign against nuclear armament, but in no circumstances to seek to impose its views by means of a general strike. At the federal executive's extraordinary meeting of 28 March there was a long and heated discussion on the question of a general strike.[41] Richter referred to the Frankfurt rally on the issue of "Fight against nuclear death", at which the writer Robert Jungk had replied to an interjection calling for the declaration of a general strike, "If the unions leaders have the courage!" Erich Ollenhauer, the chairman of the SPD, had retorted, "that it is easy to call for general strike at a rally, but leave the implementation and responsibility to others". In the executive discussion

---

40 Protokoll des 4. ordentlichen Bundeskongresses des DGB in Hamburg, 1.–6. 10. 1956 (Düsseldorf, undated), p. 729
41 See Protokoll der ausserordentlichen Sitzung des Bundesvorstandes des DGB am 28. 3. 1958, pp. 2 and 4 f. (DGB-Archiv)

Preparations for the DGB's 1958 May Day rally in Munich

on a general strike, Otto Brenner, the chairman of IG Metall, spoke in favour of "major rallies with stoppages of a few hours' duration, in conjunction with a lull in traffic". Georg Leber, on behalf of the Construction Union, also supported the staging of rallies. He said, moreover, that his union would give legal and financial assistance to building workers who refused to build launching pads for nuclear weapons. In a resolution[42] the federal executive expressed its regret at the *Bundestag* decisions, saying that it was "convinced that the majority of the German people does not support these decisions". Accordingly, the DGB would bring its misgivings to the attention of the government and the parliamentary parties and support the "Fight against nuclear death" campaign and the idea of public opinion polls. These demands were backed by large rallies in Hamburg, Bremen, Kiel, Munich, Mannheim, Dortmund and Essen on 19 April 1958. In the spring of 1958 the campaign mobilized more than 300,000 people at demonstrations and rallies, not counting those who attended the union meetings on May Day 1958, which was also devoted to the anti-nuclear movement.

Starting in March 1958 attempts were made to carry out public opinion polls on nuclear armament. Since the efforts of the SPD parliamentary party to introduce a federal law to this effect were doomed to failure, the *Länder* under Social Democratic control had a special part to play. Hamburg and Bremen, in particular, together with certain areas of Hesse, pursued the matter and enacted laws in May 1958 providing for public opinion polls, with the backing of the SPD's federal organization. But on 30 July 1958 these laws were declared null and void by the Federal Constitutional Court, as armament matters were the sole responsibility of the Federal Government. This judgment, and the outcome of the regional parliamentary elections in North-Rhine Westphalia in July 1958 – in which the CDU gained an absolute majority – prompted a mood of resignation in the SPD. Although the party executive decided on 3 September 1958 to continue supporting the "Fight against nuclear death" campaign, there was no longer any sign of Social Democratic activity on the issue.

Political problems were looming within the unions, too. On 8 July Richter informed the federal executive that their commitment to the "Fight against nuclear death" movement had led to a real test for the DGB: the Christian-social group in the DGB was taking steps to set up an independent organization. The issue was also discussed at the executive meeting of 5 August 1958; although the DGB unions once again professed

---

42 ibid.

party political independence, it was not, they said, to be equated with political neutrality (or complete abstention from politics).

These internal organizational problems and the obvious failure of the campaign both contributed to the DGB's withdrawal from the anti-nuclear movement. Neither a poll of members nor an extraordinary congress could "bring a turn-around and revitalization", feared Brenner at the DGB federal executive on 2 September 1958. Bernhard Tacke, vice-chairman of the DGB and a CDU member commented that as the movement had evidently subsided, and the rallies had been poorly attended as a result.[43] One already detects here the mood of resignation in which the DGB's federal committee decided to withdraw from the "Fight against nuclear death" campaign in October 1958.

There was little interest in the unions and the SPD for a renewed publicity offensive over this issue. In 1960 the "Fight against nuclear death" committee ceased operating. Fresh issues – especially the Berlin crisis – had overtaken the nuclear question and quickly pushed it aside. But the debate on the emergency laws was also beginning to have an impact.

The start of the conflict over the emergency laws

The conflict over the emergency laws had its origins in the government's efforts, firstly, to close a "gap" in the Basic Law, and, secondly, to attain "a sovereign state's full control over its internal and external affairs" guaranteed by the General Treaty of 1955 between the Federal Republic and the Allies.

While the SPD advocated parliamentary action over the emergency issue, the government was drawing up internal plans to amend the constitution. These intentions first came to light in a speech by the minister responsible, the Interior Minister, Gerhard Schröder, at a conference of the Police Union, which at that time did not belong to the DGB, on 30 October 1958.[44] He outlined the main features of a system of emergency measures, which were tabled as a bill of ten articles amending the Basic Law in December of the same year. It was based to a large extent on the

---

43 See Protokoll der Sitzung des Bundesvorstandes des DGB am 2. 9. 1958, p. 8 f. (DGB-Archiv)
44 Gerhard Schröder, Sicherheit heute. Sind unsere Sicherheitseinrichtungen geeignet, auch schwere Belastungsproben auszuhalten? (Sonderdruck des Bulletins des Presse- und Informationsamtes der Bundesregierung, November 1958)

general powers granted by the Weimar constitution in the event of an emergency, from the executive's legal powers to the restrictions on basic civil rights.

Schröder's ideas were overwhelmingly rejected by the Social Democrats and the unions, especially IG Metall. They took the view that the provisions of the Basic Law were quite sufficient to cope with any emergency, particularly any internal crisis. There was, however, a political signal of practical significance in the form of the semi-official contribution of the Social Democratic constitutional expert, Adolf Arndt, who recommended his party to co-operate in the solution of the emergency law problem in an article in "Vorwärts" on 21 November 1958.

More than a year later, the CDU deputy Matthias Hoogen took up Arndt's idea and proposed inter-party talks, though the scope for compromise was bound to be limited as Schröder published the "Draft Bill amending the Basic Law" (the "Schröder Bill") on 18 January 1960, shortly after the opening of the talks. This bill proposed the insertion into the Basic Law of an Article 115a, permitting the declaration of a state of emergency by a simple majority of the *Bundestag* or, in the event of imminent danger, by the Chancellor alone. In addition, it allowed essential civil rights to be set aside, such as freedom of expression (Article 5), freedom of assembly (Article 8), freedom of association (Article 9), freedom of movement (Article 11) and freedom to exercise a trade (Article 12).

The bill was tabled on 18 January 1960 by the Federal Ministry of the Interior and rejected the same day by the committee of the SPD, and a day later by the parliamentary party. The bill was also heavily criticized by the FDP.

The unions' criticism was harsher, and also more fundamental. In a statement to the press on 19 January 1960 the Engineering Union, IG Metall, condemned "the attempt to revoke at will vital democratic rights using the power of the state"; any legislation on emergency powers was to be rejected. This put the DGB's federal executive on the spot. In early February it expressly rejected the "bill tabled" and "on the basis of historical experience" repudiated the plan "to abolish the democratic rights of wage earners and their unions in times of social crisis". The majority of the unions saw the emergency legislation bills of the CDU-led government as an attack on their very existence, and as the culmination of political and legal efforts in the "Adenauer Era" to impose permanent restrictions on the trade unions' right to co-determination and the right to strike.

The position of the critics of the emergency legislation was somewhat strengthened by Schröder's statement in the *Bundestag* on 28 September 1960 that for him the emergency situation was "the hour of the executive, because this is the moment when action must be taken".[45] He could hardly have been less sensitive to the feelings of a burgeoning leftwing-liberal public opinion. It was the government's persistent attachment to a tradition of authoritarian, anti-union ways of thought that led to the first, critical articles on the problem of emergency legislation in "Gewerkschaftliche Monatshefte". Another journal, "Blätter für deutsche und internationale Politik", which was associated with the names of Wolfgang Abendroth, Heinrich Hannover and most of all Jürgen Seifert, offered a major rallying point for opponents of the legislation.

After IG Metall's congress had decided in October 1960 to oppose all plans for emergency legislation "if necessary by all legal means, including strikes",[46] the DGB leadership considered it necessary to stress that it was the umbrella organization that would have overall charge of a political strike. The conflict between the Social Democrats and the unions became apparent when the Hanover SPD party conference of November 1960 expressed majority support for the line taken by the party executive and the parliamentary party: pursuing a policy of consensus, the SPD was prepared to collaborate with the government.

The public controversy, which intensified in the months that followed, was concerned with two main issues. The first bone of contention was whether the Basic Law was just a "fair weather" constitution, or well able to cope with civil emergencies and even war. Against the backdrop of the Cold War it seemed doubtful whether a credible deterrent could be maintained against the Eastern bloc without provision for an emergency. In the eyes of the advocates of legal provisions for an emergency, the parliamentary system was too cumbersome to be capable of functioning in times of crisis. The question of replacing the right of the Allies to assume ultimate control in an emergency also played a major part. But the opponents of the emergency laws insisted that such "enabling laws" constituted a domestic political danger whose potential effects could not be foreseen – but were illustrated by the planned restrictions on the right to strike, freedom of association and other basic civil rights.

Although the Schröder Bill was debated in the *Bundestag* on 28 September 1960 and then referred to committee, the committees concerned did not even place it on their agendas. After the elections of September

---

45 Verhandlungen des Bundestages, 3. Wahlperiode, 124. Sitzung am 28. 9. 1960, p. 7177 f.
46 IG Metall (ed), Protokoll des 6. Ordentlichen Gewerkschaftstages der IG Metall für die Bundesrepublik Deutschland, Berlin, 17.–22. Oktober 1960 (Frankfurt, undated), p. 398

1961, the CSU deputy Hermann Höcherl replaced Schröder as Interior Minister. Different in his approach from his predecessor and with a realistic assessment of the Social Democrats' blocking minority, Höcherl made contact with the parliamentary parties, the representatives of the *Länder* and the trade unions and announced that a new bill would be drafted.

The SPD indicated its readiness to co-operate in a legal solution with the six-point declaration by its leading bodies on 17 March 1962, which was ratified – with an additional point – in May 1962 at the Cologne party congress. After Willi Richter, the DGB chairman, had shown understanding for the SPD's position in the his opening address, a resolution was passed calling for a number of conditions to be imposed on any legislative provision for a state of emergency. A distinction had to be made between an internal emergency, the threat of attack (times of tension) and an external emergency. There was to be no possibility of abusing the provisions to suppress political adversaries or to undermine the free, democratic system of government – particularly by imposing curbs on freedom of expression, trade union rights and the powers of the *Länder,* the Federal Constitutional Court and Parliament.[47]

In January 1962 Otto Brenner, the chairman of IG Metall, had urged the DGB leadership in a letter to stand by its position of opposition to emergency legislation, whereupon the DGB had claimed control over the issue since it affected all the unions. The position of the trade unions – especially IG Metall – became more entrenched in the summer of 1962. The situation was no doubt aggravated by a comment by Hans Constantin Paulssen, president of the Federal Association of German Employers' Federations, in June 1962. Asked why the employers had not simply rejected the unions' demands in the latest engineering pay round, he had replied that industrial disputes were such a "political liability" that "without emergency legislation and provision for state intervention" the risk could not have been taken.[48]

Of course, it should not be forgotten that at its 1962 congress IG Metall had already retreated from its two-year-old strike decision: it would not strike against a two-thirds majority of the *Bundestag.* Anyway, a general strike was the affair of the DGB, which would have to call it if the rights of the unions were curtailed. This decision was accepted by the DGB's federal committee on 24 June 1962: "If civil liberties or the independent trade

47 SPD (ed), Protokoll der Verhandlungen und Anträge vom Parteitag der Sozialdemokratischen Partei Deutschlands in Köln, 26. bis 30. Mai 1962 (Bonn, undated), p. 582 f.
48 See, for example, the Frankfurter Allgemeine Zeitung of 20 June 1962

union movement are endangered it is the duty of the German Trade Union Federation to call a general strike."[49] At its Hanover congress of October 1962 the DGB adhered – in a resolution adopted by 276 votes to 238 (54% to 46%) – to its policy of principled opposition to legislation on a state of emergency, which IG Metall's abandonment of its strike threat had helped to make possible. In view of the importance of the unions as "guarantors of the democratic governmental and social system" and after a profession of allegiance to the Basic Law's "democratic and social state under the rule of law" (Article 20, paragraph 1, and Article 28, paragraph 1) the congress rejected "any additional legal provisions governing the state of emergency and emergency service, as both projects are likely to curtail basic civil liberties, especially freedom of association, the right to strike and the right freely to express one's opinion, and to weaken the democratic forces in the Federal Republic".[50]

The debate on this resolution revealed the differences of opinion between the unions. One of the chief advocates of the SPD line was Georg Leber, chairman of the Construction Union, supported by representatives of the Mining and Power Union, the Railwaymen's Union, the Post Office Union and the Education and Science Union; in his opinion it was no longer a question of whether legislation would be introduced, merely of what form it would take. This view was resolutely opposed by IG Metall, in particular, and also by the delegates of the Printing and Paper Union, Chemistry, Paper and Ceramics Union and Trade, Banking and Insurance Union.

A few days later, on 31 October 1962, Höcherl tabled a new bill. He could hardly have chosen a worse moment. The "Spiegel" affair had just strengthened the unions' (and others') misgivings about excessive government powers. The November 1962 negotiations over the formation of a Grand Coalition also increased reservations about the Höcherl Bill, though it did contain a number of important changes. For the first time a distinction was drawn between internal and external danger and the institution of an emergency committee as an emergency parliament was mooted; the possibility of restrictions of fundamental rights, and the right to issue emergency decrees, remained similar to the 1960 Schröder bill.

This bill also encountered severe criticism from the SPD and the unions. In 1963–4 the opposition widened and became more differen-

---

49 Protokoll der Sitzung des Bundesausschusses des DGB am 24. 7. 1962, p. 12 (DGB-Archiv), published in Die Quelle 8, 1962, p. 338
50 Protokoll des 6. ordentlichen Bundeskongresses des DGB, 22.–24. 10. 1962 in Hannover (Düsseldorf, undated), p. 960 ff.

tiated. The arguments within the SPD became more incisive; the SPD's South Hesse district, in particular, achieved a sharp profile as opponents of legislation. Individual trade union congresses discussed public education and mobilization campaigns. The DGB leadership argued about the practical, political interpretation of the congress decision. Their means of exerting influence were, however, still confined to appeals to the prime ministers of the *Länder* and the federal deputies to reject the proposed legislation. But the development of a broad-based opposition movement would not have been feasible without the commitment of the Socialist German Student Union (SDS), the "Campaign for Disarmament" and IG Metall, which stepped up its information work towards the end of 1964, when the passage of emergency legislation seemed imminent.

Early 1965 saw a surge of public protest against an apparently impending agreement between the government and opposition parties on the emergency legislation; 215 professors, for example, appealed to the DGB in March 1965 to stand firm by the 1962 decision. But the DGB federal executive decided on 2 February and 4 May 1965 not to call for public rallies against the legislation. Instead it brought its influence to bear in talks and in a letter to all the *Bundestag* deputies on 15 May. So the DGB failed to live up to the expectations of the university protesters as forcefully as they would have liked. Nevertheless, collaboration between the protest of universities and intellectuals, which manifested itself in a congress, "Democracy faced with an emergency", held at Bonn University on 30 May, and the trade union opposition henceforth characterized the debate on emergency legislation, which from this point of view was a continuation of the nuclear armament controversy of the late 1950s.

It was probably due, at least in part, to pressure from the trade unions and the growing opposition of party organizations and public opinion that the SPD party executive, Shadow Cabinet and party council unanimously decided in Saarbrücken on 29 May 1965 to reject the emergency constitutional provisions as tabled by the *Bundestag's* legal committee under Ernst Benda (CDU). A balance sheet of twelve points (compared with the seven points of Cologne) and the "old" demands were repeated. In accordance with SPD's position, this bill also failed to gain the necessary two-thirds majority, after it had been presented against the votes of the SPD on the legal committee. But the years of deliberation in committee and the – secret – inter-party meetings of May 1965 had reinforced expectations that the law would probably be passed before the general elections of September 1965. The unions, in particular, were blamed by supporters of the bill for the SPD's turn-about. The CDU seized the opportunity to portray the SPD as the "prisoner of the unions" in its electoral propaganda. Partly for this reason the SPD found it necessary to emphasize its independence. In July 1965, Willy Brandt, the SPD's candidate for Chancellor, explicitly repudiated the union view, as formulated at the DGB's Hanover congress, that the provisions of the Basic Law and the constitutions of the Länder were sufficient to meet emergencies. Furthermore, he stressed the legitimacy of the SPD's position in terms of party (conference) decisions.

If the negative vote of the SPD had prevented the adoption of the constitutional amendment, the "simple" emergency bills (simple because they only required a simple instead of a two-thirds majority) were passed – bills on the economy, food supplies, transport, water supplies, civil protection, self-protection and protective building. Except for the water supply bill, the SPD voted against them. The bills had anyway been pushed through in far too much of a hurry, as demonstrated by the fact that, owing to subsequent amendments in view of the tight financial situation, the protection bills could not be brought into force until 1968.

After the *Bundestag* elections of September 1965, which once again enabled Erhard to form a CDU/CSU and FDP government, Paul Lücke took over at the Interior Ministry. He tried from the start to cultivate contacts with the SPD and the unions. The fact that the inter-party "Commission of Twelve" commenced work on the preparations for emergency legislation in March 1966 also indicated a "new style", which offered the SPD parliamentary party an opportunity to "co-operate". The SPD group's policy hitherto was given broad support at the party conference in June 1966. An attempt by the South Hesse district to gain a majority for its own position of fundamental rejection of emergency legislation, in view of the risk of a breach between the SPD and the unions, was lost by some 25–30 votes.

In the meantime there was some movement in the internal union discussions. Admittedly, in September 1965 IG Metall once again expressed its opposition to any form of legislation governing emergencies, and in May 1966 the DGB confirmed its 1962 decision by 251 votes to 182 (58% to 42%) after an impassioned debate.[51] But the resolution did not speak of a fundamental rejection of any form of emergency legislation; instead, certain specific conditions were advanced: "The unions continue to reject any emergency legislation that curtails democratic rights, especially in so far as it threatens the rights of assembly and association and the right to strike of the wage earners and their organizations." It should be noted, however, that even the 182 delegates who voted against the resolution did

---

51 Protokoll des 7. ordentlichen Bundeskongresses des DGB in Berlin, 9.–14. 5. 1966 (Düsseldorf, undated), p. 12 f.

not do so because they supported the bill tabled earlier, but because they wished to express their view that the DGB should take an active part in discussions on the emergency laws in order to obtain improvements.

To outward appearances, then, the appeals of the emergent extra-parliamentary opposition to the DGB had met with success; but in the internal DGB discussions the minority position prevailed. The DGB's emergency legislation commission set up in September 1966 at Brenner's instigation did vote in favour of the unions taking part in the congress planned for 30 October 1966 by the committee entitled "Democracy in Danger" (Notstand der Demokratie). But after an argument in the DGB executive it was decided that the DGB would take no part in the committee or in the congress. Consequently, only a handful of unions were represented at the congress at Frankfurt am Main: the Engineering Union; Chemicals, Paper and Ceramics; Printing and Paper; Commerce, Banking and Insurance; Wood and Plastics; and Leather. The "Democracy in Danger" committee, set up in August 1966, was based in IG Metall's building in Frankfurt, and the union also gave the committee financial assistance, though it was not prepared to give it a general policy mandate. The congress of 30 October 1966 was simultaneously the culmination and the conclusion of the united protest movement of students, academics and trade unionists, the collapse of which became fully apparent in "May '68" when the emergency laws were adopted.

4. *Under the impact of the "economic miracle": social change, organizational problems and a new policy direction*

Full employment, stable prices, rises in real wages and reductions in working hours – all these things meant that large numbers of working people were able to share in the growing prosperity of the 1950s (Tables 3c, 4b and 5b). The improvement in living standards, security in times of crisis and the increase in leisure had consequences which, though perceived at an early stage by the unions, were not fully analysed in terms of their implications for union activities.

*

Economic development, particularly the experience of the "economic miracle" could not fail to affect the consciousness of working people. All those who hoped that the continued existence of the private capitalist economic order would "necessarily" lead to a unified worker consciousness were – once again – disappointed. The National Socialist dictatorship and the upheavals of war and the post-war period had left deep traces in the minds of the workers. This was demonstrated by a sociological survey carried out in 1953–4 into the political awareness of iron and steel workers; apart from the feeling of "us down here" and "them up there", there were scarcely any detectable signs of a positive class consciousness or sense of solidarity.[52] The trade unions were also faced with the problem that "them up there" not only included the management and government, but also, in many cases, the works council and the union machinery.[53]

The upheavals in the traditional working class environment, which had been a major source of support for the unions, were bound to have implications. The effects of the war, refugees and deportees, the recruitment of foreign workers and the increase in internal migration shook up the traditional areas of working class housing. The trend towards "living where the grass is green" and the construction of residential estates outside city limits aided the development of socially mixed housing areas, with the result that the old solidarity networks were lost.

But it would be wrong to blame the trade unions and their home building policy, as represented by "Neue Heimat", for the disappearance of this milieu. The reconstruction of entire neighbourhoods and suburban housing estates was brought on by the acute housing shortage and the wishes of many of those in need of a home who were not attracted by the romantic aspects of overcrowding, backyards and kitchens doubling as bedrooms. But the new life style in the seclusion of one's own flat, the increasingly prevalent family evenings round the TV, the long car journey to and from work undeniably encouraged individualistic tendencies, which were also underpinned by a dismissive attitude towards all collective arrangements, after the experiences of the Third Reich. By the same token, the new way of life created and reinforced similar needs in manual and white-collar workers, which led to the erosion of social differences.

After the catastrophe so recently experienced, the desire for security became one of the most important principles governing people's lives. Promotion at work, the security of the family, improved opportunities for consumption and a refusal to take an active part in politics characterized the life style of a great many working people. A career was increasingly felt

---

52 Heinrich Popitz, Hans Paul Bahrdt, Ernst August Jüres and Hanno Kesting, Das Gesellschaftsbild des Arbeiters. Soziologische Untersuchungen in der Hüttenindustrie (Tübingen, 1957), especially p. 237 ff.
53 Heinz Kluth, Im Spannungsfeld der Organisationen, in Die Neue Gesellschaft 1961, pp. 7–15, especially p. 14 f.

to be the same as paid employment; one's true desires were realized through leisure not at work. After people had acquired the basic necessities once again, they saved for the more lasting consumer goods such as a refrigerator, followed by a television set, a car, camping equipment and travel – and, before long, Mediterranean holidays. On a scale hitherto unknown, the social reality of large sections of wage earners was determined by "quality of life" in the form of leisure and pleasure.

This improvement in the standard of living was attributed to the market economy by many wage earners – especially as the poverty and distress of the war and the post-war period and the relatively slow economic recovery in the GDR could be seen as examples of the consequences of state intervention in the economy. The "economic miracle" was the precondition for the broad recognition won by the "social market economy". Linked with this, large sections of the working population had a favourable attitude towards the private capitalist economic system, favourable at least in the sense that they believed it made a just solution to conflicts of interest possible. Moreover, many wage earners appeared to question the need for trade unions; individual promotion was seen by many as just as likely to improve their position in life.

Also large numbers of working people increasingly saw themselves as belonging to the middle class. As production grew progressively more technical, specializations and qualifications changed and as a result the workforce became increasingly fragmented. Whereas well-qualified skilled workers in a professional position could attain the income level and living standard of senior white-collar workers, the semi-skilled and unskilled, particularly women, remained on the lower rungs of society. Among civil servants and salaried staff, who had increased as a proportion of the working population between 1950 and 1960 from 20 per cent to 28.1 per cent, there developed the "special consciousness" that derived its sustenance from stressing their "differentness" from the workers. Clean office jobs, educational qualifications, proximity to management, better security socially and in industrial law and an income that rose with age all confirmed, along with higher social prestige, the white-collar workers' sense of their own worth. They considered all forms of collective representation of interests dispensable, if not actually "beneath their dignity". Although there was a process of social levelling between manual and white-collar workers in the 1950s, many of the latter clung on to their belief that they were the real representatives of the "new middle class".

But it is questionable whether one can adequately describe this development as a "levelled-off middle class society", a "levelled-off petty bourgeois, middle class society, that is no more proletarian than it is bourgeois, that is, one that is characterized by the loss of class tension and social hierarchy".[54] Certainly, there was no mistaking the tendencies towards erosion of the income differences between manual and white-collar workers and fairer access to consumption and entertainment, a fact which led to the question (alarmed or hopeful according to viewpoint), "Is there still a proletariat?"[55] But in terms of their subordinate status at work, the greater risk of unemployment, and the frequently frowned-upon manual nature of their work, discrimination against the working class continued to be a recognizable fact. The workers were not simply absorbed into the mass of the working population. And from the point of view of society as a whole, the "ideal" of the levelled-off middle class society all too obviously took no account of the problems of uneven wealth distribution, inequality in educational opportunity and differing ability to exert economic and political influence. Such problems could only be passed over because they no longer mattered much to large numbers of wage earners. As they retreated into the private sphere people tended to confine themselves – to a certain extent understandably, in view of past experience – to a spectator role in politics, a trend which also affected the trade unions.

*

As we have seen, the shift in the consciousness of "the wage earner" could not fail to have implications for the unions. Although they were able to point to successes in collective bargaining and social policy, this did not cause a marked influx of new members. The statistics, which show a steady rise in membership from 5.4 m in 1950 to 6.57 m in 1965 (Table 1c), are misleading. For measured against the increasing number of people in paid employment, which rose from 14.5 m to 21.6 m over the same period, this was certainly not a particularly impressive performance. Even counting the white-collar union DAG, whose membership increased from 343,000 (1951) to 475,00 (1965)(Table 1c), the degree of organization fell between 1951 and 1965 from 38.6 per cent to 32.6 per cent.[56]

---

54 Helmut Schelsky, Wandlungen der deutschen Familie der Gegenwart. Darstellung und Deutung einer empirisch-soziologischen Tatbestandsaufnahme, 2nd ed. (Stuttgart, 1954), p. 218
55 Hans Paul Bahrdt, Walter Dirks at al., Gibt es noch ein Proletariat? (Frankfurt, 1962, 2nd ed. 1969)
56 According to Wolfgang Streeck, Gewerkschaften als Mitgliederverbände. Probleme gewerkschaftlicher Mitgliederrekrutierung, in J. Bergmann (ed), Beiträge zur Soziologie der Gewerkschaften, pp. 72–110; these figures p. 102

This development was due to a number of quite different factors. Let us look first at the changes in the structure of the working class, which had a direct impact on the development of individual unions. The drop in employment caused by the declining importance of certain industries directly affected the unions concerned. From 1950 to 1965, the membership of the Leather Union fell from 95,000 to 74,000; Horticulture, Agriculture and Forestry went down from 98,000 to 67,000; the Woodworkers from 180,000 to 121,000; Textiles and Garments from 387,000 to 310,000; and Mining and Power from 534,000 to 319,000. The real growth unions were those in the growth industries: the Engineers' Union, IG Metall (up from 1.28 m to 1.74 m); Public Services, Transport and Communications (from 726,000 to 970,000), Chemicals, Paper and Ceramics (from 389,000 to 496,000), Construction (from 376,000 to 436,000) and the German Post Office Union (from 190,000 to 323,000). Membership showed little increase, on the other hand, in Printing and Paper (122,000 to 129,000) and Food, Beverage and Allied Trades (244,000 to 256,000).

But all the trade unions recorded a drop in the degree of organization between 1950 and 1965. In IG Metall it fell from 53 to 34.2 per cent; in Chemicals from 51.3 to 36.6 per cent; and in Construction from 30.2 to 19.2 per cent. It remained conspicuously high in the miners' union, however; although it was an industry that was shortly to be racked by crisis it had "only" experienced a decline in organization from 90.4 per cent (1950) to 68.5 per cent (1965).

Even in the 1950s the unions obviously found it hard to keep up with the changes in the structure of the working population. Although the proportion of workers to total trade union membership fell from 83.1 per cent (1950) to 77.8 per cent (1966) and the proportion of white-collar workers and civil servants increased from 10.4 to 13.2 per cent and from 6.5 to 9 per cent respectively, manual workers were still greatly over-represented, considering that they made up "only" 59 per cent of all wage earners. The trade unions were thus slow to take account of the changes in the labour force, and did so only incompletely.

The trade unions did not succeed during the 1950s in making any substantial breakthrough in organizing white-collar workers. Whereas the degree of organization among manual workers was about 40 per cent in the early 1960s, the corresponding figure for white-collar workers – DGB and DAG unions combined – was about 18–19 per cent.[57]

---

57 ibid. p. 103 f.

The organization of women also left much to be desired. The proportion of women members remained unchanged from 1950 to 1965 at about 16 per cent. Yet at least in this area the unions, which had adopted guidelines on female labour as long ago as 1949,[58] were able to keep pace, organizationally, with the increase in working women – though without improving their weak position.

Problems were also caused by the trend towards an ageing membership. While in 1963–64 only 51 per cent of male wage earners were over 35 years of age, they comprised 72 per cent of union members.[59] By stepping up their work among young workers from the beginning of the 1960s, the unions attempted to improve the age structure of the membership. They were concerned not simply with vocational qualifications but also – and more especially – with cultural events and political mobilization, the main thrust of which was symbolized by the youth magazine "ran", launched in 1970.

Changes in economic and social structure, on the one hand, and the experiences of the "economic miracle" and the Cold War on the other left their stamp on the unions' organizational successes. With the increase in white-collar workers and the growing number of working women, the recruitment of foreign workers and the integration of refugees and exiles boosted the number of wage earner groups who could only be organized with some difficulty. Recruitment was complicated by the survival of the status-minded outlook peculiar to white-collar workers, the specific problems of gender-stereotyping among women, the concentration on short-term income goals and political wariness among refugees and exiles and, in addition, linguistic barriers and traditional ties among foreign workers.

The skilled male worker continued to form the backbone of the trade unions; the unions were also strong in large companies and big cities. The results of the works councils elections in 1963 and 1965 illustrate the the relative strengths of the unions: the DGB won 82.2 and 82.7 per cent respectively; the DAG 3.6 and 3.4 per cent; other organizations (including the CGB) 1 and 0.7 per cent and non-organized 13.2 per cent. In the staff council elections of 1962 and 1966, the DGB won 73.6 and 74.8 per cent

---

58 Protokoll. Gründungskongress des DGB, München, 12.–14. Oktober 1949 (Cologne, 1950), p. 337 f. and Geschäftsbericht 1950–51, ed. DGB-Bundesvorstand (Düsseldorf, undated), p. 599 ff.

59 Walter Nickel, Zum Verhältnis von Arbeiterschaft und Gewerkschaft. Eine soziologische Untersuchung über die qualitative Struktur der Mitglieder und des Mitgliedspotentials der Gewerkschaften in der Bundesrepublik Deutschland (Cologne, 1972), p. 119

of seats respectively.[60] Although the DGB lists were overwhelmingly successful in works council and staff council elections, this cannot disguise the problems of membership structure. The unions had still found no reply to the changes in economic structure; nor did the stepping-up of agitational work at the beginning of the 1960s pay any quick dividends. Not until the political climate shifted did the trade unions catch up with the processes of social change from the mid-1960s.

*

How did the unions try to face up to this change in social reality and political *Zeitgeist?* At the end of the 1950s one approach seemed to be to strengthen the power of the organization and the leading role of the DGB; and, secondly, there were plans to replace the 1949 document "Principles of economic policy" with a new programme.

Let us first consider the efforts to reform the organization. In view of the differing strengths of the unions it is not surprising that there were repeated clashes between the unions over the duties and influence of the DGB. Whereas the smaller unions, whose mouthpiece was Georg Leber of the Construction Union, supported the strengthening of the DGB, the representatives of the large unions, headed by Otto Brenner of IG Metall, saw this as a threat to their own influence. At the DGB's 1959 congress in Stuttgart the opposing views collided head on. The conflict over the status of the DGB was eclipsed by discussions on the preparations for a new union programme, which had the backing of Willi Richter, DGB chairman since 1956, and Ludwig Rosenberg, head of the DGB federal executive's economics department. At any rate, it was decided to reform the structure of the DGB trade unions. The aim was to tighten up the decision-making structures and provide the DGB with more money and wider powers.

Three years later, at the Hanover congress of 1962, a number of changes to the statutes were adopted.[61] There was evident caution in the approach to radical reforms designed to standardize the structure of the individual unions and strengthen the umbrella organization. The executive board of the DGB was authorized to "take the necessary steps in matters of particular importance, if a decision cannot be deferred". Moreover,

---

60 Geschäftsbericht des Bundesvorstandes des DGB 1962–1965 (Düsseldorf, undated), p. 153; the same source 1965–1968, p. 128
61 DGB (ed), Protokoll. 6. Ordentlicher Bundeskongress Hannover, 22. bis 27. Oktober 1962 (Düsseldorf, undated), p. 991 ff.

Paragraph 3 of the statutes stipulated that "the decisions and guidelines of the federal congress, federal committee and federal executive shall be binding" not only on the DGB but also on the trade unions.

But in view of the efforts in the 1960s to strengthen internal union democracy, the consolidation of the position of the DGB federal executive vis-à-vis its member organizations was bound to raise problems. For one thing, the federal executive's powers over the DGB districts and regions were extended – particularly remarkable was the fact that the elected district and regional executive members could be removed from office by the federal executive. For another, the DGB districts lost their right to submit motions direct to the federal congress. The organization of the DGB was thus centralized, but it is open to question whether this amounted to a strengthening of the organization as a whole.

It was probably the fact that the SPD was on the point of drawing the policy conclusions from the changes in the social and political landscape in the 1950s with its Godesberg Programme, and the inadequacy of their own programme, that led to the decision of the DGB's 1959 congress in Stuttgart to draw up a new programme. The discussions on the reform of the statutes had not only been characterized by the divergent interests of the large and small unions but also by the clash over the unions' aims and strategy. So it was no coincidence that those who sought an increase in the DGB's power were also in favour of a policy review. It was Georg Leber, more than anyone, who now wished – in the wake of the Godesberg Programme – to commit the unions to recognizing the democratic republic and the established economic system. Social partnership and the consistent representation of economic interests on the basis of the status quo were the watchwords. Leber's most prominent supporters were Heinrich Gutermuth of the Mining and Power Union and the DGB executive, which was headed from 1962 by Ludwig Rosenberg.

Who was the new DGB chairman, whose personal charisma went a long way towards extinguishing the trade union movement's traditional image of cloth cap and class struggle. Ludwig Rosenberg was born in Berlin in 1903, the son of a businessman. After attending grammar school he joined the family business. In 1923 he joined the Social Democratic Party and took an active part in the Hirsch-Duncker white-collar trade union, for which he started working full-time in 1928. As a Jew and a trade unionist, he was forced to flee from the National Socialists, and from 1933 to 1946 he lived in exile in England, where he worked as a journalist and lecturer and belonged to the English branch of the German trade unionists' organization. On his return to Germany he took up a post as a secretary at the British zone secretariat in Bielefeld, and from 1948 with the trade union council in the united zones. From 1949 he worked for the DGB's federal executive, until 1952 as head of the foreign department; from 1954 on he was head of the economic department. In the arguments over Viktor Agartz's proposals on economic policy, Rosenberg became well-known as a champion of free-market ideas. This fact – along with an adaptability based on tolerance – recommended him for the post of the DGB's vice-chairman in 1959, before taking over as head of the organization in 1962.

His adaptability and his diplomatic skills were to be much in evidence in 1963, in the clashes over the "programme of principle", in which (naturally) IG Metall and Otto Brenner also figured. Unlike Rosenberg, Brenner took the view that Germany was still a class society. To him things were clear: "The dependent position of working people, their modest share in the national product, their general insecurity remain unchanged – not only do these live on, but so do, most importantly, the power and influence of the entrepreneurs, the enormous profits generated by the economy, which are financed and augmented at the expense of the consumers and the working people. In a word, the class society lives on." Brenner drew the conclusion that the unions should stand by the demands of the Munich Programme for "the transfer of the key industries into public ownership, co-determination and national economic planning".[62] At IG Metall's 1960 congress he also championed the central demands of 1949, since the new programme was supposed to be an "improvement and not a dilution of the old one".[63]

At the sixth DGB congress in Hanover in 1962 the opposing political viewpoints collided head on in the debate on the emergency legislation. The policy debate, on the other hand, was adjourned to an extraordinary congress as there had not been enough time to discuss the draft programme properly in the trade union organizations.

The following months were, in fact, devoted to the discussion. At the DGB's Düsseldorf congress of 1963, 262 amendments were submitted, many of them taking issue with the failure to adapt to existing conditions criticized by many of the movers. The influence of the critical motions was evident in, for example, the preamble[64], which emphasized, in the version adopted, that the "capitalist economic system has denied the worker social equality, subjected him to the arbitrary decisions of the

62 Otto Brenner, Soziale Sicherheit und gesellschaftlicher Fortschritt, in Protokoll des 5. Gewerkschaftstages der IG Metall (Nuremberg, 1958), p. 196 ff.; these quotations pp. 204 and 215

63 Protokoll des 6. Gewerkschaftstages der IG Metall, 1960, p. 230

64 Protokoll. Ausserordentlicher Bundeskongress des DGB in Düsseldorf, 21. and 22. November 1963 (Düsseldorf, undated), p. 449 ff.

employer, abandoned his labour to the laws of the market, subordinated his social security to the scramble for profit, and causes social evils and crises". And with an eye to the debate on the emergency legislation, the preamble assured that the DGB and the unions were combating "all attempts to restrict or lift the rights enshrined in the Basic Law of the Federal Republic".

Thus the "basic programme" adopted in Düsseldorf in 1963, with Ludwig Rosenberg now heading the DGB, showed signs of an integration of the differing positions. It was based on a far-reaching recognition of the economic and social structure that had developed in the post-war period. The profession of faith in the "social market economy" was, however, complemented by a demand for state controls, from the national accounts to the socialization of key industries, as instruments of an economic policy committed to an economic system in keeping with the free development of the individual and human dignity. Bipartite co-determination was one of the key demands relating to orderly administration. Taking up the ideas of an anticyclical economic policy, the trade unions took the view that the crises in economic development could be softened, if not avoided altogether, by means of counter-measures applied by the state.

To the principles of economic and social policy of 1949 were also added aims in the sphere of cultural policy. Starting from the basic idea that a democratization of society was only possible if the education system was also democratized, the programme demanded reforms in both vocational training and school and college education to give easier access to courses and create equality of opportunity. With this extension of their programme, the unions drew the logical conclusions from their own practice, which was not solely concerned with industrial disputes and social policy initiatives but also with the Ruhr festival in Recklinghausen, the Gutenberg book club, the federal association "Arbeit und Leben", the "Academy of Labour" in Frankfurt, the DGB culture prize and so on.

But the programme was not all of a piece. It contained theoretical criticism of capitalism with recognition of the market economy side by side, without combining them into a unified model of society or even a consistent strategy. It was an attempt by the unions to keep up with the times, to be "modern" – and they allowed themselves to be carried away by optimism with regard to the avoidability of capitalist crises and the chances of social levelling. The optimism was to set its stamp on the decade that followed.

The recognition of the economic status quo in the DGB's programme did not, however, go far enough for the Federal Union of Employers' Associations. It considered that a number of "the DGB's demands, which are in contradiction with our free economic and social system, [. . .] would be bound to have damaging implications for the whole nation if implemented". In particular, the demands for an extension of co-determination, central control measures, lasting redistribution and the transfer of key industries into public ownership showed, the employers claimed, that the DGB saw only the unions' rights and not their obligations as the "joint guardians of our free social system".[65]

This established the fundamental viewpoints of unions and employers as they entered a decade of social reorganization and modernization. The trade unions as a force for social reform, striving, above all, for a democratization of the state and society on the basis of existing conditions; the employers as defenders of a free economic system which – in their eyes – had proved itself and had to be protected against any claims by the state or the unions to a say in its running.

The fact was, the adoption of the "basic programme" had not managed to resolve the tensions between union demands on the future and the unions' current demands. It exposed the need, which was acted on a few years later, for a revision of the 1955 action programme. "Successes in the implementation" of this programme "and the rapid changes in living and working conditions made it necessary to adapt it to social developments", stated the DGB report for 1962–65.[66] The action programme presented to the public at a press conference on 23 March 1965 differed from its predecessor on several major points. With ten chapters instead of five, and headed by a preamble, it was partly an optimistic summary of union successes hitherto and partly a pledge to continue working for the goals still to be attained.

The "basic programme" of 1963 had already enlarged the political problem areas which the unions saw as their field of action; the action programme adopted the same approach. Alongside the traditional demands for shorter working hours, wage rises, improvements in industrial safety, the extension of co-determination, the just distribution of wealth and the safeguarding of jobs, it also addressed the question of "social infrastructure", particularly the areas of education, housing and health. But the new demands had a fundamentally pragmatic character that was unparalleled. The collective bargaining aims were a thirteenth month's wages, the provision of "fringe benefits", a contribution towards the just distribution of

65 Reprinted in Arno Klönne, Demokratischer und sozialer Rechtsstaat. Dokumente zur Gewerkschaftspolitik (Bochum, 1964), p. 133 f.
66 Geschäftsbericht des Bundesvorstandes des Deutschen Gewerkschaftsbundes 1962 bis 1. Halbjahr 1965 (Düsseldorf, undated), p. 6; also sets out the action programme

wealth and four weeks' minimum holiday. The list of demands also contained calls for the reduction of the general retirement age, adequate legal protection for tenants and the introduction of a tenth year of schooling. But as Otto Brenner, the chairman of the action programme commission, emphasized at the press conference, the centrepiece was the introduction of full economic co-determination throughout the economy. The demand for co-determination advanced to become the unions' prime objective in the 1960s, and there was scarcely any internal disagreement over this. The DAG also gave a large measure of backing to this demand at its 1963 congress, but insisted that greater account should be taken of the white-collar workers' special position in the Company Statute Law. The Catholic Labour Movement, too, professed its support for an extension of bipartite co-determination to all large concerns in its declaration of principle on social matters of 24 April 1964.[67]

The DGB's action programme was released in the spring amid a blaze of publicity and was the focal point of the 1965 May Day rallies. Whether the individual demands kindled much enthusiasm is open to doubt; in any case, it was not mass mobilization that presented the unions with real opportunities to achieve their aims but the changes in the political landscape that took place in the mid-1960s.

---

67 The DAG and KAB documents are reprinted in Klönne, op. cit., p. 135 ff.

XII. A new departure: the trade unions in the years of social reform 1966–1974/76

The end of the "Adenauer Era" and Ludwig Erhard's assumption of office as Federal Chancellor in October 1963, together with the SPD's consensus policy, which paved the way for the formation of the Grand Coalition, marked the beginning of a period that saw the political incrustations of the 1950s cast off, at first cautiously and then with increasing speed. The construction of the Berlin Wall, starting on 13 August 1961, had demonstrated the futility of the *Ostpolitik* pursued hitherto and constituted a positive challenge to rethink relations with the GDR and the Eastern bloc. The removal of the ban on the Communist Party and the creation of the DKP showed a greater degree of political and democratic self-assurance and a desire to shift the rigid fronts of the Cold War. The "educational emergency", which soon became a familiar catchphrase, appeared to jeopardized the Federal Republic's chances as a highly developed industrialized country and set up the call for the mobilization of the educational reserves of people at all levels of society. Moreover, it turned out that no sooner had the unions adapted their programme to the market economy system that – apparently – guaranteed never-ending economic growth, than there were the first clear signs of the cyclical and structural problems that developed into the recession of 1966. State intervention, which Erhard's CDU/CSU government largely replaced with appeals for moderation and the idea of the "aligned society", was increasingly acknowledged to be what the situation called for. But above all it was the youth protest of the mid-1960s – arising from opposition to the smug self-righteousness of the "CDU state", the "fustiness" that was discovered at every turn and stereotyped "friend-enemy" ways of thought – which, in alliance with numerous leftwing intellectuals, acted as the pacemaker for a shift in the *Zeitgeist* whose slogans were reform, democratization and emancipation. For a number of years it looked as if the unions were in step with the times.

1. Trade unions in politics: shared responsibility and a share in shaping events

The pressure of problems that had built up over the years, the wear and tear on the CDU/CSU leadership in the government and the resultant helplessness in the face of the political challenges of the end of the post-war period became abundantly plain in the mid-1960s. While the CDU slogan "No experiments" had met a need for security in the 1950s, the looming difficulties of the 1960s required fresh ideas and new solutions. Simply "carrying on" as before along the path of growth mapped out by the "economic miracle" was not merely considered meaningless material-ism and hence unsatisfactory; in view of the foreseeable economic uphea-vals ahead it was, in fact, no longer feasible. The market economy had passed the test of reconstruction; it now had to prove whether or not it could cope with economic setbacks.

An unmistakable sign of impending trouble was the decline in the eco-nomic growth rate, which – after the first dive to 3 per cent in 1963 – had risen again to 6.6 per cent the following year, but had then fallen, via 5.5 per cent (1965) and 2.5 per cent (1966), to –0.1 per cent in 1967. The fluc-tuations in growth rates hitherto had all been on the plus side, but in 1967 the zero barrier was broken for the first time.

From mid-1966, the economic recession was reflected in rising unem-ployment, which reached a peak for the 1966–67 crisis in February 1967 with a total of 673,000 or 3.1 per cent of the working population. Foreign workers were particularly badly hit by the recession and there was a dras-tic cut in their numbers – from 1.3 m to 900,000. Unemployment rates rose sharply, especially in the less developed regions: in Cham and Passau it reached 25.4 and 19.7 per cent respectively, in Leer and Emden 14 and 10.8 per cent. In the Ruhr district, however, there was only a slight rise in unemployment, despite the pit closures since 1964 due to the coal crisis: the worst hit town was Gelsenkirchen with an unemployment rate of 4.4 per cent.[1]

True to the liberal outlook, Erhard governed through appeals for mod-eration to the wage earners and their trade unions. But in 1966 it became increasingly obvious that wage restraint was having no effect. The backlog of long overdue social reforms and, above all, the economic recession seemed to make a broadly based government advisable. As a marginal note, perhaps we should add that the minimal opposition to this plan in

---

1 According to Geschäftsbericht des DGB 2. Halbjahr 1965–1968 (Düsseldorf, undated), p. 195 f.

parliament aroused a great deal of controversy within the SPD and, even more so, in leftwing and liberal circles. It also contributed to the development of the extraparliamentary opposition (APO).

The Grand Coalition: fighting the crisis, social policy initiatives and the adoption of the emergency laws

After tough negotiations, a Grand Coalition government was set up in December 1966 under Chancellor Kurt Georg Kiesinger (CDU) and Vice-Chancellor and Foreign Minister Willy Brandt (SPD). There was a fundamental change in the unions' attitude to the government, seen most clearly in the appointment of Georg Leber, a well-known union leader, as Transport Minister. The new government's main tasks were undoubtedly in the economic and financial sphere: to balance the federal budget for 1967 and to reflate the economy. It was the job of the Finance Minister, Franz Josef Strauss (CSU), and the Minister for Economic Affairs, Karl Schiller (SPD), to find solutions to these problems.

*

The prime task of the new government was to give a boost to the economy. On 10 February 1967 it introduced, as the first step in its economic policy, special accelerated depreciation facilities to stimulate investment. This was followed on 12 April by the Credit Financing Law, with a 2.5 billion Mark increase in state orders and, on 10 May, the adoption of the Law to Promote the Stability and Growth of the Economy. This law, which came into force on 14 June, made state intervention to control the economic cycle compulsory. A policy of "global steering" – a favourite term of Karl Schiller – was supposed to ensure growth, full employment, price stability and external equilibrium. In particular, provision for a contingency budget, permitting public bodies to spend an additional DM 5 bn, promised to give a rapid fillip to the economy. In addition, the government was empowered to raise or lower income tax by 10 per cent as required by the business cycle. To stimulate economic activity in the short term, the government should be able to finance additional state orders, in accordance with Keynesian policy, by means of loans, that is, through the national debt. When the economy was thriving – and tax revenue was flowing in – the state should build up an anticyclical reserve to prevent overheating of the economy and, in times of crisis, to prevent the national debt from becoming too big. Also in the long term, the government was obliged by the "Stability Law" to submit an annual economic report to the two Chambers, the *Bundestag* and *Bundesrat,* every January, outlining the overall economic situation and setting out the government's economic and financial objectives. Further, the government had to estimate state revenue and expenditure as part of "medium-term financial planning" for a period of five years.

The fact that this law obliged the government to relieve turbulence in the economy by state control measures was wholly in line with the course recommended by the unions, who had advocated a programme to boost the economy by state job creation measures – if necessary, financed by a deficit – back in the days of the Depression. In their "basic programme" of 1963 they had also expressed a belief in the fundamental idea of Keynesian policy, whereby the state should compensate for a cyclically induced loss of orders by stepping up public involvement.

The instruments of forward-looking economic and financial policy laid down in the Stability Law also met with the approval of the DGB, which had demanded at an early stage – in top-level talks with the BDA on 10 April 1962[2] – that a panel of experts be appointed to advise on economic development. When a panel of five wise men had been set up by the Federal President in February 1964, the DGB had declared its willingness to support all attempts to stabilize the economic cycle, provided the employers and government also contributed.[3] With the appointment of the panel of experts, compulsory annual economic reports and medium-term financial planning, the unions had seen their own objectives attained – at least in part, with regard to an economic policy based on cautious planning.

But another instrument of economic policy enshrined in paragraph 3 of the Stability Law turned out to be doubled-edged. That was the institution of "concerted action", an idea which Karl Schiller had come up with at the end of 1966. Representatives of the Federal Ministries of Economic Affairs, Finance and Labour, the Federal Bank, the Federal Cartels Office, the panel of experts, the business associations and the trade unions were to meet several times a year to discuss the economic problems facing the country. The idea was to exchange information on the expectations and positions of those involved; under no circumstances, however, were they to conclude binding agreements that would usurp the government's responsibilities or restrict the autonomy of wage bargainers.

---

2 Geschäftsbericht des Bundesvorstandes des DGB 1962 – 1. Halbjahr 1965 (Düsseldorf, undated), p. 12
3 Geschäftsbericht des Bundesvorstandes des DGB 2. Halbjahr 1965–1968 (Düsseldorf, undated), p. 247

It was in keeping with union custom that the DGB representatives at talks with the Minister for Economic Affairs, Karl Schiller, on 22 December 1966 agreed to participate in "concerted action".[4] Though it may have reminded some unionists of the *Zentralarbeitsgemeinschaft* (Central Association) set up after the First World War, or perhaps even more of the (temporary) *Reichswirtschaftsrat* (National Economic Council), they saw no option but to assume some of the responsibility for overall economic policy. From this point of view, "concerted action" was in perfect accordance with concept of the "aligned society". Erhard's concept which was based on the idea of corporative co-operation between the major sectional interests, voluntarily united by their recognition of the common good as the guiding principle of their actions.

Soon, however, the unions had to admit that they were getting nowhere in the "concerted action" meetings against the serried ranks of the employers and government representatives on fundamental questions of economic policy. At the very first meeting on 20 February 1967, all the participants were in favour of state incentives for investment; but when the unions called for a boosting of demand to stimulate the economy, their words fell on deaf ears. And at the "concerted action" meetings of 1 March and 1 June their request for an increase in purchasing power was met by the employers' soothing assurance that no wage cuts were being planned.

At the fourth round of talks on 19 July that year, the trade union representatives once again insisted that action to secure full employment be stepped up and taxation measures be taken to increase general purchasing power. In their eyes it was predictable – so they stated at the meeting of 19 November – that the policy of stimulating the economy would lead to gross inequity of income distribution, which would not be made any fairer by the surcharge on income tax set for the end of 1967. The union representatives also criticized the way wages were lagging behind profits at the talks on 14 December 1967 and 7 March 1968. Furthermore, they considered the expected growth rate of around four per cent predicted in the annual economic report too low; they saw it simply as an attempt to force wage restraint on them. The measures announced by the government on 5 July 1968 to introduce bonuses for savers and an amendment of the 312 Mark Law were not sufficient, as a contribution to the "social symmetry" so wordily advocated by Schiller, to satisfy the unions. Increasingly the unions realized that "concerted action" was placing them in a catch-22 situation. At the eighth federal congress in 1969 they emphasized that the only point of participating in "concerted action" was to ensure that wage

---

4 On this and following, see ibid., p. 251 ff.

earner interests were given greater consideration and firmly declined to accept the guidance data in the annual economic report as "wage guidelines".[5] But none the less they found that they were in actual fact caught up in a tangled web of non-binding agreements they could only ignore at the price of delivering a deliberate snub to public expectations of harmony and responsibility – which were actually shared by the unions themselves. This is evident if we take a closer look at the evolution of union pay policy, which was characterized by remarkable restraint on the part of the unions, not merely during the recession but also in the boom years.

It was the state economic policy programme, more than anything, that made for a rapid recovery from the recession of 1966–7. By October 1967 the number of unemployed was already falling to 341,000; there was a seasonal increase during the winter but it fell again, to 174,000, by September 1968. The number of foreign workers quickly increased again, reaching 1.1 m by September 1968. The unemployment trend reflected the rapidity of economy growth: the GNP actually jumped by 6.8 per cent in 1968, and by as much as 7.9 per cent in 1969 – in contrast to the predictions of the annual economic report.[6]

The anticyclical policy thus appeared to have passed the test; cyclical crises were no longer a source of dread. After the experiences of 1966–67, the general view was that a promising set of instruments for crisis-management had been created.

∗

The unions pinned great hopes on the social policy initiatives of the SPD, which was now part of the government. So how did the Grand Coalition perform in this particular area? The Law to Promote Employment, placing special responsibilities on the Federal Institution for Labour for promoting vocational and in-service training and retraining was adopted on 13 May 1969. This was followed on 12 June by the Law on the Continued Payment of Wages, which finally introduced – from 1 January 1970 – full equality between manual and white-collar workers in the event of sickness. The Vocational Training Law was passed on 14 August 1969, though it failed fully to meet the demands made at the 1966 DGB congress, followed on 19 September by the First Law on the Promotion of Training in

5 Geschäftsbericht des Bundesvorstandes des DGB 1969–1971 (Düsseldorf, undated), p. 171 f.
6 Karl Teodor Schuon, Ökonomische und soziale Entwicklung der Bundesrepublik Deutschland 1945–1981, in Lern- und Arbeitsbuch deutsche Arbeiterbewegung, vol. 2, p. 733

Individual Cases, encouraging training in the final years of schooling. The unions played a leading role in the preparation of these bills, putting forward proposals or draft bills of their own.

But they came little closer to extending bipartite co-determination to all big companies, a goal which the unions had pursued with great energy, particularly since the spring of 1968. With the setting-up of "Co-determination Action", with the submission of their own draft bill on 12 May 1968 and the May Day campaign of 1968, the unions attempted to mobilize the workers in support of co-determination. The unions' plans were for all companies meeting certain criteria to introduce co-determination arrangements similar to those in the coal and steel industry. These criteria were that the company should employ more than 2,000 people; have a balance sheet total of more than DM 75 m; or have a turnover of more than DM 150 m. The same year, the SPD took over the DGB's proposals and turned them into a bill of its own. But the Grand Coalition did not consider that it was in a position to settle the co-determination issue in accordance with union wishes. Instead – following the precept of excluding fundamentally contentious problems – it appointed a commission to look into the experience to date of bipartite co-determination in the coal and steel industry. The commission's report, drawn up under the leadership of Kurt Biedenkopf (CDU), was not submitted until 1970.

The Grand Coalition's reluctance to act over the co-determination issue was doubtless partly prompted by the polarization within the CDU/CSU parliamentary party; but a contributory factor was probably the unions' failure, even in 1968, to mobilize large-scale public support for their proposals, despite all their efforts. People did, indeed, take to the streets – particularly young people – but over other issues: in protest against the Vietnam War, the government of the Shah of Iran and the emergency laws.

*

The formation of the Grand Coalition signalled a new, decisive phase in the clash over the emergency laws. The very composition of the new government brought a note of stridency into the public debate. More than anything, perhaps, the reality of minimal parliamentary opposition fuelled misgivings over a strengthening of the executive. The worsening of the economic situation in 1966–7 helped raise the political temperature: 700,000 unemployed and the electoral successes of the NPD (Neo-Nazis) awakened memories of the last years of the Weimar Republic.

Though the Grand Coalition had certainly not been created for the sake of the emergency laws, this particular bill was one of its self-imposed tasks. In March 1967 a new bill (the Lücke Bill) was presented, containing basically the following provisions: the possibility of compulsory service for defence purposes; the setting-up of a joint committee to assume the functions of the *Bundestag* and *Bundesrat* in an emergency; powers to use the armed forces in a police role in the event of a threat from within. The provision authorizing the government to issue emergency decrees had been dropped, as had the more serious restrictions on civil liberties.

The SPD was cautious in its acceptance of the bill, deliberately leaving scope for further discussion. As a result, opposition to the "Coalition Bill" even built up within the SPD parliamentary party. On 26 June 1967, approximately 80 deputies – especially the trade unionists around Kurt Gscheidle, Helmut Lenders and Hans Matthöfer – presented a number of amendments devoted above all to the problem of guaranteeing the right to take industrial action and stage political strikes. This approach won support within the party from the South Hesse area, particularly the district of Frankfurt am Main, the seat of the Engineering Union's executive.

Critics within the Social Democratic Party were able to justify themselves by reference to the unions' position; after all, the DGB's federal committee had agreed on 17 July 1967 to reject the new bill on emergency legislation, informing all Bundestag deputies of its position by letter in September 1967. The simultaneous undertaking issued by the DGB not to arrange rallies for the time being was not accepted by all the unions and their branches.

In addition, representatives of the DGB and the individual unions expressed their reservations about the emergency legislation at the *Bundestag* hearings held in the autumn of 1967. Otto Brenner continued to reject the legislation on principle, while Ludwig Rosenberg formulated conditions on which the unions would be prepared to accept it. This approach showed a good measure of shrewdness, Rosenberg's readiness to compromise being set off to advantage by Brenner's fundamentally dismissive attitude. It shifted the ground for compromise – even as the internal Social Democratic opposition understood it – in favour of a radical revision of the bill.

At its Nuremberg party conference in March 1968, the SPD again confirmed the principles behind its policy and welcomed – with 87 nays and 6 abstentions – the "Coalition Bill". Rosenberg expressed the unions' understanding for the electoral considerations that the SPD was obliged to take into account. To accommodate the unions, a trade union council was set up; in addition, congress came out in support of the unions' demand for co-determination. The rejection of the plan to introduce the

"Star march" converging on Bonn on 11 May 1968 to protest against the passing of the Notstandsgesetze (emergency laws)

DGB indoor rally in the Westfalenhalle in Dortmund on 11 May 1968 in opposition to the emergency laws

majority vote system, as a clear signal to the FDP, led to the resignation of Lücke, who had thus seen one of his key plans defeated.

He was succeeded by Hans Benda, who had proved that he knew his stuff during the deliberations of the legal committee. As the final discussions were taking place in committee and between the political group chairmen, Helmut Schmidt (SPD) and Rainer Barzel (CDU/CSU), protest reached a head. The unions continued to insist that the existing bill should be scrapped. The student opposition also mobilized its supporters, arranging a rally that saw 40,000 marchers converging on an assembly point in Bonn on 11 May 1968. The disintegration of the anti-emergency law movement is probably best illustrated by the fact that on the same day the DGB organized a rally in Dortmund, attended by some 15,000 people.

It was chiefly the leaders of the student protest who urged the unions to stop the emergency laws through militant action. But after the partly violent attacks on SPD delegates in Nuremberg, the unions dissociated themselves firmly from these protest groups, which they considered unpredictable. On 19 May the DGB executive announced that they "are carrying out all measures solely on their own responsibility and will not be pushed into uncontrollable actions by other groups. The federal executive expressly rejects a general strike to stop the emergency legislation, considering it a breach of the principles of parliamentary democracy to call a strike against a decision taken by the Bundestag with such a large majority. [. . .] The DGB will oppose any abuse of the emergency legislation by every means at its disposal."[7]

The retreat by the unions was difficult to put across, given their fundamental opposition to the emergency laws. So in spite of this statement, May 1968 saw a spate of protest strikes, walk-outs and demonstrations in which trade unionists as well as others took part. None the less, the emergency legislation with the relevant amendments to the constitution was adopted on 30 May with the help of the majority of the SPD group's votes. It was opposed by 53 SPD deputies, one CDU member and almost the entire FDP group, which – now in opposition – had put forward its own bill as late as 1967. This result obviously gave the unions food for thought: after all, 179 of the 217 SPD deputies were members of DGB trade unions.

The version of the amendment to the Basic Law adopted in May 1968 differed in many ways from the initial drafts of the bill submitted by Schröder and Höcherl. The emergency provisions that were actually passed distinguish between times of tension, internal emergencies and

---

7 Protokoll der Sitzung des Bundesvorstandes des DGB am 19. Mai 1968 (DGB-Archiv)

defence contingencies, with different procedures laid down for government and parliament in each case. A time of tension can only be declared by a two-thirds majority of the *Bundestag;* the joint committee only becomes an emergency parliament with legislative powers in the case of an attack from without; the government's right to issue emergency decrees and many other restrictions on civil liberties had been dropped at an earlier stage of the bills' passage.

It was of special concern to the unions that the right to take industrial action and the right of resistance should be incorporated in the emergency legislation, and the two issues both raised problems. The inclusion of the right to take industrial action gave equal guarantees for strikes and lockouts; and the right to resistance laid down in the Basic Law repeatedly gave rise in the years that followed to discussion about the justification of political protests against individual decisions by a majority of the *Bundestag.*

If one examines the policies of the protagonists, there is no mistaking the fact that the SPD's steadfast insistence on the terms for accepting emergency legislation reiterated since its 1962 Cologne party conference was partly attributable to internal party opposition but chiefly to pressure from the unions and a critical public opinion. The trade unions could put the affair down as a success for their "two-pronged strategy" – rejecting the legislation on grounds of principle, while at the same time supporting the amendments proposed within the Social Democratic Party. Since they had to reckon with the adoption of the emergency laws from the outset, the unions' "maximalism" was an entirely appropriate way of shifting the ground for compromise in their own direction so as to achieve partial successes with regard to the contents of the bill.

While feelings ran high in the spring of 1968, soon afterwards the argument over the emergency laws was forgotten. In the following months the SPD managed to present itself credibly as the party of social reform, with Willy Brandt's promise to "risk more democracy", and after the elections of 18 September 1969 it was charged with the formation of a new government along with the FDP.

The first years of the Social-Liberal coalition: social reforms – aims and realities

Union involvement in politics became fully apparent with the formation of the Social-Liberal coalition under Willy Brandt (SPD) and Walter Scheel (FDP) in October 1969. Many leading trade unionists accepted

26 October 1962: Ludwig Rosenberg takes over as head of the DGB from Willi Richter, who stepped down for age reasons

Heinz Oskar Vetter in discussion with college students (September 1970)

posts in the government: Georg Leber and Walter Arendt, followed later on by Hans Matthöfer, Herbert Ehrenberg and Kurt Gscheidle. The high degree of union commitment to the policy of the Social Democrat-dominated government made it necessary to clarify the (party) political attitudes of the unified trade unions. There was all the more reason to do so as the man elected to head the DGB in May 1969, Heinz Oskar Vetter, was a member of the SPD.

Vetter was a man from the "second rank" of the DGB. Born the son of a senior local government official in Bochum-Werne in 1917, he started work as an engine fitter in the mining industry. At the same time he studied for his *Abitur,* but was then conscripted into the army and did not return from imprisonment as a POW until 1946. Again he worked as a fitter in the mines and joined the Miners' Union, IG Bergbau, with which he took up a full-time post in 1952. In 1960 he was elected on to the executive, and in 1964 became vice-chairman of IG Bergbau. Though he only obtained 267 votes out of 427 in the election for DGB chairman, he was confirmed in office by an overwhelming majority in 1972. He had established a political profile of his own much faster than people had expected. He made the DGB's co-determination initiatives very much his own business and his 1977 proposal that reductions in working hours should be agreed even without full compensation caused a considerable stir. Though Vetter, who was president of the ETUC from 1974 to 1979, entered the European Parliament for the SPD in 1979, he always tried to draw a dividing line between the union and the Party.

At the third extraordinary federal congress of May 1971[8], he stressed that a "critical distance" should be maintained between the unified trade union and political parties. It was the duty of the unions, as the "old style" workers' parties were no more, "now more than ever to draw up and pursue aims as a true union of wage earners'. The unions should not become a substitute for parties; but they themselves should draft and develop political plans for the emancipation and equality of working people, political models for the society of tomorrow".

As Vetter made it clear in May 1971, ever since their beginnings the trade unions had had "the dual task, as militant self help organizations, of protecting their members from the consequences of their economic and social inferiority and, as a political movement, of improving the dependent and under-privileged position of working people in society". The two tasks – "the protective and the formative functions – can and must not be

---

8 Heinz Oskar Vetter, in Protokoll des 3. Ausserordentlichen Bundeskongresses am 14. and 15. Mai 1971 in Düsseldorf (Düsseldorf, undated), p. 15 ff.

divorced one from the other. Effective and lasting protection is only possible through social change". The unions, he said – taking on the proponents of the social partnership and "regulative function" ideologies – are thus "in equal measure protective associations and a political movement".

Through this definition of the unions' twin tasks, Vetter attempted to take the wind out of attempts to pin the unions down to one or the other, a regulative factor *or* a counterforce.[9] He was thus opposing extreme expectations of social reform or revolution as much as the corporatist obligation on the unions to work within the status quo. The dual role of protecting the workers and shaping society assigned to the unions by Vetter was reflected in the early 1970s by a flood of policy documents, of which we shall mention only a few here. 1972 alone saw the publication of a new action programme, demanding, in particular, measures to change the structure of society, such as co-determination, wealth creation, job security and fiscal policy. It also addressed the questions of tenants' law and land law, public transport and environmental protection. In 1972 special "DGB guidelines" on the environment were issued and these were given a tangible form in the DGB's 1974 environmental programme. The same year – which, incidentally, had been declared the "Year of the Female Employee" – the DGB published a "Programme for Female Employees", a "Health Policy Programme",[10] "Vocational Training Demands", calling for the amendment of the 1969 Vocational Training Law, and a list of "The DGB's Educational Proposals". In 1973 there followed "The DGB's Demands for Reform of Tertiary Education". The aim of the programmes was to eliminate discrimination against working-class children by creating equality of opportunity; with regard to content, the educational system should foster the critical faculties and a democratic mentality. Furthermore, the proposals for the "Humanization of Working Life", which embraced (almost) all the individual union demands from industrial safety to co-determination, were issued in programme form.[11] It should also be mentioned that in 1971 the white-collar union DAG issued a "programme of principle", the basic tendency of which was entirely in line

9 See, for example, Eberhard Schmidt, Ordnungsfaktor oder Gegenmacht. Die politische Rolle der Gewerkschaften (Frankfurt am Main, 1971)

10 Reprinted in Gerhard Leminsky and Bernd Otto, Politik und Programmatik des Deutschen Gewerkschaftsbundes (Cologne, 1974), p. 218 ff. and 365 ff.

11 Heinz Oskar Vetter, Humanisierung der Arbeit als gesellschaftspolitische und gewerkschaftliche Aufgabe. Protokoll der DGB-Konferenz vom 16./17. 5. 1974 in München (Frankfurt/M and Cologne, 1974)

with that of the DGB programme of 1963.[12] Thus, with an abundance of policy statements the unions, both moulded and driven by the spirit of upheaval of the late 1960s and early 70s, tried to influence political decisions in their own favour.

*

The Social-Liberal coalition initially benefited from the economic upturn after the 1966-7 recession. In 1968, the growth rate reached 6.8 per cent and in 1969 went even higher, to 7.9 per cent; but after that growth dropped off, declining to 5.9 per cent in 1970, 3.3 in 1971 and 3.6 in 1972, rising again to 4.9 in 1973 and then falling back down to 0.4 and -1.8 per cent (1974 and 1975 respectively) as the first oil crisis hit Europe and the economic crisis of the 1970s set in. Until 1971 the unemployment rate remained below one per cent; in 1972 it rose to 1.1 per cent and continued mounting, reaching 1.2 per cent in 1973 and – with the onset of the worldwide economic crisis – 2.6 per cent in 1974 (Table 5b).

Despite the falling growth rate and rising unemployment, the annual rate of inflation increased from 1969-70 onwards: from 1.9 per cent in 1969 and 3.4 in 1970, inflation rose to 5.3 and 5.5 per cent in the next two years and continued to rise, reaching 6.9 and 7 per cent in 1973 and 1974 respectively. Rising prices were to become one of the major issues in the debate on economic policy, as can be seen from the DGB's policy statements from the early 1970s.

It became increasingly apparent as the 1970s went on that economic development, which had powered the reform policies of 1968-9, was now putting a damper on exaggerated expectations. The limited room for financial manoeuvre soon meant that there could be no trail-blazing innovations in the Social-Liberal coalition's social legislation. Rather, it stayed within the framework established by the decisions of principle taken in the 1950s – though, admittedly, with distinct improvements. A glance at the chronology of laws in the field of social policy demonstrates this. By the decision of 13 December 1969, war victims' pensions were index-linked – that is, from January 1971 they were tied to the general movement of incomes, as old age pensions already were. On 27 June 1970 the amending law to the Capital Formation Law doubled the concessionary savings amount to DM 624 from 1 January 1971. The Pension Reform Law of 21 September 1972 introduced the flexible retirement age,

---

12 Grundsatzprogramm der DAG, in Protokoll des 10. DAG-Gewerkschaftstages 1971 (Hamburg, undated), p. 473 ff.

making it possible to retire from the age of 63 on. Although the unions had called for the retirement age to be reduced to 60, they welcomed the new law as a "first step" in the right direction. They also welcomed the opening of the pension insurance scheme to the self-employed and housewives and the raising of the lowest pension classes.[13] Lastly, one should not forget the introduction of bankruptcy default payments from July 1974, protecting employees against loss of wages should the employer be unable to pay, and the income tax reform of 25 July 1974, which replaced tax allowances for children with a fixed child benefit, did away with progressive tax scales in the lower and middle-range income groups and doubled the earned income allowance from DM 240 to DM 480.

Among the other reforms that determined the climate of these years was the reform of marriage, family and divorce law, and Paragraph 218 of the Penal Code on abortion. Both reforms were firmly supported by the unions with policy statements and legislative proposals of their own.

The reform momentum of the first years of the Social-Liberal coalition was, however, soon slowed down by growing opposition. Signs of this were, for example, the fate of the government's Vocational Training Bill of April 1975. Partly in accordance with union demands, the bill encountered determined employer opposition and was finally voted down by the CDU/CSU majority in the *Bundesrat*. True, the Law to Promote Training and, in December 1975, and the Higher Education Framework Law were passed – but the latter was confined to the limits set by the Federal Constitutional Court. With regard to the programme to "humanize working life", only the industrial safety proposals in the narrow sense were enshrined in law, in the shape of the Industrial Safety Law (1973) and the Workplace Order (1975). Safeguards against rationalization remained within the ambit of collective bargaining, which requires separate treatment, as does the government's co-determination legislation.

The boost to social policy in the 1960s and 1970s resulted in a slow increase in social insurance benefits as a proportion of GNP. The ratio increased from 17.1 percent (1950) to 18.7 (1960) and 24 (1965) and then to 26.1 (1968) and 26.8 per cent (1972). The economic crisis of 1974 then brought a marked increase.[14] The reform laws, some of which were quite costly, led to a gradual increase in federal debt. Whereas net federal borrowing had been no more than DM 1 million in 1969, from 1970 on it

---

13 Geschäftsbericht des Bundesvorstandes des DGB 1969–1971 (Düsseldorf, undated), p. 118
14 Bernhard Schäfers, Sozialstruktur und Wandel der Bundesrepublik Deutschland (Stuttgart, 1981), p. 190

grew from DM 1.11 billion to 1.44 bn (1971), 3.98 bn (1972), 2.68 bn (1973) to reach 9.48bn in 1974. In 1971 the Federal Finance Minister, Alex Möller (SPD), resigned over the budget situation, considering that departmental demands were jeopardizing stability.

∗

On the other hand, it would have cost "nothing" to put the unions' long-standing call for co-determination into effect. And after Willy Brandt's government statement of 28 October 1969 announcing a reform of the Company Statute Law and an extension of co-determination, the unions believed that they had attained their goal. But both issues turned into problems for the coalition.

First, reform of the Company Statute Law. After clearly criticizing the government bill of 29 January 1971[15], the DGB tried once more to show off its plans to their best advantage in spring 1971 by writing to all the *Bundestag* deputies on 8 February and by campaigns "For a better Company Statute Law".[16] But the unions obviously did not have a decisive influence on the revised version of the Company Statute Law passed on 10 November 1971 with the votes of the coalition parties plus 27 CDU deputies. Nevertheless, the law was an undeniable improvement on the 1952 version in a number of respects: for the first time the individual employee was given his own place in company statute law; the co-determination and participation rights of the works councils were extended and consolidated; the representation of young people was increased; and finally the unions' position in the company statute was recognized and guaranteed.

So all in all the unions saw the new law as a "major step forward". Although the Company Statute Law did not satisfy all the DGB's demands, it had to be regarded as "a major success in the trade union battle for improved co-determination at work".[17] Vetter saw it as a "positive contribution to the reform of society".[18] Criticism was chiefly levelled at

---

15 Gerd Muhr, Vorwort, in DGB-Bundesvorstand (eds), Für ein besseres Betriebsverfassungsgesetz. Eine vergleichende Darstellung zum Regierungsentwurf (Düsseldorf, undated) (1971)

16 Heinz O. Vetter and Gerd Muhr to all Bundestag deputies on 8 February 1971, reprinted in Leminsky and Otto, Politik und Programmatik des Deutschen Gewerkschaftsbundes, pp. 124–6

17 Geschäftsbericht des Bundesvorstandes des DGB 1969–1971 (Düsseldorf, undated), p. 144 f.

18 H.O. Vetter, Gewerkschaftspolitische Bilanz des Jahres 1971, in Die Quelle 12, 1971, pp. 481–3

the new law's virtual lack of effective co-determination rights for works councils in economic matters. Other features, too, turned out to be problematic as far as the unions were concerned. Co-operation between unions and works councils was not adequately covered by the law, and the breakdown of the workforce into workers, salaried staff and senior salaried staff (executives) entrenched sectional differences, thus making a united defence of their interests more difficult. The last provision was very much in line with Christian trade union thinking and also that of the DAG, which had been calling for "minority protection" for years in its declarations of principle and now received backing from the FDP.

Particularly the problem of distinguishing "senior salaried staff" or executives from others led to a great many disputes between unions and management in the years to come and the matter soon came before the courts. The narrow definition laid down by the Federal Labour Court in its ruling of March 1974, which deemed executives to be solely senior staff with management decision-making duties, did, in fact, support the union position[19] – but it was not a dramatic success of the kind that might have had implications for the framing of the Co-determination Law.

Nor was the Staff Representation Law (Personalvertretungsgesetz) adopted on 12 December 1973 by any means entirely in line with union thinking. The unions had subjected both the 1972 officials' draft and the 1973 government bill to stiff criticism.[20] Although the DGB welcomed the revised law as "more progressive" than the bill, it also pointed to serious flaws.[21] In particular, the far too limited co-determination rights of the staff councils and the division into workers, salaried staff and civil servants clashed with union aims. The Public Service Union ÖTV underscored the union view that "the current laws on collective bargaining and the public service should be replaced by a new, uniform public service law established by collective agreement". It also called for the creation of a uniform staff law guaranteeing "unrestricted rights of association for officials of the public service".[22]

19 DGB-Nachrichtendienst ND 47/74, Düsseldorf, of 6 March 1974
20 DGB-Nachrichtendienst No. 168 of 25 May 1972 and No. 113 of 2 April 1973; DGB-Bundesvorstand (eds), Für ein besseres Personalvertretungsgesetz. Vergleichende Darstellung des DGB zum Regierungsentwurf zur Änderung des Personalvertretungsgesetzes (Düsseldorf, undated) (c. 1972–3)
21 DGB begrüsst Personalvertretungsgesetz, in DGB-Nachrichtendienst No. 428/73 of 13 December 1973
22 Gewerkschaft ÖTV (ed), Modernisierung im öffentlichen Dienst. Einheitliches Personalrecht 3 (Stuttgart, 1976), p. 5

But how about the "number one demand", as Heinz Oskar Vetter described it at the DGB's 1972 congress – co-determination at company level? Since spring 1972 the DGB had been trying to focus more attention on this issue. Bipartite representation on the supervisory boards of large companies was not the only union demand. The unions were still seeking the creation of a Federal Economic and Social Council to inform and advise government and parliament. This council would replace corresponding bodies at regional level and would also be empowered to initiate legislation.[23]

But the difficulties of achieving these demands were obvious. The "Biedenkopf Commission" had not submitted its report on experience of bipartite co-determination until 1970[24]. Although it gave a thoroughly favourable assessment of co-determination in the coal and steel industry, the commission could not bring itself to recommend the extension of the coal and steel provisions to all large companies. As a result of this, both advocates and opponents of bipartite co-determination could claim to have its backing. In any case, the commission did not devise a compromise between SPD and FDP thinking on co-determination. The SPD stuck to its 1968 bill, while the FDP presented the "Riemer Bill" at its 1971 party conference in Freiburg, based on the Biedenkopf recommendations and proposing that the management side be given a dominant position on supervisory boards, with shareholders, management and employees being represented in the ratio of 6:2:4. The same year the CDU party conference approved a scheme giving shareholders and employees seven and five seats respectively on the supervisory board.

Thus apart from the SPD draft, the DGB was fairly isolated. It could, of course, point to the smooth working of co-determination in the coal and steel industry. Evidence for this was the fact that in numerous pit closures social hardship (and disturbances) had been prevented by social welfare planning.[25] But getting the union demands accepted and enshrined in law proved to be difficult. At the end of March 1974, the employers' association, the BDA, held a conference in Cologne called "Market economy or trade union state", a title that recalled the confrontations of the Weimar period. The unions attempted to counter this with an analysis by the Institute of Economic and Social Sciences entitled "Trade union state or

23 According to Leminsky and Otto, op. cit., p. 147 ff.
24 Mitbestimmung im Unternehmen. Bericht der Sachverständigenkommission zur Auswertung der bisherigen Erfahrungen bei der Mitbestimmung (Mitbestimmungskommission), Bochum, im Januar 1970 (Bundestags-Drucksache VI/334)
25 Geschäftsbericht des Bundesvorstandes des DGB 2. Halbjahr 1965 – 1968, p. 275

entrepreneurs' state".[26] But in terms of public opinion the employers won on points with their theory of the necessary correlation between a free economy and a free society, which they claimed would be jeoparized by co-determination. And thanks to the FDP, basic liberal economic ideas of this kind did leave their mark on the government's 1974 Co-determination Bill, which was subsequently adopted by the *Bundestag* with a number of changes on 18 March 1976.[27]

The new law introduced co-determination in companies with their own "legal personality" normally employing more than 2,000 people. The supervisory boards of such companies must be occupied by equal numbers of shareholder and employee representatives, the size of the board depending on the number of staff employed. The composition of the employee side was more complicated than in the coal and steel scheme. A proportion of the employee seats are reserved for the unions represented in the company; the others are distributed among the workers, salaried staff and executives in proportion to their share of the total workforce, though each of these groups has at least one seat. All the employee representatives, including the unionists, are elected by the staff. In companies with less than 8,000 employees direct elections are held; otherwise via an electoral college. One feature that concerned many people – not just the unions – was that executives, who according to the Federal Labour Court ruling of March 1974 had to exercise management functions, were supposed to belong to the employee side. Furthermore, in the event of repeated tied votes the chairman of the board, who was appointed by the management, had a casting vote. Finally, the unions criticized the fact that the employee side did not have a decisive say in the appointment or rejection of the worker-director on the management board (*Vorstand*). For these reasons the unions reacted to the law with undisguised disappointment.

Nor were the employers satisfied with the law. They held that the guarantees in the Basic Law covering private property and entrepreneurial freedom had been breached by the Co-determination Law. Furthermore, the unions' participation in the supervisory board gave them an information advantage which set aside autonomy in negotiating wage rates. Despite the clearly non-bipartite composition of the supervisory board, the employers lodged an appeal against the Co-determination Law with the Federal Constitutional Court. The unions took the opportunity to

---

26 Gewerkschaftsstaat oder Unternehmerstaat (Sonderheft der WSI-Mitteilungen, August 1976)

27 Der Bundesminister für Arbeit und Sozialordnung (ed.), Mitbestimmung, p. 83 ff.

announce that they were ceasing to participate in "concerted action", of which they were growing increasingly critical as it was. Although the Constitutional Court did not allow the employers' appeal in its judgment of 1 March 1979, the limits of any wider ranging forms of co-determination were drawn so tightly that an extension of bipartite co-determination receded into the far distance.[28]

2. Collective bargaining: from a low profile, via spontaneous strikes to a more aggressive approach

In view of the personal links and the similarity between the political thinking of the union and SPD leaders on the one hand, and the economic recession on the other, it is not surprising that the unions practised wage restraint in the second half of the 1960s. They were also concerned with the step-by-step introduction of the 40-hour week, the cost of which was added to the rate of increase in wages. The trade unions indicated at the wage talks – contrary to their official pronouncements – that they were quite prepared to take official guidance data into account.

A glance at the wage agreements concluded in 1967 and 1968 shows – in the words of the DGB – "quite clearly the reasonable conduct of the unions".[29] With only nominal wage rises being negotiated in these years, real wages fell in 1967 by 1.7 per cent and in 1968 by 1 per cent, but then increased in the next two years by 1.4 and 5.5 per cent. The development of real wages is also reflected in the fluctuations in gross income from paid employment as a proportion of national income: from 55.7 per cent in 1967, it dropped to 53.6 in 1968. Despite substantial wage rises in 1970–71, it only gradually recovered from this low but then it continued rising again until 1973.[30]

The unions' readiness to show moderation over pay led some sections of the membership and of the workers as a whole to lose confidence in them. With company profits increasing by leaps and bounds but real wages stagnating, the outcome was the "wildcat" strikes of 1969. The immediate cause of the spontaneous strikes was the merger of two companies, the Dortmund-Hörder-Hütten Union and the Hoesch AG Dortmund, on 1 October 1969, necessitating the internal levelling-out of wages

---

28 Reprinted ibid., p. 251 ff.
29 Geschäftsbericht des Bundesvorstandes des DGB 2. Halbjahr 1965–1968 (Düsseldorf, undated), p. 285
30 According to F.Deppe, Autonomie und Integration, pp. 62 and 64

and salaries. The workers at Hoesch AG Hüttenwerke in Dortmund downed tools on 2 September, demanding an immediate pay rise. The strike ended the next day, when the company swiftly agreed to increase hourly rates by 30 Pfennigs. But in view of the profits explosion of 1968–9, the strike sparked off similar actions at other companies in the iron and steel industry, coal mining, engineering, textiles and the public services. In early September alone, 230,000 days were lost in the iron and steel industry, and 49,000 shifts lost in coal mining, through strike action. In all cases the strikers soon managed to obtain pay rises that were paid out even before their collective agreements expired.

The unions had complained before about the way wages were lagging behind soaring profits and had frequently demanded that pay talks be brought forward – but to no avail. These spontaneous strikes, however, helped to underline the unions' demands for talks. Consequently, substantial pay rises were achieved and collective agreements with a shorter period of validity were accepted.

But by the early 1970s the two sides were again adopting tougher attitudes. With the mass influx of dollars putting price stability at risk, a risk increased by the workers' pay demands but also jeopardizing exports (as exchange rates had been allowed to float), the employers pressed for low-level pay rises. The two sides clashed in Baden-Württemberg in 1971.

What triggered the dispute was IG Metall's 11 per cent wage demand, made when it gave notice on 30 September 1971 that it was terminating its collective agreements. At first the employers made no offer at all, but then settled on 4.5 per cent. Owing to the stubbornness with which both sides clung to their positions, the talks were declared deadlocked on 17 October. Arbitration proceedings began on 28 October. On 2 November the mediator's proposal (7.5 per cent over a period of seven months) was rejected by the employers. At this, IG Metall (who had accepted the mediator's proposal) decided to hold a strike ballot on 12 November: it showed 89.6 per cent of the membership in favour of a strike.

IG Metall decided on selective strikes. On 22 November 55,000 workers at Daimler-Benz, Audi-NSU and Graubremse Heidelberg came out on strike. They were followed the next day by another 60,000 workers at 76 companies. The employers now decided to respond with a lockout, which – beginning on 26 November – affected a total of 304,823 employees at 530 companies. Further attempts at mediation and even the intervention of the Chancellor proved fruitless. But since the unions did not seem minded to give way and the growing opposition to the lockouts had begun to mobilize in protest rallies – for example, 45,000 workers gathered in Stuttgart on 8 December – agreement was reached on 10 December. After an industrial dispute that had cost 4,138,000 lost days (according to official sources) or 5,130,000 (according to union sources) and loss of production put at DM 2 billion, the employers accepted wage rises of 7.5 per cent over 12 months; for October to December a lump sum of DM 180 net was paid out; in addition to this, a "thirteenth month", worth up to 40 per cent of a normal month's income, was written into the agreement.

This outcome was approved by 71.2 per cent of the membership. It should not be forgotten, however, that the employers had again pushed through the principle of central wage negotiations. Also, the fact that the terms agreed for North Baden-North Württemberg set the latitude for the other agreements entailed an overall stabilization of real wages – but did not secure the additional increase the employees had demanded. In fact, to a large extent the employers' position had prevailed.

For this reason the employers could interpret the outcome of the dispute as a victory. A newspaper advertisement on 15 December published by the engineering industrialists said: "Our thanks to the firms affected, who have born the brunt of the dispute. But it has paid off for all companies: the result is below the preceding mediation proposals. [. . .] The total burden on companies, spread over 15 months, works out at approximately 7 per cent. The 15 month validity gives the engineering industry a sensible basis for its calculations and provides the peace necessary in these economically difficult times."[31]

The pressure on IG Metall, which had to dispense some DM 80 m altogether in strike pay was stepped up by the extension of the dispute by production standstills in firms not directly involved. About 100,000 workers, chiefly in the car industry, were drawn into the dispute through "cold" lockouts (that is, they were locked out before taking any industrial action). In accordance with the state neutrality requirement in industrial disputes, the Federal Institution for Labour decided, pursuant to Paragraph 116 of the Law to Promote Employment of 25 July 1969, not to pay benefit to workers only indirectly affected, since – as it said in the decree of 22 November 1971 – "experience shows" that these employees would also benefit, should the aim of the strike be achieved. On 2 December, however, the advisory board of the Institution did grant the employees concerned unemployment or short-time benefit – though this decision was later deemed unlawful by the Regional Social Court of Baden-Württemberg on 27 November 1972.

31 Quot. Regine Meyer, Streik und Aussperrung in der Metallindustrie. Analyse der Streikbewegung in Nordwürttemberg–Nordbaden 1971 (Marburg, 1977), p. 346

The temporary closures could certainly be considered "cold" lockouts. Doubts about the need for such action were reinforced by the fact that many closures were effected, or notice of closure given, on only the fourth day of the strike. The fact that Daimler-Benz announced that work would be resumed at its Berlin works on the day after the second strike ballot, although production in the strike-hit area did not get going again properly until after the ballot, also appeared to justify such doubts.

The Federal Labour Court judgments of 1955 and 1971, which placed tight restrictions on the use of the lockout but permitted it in principle, the lockout in the engineering industry in 1971 and, lastly, the conduct of the Federal Institute of Labour, had made strikes an incalculable risk for the trade unions. The principle of "proportionality"*, the yardstick for which was outside union control and fell within the purview of the state and (especially) the employers, together with the free use of lockouts by the employers, clearly limited the unions' scope for action. Moreover, "concerted action" and the annual expert reports restricted the unions' autonomy in drawing up their objectives back at the opinion-forming and decision-making stage. The risk of incurring incalculable financial burdens if they escalated industrial action restricted their freedom to act; in addition, the expense of major disputes weakened the unions financially to such an extent that the unions could be taught a lasting lesson by the employers. Thus in the early 1970s industrial relations became increasingly confrontational and this was to become fully apparent with the recession of the mid-1970s.

The results achieved by union pay policy in the early 1970s are impressive. In the attempt to make good the loss of confidence revealed by the "wildcat" strikes of 1969 and to catch up with real wages (which consistently outstripped the agreed rates), the unions were demanding wage rises of 10 per cent and more in the early 1970s. In fact, in several industries they succeeded in securing pay rises of this magnitude. It is noticeable that with economic difficulties looming up ahead, the public service and transport union ÖTV started acting as pacemaker for the first time, for example with its 1974 wage rise of 11 per cent, achieved after a strike, an episode which rather cast a shadow on the image of the Chancellor, Willy Brandt. IG Metall followed this up by securing a good 12 per cent. Despite the clear rise in agreed wage rates in the early 1970s, real wages were often even higher. For this reason, the DGB unions decided at their 1975 Hamburg congress to push harder to secure these actual wages.

---

* Translator's note: "Verhältnismässigkeit": stipulation that any retaliatory industrial action must be in proportion to the original action taken

Owing to their increased militancy and the generally favourable development of the economy, the unions managed to secure significant improvements in their members' real wages. After the losses caused by the recession, real wages rose by 1.4 per cent in 1969, 5.5 per cent in 1970 and 2.3 per cent in 1971; in 1972 they fell slightly by 0.3 per cent, and then rose again in 1973 and 1974 by 1.5 and 3 per cent respectively (Table 3c). Gross income from paid employment as a proportion of national income also rose from a low of 53.6 per cent in 1968 to 54.1 (1969) and 54.8 (1970) and continued rising slowly to 55.8 (1971 and 1972) and 56.6 per cent in 1973.[32]

But wages were not all the unions fought for. As a result of the intensification of work, the increase in night work and shift work and the speeding up of the work rate, trade union bargaining policy came to focus on issues such as the "humanization of work" and safeguards against rationalization.

In the late 1960s the trade unions had already given increasingly urgent warnings of the dangers of the uncontrolled development of technology. Since then agreements on rationalization safeguards had become much more common. The Engineering Union and the Chemical, Paper and Ceramics Union had led the way, for instance with the 1968 agreements covering some 10 million employees. Although the demand for rationalization safeguards in the 1965 action programme had been directed at the legislators, after the limited success of efforts in this direction (the Law to Promote Employment of 1969), the unions concentrated on achieving this objective through collective agreement.

Rationalization safeguards were considered an essential part of the humanization of work, which the unions sought to achieve through adopting a dual strategy – the law and collective agreement. Here, too, the unions shifted the emphasis on to collective bargaining in view of their lack of political success. One of their principal achievements was the October 1973 outline agreement on pay II for the North-Württemberg–North Baden engineering industry. After two-week selective strikes involving some 57,000 employees at Bosch and Daimler-Benz, a collective agreement was concluded, which not only set limits on the company standards for the production process (for example, the time allotted for a specific operation) but also improved the rules governing breaks. Every worker on piece-rates or bonus was henceforth entitled to five minutes

---

32 Deppe, op. cit., p. 62 and 64

recovery time and three minutes personal time per working hour – for these periods he was paid the going rate.

*

Although the recession of 1966–7 had destroyed the dream of an everlasting "economic miracle", living standards continued to rise unabated throughout the 1960s for large sections of the community. If we compare, for example, the possession of consumer durables in 1962 and 1973, we find the following changes: in 1962 only 52 per cent of households had a refrigerator – in 1973, 93 per cent; for vacuum cleaners, television sets and cars the figures are 65/91 per cent, 34/87 per cent and 27/55 per cent.[33] Thus the post-economic miracle period continued to be characterized by consumerism and rising living standards. But this was by no means linked with a fairer distribution of wealth: in the early 1970s, 1.7 per cent of all households owned 74 per cent of all the private wealth produced by the economy.

It became increasingly clear that changing this was one of the trade unions' objectives.[34] The DGB federal executive's statement on wealth formation of October 1968 for the first time drew a distinction between encouraging saving and granting workers a share in the wealth produced. The "DGB Guidelines on Wealth Formation' of March 1970 set these ideas out in more specific form. While measures to encourage saving were approved, they were not expected to achieve any real redistribution of wealth. Accordingly, wealth formation was to be achieved by the encouragement of saving and inter-company wage-earner profit-sharing. Companies would channel part of their profits into funds, which would have to issue share certificates to employees. Although the 1972 action programme also stated that wage earners should be granted an appropriate share of the wealth produced through an inter-corporate system of profit-sharing, the draft resolution to this effect was defeated at the ninth DGB federal congress in 1972. This was a victory for IG Metall's view that priority should be given to pay policy. Wealth formation funds, on the other hand, would lead to a direct reduction in all employees' disposable incomes – in return for share certificates that were not even saleable. The DGB federal committee submitted a new paper, by a narrow majority, on 4 April 1973, dealing with the issue of securing a share in the profits for employees. Starting from the perception that capital-forming collective

---

33 According to Schuon, op. cit., p. 734
34 See Leminsky and Otto, op. cit., p. 164 ff.

agreements, savings benefits and investable wages* do not effect redistribution and that company plans for employee participation are more designed as measures to prevent mobility, the participation by employees in the wealth produced was to be achieved through regional funds, into which the companies were to siphon off part of their profits. But no actual agreement was reached.

3. Good times for trade union organization: increase in membership and the heyday of the "co-operative economy"

After a phase of slow membership growth in the 1960s, the new decade brought a marked rise in union membership – from 6.5 m (1966) to 7.4 m (1976). But these overall figures (Table 1c) concealed a number of counter-trends, since the increase in membership was not evenly spread across the unions and trades. The unions that profited from the increase were Commerce, Banking and Insurance; Education and Science; the German Post Office Union; the Engineering Union; Chemicals, Paper and Ceramics; and Public Services, Transport and Communications. Those that lost members or stayed at the same level were Horticulture, Agriculture and Forestry; Leather; Mining and Power; and Textiles and Clothing – all unions in declining industries. To give just one example: in 1958 the mining industry employed over 650,000 people in 622 companies; in 1976 this had fallen to 250,000 workers and 383 companies.

All in all, the unions were able to consolidate their position in the "reform climate" of the 1970s. The DAG and the German Civil Servants' Union also took part in this process of consolidation, registering 471,000 and 803,000 members respectively in 1976. As far as the CGB was concerned, however, this only applied to a lesser extent. In April 1966, for example, the Union of Christian Mining and Power Workers (Saarland) had dissolved itself and taken its 20,000 members to the Mining and Power Union.[35] In addition to membership statistics, the results of the works council elections give some idea of the relative strength of the unions. Taking the engineering industry as an example, we find that the DGB lists took some 80 per cent of the vote throughout the 1960s and 70s; the DAG lists between 2 and 4 per cent; the CGB lists barely 1 per cent; the rest of the votes went to lists of non-unionized candidates. Incidentally, in

---

* Translator's note: Scheme by which employee's share of a company's profits is invested in the company itself.

35 Geschäftsbericht des Bundesvorstandes des DGB 2. Halbjahr 1965–1968, p. 82

1968 only 11.2 percent of all works council members were women[36] – a proportion that did not change much in the 1970s.

The shift in union membership reflected a process of social change, which was clearly leading to the "service society". Those engaged in manufacturing as a proportion of the total working population were down to 46 per cent by 1975 and 45 per cent by 1979; the proportion accounted for by agriculture and forestry shrank to 7.2 per cent in 1975 and 6 per cent in 1979. The service industries, on the other hand, accounted for 47 per cent in 1975, rising to 49 per cent in 1979.

The unions were no better at keeping pace with the changing structure of the working population in the 1970s than in earlier decades. The proportion of manual workers declined steadily – from 75.8 in 1970 to 71.2 per cent in 1976. While the proportion of civil servants stagnated at 9.5/9.4 per cent, the proportion of white-collar workers rose from 14.7 to 19.4 per cent. The proportion of women also grew – from 15.3 to 18.3 per cent. Overall, then, manual workers were clearly over-represented in 1976, as in earlier years, since they "only" made up 49.5 per cent of all wage earners.[37]

With the growth in membership, the degree of organization increased from 32.4 to 36.6 per cent between 1966 and 1975; the degree of organization of female employees also rose, from 15.7 to 19.3 per cent, though it still lagged a long way behind that of male workers (in 1975, roughly 50 per cent). Despite the increase in the degree of organization, the German trade unions cut rather a poor figure in comparison with other advanced capitalist countries. In the first half of the 1970s, the unions in Sweden had a degree of organization of 87 per cent, in Belgium 70 per cent, in Denmark and Austria (1968) 66 per cent, in Norway 55 per cent, in England 50 per cent and in the Netherlands 47 per cent; while in the United States (28 per cent) and in France (25 per cent) the figure was lower than in the Federal Republic.[38]

If one considers the degree of organization of the individual unions, no consistent picture emerges. The positive trend predominated between 1966 and 1975. A few examples must suffice. The following unions were able to increase their degree of organization: the Engineering Union from 34.1 to 43.6 per cent; Chemicals, Paper and Ceramics from 35.9 to 40.1 per cent; Mining and Power from 72.8 to 86.7 per cent; Printing and Paper

---

36 Geschäftsbericht des Bundesvorstandes des DGB 1969–1971, p. 318
37 Deppe, op. cit., p. 52
38 According to Wolfgang Streeck, Gewerkschaften als Mitgliederverbände. Probleme gewerkschaftlicher Mitgliederrekrutierung, in J. Bergmann, op. cit., p. 102 ff.

from 31.8 to 36 per cent; Textiles and Garments from 25.2 to 32.5 per cent. Stagnation or decline affected the Construction Union (19.5 to 20.5 per cent), Wood (19.1 to 18.6) and Food, Beverage and Allied Trades (18.2 to 16.4).[39]

The encouraging picture of membership trends overall is in no small measure attributable to a drop in turnover. Between 1965 and 1975 turnover fell – with some, partly quite conspicuous fluctuations – in Chemicals, Paper and Ceramics from 13.1 to 9.4 per cent, in Commerce, Banking and Insurance from 18.6 to 12.9 per cent, in the Engineering Union from 15 to 10.9 per cent and in Textiles and Garments from 18.8 to 16.5 per cent.[40]

One may assume that the problem of membership turnover was reduced by the new methods of collecting unions dues.[41] There was a sharp increase in the proportion of dues collected by direct debit from a bank account between 1965 and 1975. In addition, more trade union members had their dues deducted at source and passed on to the union by the wages department. These methods of collecting dues were symptomatic of the increasingly impersonal relationship between the unions and their members, a trend that was reinforced by the closure of administrative offices by several unions, for example, Mining and Power (from 50 down to 23), Chemicals, Paper and Ceramics (from 83 to 68), Commerce, Banking and Insurance (from 371 to 45), Engineering (from 186 to 168) and Textiles and Garments (from 136 to 79). True, this was accompanied by a rise in average staffing levels, but we are still left with an impression of increasing distance between the unions and the grass roots.

*

The development of co-operative enterprises was a clear sign of the unions' organizational and financial consolidation in the 1960s and 70s. There follows a brief presentation of the most important groups.[42]

In 1969 more than a hundred individual consumer co-operatives merged to form the Coop Group, a nationwide group of companies, for which a holding company, the Frankfurt Coop-Zentrale (soon Coop AG)

39 Gewerkschaftliche Monatshefte 11, 1979, p. 741 f.
40 According to Streeck. op. cit., p. 109
41 ibid., pp. 107 and 110. See also Klaus Armingeon, Die Entwicklung der westdeutschen Gewerkschaften 1950–1985 (Frankfurt and New York, 1988), p. 89 ff.
42 The following information is taken from Achim von Loesch, Die gemeinwirtschaftlichen Unternehmen der deutschen Gewerkschaften. Entstehung, Funktionen, Probleme (Cologne, 1979)

was set up in 1974. In 1978 the share capital of this central company amounted to DM 150 m, 40 per cent of which was held by the Federation of German Consumer Co-operatives, 22 per cent by the central co-operatives of Switzerland, Denmark and Sweden and 38 per cent by the Finance Company for Co-operative Economy (BGAG), created in 1974.

The "flagship" of the co-operative enterprises was the "Neue Heimat" (New Home) Group, the biggest housing development corporation in Western Europe, with its seat in Hamburg. In 1977 it administered 418,000 apartments and houses throughout the Federal Republic, of which it owned 320,000, and roughly 87,000 commercial properties. On top of this there was Neue Heimat International with numerous foreign interests. It can hardly be said to have dominated the market, however: of the roughly 450,000 units built annually during the mid-1970s, some 12–15,000, or about 3 per cent, were constructed by Neue Heimat. Its share of the total housing stock amounted to a mere 1.5 per cent. The shareholders in the Neue Heimat Public Utility Housing and Development Company were the asset management and trust companies of the DGB and the individual unions. The company's ordinary capital amounted to DM 60 m, of which the major shares were held by the DGB, with 33.9 per cent, the Construction Union (25.4 per cent) and IG Metall, the engineering union (18.5 per cent). The Finance Company for Co-operative Economy had a 49.9 per cent holding in Neue Heimat Städtebau (Urban Development), set up in 1977; half the company's ordinary capital of DM 120 m was held by the DGB's managing companies and by unions affiliated to the DGB.

The Volksfürsorge (Public Welfare) Insurance Company also enjoyed a tremendous boom in business. At the end of 1977 it had 5.8 m policies in force, with a total sum insured of DM 34.2 billion, making it one of the largest German insurance companies.

Things went just as well for the Bank für Gemeinwirtschaft (BfG – Bank for Co-operative Economy), headed by Walter Hesselbach. Its balance sheet total grew from DM 133 m in 1950 to more than DM 2.1 bn in 1958 and DM 35 bn in 1978. The BfG played a growing part in the internal banking business. In 1973 it opened a branch in London, followed in 1976 by branches in New York, Sao Paulo and Hong Kong. In 1974 it joined the Israeli bank Hapoalim to set up the Israel Continental Bank.

The co-operative travel agency, Gut-Reisen, created in Frankfurt in 1969, was less successful. As its market share of charter flights stayed below 10 per cent and its car holiday and self-catering sections refused to rise above 6 per cent, the non-competitive enterprise was soon sold to NUR-Neckermann und Reisen.

With the increasing expansion of the public utility enterprises, they not only became detached from their co-operative origins; with the adoption of capitalist legal forms they also took over and developed the principles of hierarchical organization, that is, the distinction between the entrepreneurial, management role and the practical role. Moreover the success of the trade union enterprises' business activities increasingly raised the issue of their commitment to the unions' moral claims and political objectives. The more public utility enterprises came to resemble "formally and structurally [. . .] the private enterprise type", the more blurred their specific profile became. In actual fact, it was hard for "outsiders" to tell the difference between public utility and private companies (and this was admitted); it was a difference of principle, however, as it was part of the company's aim to use profits in a publicly responsible manner, in contrast to the private appropriation of profit.[43]

Probably in view of the economic success of the public utility enterprises but no doubt also because they had lost some of their earthy trade union aroma, in the early 1970s the unions believed that they had to give their public utility enterprises a more clearly formulated justification and set of duties. Trade unionists as businessmen – they claimed – had demonstrated that they could not only hold their own against private entrepreneurs in tough competitive conditions, but could also contribute to the running of the market economy. In addition, they fulfilled "in an exemplary fashion trade union demands with regard to social policy and society as a whole" and proved "that in a competitive economy socially owned capital can be successfully managed in the service of the public". The plan for "the task and duties of the public utility enterprises of the DGB and its trade unions" adopted by the DGB's federal committee in December 1978 also referred proudly to the successes achieved in conjunction with the establishment of the Finance Company for Co-operative Economy (BGAG) in 1974, as "the interests held were now easy to grasp and transparent in according with trade union thinking".[44]

43 ibid., p. 143 f.
44 Ziele und Funktionen der gemeinwirtschaftlichen Unternehmen, beschlossen vom DGB-Bundesvorstand gemeinsam mit den gemeinwirtschaftlichen Unternehmen, Düsseldorf, Nov. 1972; Auftrag und Augaben gemeinwirtschaftlicher Unternehmen des Deutschen Gewerkschaftsbundes und seiner Gewerkschaften, beschlossen vom Bundesauschuss des DGB am 6. 12. 1978, both reprinted in A. von Loesch, op. cit. pp. 383–394

In view of the membership trends of the 1960s and 70s and the growing anonymity of the "trade union machinery", the need was increasingly felt to reform internal grass-roots participation in the organization and the relations of the individual unions with one another and with the federation. This became even more urgent as the predominance of the big unions within the DGB increased. By 1975, the three largest unions – IG Metall, the ÖTV and Chemicals, Paper and Ceramics Union – accounted for more than half of all trade union members.

The problem of the individual unions' differing size and importance along with the relations of the (major) unions with the umbrella organization was still in need of clarification. The debate about the rules flared up in the 1960s, fuelled by the need to carry out internal economies (implemented chiefly in the areas of training and group targeting, in accordance with the Springen decisions of 1967) and a rules commission was appointed. The narrow limits of its brief were demonstrated by the position adopted by IG Metall, against which no real reform could be carried out. Otto Brenner, for example, advocated a tightening-up of the organization but rejected any limitation of each individual union's autonomy.[45] Since a two-thirds majority was required for any rule change and IG Metall on its own accounted for 131 of the 430 delegates at the extraordinary congress of 1971 and knew that the other big unions had similar reservations about any reforms that went too far, the outcome of the reform debate was predictable.[46] The formula for allocating delegates was not changed in favour of the smaller unions. No new division of duties between the federation and the individual unions was agreed. The proposed press merger was defeated. Only the enlargement of the federal committee, on which each union is now entitled to three seats, can be seen as supporting the idea of co-operation on equal terms between the DGB unions.

The rule changes of 1971 were thus no great accomplishment. The centralization plans designed to tighten up and strengthen union organization were once again frustrated by union in-fighting. So from this angle the unions were hardly well-prepared for the critical years ahead. The same, incidentally, is true of international union co-operation. In an age in which vast corporations have shifted capital and production across national borders, without giving the unions or governments a chance to

---

45 Otto Brenner, Was bedeutet Reform des DGB? in Gewerkschaftliche Monatshefte 4, 1971, pp. 209–12
46 Satzung, in Protokoll des 9. Ordentlichen Bundeskongresses in Berlin vom 25. bis 30. Juni 1972 (Düsseldorf, undated)

monitor them, more attention had to be given to stepping up union co-operation. With a view to European union, the ICFTU (International Confederation of Free Trade Unions) was joined by the ECFTU (European Confederation of Free Trade Unions) in April 1969. Otto Brenner was elected its president. After the enlargement of the EEC on the accession of the United Kingdom, Ireland and Denmark, the ECFTU was reconstituted as the ETUC (European Trade Union Confederation). Owing to its limited capacity to influence the European institutions and the reluctance of the national unions to relinquish powers to the ETUC, there was little likelihood of this body developing into a powerful federation of trade unions. So nor should the international muscle of the unions be overrated on the threshold of a period of serious economic problems, the solution to which certainly did not (and does not) lie in a series of solo efforts by individual nations.

XIII. Power and impotence of the trade unions in the crisis of the 1970s and 1980s

The oil crisis following the Yom Kippur War between Egypt and Israel in autumn 1973 marked the onset of a worldwide recession that affected all the industrialized nations of the West. The effects of the slump on the employment situation were exacerbated by the structural problems of specific industries (for example, ship-building, steel and textiles) and the consequences of the third industrial revolution, the advance of microelectronics. From the end of the 1970s on, mass employment was a dominant part of the picture. Time and again the growing power of the employers and a government that was increasingly resolute in sticking to its objectives threatened to force the trade unions on to the defensive.

1. *Cyclical and structural crises, mass unemployment and organizational stagnation*

The upturn in the economy of 1972–3 was rudely interrupted by the oil crisis of 1973, which culminated in the slump of 1974–5. Economic growth, as high as 4.7 per cent in 1973, fell to 0.4 per cent in 1974 and –1.4 per cent in 1975. Business activity soon picked up again, with the economy growing by 5.6 per cent in 1976. But the recovery did not have the vigour of earlier years and turned back into recession in 1981–2, following the second oil crisis in 1979, with growth rates of 0 and –1 per cent. The transition from the 1970s to the 1980s was dominated by high inflation and growing unemployment.

There were a number of reasons why the upturns in the economy had been growing constantly weaker since the 1960s. First of all, the normalization of need: after the reconstruction phase, which lasted until the end of the 1950s, the domestic market started to show obvious signs of saturation. To meet this, exports were stepped up; developing economic cooperation between the European countries and the expansion of world trade increasingly took the place of German domestic sales. This trend entailed export and balance of payments surpluses on the one hand, and dependence on trends in foreign trade on the other. Changes in the structure of production were another factor. As an example we may point to the crisis in coal-mining, the importance of which diminished as coal was overtaken by other sources of power (oil, gas and nuclear power). There were also crises in shipbuilding and steel, triggered off by new materials (plastics) and international competition. Finally, there was the increased use of new production techniques; their effects in terms of rationalization in industry and the service sector were far in excess of their ability to create jobs. From the mid-1970s on, microelectronics prompted a fresh wave of rationalization – including the service sector, which was thus unable to absorb people who had lost their jobs in manufacturing, as it had done following earlier spates of rationalization.

In conditions of higher raw material costs and stagnating world trade almost all Western countries suffered cyclical and, above all, structural problems, which were initially given the name "stagflation" – meaning that economic growth was nil (or minimal) while unemployment and prices rose. In West Germany inflation rose from 1.9 per cent in 1969 to 5.5 in 1972, 6.9 in 1973 and 7 per cent in 1974; after that it fell to 3.7 per cent (1977) and 2.7 per cent (1978), only to resume its upward climb in 1979–82 (4.1, 5.5, 5.9 and 5.3 per cent). From 1972 on, unemployment grew steadily worse, increasing in leaps and bounds in the second half of the 1970s: from 1.1 per cent in 1972 it was up to 4.7 per cent by 1975; in 1979 and 1980 it levelled out at 3.8 per cent, but subsequently rose to 5.5 (1981), reaching 7.5 per cent in 1982 (Table 5b).

Shortly after the political watershed of autumn 1982 a new economic upturn commenced, with growth rates of 2–3 per cent. This was accompanied by a clear trend towards price stabilization: in the years that followed, the rate of inflation reverted to 1–2 per cent (1987–8). Yet despite steady economic growth, which neither the crash on the New York stock exchange on 19 October 1987 nor the international debt crisis has (so far) seriously disrupted, unemployment rose again, reaching more than 8 per cent in 1983 and staying at this high level (Table 5b). Excluding the "silent reserves", the number of registered unemployed has exceeded 2 million every year since 1983. Since the start of the employment crisis in 1974, almost one worker in three has at some time been out of work, at least temporarily. Unemployment has become an experience familiar to the mass of working people.

*

Since the beginning of the 1970s, the membership of the DGB-affiliated unions (including, since 1978, the Police Union) had been growing, reaching 7.9 m in 1981. But then for three successive years membership fell: in 1984 the DGB unions were down to "only" little over 7.6 m. From 1985 membership stabilized and then rose slightly, remaining at just over 7.6 m in 1986–8. The trend was the same in the DAG: with small fluctuations their members increased from roughly 470,000 in 1974–7 to 501,000 in 1982. The 1982–3 fall to 497,000 was contained and soon, from 1985 on, turned into an upward trend once again (Table 1c). The membership of the Christian Trade Union Federation was a steady 300,000 throughout the 1980s. There are several reasons for the decline in membership of the DGB unions in the first half of the 1980s. Foremost among them was the crisis of confidence in the unions, which the "Neue Heimat" affairs in early 1982 and 1986 may not have actually triggered off but certainly aggravated. Other major factors affecting the unions were the structural crises and the permanent decline of certain industries: the loss of members in the construction, mining and textiles unions, for instance, reflected the problems in the industries for which they cater.

In one area, at least, the unions responded to the shift in emphasis due to the structural economic change with the beginnings of organizational reform. After months of discussion, the transitional rules for the future industrial union Media, Printing and Paper, Journalism and Art (IG Medien) were submitted in summer 1985. Finally set up in 1989, IG Medien was an amalgam of the Printing and Paper Union, the Art Union and the Radio, Television and Film Union.

It is noticeable how the predominantly white-collar union Commerce, Banking and Insurance continued to grow even during the crisis on the labour market. That also applies to the two largest unions, the Engineering Union and Public Services, Transport and Communications; increases in growth were also recorded – even in the lean years of 1986–7 – by the Chemicals Union, Printing and Paper, and Food, Beverage and Allied Workers' Union.

In contrast to earlier periods, the economic crisis and mass unemployment of the 1970s and 1980s did not cause a breakdown in trade union organization, though improving the degree of organization was out of the question in this period. After a slow climb to 34.2 per cent in 1978, it declined steadily – levelling out at 32.9 per cent in 1984 and 1985.

The organizational problems that had dogged the unions in the past were not resolved in the 1970s or 80s, either.

Foremost among them, as in the Depression of the 1930s, was the problem of the unemployed. There was and is no uniform arrangement enabling the unions to accept the unemployed as members, even if they have never worked before. What is more, the offers open to the jobless – such as the benefits provided by some unions after more than a year's continuous unemployment and the jobless schemes mostly organized at local level – are not widely known.

The proportion of white-collar workers to union members overall (22.8 per cent in 1987) remained a long way behind their proportion of the total workforce (44 per cent). The membership structure of the DGB trade unions was still geared to the employment patterns of the 1950s. It should also be pointed out that the proportion of male white-collar workers belonging to unions changed little in the 1980s, so that the increase in white-collar workers must be attributed to the growing union activity of female employees. Even though the growth in membership of the 1970s was chiefly due to women, the degree of organization among women (23 per cent in 1987) was still much lower than their proportion of all employed persons (38 per cent in 1987). Apart from gender-specific handicaps of a more general nature, one reason for women's reluctance to join the trade unions may have been the small numbers of women in elected posts and leading positions. Even at the DGB congress of 1986, only 79 of the 516 union delegates (or 15.3 per cent) were women. Of the nine seats on the DGB's federal executive only two were occupied by women – Irmgard Blättel and Ilse Brusis. Only one woman is chairman of an industrial union – Monika Wulf-Mathies of the ÖTV – and none of the nine DGB regions is headed by a woman. These figures illustrate how career patterns for men and women within the trade unions continue to differ.

The figures for young trade union members reflected the problem of an ageing membership with which the unions were faced, reinforcing demographic trends in the the population at large. This problem was rendered even more acute by the fact that young members figured prominently among those who left the unions in 1982–3. The reasons for this may be the oft-quoted "change in values", an aversion to "large, anonymous machineries" or the credibility crisis brought to a head by the "Neue Heimat" affair.

Finally, the changes in production techniques and structures in recent years have posed a number of organizational problems for the trade unions. The increase in part-time and home working and the increasing flexibility of working hours have swelled the categories that had always been reluctant to join. At the same time, the number and importance of the traditional industrial workers have declined, with the result that the trade unions' established social basis has been shrinking steadily. In addition, redundancy has forced a large number of workers out of the sort of jobs that are covered by collective agreements – or they have left voluntarily. But there never has been any place for the trade unions in the underground economy or in the self-employed small business world where self-realization often verges on self-exploitation.

The charge has often been levelled at the unions that because of the recession they were tending to cater exclusively for "job holders". The internal discussion of the aims and strategies of trade union policy, which had been stepped up since the mid-1980s, and plans to match members' aspirations more closely with the action taken by the executives, showed that the erosion of solidarity caused by the employment situation and the trade unions' loss of credibility had been recognized but not overcome. The main ways put forward for getting out of this crisis were organizing the unemployed, strengthening internal democracy, revitalizing union work at company and local level and increased targeting of specific categories – such as foreign workers, young people, women and white-collar workers.[1] The future will show whether these proposals are genuinely heeded and put into effect.

∗

Among the most important changes in the field of trade union policy proper was the sale of public utility enterprises triggered by the "Neue Heimat" scandal. Both inflicted severe damage on trade union credibility which was difficult to repair. As early as the beginning of 1982, the magazine "Der Spiegel" had exposed the inadequacies of the Neue Heimat management under Albert Vietor. Although changes of staff were rapidly undertaken as a result, the awkward question of the unions' monitoring role left the trade union leaders with egg on their faces – after all, they did have representatives on the supervisory board of Neue Heimat.

Unfavourable trends in the construction and property business made it more difficult to carry out a thorough rehabilitation of Neue Heimat, which had clearly overstretched itself with its many foreign and domestic ventures. The sale of Neue Heimat in September 1986 to a hitherto unknown Berlin bread manufacturer, Horst Schiesser, for the nominal price of one Mark was a panic reaction difficult to comprehend. Mismanagement, the sale and then the repurchase of Neue Heimat and its placing in the hands of a trustee all cost the trade union movement a great deal of prestige and pushed it to the verge of an identity crisis.

The unions tried to cope with the financial consequences of the Neue Heimat débâcle by selling off most of the Bank for Co-operative Economy, reorganizing and finally selling the Coop Group as a limited company and drawing up plans to sell other public utility enterprises such as Volksfürsorge insurance. At the same time they dropped a number of

---

1 See Ernst Breit, Fortschritt – gegen, ohne oder durch die Gewerkschaften, in Gewerkschaftliche Monatshefte I, 1985, pp. 1–19

trade union activities that were often seen as something of a liability because of their internal contradictions. At the conference on "Trade Unions and the Co-operative Economy" held on 14 October 1987, Franz Steinkühler (chairman of IG Metall since October 1986) called for the curtain to be rung down on this chapter of trade union history. It was not possible, he said, for trade unions to "run public utility enterprises in a capitalist environment". The only possible conclusion that could be drawn from developments to date was to get out of the "co-operative economy" – no matter how painful it might be. The trade unions could not afford critical headlines over the issue again. But Hans Matthöfer, the chairman of the Finance Company for Co-operative Economy (BGAG) was opposed to "making any premature commitments for the future [. . .] now, out of disappointment", referring to the need for hard-hitting adjustments. And Walter Hesselbach, the "father of the co-operative economy", advised the movement not to sever all links with its history despite the prevalent mood of anger.[2]

The question of the future of the co-operative economy in a capitalist setting is quite justified, especially as the specific hallmarks of public utility enterprises were hard to detect. Throughout the 1980s, however, people continually asked whether an attempt should not be made to revive the co-operative tradition – before the trade unions completely abandoned it. If such an attempt were to be made, a flair for business and a monitoring system, both guided by the right values, a clear-cut co-operative economic philosophy, an organizational culture and individual economic morality would all be vital elements.[3]

2. *On to the political defensive*

The unions were badly hit by the cyclical and structural problems of the 1970s and 80s; even during Helmut Schmidt's chancellorship they felt as though they (like the "social state") were fighting an uphill struggle[4], and this was before they suffered a drastic loss of influence on government

2 According to Frankfurter Rundschau of 15 October 1987
3 Klaus Novy, Wieviel ist verloren – "Neue Heimat", Gemeinwirtschaft oder mehr?, in WohnBund 10, 1986, p. 4; also Wilhelm Kaltenborn, Wie die Theorie der Gemeinwirtschaft auf die Praxis kam – und was sie vorfand, in Gewerkschaftliche Monatshefte 3, 1987, pp. 186–90
4 Friedhelm Hengsbach, Der Sozialstaat im Gegenwind – eine Bilanz der 13 Jahre SPD/FDP-Regierung, in Gewerkschaftliche Monatshefte 1, 1983, p. 1

policy after the "watershed" of 1982. In addition, there was the appearance of new social movements – from the peace movement and women's movement to the environmental groups – which rather put the trade unions (and the SPD) on the political sidelines at first. They sought escape from this predicament by attempting to overhaul their political programme.

The "Schmidt Era": the start of an uphill struggle

1974 marked a political turning point: in May of that year Willy Brandt resigned in the wake of the Günter Guillaume "spy in the chancellery" affair. The era of reform that had started with such high hopes thus came to an end. But the change of policy that accompanied Helmut Schmidt's appointment to the chancellorship should not be turned into a question of personalities. The espionage affair was the reason given for Brandt's resignation not the real cause. In the early 1970s it had already started to become clear that demands and expectations with regard to the extension of the "social state" were conflicting with the limited scope for fulfilling these hopes. The Schmidt government tried to take the appropriate action in its economic and financial policy, allowing for the limitations imposed by the recession on the government's freedom of action; this inevitably brought it into conflict with the trade unions' objectives.

From 1974 onwards the limits of state anticyclical economic policy became obvious. The comprehensive controls financed by debt proved quite incapable of giving a lasting boost to the economy and curbing unemployment. In view of the increasing national debt and inflationary price trends, the government henceforth sought to enforce a restrictive monetary and credit policy. The first sign of this new course was the Cabinet decision of 10 September 1975 to introduce spending cuts to improve the budgetary position from 1 January 1976. Spending under the Law to Promote Employment, pension funding and public services were cut and employee contributions to the unemployment insurance scheme increased. Further steps were taken to cut welfare benefits in the shape of the Law to Moderate the Cost of Health Insurance and the Twentieth Pensions Adjustment Law of March 1978, upping contributions and introducing health insurance contributions for pensioners from 1982.

In tandem with this policy of retrenchment in the field of social welfare the Schmidt government pursued a costly plan to deal with employment problems. In March 1977 the government agreed on an investment programme to make DM 16 bn available for action to improve the environment, water supply and distribution, and energy conservation. In November 1977 the government also agreed a federal programme worth DM 190 m to encourage urban renewal in accordance with the Law to Promote Urban Development; in May 1978 the programme was supplemented by an amendment to the Housing Modernization Law involving a total outlay of DM 4.35 bn.

The DGB welcomed the federal government's investment programmes, while criticizing them for providing too little too late.[5] In fact, the Schmidt government's measures in the field of labour market policy were largely in accord with the ideas contained in the DGB's "Proposals for restoring full employment" of July 1977 and reiterated on numerous occasions. It demanded action to promote qualitative growth in selected areas of the economy, to "humanize" work and, above all, to reduce working hours. The principle demand, however, was for an active employment policy, that is, for more and bigger public job creation programmes.

Demands for safeguarding or creating jobs were also given a key position in the fifth action programme of June 1979. In March 1981 trade union plans for combating the crisis were augmented by the demand for an "investment programme to safeguard employment[6] by means of qualitative growth" to a tune of DM 10 bn. The money was supposed to come from a general labour market tax levied on those in high and very high income tax brackets. The programme set out a list of measures for energy saving, housing renewal and urban redevelopment, the expansion of public transport, the upgrading of waste disposal systems (sewage works, etc.) and improvements in education and research.

The longer the jobs crisis lasted and the more widely its effects were felt, the more the business community and the FDP opposed a state job creation policy that had not only proved ineffective – as the rising unemployment figures appeared to prove – but was rocking public budgets and hence the whole credit system. More than anything it was the growing national debt that triggered this rethink. As the employment crisis worsened, net federal borrowing soared from DM 2.7 bn in 1973 to DM 9.5 bn in 1974 and almost DM 30 bn in 1975. Annual new federal borrowing remained at roughly this level, fluctuating between DM 22 and 27 bn, until 1980, before rising once again to DM 37 bn in 1981 and 1982.

5 DGB (ed), Das Programm für Zukunftsinvestitionen der Bundesregierung vom Frühjahr 1977 (Düsseldorf, 1978)
6 DGB (ed), Vorschläge zur Wiederherstellung der Vollbeschäftigung (Düsseldorf, 1977)

The growing national debt was increasingly laid at the door of the SPD and the unions by the employers, the FDP and the CDU/CSU. It was a common complaint that their policies were encouraging the "outmoded expectations" of citizens gently swaying in the "hammock of the social safety net". In the late 1970s, the employers were pressing more urgently than ever before for a political "change" to put the unions in their place. The slogan about the "trade union state" was dusted off. A "federation law" would tame the unions and with a "list of taboos" the employers limited the scope for negotiating issues and compromises with the trade unions. Further proof of the employers' "roll-back strategy" was the attempt by the Mannesmann AG in June 1980 to get round co-determination on the coal and steel model by incorporating the iron and steel works into the pipe works. This question acted like a canker within the SPD-FDP coalition; not until 1981 were they able to reach a compromise safeguarding co-determination until 1987, which was admittedly not likely to satisfy the trade unions.

Furthermore, in 1978–9 the trade unions' self-confidence and ability to act were badly hit by the campaign against "backscratching" in relations between the unions and the SPD. Proposals by sections of the CSU to form party political groups in the DGB unions or to consider strengthening the Christian Trade Union Federation, were firmly rejected by the DGB unions.[7] Charges of alleged Communist subversion[8] in some unions were considered by many unions as without foundation – especially as at the end of the 1960s and beginning of the 1970s they had passed incompatibility decisions to protect themselves against the influx of new members from the ranks of the extraparliamentary opposition and the DKP (Communist Party), set up in 1968 to replace the KPD banned in 1956.[9]

The conflicts between the employers, the FDP and CDU/CSU on the one hand and the SPD and the trade unions on the other became more acrimonious in the early 1980s, particularly over budget discussions. It also emerged that even the ruling Social Democrats and the unions were not always in agreement on the basic principles of policy. The 1982 budget consultations were very much dominated by a policy of entrenchment – at

---

7 IG Metall (ed), Spalte und herrsche: F.J. Strauss und die Einheitsgewerkschaft (Frankfurt, undated); Frank Deppe, Detlef Hensche, Mechthild Jansen and Witich Rossmann, Strauss und die Gewerkschaften. Texte, Materialien, Dokumente (Cologne, 1980)

8 Ernst Günter Vetter, Die Roten sind auf dem Vormarsch, in Frankfurter Allgemeine Zeitung of 21 April 1979

9 Rotbuch zu den Gewerkschaftsausschlüssen (Hamburg, 1978)

the expense of the social security system. In more detail, "Operation 82" laid down: curbs on the right to claim unemployment benefit, a rise in contributions (from 3 to 4 per cent) and cuts in benefit; cuts in child benefit for the second and third children by DM 20 each; an contributory element in medical costs; deletion of the educational requirement in the basic vocational training year; and a cut in federal life assurance subsidies.

The protests of the trade unions were of little avail. On 8 November 1981 there was a demonstration of 70,000 workers in Stuttgart. Franz Steinkühler, then regional head of IG Metall, called for "resistance to the rundown of the welfare system" and recalled the lessons to be learned from Brüning's mistaken policy of retrenchment.[10] Partly as a result of union pressure, a front in favour of a job creation policy was once again set up within the SPD. In response the federal government decided in February 1982 to create a "common initiative for jobs, growth and stability", which took up, for example, the trade union demand for combating youth unemployment by means of a DM 400 m programme; the centrepiece, however, was a temporary investment allowance, intended to stimulate total investment of DM 40 bn by means of budget expenditure in the region of DM 4 bn.

The trade unions hardly recognized their demands in the government's economic measures – even less in its social measures. Disappointment in the late 1970s and early 1980s at the government's economy programme were now followed by bitter protests. Their basic mood was indicated by the slogan "Enough is enough".[11] Though the unions stressed that they wanted "no other government, we want another policy" (Leonard Mahlein, chairman of the Printing Union[12]), in fact the ruling Social Democrats and the trade unions drifted apart at this time, under the pressure of the compromises necessary to keep the coalition with the FDP going and the CDU/CSU majority in the *Bundesrat*.

While, despite all the economies, the SPD clung on to the idea of state job creation through economic policy programmes financed by budgetary deficits, the FDP – under the ideological leadership of Otto Graf Lambsdorff – demanded a political "about-turn". An end to state control of the

10 According to Hans-Joachim Schabedoth, Bittsteller oder Gegenmacht? Perspektiven gewerkschaftlicher Politik nach der Wende (Marburg, 1985), p. 81
11 Karl-Heinz Janzen, Das Mass an Zumutungen ist voll. Zu den Haushaltsbeschlüssen 1983, in Neue Gesellschaft 8, 1982, pp. 774–7; Claus Schäfer, Verteilungs- und Beschäftigungswirkungen von Operation '82, Gemeinschaftsinitiative und Operation '83, in WSI-Mitteilungen 10, 1982, pp. 579–87
12 According to Klaus Bohnsack, Die Koalitionskrise 1981/82 und der Regierungswechsel 1982, in Zeitschrift für Parlamentsfragen 1, 1983, p. 11

Ernst Breit, chairman of the DGB, making his speech on general principles at the thirteenth DGB congress in 1986

economy and cuts in production costs, taxes and social expenditure – with goals such as these the FDP was on a collision course with the SPD, while the rumblings of discontent at various government measures, from the NATO twin-track decision to the rundown of the social security system, grew louder and louder within the SPD itself, as the 1982 Munich party conference showed.

The coalition finally broke down over the 1983 budget consultations. Although the thinking of both ruling parties was broadly in line with the 1982 budget decisions, the proposed economies did not go far enough for the FDP's liking. "Denationalization", "deregulation" and "relaxation" of the economy and the employment market were the new slogans with which the FDP under Hans-Dietrich Genscher sought to initiate a "spiritual and moral watershed" together with the CDU/CSU under Helmut Kohl.

After the "watershed" of autumn 1982: on the sidelines

For Ernst Breit, who was elected chairman of the DGB in May 1982, his new job was no sinecure, even though in him the DGB had chosen a highly experienced trade unionist to lead it. Born the son of a toolmaker in Rickelshof, Kreis Dithmarschen in 1924, he attended technical school and in 1941 became a trainee inspector in the post office. After serving in the army and a period as a prisoner of war, he returned to the post office and gradually rose to a senior position. In 1946 he joined the German Post Office Union, joining the executive in 1953 and heading the union from 1971 on. His level-headed approach to his work and his sense of realism obviously recommended him to the vast majority of delegates as a suitable man to tackle the problems looming up in the early 1980s.

The previous year the DGB had adopted a new basic programme that was to serve as a pointer in the foreseeable conflicts over social and economic policy, the peace issue and the environment. But in the final years of the Social-Liberal coalition it had become evident how difficult it was for the trade unions to find a united and consistent political line on such contentious issues that satisfied the increasingly urgent wishes of the membership without being disloyal to the ruling Social Democrats. Furthermore, the unions' credibility was badly damaged by the "Neue Heimat" scandal, the first part of which – Albert Vietor's mismanagement – became public knowledge early in 1982 and overshadowed the departure of Heinz Oskar Vetter.

Then, in September 1982, the trade unions were faced with a new government coalition, comprising the CDU/CSU and FDP under Helmut Kohl, who could certainly not be suspected of excessive friendliness to the unions. As supporters of the supply-side economics of Margaret Thatcher and Ronald Reagan, the politicians responsible for economic and social affairs in the new government relied on giving a boost to investment by relieving business of some of the burden of taxes, social insurance contributuions and wage-costs as well as legal obligations that were felt to be a hindrance. These new forces for growth would, it was hoped, also reduce unemployment.

The trade unions by no means stood back idly and watched this political "watershed" and the rundown of the social services. As planned before the change of government, the DGB arranged a series of rallies in the autumn of 1982 in Frankfurt, Nuremberg, Dortmund, Stuttgart, Hanover, Hamburg and Saarbrücken, at which more than half a million workers gathered to protest at the policies of the (new) government. It was certainly no premature move: this much was evident from the various plans, ideas, proposals and projects floated by the government camp in months that followed.

The critical, indeed at times anti-union, thrust of "watershed politics" could not escape anyone reading the various policy documents in circulation in 1982–3.[13] First there was the memorandum of March 1982 from the Federal Association of German Employers' Federations on "Social security in the future", with its calls to redefine the "social state". These ideas were taken up by Lambsdorff in September 1982 and, after the 1983 elections, by the CDU parliamentary party's spokesman on social affairs, Heimo George, who in July 1983 presented "Proposals for stemming unemployment", which advocated freeing the private economy from all the dictates and fetters restricting it. His solution was to make labour cheaper, and to this end he recommended "limited undercutting of scheduled wage rates". He considered laws protecting the disabled and young people an obstacle to recruitment and held that they should therefore be abolished. In August 1983 Ernst Albrecht, the Christian Democrat Prime Minister of Lower Saxony, followed up with "Ten theses on the problem of unemployment", which gave priority to removing the tax burden from companies and stripping away the "ossified husk encasing the economic and social system' by relaxing laws on dismissal, the protection of youth and co-determination. The long-term aims of Christian Democratic eco-

---

13 According to Schabedoth, op. cit., pp. 89 and 113 f.

nomic and social policy were gathered together at the end of 1983 by the CDU's economic council and published in a policy document entitled "Freedom and performance as a strategy for the future". Lastly, Helmut Haussmann, the FDP secretary general again pinned down the thrust of the "new politics" in an interview in the magazine "Der Spiegel" when he said, "Collective agreements must become much more flexible, not only upwards but also downwards."[14] The FDP backed its secretary-general, for "what we need are wages adjusted to meet specific market conditions, differentiation by work, industry, region".[15] The Minister for Economic Affairs, Martin Bangemann (FDP), hastened to come out in favour of greater flexibility and differentiation in pay policy by industry and region.[16] Since in fact pay policy already makes precisely this sort of differentiation, the trade unions not unreasonably suspected that such statements concealed an attack not only on the level of wages but also on the collective agreement qua institution.

The trade unions saw these programmatic statements on the "future of the social state"[17] as an assault on the very basis of their policies. Behind the eulogy in praise of individual responsibility they detected the intention to dismantle the social security system. The plaint about dwindling entrepreneurial freedom they regarded as a full frontal onslaught on the co-determination arrangements and industrial safety laws. They interpreted the new buzzwords of "relaxation" and "deregulation" as attacks on the system of collective bargaining for settling wages, working hours and conditions; and the slogan "Hard work must pay once again!" appeared to hark back to the ruthless old "dog-eat-dog" society.

*

The trade unions continually attempted to show that the price of such a "watershed" policy was high, and that it was paid by wage earners, pensioners, the unemployed and the sick. The economies announced by the Kohl government in autumn 1982 cut unemployment benefit, imposed charges under the health insurance scheme and scrapped scholarships for school pupils. The budgets of the following years were entirely in line with the initial decisions of autumn 1982: social retrenchment with the aim of

---

14 Der Spiegel of 15 April 1985, p. 21 ff.
15 Freie demokratische Korrespondenz, Pressedienst der FDP, Ausgabe (press release) 116 of 23 April 1985
16 General-Anzeiger (Bonn) of 19 April 1985, p. 1
17 Kurt Biedenkopf, Die Zukunft des Sozialstaates, in Gewerkschaftliche Monatshefte 8, 1984, pp. 494–500

consolidating the public budgets and redistribution to encourage businesses to invest. But it soon turned out that the repayment of the national debt could not be maintained in the face of constant new demands. Net federal borrowing was reduced from DM 31.5 bn in 1983 to DM 28.3 bn in 1984 and roughly DM 22 bn in 1985 and 1986; but the following year it rose to DM 26.3 bn and in 1988 exceeded DM 30 bn.

The programme of economies was accompanied by a series of laws designed to "denationalize" or "deregulate" employment conditions, and thus at the same time weaken the position of the unions. Let us recall the Law to Promote Employment of 19 April 1985. In the face of strong union protests, this law made it easier to employ staff on temporary contracts. The trade unions feared that temporary appointments, limited to 18 months, would create a "two-class" set of laws for employees – which could be used by the employer as an "effective means of discipline".

The slogan about the "state's retreat from the economy" also covers measures planned or already implemented to privatize public enterprises, ranging from the part-sale of federal holdings in Lufthansa and Volkswagen to the restructuring of the post office. All these measures met with strong protests from the unions, which denounced this policy – to no avail – as a wanton waste of public resources.[18]

In this connexion we should also mention the plans to amend the Company Statute Law to strengthen the protection of minorities at the expense of the DGB unions. The idea is to change the rule requiring all candidatures in the works council elections to be endorsed by a list of names so as to allow any trade union represented in the company to submit candidates. This would make it easier for members of the smaller unions – such as the Christian trade unions and the DAG – to get on to the works councils. The same idea is behind the FDP's proposal to set up legally recognized "mouthpiece committees" (Sprecherausschüsse) for senior employees. In a conversation with Chancellor Kohl, Ernst Breit stressed that the laboriously forged contacts between government and unions might be strained past breaking point, should such plans go ahead.[19]

In these conditions it seemed (almost) futile for the DGB to announce in 1982 a new offensive over co-determination.[20] In view of government plans, this assessment certainly applies to the co-determination drive of

18 See Rudolf Kuda, Wirtschaft, in Michael Kittner (ed.), Gewerkschaftsjahrbuch 1985. Daten, Fakten, Analysen (Cologne, 1985), p.178 f.
19 Der Spiegel No. 50, 1984
20 Ernst Breit, Mitbestimmungsinitiative: Abbau der Arbeitslosigkeit – Demokratisierung der Wirtschaft, in Gewerkschaftliche Monatshefte 10, 1982

1985, launched in March by a conference on "full employment, co-determination and the shaping of technology" in Cologne. The fact that co-determination became one of the stock themes of trade union congresses did little or nothing to achieve the desired end. And the same, incidentally, must be said of the need (which the unions were rather slow to see) to press for improvements in workplace co-determination rights, especially when it comes to the introduction of new technology.[21] Chances of achieving the continually voiced call for the introduction of national economic co-determination arrangements – with economic and social councils and bipartite participation (involving the trade unions) in chambers of commerce and industry and trade corporations – were probably just as remote.[22]

With resolutions and policy pamphlets, academic conferences and rallies, the trade unions tried to draw public attention to their plans for the economy and society. The issues covered ranged from the education conference "Education for all – encouragement not selection" in November 1983 to the IG Metall conference entitled "The Other Future. Solidarity and Freedom" in October 1988. And after the protests of autumn 1982, the DGB arranged a whole "week of protest" from 14 to 20 October 1985 against the policies of the Kohl-Genscher government. Under the slogan "Solidarity is our strength", the DGB took issue with government policy. "Freedom through flexibility?" it asked, and supplied the answer, "Only for employers! For wage earners the edifice of reliable industrial relations will collapse."[23]

But not all government measures were unanimously opposed by the trade unions. While some, notably IG Metall, were aiming at the introduction of the 35-hour week by demanding cuts in working hours, others such as the Chemicals Union and Food, Beverage and Allied Workers' Union accepted the plans of the Federal Ministry of Labour to introduce new arrangements for early retirement to shorten employees' working lives and make the pensionable age flexible.[24] The unions that had initially rejected this scheme as an obstacle to achieving a cut in the working week had obviously been persuaded by the facts that both methods of securing a

---

21 DGB (ed.), Konzeption zur Mitbestimmung am Arbeitsplatz (Schriftenreihe Mitbestimmung, No. 7, Düsseldorf, March 1985); cf. IG Metall (ed.), Aktionsprogramm: Arbeit und Technik – "Der Mensch muss bleiben!", November 1984

22 DGB (ed.), Gesamtwirtschaftliche Mitbestimmung – unverzichtbarer Bestandteil einer Politik zur Lösung der wirtschaftlichen und gesellschaftlichen Krise (Schriftenreihe Mitbestimmung, No. 6, Düsseldorf, December 1984)

23 DGB (ed.), Solidarität ist unsere Stärke (Düsseldorf, 1985)

24 Bundesminister für Arbeit und Sozialordnung (ed.), Vorruhestand (Bonn, May 1984)

reduction in working time made sense. At any rate, when the government wished to allow the early retirement scheme to lapse in 1988, there were broad-based protests from the unions, particularly over the implications for employment. The protests received the backing of the CDU's social committees, and the outcome was the renewal of the law in a slightly altered form.

There was by no means agreement between the DGB unions on all major topics; this was evident from the way the NATO twin-track decision was handled. Whereas as recently as 1981 the trade unions in general had found it hard to co-operate with the peace movement and had distanced themselves from the "Krefeld appeal", in particular, by passing a resolution of their own[25], many trade unionists took part in the 1982 Easter marches and the Bonn peace demonstration of June 1982. The rallies on Anti-War Day, 1 September 1982, also helped bring the unions and the peace movement closer together. With the end of Schmidt's term of office, the SPD's change of direction and the missile deployments of 1983–4, the unions became fully committed to opposing increases in nuclear arsenals. IG Metall wanted to hold a general strike of 10–15 minutes to protest against "modernization"; the Chemicals Union, IG Chemie, also came out against an increase in arms but regarded a political strike of that type as an impermissible attempt to put pressure on parliament. So the DGB federal executive finally decided to call on union members to down tools for five minutes in support of disarmament. In addition, the DGB staged numerous rallies every year on Anti-War Day, 1 September; the 1988 rally, for instance, focused on the slogan "Money from arms for the social services" and made the following demands: an end to the arms race, the scrapping of nuclear weapons, a freeze on the development of new missile systems, mutual reductions in troop strengths, a ban on chemical and biological weapons, and a ban on arms exports to the Third World.

One of the long-running disputes over economic and financial policy between the government and the unions was the tax reform announced amid great publicity in 1985 – the one that the government claimed would make hard work pay again. Quite apart from the problems of detail that kept on cropping up – from tax exemption for aviation spirit to the introduction of a tax on gas – the unions held that the thinking behind the tax reform was fundamentally flawed. The trade unions demanded that the planned tax relief worth roughly DM 20 bn should be divided into two

---

25 Reprinted in Leminsky and Otto, op. cit., p. 73 ff.

parts. Half the sum should go to help families with children and those on low and average incomes; the other half should be spent on job creation measures.

The clash between the government and the unions came to a – temporary – head early in 1986 during the debate on the amendment of Paragraph 116 of the Law to Promote Employment (AFG).[26] The impetus for a change in the law had been provided by the 1984 dispute in the engineering industry. The government, with the Labour Minister Norbert Blüm (CDU) at the forefront, stated that the purpose of the amendment was to ensure the neutrality of the Federal Institute of Labour in the event of an industrial dispute. But the unions discerned a desire to prevent the payment of benefit to those not directly involved in a pay dispute, thus encouraging the employers to go ahead with their tactics of the "cold lockout" (that is, locking out workers not engaged in industrial action), which were designed to bring the unions quickly to their knees.

Contrary to expectations, the unions managed to conduct a campaign on this apparently rather flimsy issue and mobilize large numbers of wage earners at rallies and demonstrations. On 6 March alone, more than one million workers attended 200 DGB rallies to protest against the amendment of Paragraph 116 of the AFG. And in an "employees' opinion poll" conducted by the DGB, 7.6 m ballot papers were handed in, of which 95 per cent were against the government proposal. The "reform of AFG 116" was obviously seen as a pointer to government policy, though the trade unions were not agreed about which road to take. While some, notably IG Metall, advocated "warning strikes", IG Chemie, headed by Hermann Rappe, rejected any attempt to put pressure on parliament. Despite the unions' protests, the amendment was adopted – with insignificant concessions to the unions – on 10 March 1986 by the governing majority in a roll call vote. It came into force on 1 May the same year.

Thus on virtually all economic and social policy decisions there were serious disagreements between the unions and the government. At the end of the first full legislative period of the "watershed government" it was evident that the unions had been shunted aside, their demands and protests ignored. This trend was reflected in the list of demands that the DGB published along with its "election acid test"[27] for the general elections of 25 January 1987.

---

26 See Michael Kittner (ed.), Gewerkschaftsjahrbuch 1986 (Cologne, 1986), p. 403 ff., and ditto 1987 (Cologne, 1987), p. 360 ff.
27 Wahlprüfsteine vom Oktober 1986, in ötv-magazin 11, 1986, p. 7

Chief among union demands was the call for "more public initiatives for work, the environment and the quality of life", including investment programmes worth DM 100 bn over a five-year periód; to fund all this the tax reform scheduled for 1988 and 1990 should be dropped. They demanded the immediate repeal of the provisions of the Law to Promote Labour that encroached on workers' rights, and the same for the changes in protection for the disabled and young people. Under the rubric "The expansion of co-determination at all levels of the economy", the DGB called for the withdrawal of draft amendments to the Company Statute Law and the Staff Representation Law, improved rights of co-determination in connexion with rationalization and the introduction of new technologies, the safeguarding of co-determination in the coal and steel industry, the extension of bipartite co-determination to cover all large companies and the introduction of national economic co-determination with economic and social councils. Finally they wanted the unions' ability to take strike action to be guaranteed by the repeal of the amendment to Paragraph 116 of the Law to Promote Labour and a ban on lockouts.

The ruling coalition of CDU/CSU and FDP emerged victorious from the *Bundestag* elections of 25 January 1987, though they polled fewer votes than at the previous general election. This was considered to be due to the fact that the Christian Democrats had forfeited "the votes of many wage earners" who "did not agree with the pro-employer and anti-union government policies of the tenth legislative period" from 1983 to 1986.[28] Admittedly, the trade unions suffered a clear drop in the proportion of unionized deputies, principally due to the SPD's electoral losses. This may not have been such a hard blow, however, as the unions had often had occasion to note that union membership was no guarantee that the deputy in question would champion trade union interests in parliament.

*

The problem of the "acid test" (which expressly avoided recommending which way to vote) caused the issue of the unions' party political neutrality or independence to flare up again and again. The unions' political commitment remained a controversial point. However plausible the DGB's position that the unified union was "independent of political parties but neither politically neutral nor non-political", it was, and is, difficult to put this claim into practice. It was little use Dieter Wunder, chairman of the

---

28 Klaus Richter, Gewerkschafter im Elften Deutschen Bundestag, in Gewerkschaftliche Monatshefte 3, 1987, pp. 182–5

Education and Science Union, stressing that the unions were "not opponents of the CDU or CSU but are combating the present employment and social policies of the government that comprises these parties".[29] After the "heated debate" of 1978–9 CDU/CSU politicians had constantly condemned any critical comments on government policy since 1982 – such as the "protest weeks" of October 1985 and 1988 – as a breach of the unions' commitment to "party political neutrality".

Reservations of this kind received a boost by controversial personnel decisions, as when the delegates at the eleventh congress of the ÖTV union in Hamburg in June 1988 refused to vote a CDU member on to the executive because of his views on the reform of Paragraph 218, which differed from that of the majority of delegates. Ulf Fink, then chairman of the Christian Democratic Wage Earners and elected vice-chairman of the DGB in 1990, interpreted the congress's decision as "a danger to the unified trade union". The vote had not merely been directed against the candidate as an individual but was an affront to all CDU members in the organization, he claimed.[30]

In fact, the unions and the SPD are tightly interwoven. Of the 193 members of the SPD parliamentary party following the 1987 elections, 188 are members of trade unions, as are all 42 members of the party executive. Looked at from another angle, 16 of the 17 trade union chairmen are Social Democrats, as are 7 of the 9 members of the DGB federal executive; of the DAG's 9 federal executive members, 7 including the chairman are Social Democrats.

Nevertheless, the relationship between the unions and the SPD was (and is) not free of conflict. Let us recall the disagreements over the economy programme introduced under Chancellor Schmidt in 1981–2; or the irritation aroused by the "Neue Heimat" affair, which was seen by the Social Democrats as a millstone in the election campaigns of 1982–3 and 1986–7; or the proposal floated by the Prime Minister of Saarland and vice-chairman of the SPD, Oskar Lafontaine, for a reduction in working hours without full compensation (at least for higher earners) – right in the middle of the confrontation in the pay negotiations for the public services early in 1988. After a top-level discussion on 25 April 1988 it was possible to calm things down, but the dispute between the party and the unions over each side's claim to independence went on seething under the surface, and erupted once again at the Münster SPD party conference at the

---

29 ötv-magazin 11, 1986, p. 7. Dieter Wunder, Gewerkschaften – eine Kraft der Vergangenheit?, in Gewerkschaftliche Monatshefte 2, 1985, pp. 65–73; this quot. p. 71
30 General-Anzeiger (Bonn) of 22 June 1988, p. 1

end of August and beginning of September 1988 with "fresh vehemence". Against this background it is not hard to understand the plea of the party chairman, Hans-Jochen Vogel, for ways of resolving conflicts that do not lose sight of the need for future co-operation, especially as "to weaken one is as a rule to weaken the other, and thus to strengthen the conservative, if not reactionary, forces".[31]

However often the trade unions felt left in the lurch by the SPD, there was no alternative to co-operation over policy and strategy with the Social Democrats, nor does it seem likely that there ever will be. Despite the many irritants in relations between the two, they have never prompted the unions to consider proclaiming themselves a "replacement worker's party". One key factor behind this reserve is no doubt the danger of factions forming inside the unions along party political dividing lines; another is certainly the limitations any such move would immediately impose on their political influence in parliament.

In 1987–8, then, the CDU/CSU had suffered a big drop in electoral support – not only in the *Bundestag* but also in a series of regional parliamentary elections. This may well have given them food for thought, along with the realization that the economic and financial policy pursued hitherto, owing to unused capacity in individual industries and the speeding-up of technological change, had not taken the pressure off the employment situation. Early in 1988 the government and the trade unions started to close the gap between them. This was, in part, a reaction by the government to the widespread criticism manifested in the election results and the growing pressure of problems building up. The government was no doubt also worried by the mobilization, in certain regions, of workers and their families threatened or actually affected by factory closures and mass redundancies, a phenomenon that was at first spontaneous and then orchestrated by the trade unions. The self-healing powers of the market, on which the government had pinned its hopes, had obviously not been sufficient to solve the structural problems of the shipyards, the steel industry and mining. Entire regions – the coastal *Länder,* the Ruhr district, the Saarland – had been badly hit by the consequences of restructur-

---

31 Hans-Jochen Vogel, SPD und Gewerkschaften (slightly abridged version of an address given to the "Trade Unions and Politics" discussion group of the Friedrich Ebert Foundation political club in Bonn on 5 May 1988) in Gewerkschaftliche Monatshefte 7, 1988, pp. 385–98; this quot. p. 389 f.

ing. It was only following the protests staged by workers at the Krupp steelworks at Duisburg-Rheinhausen threatened by mass redundancy that the federal government decided to agree a joint approach with the two sides of industry and the governments of the *Länder*. The Ruhr district conference early in 1988 and the coal and steel conference of July the same year, which also agreed to earmark financial resources for structural aid, harked back to the old "concerted action" idea. Whether or not such conferences will bear any practical political fruit (unlike their failed predecessor) we shall find out sooner or later. On one point, though, a lesson had been learned from the errors committed by "concerted action": the number of participants and the agenda are tightly controlled. And what is more, there are signs of a change of course most welcome to the unions: a move away from welfare planning towards planning alternative jobs for those affected by works closures.

Anyone who suspected that corporatist crisis strategies were being revived at the conferences of government and trade union representatives in the first half of 1988, was soon undeceived. The DGB's "week of action" in October 1988 – which Chancellor Kohl construed in advance as a sign of the "enmity" with which the unions regarded the government – demonstrated that the unions were sticking to forms of protest and mobilization designed to focus maximum attention on the divergent positions of government and unions. A spin-off that may not have been entirely unwelcome was the fact that a number of disagreements between individual trade unions – for example, between H. Rappe (IG Chemie) and F. Steinkühler (IG Metall) over the issue of weekend working – were thrust into the background in the process.

3. *The unions fall back on their own strength: collective bargaining on a collision course*

The more the trade unions' influence on economic policy diminished, the more they concentrated once again on collective bargaining. "In assessing the political trend and political action, trade union work in the years ahead will no longer be standing in the lee of a state reform policy. A return to the independent power of the trade union movement and "help to self help" are the basis on which wage earners' interests [. . .] will have to be defended."[32] Though since the second half of the 1970s the unions

---

32 Siegfried Bleicher, Ergebnisse und Aussichten der Technologiepolitik und der Humanisierung der Arbeit nach einem Jahr Regierung Kohl/Genscher, in Gewerkschaftliche Monatshefte 3, 1984, pp. 166–75; this quot. p. 175

had not succeeded in putting their ideas on economic and social policy into effect – they had suffered bruising defeats in these areas during the "Schmidt Era" – the shrinking scope for distribution of wealth put employers and trade unions in a state of readiness. Since the 1970s there had been three main problem areas: raising and safeguarding wage levels, protection against rationalization and the reduction of working hours.

*

Let us first look at pay policy. It is no matter for surprise that the trade unions came up against bitter resistance from the employers in the years of recession. Once again the employers blamed high wages, causing high wage incidentals and hence insufficient profits, for lack of investment, poor growth and high unemployment. Wage restraint (implying a voluntary cut in income) was considered the best means of curbing unemployment.[33]

The trade unions had been forced on to the defensive over wages, at least; this was seen most clearly in the fact that since the second half of the 1970s strikes in support of wage claims had become a rarity. An exception to this trend was the industrial dispute in the printing industry in 1976.

What touched off this dispute was a wage claim by the Printing and Paper Union seeking a 9 per cent rise and a minimum of DM 140; the employers' offer was 4.7 per cent. The latter clearly influenced the arbitration proposal of 5.4 per cent put forward on 2 March 1976; understandably it was rejected by the printers' executive committee. The union position was supported by an initial spate of warning strikes from 31 March to 2 April, affecting some 40 companies. After the arbitration process had failed to result in agreement at the Supreme Arbitration Office in Munich, it was decided to hold a strike ballot. On 27 April, the membership was ballotted and 88.2 per cent voted in favour of a strike. The start of the strike was set for the next day.

The Printing Union opted for "selective" strikes, concentrating initially on certain large, highly profitable newspaper companies where the union had a high level of membership and, in view of the healthy profit situation, it would be reasonable to take industrial action to secure wage rises. This staggered approach also saved the union money. As the second

---

33 "Für mehr Beschäftigung". Zwanzig-Punkte-Programm der Bundesvereinigung der Deutschen Arbeitgeberverbände (Cologne, 1985), especially p. 16; Innovationen für mehr Wachstum und Beschäftigung. Ein wirtschaftliches Konzept des Bundesverbandes der Deutschen Industrie (Cologne, 1986), esp. p. 33

stage it was planned to extend the strike to the intaglio (magazine) printing presses, and in the third stage to all companies. The first stage affected 48 companies, where roughly 16,000 workers downed tools. A few hours after the start of the strike the employers announced an official lockout. This action, which lasted from 30 April to 3 May, ended up affecting some 69,000 workers in more than 700 printing works, or nearly half the country's 145,000 printing workers. The lockout was fully observed only by the major newspaper and magazine publishers with their own printing works, which were involved in the strike. Small and medium-sized companies, on the other hand, were by and large reluctant to take part in the lockout.

On 3 May the lockout was lifted, and the next day fresh talks were held, leading to a 5.9 per cent offer – which was, however, rejected by the Joint Working Party on Pay (Tarifkommission) on 5 May. The Printing Union decided to go ahead with the second stage of the strike. On 6 May some 68,000 workers came out on strike, and by the following day it was 69,000. In a press statement of 8 May, however, the union announced that from 10 May the scope of the strike would be slowly reduced out of consideration for the financial plight of small businesses and local newspapers. At the same time there was a fresh attempt to reach a settlement on 12 May, this time chaired by Friedhelm Farthmann, the Labour and Social Minister of North Rhine-Westphalia. The proposal worked out on this occasion provided for an average pay rise of 6 per cent spread over 10 months; the other two months would be covered by an across-the-board lump sum payment of DM 245. In the second ballot held on 18 May, 55.7 per cent of the union's members voted for acceptance of this offer.

A particular bone of contention was the refusal of workers on the "Frankfurter Neue Press" and the Hanover edition of "Bild" to type-set or print leaders arguing against the strike; they refused after their demand for the simultaneous insertion of an article presenting the opposing view was turned down. So both newspapers appeared with blank spaces on 4 May to draw attention to the "censorship" of content by the workers. While some people saw the action of the printers and compositors as an attack on the freedom of the press, others viewed the planned editorials as weapons in the dispute, the effect of which on public opinion at least ought to have been balanced by the publication of an article supporting the strikers.

Pay policy demonstrated more graphically than anything else that the unions had been forced on to the back foot by economic recession and mass unemployment. They continually called for wages to be raised to help increase purchasing power and thus get the economy moving, but such unions as IG Metall, IG Chemie and the ÖTV actually confined themselves to catching up with price rises. The safeguarding of living standards became the key phrase in the confrontations over pay in the 1970s. Yet it is obvious that this policy could never increase the purchasing power of the great majority; and the way in which some unions commended the pay deals they reached as moderate and responsible reveals contradictions in union reasoning on pay levels.

Moreover, the crisis of the 1970s and 80s focused attention on the problems that are built into trade union pay policy. They did not succeed in getting real wages incorporated into collective agreements, nor did they achieve full equality between men's and women's wages. Controversy still surrounded the introduction of a basic flat-rate payment as part of pay deals, to prevent wage differentials widenening still further as a result of rises being calculated solely in percentages.

On one issue, however, there was a breakthrough. In July 1988 a settlement came into force in the chemical industry which was hailed as the "agreement of the century", in which the difference between wages and salaries was abolished in favour of a graduated pay scale with 13 steps applying to all manual and white-collar workers. The other unions, including the Engineering, Post Office and Construction Unions, recognized that this pay agreement pointed the way ahead.

The inflation rates of the 1970s demonstrated how companies could pass on increased costs in the form of higher prices, at least in the short term. This allowed the employers to be relatively generous in wage negotiations, provided pay deals did not exceed the limits set by productivity and price increases. Thanks to this pay policy, until the early 1980s the trade unions were able to prevent a sharp fall in the wage and salary ratio, that is, the ratio of total earned income to national income as a whole.

But what did wage and income trends mean for the distribution of national income? Even during the 1970s it was found that gross income from business activities and wealth grew faster than income from paid employment. According to the government's annual economic reports, the former increased from 1975 to 1978 by 9–11 per cent per year – in 1976 by as much as 12–14 per cent; income from paid employment, on the other hand, rose by only 6.5–8.5 per cent annually over the same period – in 1978 by only 5.8 per cent.[34] And comparing trends in net wages and net profits, we find that total net wages tripled between 1965 and 1986, while net profits increased more than fourfold.

---

34 According to Otto Jacobi, Gewerkschaftliche Lohnpolitik unter dem Druck anti-keynesianischer Wirtschaftspolitik, in Bergmann, op. cit., pp. 326–362; these data p. 342

It is the logical consequence of this trend that net wages diminish as a proportion of national income in favour of net profits. Income from paid employment fell as a proportion of national income from 70–71 per cent in 1981–2 to around 65 per cent in 1987; gross entrepreneurial income and income from wealth, on the other hand, rose as a proportion of national income from 29.5 to 35 per cent. The wages and profits ratios were thus broadly the same in 1986 as they had been in the early 1960s. These figures proved, the unions stressed, that wage levels, at any rate, were not to blame for unemployment. They could not be, if the wages and salaries ratio was the same in the early 1960s, when there was full employment, as it was in the late 1980s, with mass unemployment in excess of two million.[35]

∗

Industrial disputes grew undeniably tougher during the 1970s. They were mainly centred on the engineering and printing industries. Two factors combined to bring conflict to these two industries. The first was the traditionally assertive policies of these unions; the second, and more important, was the attempted introduction of new technologies in these industries, leading to job losses.

Both the Printing Union, IG Druck und Papier, and the Engineering Union, IG Metall, had to wage punishing disputes in 1978. IG Druck und Papier was engaged in a dispute from 27 February to 19 March, involving 19,000 strikers and 53,000 workers locked out, over the introduction and use of computer-based word processing systems, with serious implications for skills and the number of jobs, which the union sought to mitigate as far as possible. In 1976 the union had already had to pay out DM 33 m in benefits, spent in roughly equal proportions on strikes and lockouts. In 1978 the cost of the dispute amounted to DM 15 m, 81.5 per cent of which went on lockouts and only 18.5 per cent on the strike. This exhausted the union's industrial funds, and in future it had to rely on the aid of the DGB and some individual unions.

The industrial dispute in the Baden-Württemberg engineering industry assumed even greater dimensions, being concerned not only with pay rises but also and most importantly with protection against regrading

---

35 Hartmut Görgens, Zur Entwicklung von Löhnen, Gewinnen und Kapitalrendite in der Bundesrepublik Deutschland, in Gewerkschaftliche Monatshefte 6, 1987, pp. 353–61; this information p. 354. Cf. Michael Kittner (ed.), Gewerkschaftsjahrbuch 1988 (Cologne, 1988), pp. 107 and 135

(on lower pay scales) for workers affected by the introduction of new technologies. This dispute, which lasted from 15 March to 7 April 1978, saw 80,000 engineering workers out on strike and 200,000 locked out. Once again, the employers made free use of the "cold" lockout. Daimler-Benz, for example, put 3,000 workers on short time from 20 March and another 14,000 the next day; just as swiftly the number dropped to zero once the strike was over. At the peak of the conflict – on 5 April – 77,000 workers were affected by cuts or halts in production, so that owing to the use of the "cold" lockout more than 500,000 working days were lost. Five large companies alone – Daimler-Benz, Bosch, Ford, Audi-NSU and BMW – accounted for roughly 80 per cent of the short time. This dispute cost IG Metall DM 130 m; the next one was to swallow another DM 120 m.

Since the mid-1970s all industrial disputes had been overshadowed by the high rate of unemployment, which lay behind the trade unions' refusal to countenance precipitate rationalization measures and their demands for safeguards for jobs. The call for a reduction in working hours, which also gave rise to clashes from the late 1970s on, was very much in the same vein.

*

While a shorter working week and longer holidays were initially promoted by the trade unions as steps towards the "humanization of working life" and a better "quality of life", with the growth in unemployment their arguments came to focus more on the beneficial effects on employment.

After successes in getting longer annual holidays and rest break arrangements regulated by collective agreement and a flexible retirement age laid down by law (1972), public interest once again focused on the working week. Again it was IG Metall that paved the way over the reduction of working hours. At its 1977 Düsseldorf congress, the first calls were heard for the "introduction of the 35-hour week". The increase in unemployment gave extra impact to the union argument; but the poor economic growth since the end of the 1970s contributed to a hardening of the employers' position – after all, there was no scope for wealth distribution on the scale of the 1950s. The 1978 list of "non-negotiable topics" and the 1978-9 dispute in the iron and steel industry of North Rhine-Westphalia were a clear indication of the employers' dismissive attitude towards any reduction in the working week to less than 40 hours.

The dispute of 1978-9 was sparked off when the Large Working Party on Pay (*Grosse Tarifkommission*) for the iron and steel industry of North Rhine-Westphalia gave notice that it was terminating the covering wage agreement as from 30 June 1978. Its main demand was a cut in the sche-

DGB solidarity demonstration on 12 December 1978 during the 1978-9 dispute in the iron and steel industry in North Rhine-Westphalia over the introduction of the 35-hour week

duled working week, with no cut in pay, leading to the 35-hour week. The unions justified the demand by citing the particularly heavy nature of work in the industry (the humanitarian aspect) and also the employment benefits (the safeguarding of jobs). In negotiations on 22 August, 13 September and 16 October 1978, the employers rejected any reduction in working hours – for financial reasons, and also because they claimed it would pose a threat to jobs rather than safeguard them.

After terminating the agreements on wages, salaries and training allowances, the Large Working Party agreed the following demands on 19 October: a 5 per cent rise in scheduled wages and salaries, a DM 40 rise in training allowances in the first and second years of training and DM 30 in the third and fourth years. After the talks of 7 November had failed to bring the two sides any closer together, the employers declared a deadlock over working hours, whereupon the unions responded by declaring the talks on wage levels deadlocked. The Engineering Union set the strike ballot for 18-21 November. After a huge rally on 17 November, at which some 120,000 workers backed the call for the introduction of the 35-hour week, 86.9 per cent of members voted in the ballot for a strike. The strike was scheduled to begin on 28 November, with 40,000 engineering workers at Thyssen, Mannesmann, Hoesch, Krupp and other companies being called out. On 27 November the employers in the iron and steel industry had already decided to respond to the strike with a lockout of the strikers and a further 30,000 workers starting on 1 December. On 30 November IG Metall held a rally in the Ruhrland Hall, Bochum, to protest against the employers' use of the lockout. Approximately 145,000 people took part in other similar protests – accompanied by sympathy strikes – on 8 and 12 December. Meanwhile, lockouts at nine companies targeted for strike action had affected 40,000 strikers, and some 30,000 workers were locked out at another eight companies, making 70,000 in all. At this, IG Metall announced on 22 December that it intended to call out another three plants with roughly 20,000 employees from the beginning of 1979.

With the threat of escalation in the background, a compromise was reached on 6 January 1979 after tough negotiations. Including the free shifts agreed for those on night shift and older workers, the outcome was, for two-thirds to three-quarters of workers employed in the iron and steel industry, an average working week of 38.5 hours. This (and the longer annual holidays) was a long way removed from IG Metall's goal of a 35-hour week. This is also reflected in the rather high level of dissatisfaction with the outcome of the negotiations among the workers concerned: in the second ballot of 8-10 January 1979, the result was approved by 54.4 per cent, but turned down by 45 per cent.

It is hardly surprising that the trade unions had been pressing since 1971 for restrictions on the employers' use of the lockout, in view of the frequency with which they had exercised this weapon in the 1970s. In 1955 and 1971 the Federal Labour Court had recognized the lockout as a means of ensuring "parity" between the unions and employers, ruling that a lockout did not cancel the employment contract but simply suspended it. The trade unions now launched a campaign of mass petitions and demonstrations aimed at getting lockouts banned. This was to gain support for the struggle against the lockout and to politicize the confrontation. But the judgment announced by the Federal Labour Court in June 1980 upheld the right to stage a lockout, though stressing the fact that it merely suspended the contract of employment and laid down a number of restrictions. The lockout was not to be employed against trade union members only; it must be confined to one area of collective bargaining; it must only be employed in response to a strike, and must be commensurate with it. The judgment's practical significance was soon to become apparent.

In time for the next round of pay talks in the engineering and printing industries, the employers launched their campaign for greater flexibility in working hours, which was designed to forestall the union demand for a general reduction.[36] In fact, the call for a 35-hour week in 1983-4 was not particularly popular, either in the media or with working people. The government also rejected the demand, the Chancellor denigrating it at the Young Union's Germany Day on 12-13 November 1983 as "absurd, stupid and foolish". Moreover, the DGB unions were not all in agreement over the correct strategy for achieving a cut in working hours: should it be counted over a lifetime – or over a week? None the less, IG Metall managed to achieve a change of mood in many working people through a comprehensive publicity and propaganda drive, in keeping with the idea of the "new mobility".* They were aided by the employers' stubborn refusal to contemplate any sort of compromise agreement; indeed, in 70 meetings spread over three months of negotiations they had not proved the slightest bit accommodating. And the talks in the printing industry also

---

36 Institut der Deutschen Wirtschaft in Zusammenarbeit mit der Bundesvereinigung der Deutschen Arbeitgeberverbände (ed.), Auf dem Prüfstand: Die Verkürzung der Arbeitszeit (Cologne, 1983); Bundesvereinigung der Deutschen Arbeitgeberverbände (ed.), Flexibilisierung der Arbeitszeit. Neue Tarifregelungen als Chance (Cologne, 1984); Bundesvereinigung der Deutschen Arbeitgeberverbände (ed.), Mehr Beschäftigung durch flexible Teilzeitarbeit (Cologne, 1984)

* Translator's note: the use of short, selective strikes and other forms of industrial action.

stalled over the employers' insistence on linkage between a new wage structure and formal recognition of the 40-hour week.

The printing and engineering unions were struggling more or less simultaneously for a reduction in the working week. The printers' strike, which lasted from 12 April to 6 July 1984, was based around selective strikes of limited duration, in which a total of 46,000 workers in 563 companies took part for at least one day. The negotiations conducted concurrently with the strike finally went to arbitration. But the arbitration offer was turned down by the employers – probably because no end was in sight to the dispute in the engineering industry.

IG Metall conducted its dispute in two areas at once – Hesse and North Württemberg-North Baden. Strikes were initially aimed selectively at suppliers to the car industry, but then regional strike centres were set up. After warning strikes on 11 March, 33,000 manual and white-collar workers came out in the administrative districts of Kassel, Darmstadt, Frankfurt and Hanau on 21 March 1984. In North Württemberg-North Baden 11,500 employees at the Daimler-Benz works in Sindelfingen were brought into the strike on 16 May, two days after it started. The employers contributed to the spread of the dispute by making use of the lockout. Hundreds of thousands of workers outside the areas to which the dispute applied were affected by "cold" lockouts. On 18 May the Federal Institute for Labour issued the "Franke Decree", refusing any financial assistance to those affected by "cold" lockouts. After several Social Courts had condemned this decision as unlawful, the Federal Institute paid out shorttime benefit "with reservations". On 28 May IG Metall arranged a big rally, "For labour and the law – against lockouts and breaches of the law", in Bonn. Meanwhile the industrial dispute continued, at the same time as arbitration talks for the engineering industry of North Württemberg-North Baden, which began on 20 June. Only when the Federal Government called for moderation, did the employers' association, Gesamtmetall, accept Georg Leber's arbitration proposal, which provided for a reduction of the working week by 1.5 hours. From 3 July work was resumed in the North Württemberg-North Baden engineering industry and on 5-6 July work in Hesse and in the printing industry. Under the impact of the dispute, the 38-hour week was also introduced in the steel industry in October 1984.

The next round in the fight for the 35-hour week was fought in 1987. Though the employers had retracted their blank "no" since the 1984 dispute, the trade unions, with IG Metall again at the forefront, were faced with the amended Paragraph 116 of the Law to Promote Employment, which raised the financial risk of a strike for the unions overall. The scandal over "Neue Heimat" had caused the unions a considerable loss of credibility. IG Metall therefore sought from the outset to tie the dispute over the reduction of working hours to a mass movement against mass unemployment, the rundown of the social welfare system and curbs on wage earners' rights.

After initial warning strikes in the engineering industry in early to mid-March 1987, representatives of IG Metall and Gesamtmetall met for top-level talks in Bad Homburg on 22-3 April 1987. The most important results were: wages and salaries to be raised by 4 per cent from 1 April 1987; the working week to be cut to 37.5 hours and pay to go up by 2 per cent from 1 April 1988; the working week to be cut to 37 hours and pay to increase by 2.5 per cent from 1 April 1989. The key points of the engineering agreement were taken over by the printing industry in an arbitration deal on 6 May 1987.

Lastly, the public service union ÖTV scored another success in pushing through a cut in the working week in the 1988 pay round, which was marked by the confrontational strategy of the public employers, headed by the Federal Minister for the Interior, Friedrich Zimmermann (CSU), and the "ideas" of the SPD vice-chairman and Prime Minister of Saarland, Oskar Lafontaine, on a reduction in working hours *without* full compensation for wage earners. The ÖTV and the DGB federal executive rejected this firmly as an attack on autonomy in negotiating wage claims. Against the opposition of large sections of public opinion, the ÖTV managed to force the employers to accept the arbitration proposal put forward by Hermann Höcherl (CSU), which laid down a very cautious transition to the 35-hour week in two stages: by 1990 the 38.5-hour week would be arrived at in two stages. At the same time wage increases were fixed: 2.4 per cent from 1 March 1988; 1.4 per cent from 1 January 1989 and 1.7 per cent from 1 January 1990. This marked the breakthrough of the 35-hour week in another industry.

The Textile and Clothing Union trod the same path in June 1988, securing reductions in the working week of one hour from 1 May 1989 and a further half-hour from 1 May 1990 in the Baden-Württemberg textile industry. IG Chemie also concluded a new collective agreement in July 1988 providing for a one-hour cut in the working week from summer 1989; employees over 58 years of age would then only have to work 35 (instead of 36) hours; from 1990, the 35-hour week was extended to 57-year-olds. This made the construction industry the only major industry that had failed to agree on a working week less than 40 hours by mid-1988.

*

To sum up, since the mid-1970s the trade unions had been confronted by an increasingly tough employers' policy. Indications of this change were the appeal to the Federal Constitutional Court against the Co-determination Law of 1976 (which the unions anyway considered inadequate), the 1978 list of proscribed topics and, above all, the free use of lockouts, which had increased the cost of industrial action to the unions immeasurably.

The unions responded to this hardening of employer attitudes with a readiness to engage in industrial action hitherto not experienced in times of recession and mass unemployment, principally in order to secure acceptance of the demand for cuts in working hours. Strikes peaked in 1978, 1981, 1984 and 1986 (Table 2d); they took the form of a "new mobility", that is, they were selective and of short duration, so as to make it more difficult for the employers to respond by, for example, moving production or staging lockouts. The lockouts of 1978–9 and 1984 had a major impact on the statistics for industrial action, almost doubling the number of working days lost owing to strikes in 1978–9 and more than doubling them in 1984.[37]

With this aggressive bargaining policy the trade unions achieved considerable success in stabilizing wage levels and especially in cutting working hours – without, however, making any significant inroads on mass unemployment. The protection of the living standards and jobs of those in work may not have been the primary objective of the trade unions – but that was, in fact, their main achievement in the field of collective bargaining. It is not surprising that a policy of this kind did not meet with the approval of the unemployed.

4. *A phase of reorganization: problem areas in trade union policy*

Industrial society has entered a phase of accelerating change. New technologies, particularly microelectronics, are changing working life and living conditions in general. The destruction of the natural environment has reached such proportions that a radical rethink and change of direction are urgently required. What we need are ideas for the social and ecological conversion of industrial society – into the post-industrial society.

---

37 Ingrid Kurz-Scher, Tarifpolitik und Arbeitskämpfe, in Michael Kittner (ed.), Gewerkschaftsjahrbuch 1987. Daten, Fakten, Analysen (Cologne, 1987), pp. 69–120; this information p. 120

It is not easy in the present circumstances to confront this challenge. With the economy in the doldrums, forces capable of engendering a resurgence have been given high priority, since the problems of restructuring and redistribution are more easily dealt with if the GNP is rising. Mass unemployment also prevents a change of direction in industrial policy, owing to the false contradiction between environmental protection and job security.

It is also a challenge to the trade unions, which have been concerned with the problems of the future of industrialized society ever since the 1970s. But like industrial society itself, the trade unions are not well equipped in times of recession to meet this challenge. Organizational problems, loss of political credibility and internal differences within and between the unions all make it difficult for them to formulate the overdue realignment of their policies.

One fundamental problem, as far as trade union policy-making is concerned, is the loss of their earlier uncritical belief in progress, which took far too optimistic a view of future technological and economic developments, seeing them as contributing to the upward trend in social welfare. The visible and tangible "limits of growth" and the less pleasant concomitants of technological change, fostered the spread of an apocalyptic mood from the mid-1970s on. And since in times of crisis the trade unions – as Ernst Breit admitted – "tend to defend existing conditions of work, [they] now arouse in superficial observers the suspicion that they have developed into a conservative force".[38] In fact, the trade unions made heavy weather of reaching a definitive position on the advance of new technologies, from the computer and microelectronics to biotechnology and genetic engineering. Traditionally, the unions have been favourably inclined towards technical progress; but in recent years – unlike earlier periods of rapid rationalization – they have turned their attention more to the undesirable side-effects and consequences: the increased intensification of labour, the pressure to adjust flexible working hours to meet the requirements of production and, most importantly, the loss of jobs – all factors which the unions would like to see included in the discussion. As a result, they left themselves open to the charge of being enemies of progress – which makes it more difficult for them to push through rules and arrangements to temper the social consequences of new production technology – as is no doubt the intention.

With their integration into the status quo the unions appear to many younger people, in particular, to have taken leave of their own history.

---

38 Ernst Breit (1985), op. cit.

The DGB has tried to compensate for this oft-criticized lack of historical awareness by arranging several historical conferences[39], thus recalling the trade union movement's tradition as a liberation and human rights movement.

The debate about the "programme of principle" of 1981 also showed an effort to make up for the loss of history, and hence a real utopia. Or was the intention to seek in history the self-assurance that the future did not (any longer) hold in store? At any rate, it seemed necessary to redefine the movement's own ties with tradition. For one thing, the unions had to try and take the steam out of the 1979–80 attacks by Christian Social politicians on the DGN unions' "party political bias"; and for another – partly in view of the "History of the German Trade Union Movement", a book first published in 1977[40] – they had to decide what part the Communists had played in the development of the trade unions. The first problem was solved by a willingness to make concessions. The second was solved by avoidance, on the lines proposed by Heinz Oskar Vetter at the start of the programme debate: members of the German Communist Party would be accepted as trade union members, provided they did not attempt to form a cadre or indulge in cadre politics.[41] Against this background it is understandable that the preamble of the "programme of principle" professed more clearly than before allegiance to the unions' libertarian-socialist and Christian-social tradition. With its historical perspective and analysis of the present position, the programme, which was adopted im March 1981 at the Fourth Extraordinary Congress in Düsseldorf, made an important contribution to the review of union policy in circumstances of recession and mass unemployment, the environmental crisis and the arms race.[42] It also addressed a number of matters directly for the first time, such as the policy of full employment, the position of the Basic Law in and with regard to the "social state", the implementation of new technologies, and environmental protection. At the same time, traditional demands – the

39 Heinz Oskar Vetter (ed.), Aus der Geschichte lernen Zukunft gestalten. Dreissig Jahre DGB. Protokoll der wissenschaftlichen Konferenz zur Geschichte der Gewerkschaften vom 12. und 13. Oktober 1979 in München (Cologne, 1980); Ernst Breit (ed.), Aufstieg des Nationalsozialismus. Untergang der Republik. Zerschlagung der Gewerkschaften. Dokumentation der historisch-politischen Konferenz des DGB im Mai 1983 in Dortmund (Cologne, 1984)

40 Frank Deppe, Georg Fülberth and Jürgen Harrer (eds.), Geschichte der deutschen Gewerkschaftsbewegung (Cologne, 1977)

41 Heinz Oskar Vetter, Zum Beginn der Diskussion um ein neues Grundsatzprogramm, in Gewerkschaftliche Monatshefte 1, 1980, pp. 1-12

42 DGB-Bundesvorstand (ed.), Grundsatzprogramm des Deutschen Gewerkschaftsbundes (Düsseldorf, 1981)

right to work, the humanization of working life, the fair distribution of income and wealth, checks on economic power, education policy – retained their places as key issues of trade union policy.

Because of the attempts by the employers and their political allies at a "roll-back" policy described above, the 1981 "programme of principle" was an attempt to define precisely and realistically the goal of the "social state" as set out in the Basic Law and the function of the trade unions in the social state based on private capitalism. The trade unions could not and should not allow themselves to be reduced to one of the alternatives, a regulatory factor or a counterbalance. Instead – as the preamble stated – they had a twin thrust: both a protective and a creative function.

The "programme of principle" was the trade unions' attempt to set out their views on the urgent problems of current concern. This effort also left its mark on the DGB action programme, which Ernst Breit presented to the press on 7 September 1988.[43] Combating unemployment with a five-year investment programme costing DM 100 bn on the one hand, activating environmental policy on the other – these were the two vital areas of the programme, which also included the most important demands contained in the "programme of principle" in updated form.

Neither of these programmes marks the end of the trade unions' policy debate, of course – especially as, to some of the issues addressed in the programmes, there are no clear answers in sight that are acceptable to all the individual unions. This is particularly true of environmental protection: the unions stressed the need for it early on, but it has proved difficult for them to set about it in a realistic way. As organizations representing the interests of employees in all industries – including the chemical and power industries – it was not easy for them to square environmental points of view with the economic and social interests of the employees concerned. The plan entitled "Environmental Protection and Qualitative Growth" adopted by the DGB federal executive in March 1985 attempted to combine economic and ecological objectives, the realistic nature of which still had to be put to the test in actual cases of conflicting interests. The way the environmental programme is worded, however, is a clear indication of the ponderousness of DGB policy during the review phase. The goal of environmental protection was embedded in thoroughly traditional ways of thought – from creating employment through (qualitative) growth to bipartite co-determination as one way of ensuring that "false

43 DGB-Bundesvorstand (ed.), Aktionsprogramm des Deutschen Gewerkschafts-bundes (Düsseldorf, October 1988)

confrontations between employment and environmental problems do not arise in the first place".[44]

One acid test of the seriousness of the unions' desire for a change of course is undoubtedly their attitude to the continued use of nuclear power. The unions are in danger of making themselves political pariahs by employing verbal compromises to dodge the issue. It will soon be apparent whether, or to what extent, this danger was avoided by the decisions taken at the DGB's 1986 congress in Hamburg and the 1987 DAG congress in Hanover to end reliance on nuclear power.

It is hard to see any solutions to the dilemma of choosing between the possible risk to jobs and the rundown of the arms industry. The question of alternatives to a policy of economic growth through increasing arms spending and arms exports requires a concrete answer.

Meanwhile, the challenge of the 1990s is to resolve the partition of Germany and of Europe. It is now one of the major tasks of the DGB unions – headed since May 1990 by Heinz-Werner Meyer, Ursula Engelen-Kefer and Ulf Fink – to support the formation of independent trade unions, to work to ensure the welfare of working people and to assist in the development of pluralist democracies in the countries of central and eastern Europe.

The issue of human rights must also remain a central concern of trade union policy. It is not simply a matter of safeguarding and extending democratic and social rights in the Federal Republic, and championing the rights of foreign workers and asylum seekers; it is also necessary, in this context, to show a commitment to the struggle for a decent life in other countries of the world, from Chile to South Africa.

One area that has been little explored to date is international trade union co-operation and the possibilities it offers of getting to grips with worldwide economic and employment problems and the political dilution of national decision-making in favour of supraregional and international bodies, and also of counteracting the power of the multinationals. In the International Confederation of Free Trade Unions and the European Trade Union Confederation, founded in 1973, we have two international organizations; but their political effectiveness is very limited. In view of the steady progress of European integration – that is, the creation of the common internal market in 1992 – and the political changes in central and eastern Europe, it is essential to step up European trade union co-

---

44 DGB-Bundesvorstand (ed.), Umweltschutz und qualitatives Wachstum. Bekämpfung der Arbeitslosigkeit und Beschleunigung des qualitativen Wachstums durch mehr Umweltschutz (Düsseldorf, March 1985)

Heinz-Werner Meyer, chairman of the DGB since May 1990

operation. Many German trade unionists view the attempt to bring the European sister unions together "under one roof" as a Sisyphean task as it is.[45] It should be added, however, that since the 1970s the German trade unions have been more inclined to acknowledge that the question of European unity is no longer just one problem of international politics among others but a task that affects virtually all areas of union activity.

The commitment of trade union policy to the European arena and the unions' concentration on the struggle against the rundown of the welfare system and unemployment must not, however, result in other issues being pushed aside – issues such as the involvement of the unions in East-West and North-South relations, the international problems of economic power, violations of human rights, the threat to peace and the worldwide destruction of the environment. Only time will tell if this plethora of national and international tasks proves too much for the trade unions. But a look back at their own history may encourage the unions to face the problems of the modern world with self-assurance.

---

45 Hermann Rappe, according to the General-Anzeiger (Bonn), 27-28 August 1988

Conclusion: an appraisal of the achievements and prospects of trade union policy

In conclusion we cannot offer the reader a summary of trade union history, with all its successes and setbacks, its crises, crushing defeats and lasting accomplishments. Instead – taking the questions posed in the introduction as our starting point – we shall attempt an appraisal of more than a hundred years of trade union policy in Germany and address the issue of the "end of the trade unions" or the "end of the labour movement" so often predicted in recent years.

*

Trade unions are not an end in themselves. Therefore the following appraisal cannot and should not centre on their organizational achievements or policy statements. The question to ask is whether they have helped improve the economic and social conditions of working people and contributed to political equality.

An assessment of trade union policy is, of course, also an appraisal of social history ever since industrialization gathered momentum. Without a doubt, the trade unions have been a vital driving force behind the struggle of working people against exploitation and political oppression, though they have not been alone in this. Although it is not possible to calculate exactly what share the trade unions have had in the social development of the past 100–120 years in relation to the labour movement as a whole and the bourgeois social reformers, one may safely say that for much of its course German social history would have been bumpier without the trade unions.

Let us first consider the areas that comprise the core of trade union policy. Since the late nineteenth century, workers' incomes have increased many times over – sometimes slowly, sometimes faster – not merely their face value but in real terms (Table 3d). One of the major successes attributable to the unions is the reduction in working hours. Since the mid-nineteenth century the working week in industry has been virtually halved (Tables 4a,b). This, together with longer holidays and better pay, has contributed to an undeniable rise in living standards for broad sections of the population.

The improved "quality of life" of working people also stems from the steady extension of financial safeguards against the social consequences of all the hazards that in earlier times – until the end of the nineteenth century, and again in the Depression of the 1930s – led to poverty and misery. Insurance against sickness and disablement are now as natural a part of welfare provision as unemployment benefit and old age pensions.

Conditions of life which are nowadays often taken for granted are in fact social rights that were fought for and won with much effort by the trade unions: freedom of association, the right to strike, collective agreements, industrial health and safety standards, industrial law, universal suffrage, co-determination and worker participation at workplace and company level, and representation on public bodies responsible for everything from social insurance to radio.

As a glance at their membership figures shows, the trade unions proved to be the largest organized force working not only for social reform but also for democracy. Alongside other associations and parties they fought and suffered – in part against substantial opposition – to tame the system of private capitalism and force it in the direction of the "social state", to secure and implement basic liberal rights, and to build up and extend parliamentary democracy. With their ideal of solidarity transcending the barriers of trade, class and geography, with structures providing for the internal development and expression of an informed opinion and the idea of the collective defence of interests within the framework of a pluralist society, the trade unions were (and are) the "schools" and at the same time guarantors of democracy. The trade unions have never sought to claim absolute power for themselves; though often accused of wanting a "trade union state", in fact this has never been their goal at any time.

The trade unions have always been (and this also applies to the majority of Christian unions during the Weimar Republic) the pioneers and champions of the free, democratic social state based on the rule of law, the foundations of which they helped to lay in 1918–19. Again, after the Federal Republic came into being, they gave vigorous assistance in building it up and monitoring its development with a critical eye – as the clash over emergency legislation demonstrated. In doing so, they proved immune to the temptations of totalitarianism, whose advocates, in turn, were (and are) unwilling to tolerate an independent trade union movement.

But the successes should not be allowed to eclipse the darker side of the trade union balance sheet. Let us begin with pay policy. The difference between men's and women's wages (Table 3e), the imbalance between the income of the self-employed and wage earners and the extremely inequitable distribution of the wealth produced by the economy indicate the limits of trade union objectives and their ability to achieve them. Even cuts in working hours have their drawbacks: made possible by increases in productivity, they went hand in hand with the intensification of labour and an increase in shift and night work.

Even the most impressive provisions of social policy have their weak spots. Even today many who are sick, the long-term unemployed and the old, especially women, sink below the poverty line. The "two-thirds" society* is a bitter reality. The constant clashes over the cost of social insurance, leading to benefit cuts or freezes in times of recession, when they are most needed, clearly demonstrate that even the advances made in social policy hitherto are still liable to suffer attacks and setbacks. This also applies, incidentally, to the protection afforded by industrial law and co-determination and worker participation arrangements. Practically all legal provisions – from workplace co-determination to influence over corporate investment and production – have loopholes and weak spots, making them vulnerable to efforts to demolish positions which have already been taken. The confrontations over the right to strike and the union call for a lockout ban also confirm the impression that the problems surrounding the legal position of employees and their trade unions have by no means all been – permanently – resolved. It has not yet proved possible to detach social policy and industrial law from their dependence on economic development and economic and financial decisions, in which the unions have at best a conditional say and at worst little or no say, as demonstrated by the fate of their plans for securing and maintaining full employment.

Ultimately, any assessment of trade union policy cannot overlook the fact that the unions did not succeed in preventing the disasters of German history. The general strike debate together with the "policy of August 1914" and the helpless course between compliance and protest of spring 1933 show the trade unions' fatal tendency to underrate the ruthlessness and radicalism of their opponents and the enemies of a socially oriented, democratic society.

These defeats illustrate in heightened form the trade unions' painful experience that wage rises and advances in social policy can be clawed back. Thus many employers regularly try to take back the allegedly extravagant "benefits" of the social state in times of economic crisis by adopting a 'roll-back' strategy – as if working people had not already paid for them through wage restraint, contributions and taxes.

*

* Translator's note: The sort of society in which "two-thirds" fare quite well, while the other third fare badly.

During slumps the structural weakness of the trade unions becomes evident: unemployment, the threat of job losses and a drop in incomes on the one hand, and membership losses and the "prevailing opinion" on the other sap the determination and stamina of the workers and their unions. To put it another way, these are the conditions in which trade union policy has to operate successfully. Some of the principal prerequisites of success are: a sound economy, giving scope for wage awards and for conducting industrial action; clear aims, related to the workers' needs and yet at the same time going beyond the narrow bounds of immediate demands and envisaging structural changes, too; sufficient organizational strength and a membership willing to be mobilized in the area of the dispute, rendering the militancy of the union a potential threat to be reckoned with; party political backing and broad popular support – for example, from statements in the media.

While these prerequisites of success depict an ideal situation, so to speak, this list details the initial position that is most desirable from the unions' point of view in the event of a dispute. Because economic development is only rarely or indirectly subject to trade union influence – in times of crisis the unions' influence on politics and public opinion is inclined to be rather small – the two other features of successful trade union policy are all the more important. It is in this area that internal union plans propose to strengthen the trade unions' credibility, efficiency and political competence, all aspects which suffered heavily during the crisis of the 1970s and 80s.

There are a number of organizational requirements – such as the expansion of the trade union press, the consolidation of internal democracy and revitalization of cultural activities – which, if achieved, might boost the cohesion and appeal of the unions. But for one thing their financial predicament evidently forces them to take decisions that have quite the opposite effect – for instance, their attitude to the weekly newspaper, "Welt der Arbeit" (World of Work) and the plans for structural reform of the DGB. For another, such measures would probably not be an adequate response to the present upheaval.

*

However impressive the record of trade union policy may appear when looking back over the past 100 years of German social history (despite all its weak spots and less attractive aspects), the current outlook is anything but sunny. With the development of new production, office and communications systems, changes are taking place in working life and the consciousness of working people, the implications of which can scarcely be guessed at as far as the formulation and defence of workers' interests are concerned. Traditional collective interpretations of conflicts collide with the new individualism of wage earners at work and at leisure. The trade unions are being caught up by a development which they themselves have helped to shape. Today's fiercely asserted demands for an individual life style are, in fact, largely a result of precisely the generally high quality of life and social security that the unions have helped to create.

A look at history teaches us, however, that the current crisis in the labour market, the anti-union crisis plans and the unions' loss of influence are not "new". What is "new" is the fact that blind economic growth, whose chief proponent is industry and on which trade union successes of the past were largely based, can and must no longer be desirable in view of the furious pace at which the environment is being devastated. And the other "new" factor is the contraction of the trade unions' social base (that is, male industrial workers) as post-industrial society emerges: in 1987, white-collar workers outnumbered manual workers for the first time (Table 6b). In important industries – coal, steel, ship building – the trade unions have slipped into the role of defending structures that have out-lived their usefulness, while employees in other, up-and-coming industr-ies and services remain aloof or reject them. The phrase "the end of the trade unions" is often heard.

None the less, the trade unions have every reason to address this pro-blem in a purposeful way. There are three main aspects to it.

Firstly, they have shown in the past that they are perfectly capable of fusing together heterogeneous groups of workers. The most impressive example of this was the way in which they overcame the limitation to skilled workers; admittedly, they were not so successful in attracting female and white-collar workers, or, for that matter, in integrating foreign workers from the early 1960s on. The trade unions always made heavy weather of the social heterogeneity of wage earners whenever it was a matter of forming an association that extended beyond the industrial labour force. But despite any amount of justified scepticism, the growing numbers of white-collar and female workers as a proportion of the mem-bership make it impossible simply to deny that the trade unions have any chance of organizing broad-based solidarity among wage earners. In any case, solidarity has never arisen naturally, as it were, even in the age of a relatively intact working class milieu; solidarity always had to be worked for and asserted and tempered in the face of opposition.

Secondly, throughout their history trade unions have proved to be tho-roughly adaptable. They have adjusted to changes in overall circumstances and the conditions in which they have waged their struggle, without losing sight of their core objectives. The same goes for their organizational form. Local trade associations gave rise to national organizations, which later evolved into the industrial unions of today. The fact that the personal proximity of the local union leadership and members long ago gave way to the remoteness of the union "machinery" from the "grassroots", institutionalized by the principle of delegation, may be a consequence of large-scale organization; none the less, it needs correcting. But the process of change has, crucially, embraced the position and function of the trade unions, too. Today they enjoy widespread recognition in law, by employers and by public opinion, though this recognition extends primarily to the function which they have gradually assumed as a regulatory factor under the existing economic and social order. As the capitalist economic and social system has proved its viability and ability to develop into a "social state", the trade unions have acquired a lot of new duties and at the same time slotted into this system.

And yet the unions' dual role as a regulatory factor and a counterbalancing force, the protective and creative functions that pervade the 1981 "programme of principle", are more than merely declamatory in character. Although the unions see themselves as "service" organizations under existing conditions, they are still pressing for structural changes in line with the "social state" precept of the Basic Law. The fact that this has frequently given rise to conflict, and still does, is indicative of the trade unions' position as a counter-force, which it defends more militantly at certain times than at others. Despite the shift in their duties and function in the direction of "public" institutions, the trade unions' tradition as militant organizations lives on in a readiness to take autonomous action. This militant reformism must be preserved.

Thirdly and lastly, the conflicts that gave rise to the trade unions in the first place persist. For the end – or rather, the relative decline in importance – of industrial work will not mean the end of paid employment. It is important and right to define the concept and the importance of work in modern society; it is quite unrealistic, on the other hand, to adumbrate a social system able to manage without paid employment in the foreseeable future. But if paid employment continues, there remain certain key problem areas that belong to the trade unions' "traditional" set of duties.

It would be insufficient if the trade unions were to respond to the trend towards a post-industrial society and the shift in values associated with it simply by "improving" their solution, dismissing as "false consciousness" the wish for individualization shared by, say, women, young people, white-collar workers and the technical intelligentsia, as they did in their earlier agitation among white-collar workers. The trade unions will have to affirm the development of new, individual needs and possibilities of freedom, which ought to come all the more easily to them as they helped create the social preconditions for this trend.

The desire for individualization is undoubtedly reinforced by the breakdown of those systems that, by labelling themselves "socialist", have tainted every demand for fundamental social reforms with notions such as lack of political liberty and a low standard of living. The knee-jerk identification of "actual existing socialism" with the trade union idea of the "social state", propagated through the liberal-conservative slogan of "freedom, not socialism", serves to discredit not only Social Democracy but also the unions, which must face this political and programmatic challenge.

So the trade unions need to reorientate themselves on new lines. For the industrial society in transition it is not enough to hark back to the 'bad old days' in order to effect the integration of broad strata of wage earners required to exert political influence. The employees of today have less cause than ever to identify with the fate of the exploited workers of the last century. From studying the early years of industrial capitalism they might learn how it feels for wage earners to be exposed to the employers' 'deregulation' and 'relaxation' strategies without the support of trade unions – though this can never replace first-hand experience of conflict, individual powerlessness and trade union solidarity. The trade unions thus need an image of the wage earner in which – in contrast to the past – it is not only the skilled worker's individual sense of his own worth that counts but that of all wage earners, including white-collar workers. Only then will the trade unions be appropriate partners with whom to discuss the solution of workplace disputes and welfare problems. Their policies must be founded on the perception that there is no such thing as *the* workers or *the* wage earners – nor has there ever been.

Recognizing the highly disparate life-styles and interests of working people does not mean that the trade unions must abandon a comprehensive vision of the society they want. But they must be more specific than before about their goal of a solidarity-based society, centred not on technology or economics but on human beings, and bring it into line with the multifarious needs and wishes of wage earners. There are signs of this: for instance, when IG Metall proposes the conclusion of collective agreements on working hours that include several alternatives, from which the works council and the employer are free to select jointly the best arrangement for the company and workforce concerned. Or when consideration is given to union ideas on organizing work to take account of opportunities of personal self-fulfilment through leisure as well as work. Or in attempts to break down the trade unions' remoteness from the company and the workplace, which is rooted in the German trade union tradition.

As so often in their long history, the trade unions must modify their theory and practice in step with the world which their policies have helped to change. Points of reference for this process of change are provided by the problem areas of trade union policy explored in more detail in the account given above of the current trade union programme debate. Dealing with these problem areas will also afford opportunities for working together with the new social movements. The trade unions certainly have no call to give up their basic principles in the process. Social justice, human solidarity, libertarian democracy and international co-operation are cornerstones of trade union policy which, given worldwide poverty, exploitation, political manipulation and oppression, the destruction of the environment and the danger of war, have lost none of their topicality. The trade unions face radical changes – probably more far-reaching than ever before in their history. But they have not come to the end of the line; new tasks lie ahead.

Appendix

I. Tables*

1. Membership of the national trade union federations

*a) The Free, Christian and Hirsch-Duncker trade unions,
   1868–1932*

Year	Free Trade Unions	Christian Trade Unions	Hirsch-Duncker Trade Associations
1868	(. . .)		(Foundation)
1869	47.192		30.000
1870	(. . .)		?
1871	(. . .)		6.000
1872	19.695		18.803
1873	(. . .)		18.883
1874	(. . .)		22.000
1875	(. . .)		19.900
1876	(. . .)		(. . .)
1877	52.511		(. . .)
1878	56.275		16.525
1879	(. . .)		14.912
1880	(. . .)		21.000
1881	(. . .)		19.893
1882	(. . .)		24.558
1883	(. . .)		29.330
1884	(. . .)		47.681
1885	85.687		51.000
1886	(. . .)		52.162
1887	85.106		53.691
1888	111.245		56.655
1889	174.608		62.688

* Note: For technical reasons numbers are printed with full stops, as in German, instead of commas; similarily, commas are employed instead of decimal stops.

Year	Free Trade Unions	Christian Trade Unions	Hirsch-Duncker Trade Associations
1890	294.551		62.643
1891	291.691		65.588
1892	215.511		45.154
1893	218.972		61.154
1894	245.723	(Foundation)	67.078
1895	255.521	5.500	66.759
1896	329.230	8.055	71.767
1897	412.359	21.000	79.553
1898	493.742	34.270	82.755
1899	580.373	56.391	86.777
1900	680.427	76.744	91.661
1901	677.510	84.497	95.057
1902	733.206	84.667	102.561
1903	941.529	91.440	110.215
1904	1.116.723	107.556	111.889
1905	1.429.303	188.106	116.143
1906	1.799.293	247.116	118.508
1907	1.873.146	284.649	108.889
1908	1.797.963	260.767	105.633
1909	1.892.568	280.061	108.028
1910	2.128.021	316.115	122.571
1911	2.400.018	350.574	107.743
1912	2.559.781	350.930	109.225
1913	2.525.042	341.735	106.618
1914	1.502.811	218.197	77.749
1915	994.853	162.425	61.086
1916	944.575	178.907	57.766
1917	1.277.709	293.187	79.113
1918	2.866.012	538.559	113.792
1919	7.337.477	1.000.770	189.831

Year	Free Trade Unions	Christian Trade Unions	Hirsch-Duncker Trade Associations
1920	8.032.057	1.105.894	225.998
1921	7.751.589	1.028.900	224.597
1922	7.821.558	1.033.506	230.612
1923	5.817.258	806.992	216.497
1924	4.023.867	612.952	147.280
1925	4.182.511	582.319	157.571
1926	3.932.935	531.558	163.451
1927	4.415.689	605.784	167.638
1928	4.866.926	647.364	168.543
1929	4.948.267	673.127	168.726
1930	4.716.569	658.707	163.302
1931	4.134.902	577.512	149.804
1932	3.532.947	?	?

Sources: For 1868–1889: Gerd Hohorst, Jürgen Kocka and Gerhard A. Ritter, Sozialgeschichtliches Arbeitsbuch. Materialien zur Statistik des Kaiserreichs 1870–1914 (Munich 1975), p. 135 ff.; for 1890–1932: Erich Matthias and Klaus Schönhoven (eds), Solidarität und Menschenwürde. Etappen der deutschen Gewerkschaftsgeschiche von den Anfängen bis zur Gegenwart (Bonn 1984), p. 369 f.

b) Free, Christian-national and Hirsch-Duncker salaried employees' federations 1920–1931

Year	General Free Union of Salaried Staff (AfA-Bund)	General Association of German Salaried Staffs' Unions (Gedag)	Trade Union Federation of Salaried Staff (GdA)
1920	689.806	463.199	
1921	609.626	422.845	300.357
1922	658.234	460.086	302.254
1923	618.097	408.773	294.241
1924	447.201	393.559	260.796
1925	428.185	411.113	273.016
1926	400.155	418.700	275.352
1927	395.259	456.980	288.134
1928	421.106	501.635	301.967
1929	450.741	557.420	320.117
1930	459.840	591.520	335.428
1931	434.974	593.800	327.742

Source: Dietmar Petzina, Werner Abelshauser and Anselm Faust, Sozialgeschichtliches Arbeitsbuch III. Materialien zur Statistik des Deutschen Reiches 1914–1945 (Munich 1978), p. 112.

c) German Trade Union Federation (DGB) and German Salaried Employees' Union (DAG) 1951–1987

Year	DGB total	No. of female members	DAG total	No. of female members
1951	5.912.125	1.011.436	343.500	107.700
1952	6.004.476	1.028.713	360.388	117.365
1953	6.051.221	1.046.148	384.365	127.819
1954	6.103.343	1.055.213	406.473	140.091
1955	6.104.872	1.047.805	420.540	146.132
1956	6.124.547	1.043.241	431.483	149.217
1957	6.244.386	1.077.652	437.068	151.782
1958	6.331.735	1.089.527	438.142	152.238
1959	6.273.741	1.070.762	440.011	152.777
1960	6.378.820	1.093.607	450.417	155.554
1961	6.382.036	1.078.257	461.513	157.395
1962	6.430.428	1.058.453	471.902	159.797
1963	6.430.978	1.033.842	479.457	161.209
1964	6.485.471	1.022.052	475.415	157.991
1965	6.574.491	1.030.185	475.561	159.311
1966	6.537.160	1.014.833	477.982	159.300
1967	6.407.733	976.793	481.286	160.227
1968	6.375.972	971.590	471.147	154.528
1969	6.482.390	984.074	467.796	151.496
1970	6.712.547	1.027.150	461.291	147.820
1971	6.868.662	1.050.488	469.932	153.189
1972	6.985.548	1.115.266	468.880	154.227
1973	7.167.523	1.179.762	463.370	155.895
1974	7.405.760	1.284.500	472.035	160.284
1975	7.364.912	1.313.021	470.446	163.537
1976	7.400.021	1.353.958	473.463	167.068
1977	7.470.967	1.402.643	475.372	169.920
1978	7.751.523	1.482.349	481.628	176.099
1979	7.843.565	1.540.832	487.743	182.178
1980	7.882.527	1.596.274	494.874	188.604
1981	7.957.512	1.650.773	499.439	194.121
1982	7.849.003	1.649.399	501.037	198.196
1983	7.745.913	1.644.770	497.346	200.698
1984	7.660.346	1.654.508	497.724	201.228
1985	7.719.468	1.705.131	500.922	205.271
1986	7.764.697	1.755.963	496.299	205.866
1987	7.757.039	1.788.361	494.126	211.639

Note: Figures for the DGB are totals for 30 September until 1959; after that, for 31 December. Figures for the DAG are for 30 September until 1975; after that for 31 December.

Source: Statistische Jahrbücher für die Bundesrepublik Deutschland 1952 ff.

387

2. Industrial action

a) Industrial disputes in 1848, 1869, 1871–1882 and 1884–1890

Year	No. of disputes	Year	No. of disputes	Year	No. of disputes
1848	49	1876	84	1884	60
1869	152	1877	67	1885	146
1871	158	1878	41	1886	77
1872	352	1879	15	1887	125
1873	283	1880	19	1888	100
1874	129	1881	15	1889	280
1875	88	1882	27	1890	390

Note: 1848 figures are for the German Confederation excluding Austria; from 1869 onwards, for the German Reich. The figures are not consistent, as they were compiled at a later date from various different sources (newspapers and periodicals, particularly from the labour press, archive material, and so on). They are therefore only to a limited extend open to comparison, and are intended to give a broad picture of fluctuations over the years.

Source: Klaus Tenfelde and Heinrich Volkmann (ed.), Streik. Zur Geschichte des Arbeitskampfes in Deutschland während der Industrialisierung (Munich 1981), p. 294.

b) Industrial disputes conducted by the Free trade unions, 1890–1898

Year	No. of disputes	Nos. affected	Total duration (in weeks)
1890/91	226	38.536	1.348
1892	73	3.022	507
1893	116	9.356	568
1894	131	7.328	879
1895	204	14.032	1.030
1896	483	128.808	1.923
1997	578	63.119	1.921
1898	985	60.162	4.848

Note: The table shows all industrial disputes commencing in the year in question in which the Free trade unions were involved. No distinction was made between strikes and lockouts. The total duration in weeks refers to the total duration of all industrial disputes, regardless of the numbers involved.

Source: Correspondenzblatt der Generalkommission der Gewerkschaften Deutschlands Nr. 29, 1901, p. 454.

c) Industrial disputes (strikes and lockouts) affecting workers in trade and industry 1899–1933

Year	Disputes	Companies affected	Workforces of these companies	Total no. of strikers and workers locked out (incl. those prevented from working)	Days lost
1899	1.311	7.548	265.148	116.531	3.381.000
1900	1.468	8.347	321.281	141.121	3.712.000
1901	1.091	4.799	149.200	68.191	2.427.000
1902	1.106	4.385	149.791	70.696	1.951.000
1903	1.444	8.740	251.177	135.522	4.158.000
1904	1.990	11.436	309.676	145.480	5.285.000
1905	2.657	18.340	965.510	542.564	18.984.000
1906	3.626	19.026	838.988	376.325	11.567.000
1907	2.512	18.379	574.728	286.016	9.017.000
1908	1.524	6.532	280.657	119.781	3.666.000
1909	1.652	6.560	290.701	130.883	4.152.000
1910	3.228	19.110	680.651	390.706	17.848.000
1911	2.798	12.573	895.813	385.216	11.466.000
1912	2.834	9.813	1.030.948	493.749	10.724.000
1913	2.464	15.586	655.398	323.394	11.761.000
1914	1.223	6.046	238.195	98.339	2.844.000
1915	141	185	48.356	15.238	46.000
1916	240	437	422.591	128.881	245.000
1917	562	3.399	1.468.328	668.032	1.862.000
1918	532	1.095	715.742	391.591	1.453.000
1919	3.719	33.840	2.760.767	2.132.547	33.083.000
1920	3.807	42.268	2.008.732	1.508.370	16.755.000
1921	4.455	55.237	2.036.070	1.617.225	25.874.000
1922	4.785	47.501	2.565.554	1.895.792	27.734.000
1923	2.046	24.175	1.917.265	1.626.753	12.344.000
1924	1.973	28.430	2.066.334	1.647.143	36.198.000
1925	1.708	25.122	1.115.036	771.036	2.936.000
1926	351	2.617	131.292	97.157	1.222.000
1927	844	10.373	685.851	494.544	6.144.000
1928	739	7.852	985.690	775.490	20.339.000
1929	429	8.558	268.499	189.723	4.251.000
1930	353	3.403	302.190	223.885	4.029.000
1931	463	4.753	297.013	172.139	1.890.000
1932	648	2.610	171.555	129.468	1.130.000
1933	69	337	13.162	10.475	96.460

Note: "Days lost" for 1899–1922 are calculated on the basis of the number of workers involved in industrial action and the length of disputes in days; from 1923 on, the number of working days reported as having been actually lost is given. No industrial disputes were recorded after April 1933.

Source: Statistisches Jahrbuch für das Deutsche Reich 1934, p. 321.

d) Industrial disputes 1949–87

Year	Companies affected	Employees affected	Days lost
1949	892	58.184	270.716
1950	1.344	79.270	380.121
1951	1.528	174.325	1.592.892
1952	2.529	84.097	442.877
1953	1.395	50.625	1.488.218
1954	538	115.899	1.586.523
1955	866	597.353	846.647
1956	268	25.340	263.884
1957	86	45.134	2.385.965
1958	1.484	202.483	782.123
1959	55	21.648	61.825
1960	28	17.065	37.723
1961	119	21.052	65.256
1962	195	79.177	450.948
1963	791	316.397	1.846.025
1964	34	5.629	16.711
1965	20	6.250	48.520
1966	205	196.013	27.086
1967	742	59.604	389.581
1968	36	25.167	25.249
1969	86	89.571	249.184
1970	129	184.269	93.203
1971	1.183	536.303	4.483.740
1972	54	22.908	66.045
1973	732	185.010	563.051
1974	890	250.352	1.051.290
1975	201	35.814	68.680
1976	1.481	169.312	533.696
1977	81	34.437	23.681
1978	1.239	487.050	4.281.284
1979	40	77.326	483.083
1980	132	45.159	128.386
1981	297	253.334	58.398
1982	40	39.981	15.106
1983	114	94.070	40.842
1984	1.121	537.265	5.617.595
1985	53	78.187	34.505
1986	96	115.522	27.964
1987	119	154.966	33.325

Source: Statistische Jahrbücher für die Bundesrepublik Deutschland 1952 ff.

3. Wages and Salaries

a) Real wages of workers in trade and industry under the Empire 1871–1913 (1895 = 100)

Year	Index	Year	Index
1871	70	1895	100
1875	87	1900	111
1880	79	1905	114
1885	89	1910	119
1890	96	1913	125

Source: G. Hohorst et al., Sozialgeschichtliches Arbeitsbuch, p. 107.

b) Real wages of workers in trade and industry under the Weimar Republic, and the "Third Reich" 1925–39 (1928 = 100)

Year	Index	Year	Index
1913/14	97	1933	89
1925	81	1934	94
1928	100	1935	92
1929	102	1936	95
1930	96	1937	98
1931	91	1938	105
1932	86	1939	110

Source: Günter Menges and Heinrich Kolbeck, Löhne und Gehälter nach den beiden Weltkriegen. Tabellen und Schaubilder aufgrund statistischer Untersuchungen (Meisenheim 1958), p. 31.

c) Real gross hourly and weekly wages of workers in West German industry, 1950–78 (1970 = 100)

Year	Index of gross hourly wages	Index of gross weekly wages	Year	Index of gross hourly wages	Index of gross weekly wages
	1970 = 100	1970 = 100		1970 = 100	1970 = 100
1950	32,9	35,7	1965	77,9	78,2
1951	34,9	37,8	1966	80,3	79,9
1952	36,9	39,9	1967	81,7	78,3
1953	39,4	42,7	1968	84,2	82,5
1954	40,3	44,2	1969	89,9	89,7
1955	42,4	46,6	1970	100	100
1956	45,5	49,0	1971	105,6	103,5
1957	48,4	50,5	1972	109,2	106,1
1958	50,6	51,9	1973	112,9	109,7
1959	52,8	54,0	1974	116,5	110,8
1960	56,9	58,2	1975	118,4	109,2
1961	61,3	62,7	1976	120,4	113,1
1962	66,4	67,2	1977	124,4	117,2
1963	69,3	69,5	1978	127,9	120,4
1964	73,4	73,4			

Source: Erich Wiegand, Zur historischen Entwicklung der Löhne und Lebenshaltungskosten in Deutschland, in: Erich Wiegand and Wolfgang Zapf (ed.), Wandel der Lebensbedingungen in Deutschland (Frankfurt and New York 1982), pp. 65–153, this table p. 141.

d) Average gross wages of workers in industry in 1913–14 and 1925–86 (1980 = 100)

Year	Index of gross hourly wages	Index of gross weekly wages	Year	Index of gross hourly wages	Index of gross weekly wages
1913/14	3,7	5,0			
1925	5,4	6,1	1960	20,6	22,5
1926	5,8	6,5	1961	22,8	24,8
1927	6,4	7,2	1962	25,4	27,3
1928	7,1	8,3	1963	27,3	29,2
1929	7,5	8,5	1964	29,6	31,5
1930	7,2	7,8	1965	32,4	34,7
1931	6,7	6,9	1966	34,6	36,7
1932	5,6	5,7	1967	35,7	36,4
1933	5,4	5,8	1968	37,3	38,9
1934	5,6	6,2	1969	40,6	43,1
1935	5,7	6,4	1970	46,6	49,6
1936	5,7	6,6	1971	51,7	54,1
1937	5,9	6,9	1972	56,3	58,3
1938	6,1	7,2	1973	62,2	64,4
1939	6,2	7,5	1974	68,5	69,5
1940	6,4	7,6	1975	73,9	72,6
1941	6,7	8,2	1976	78,6	78,8
1942	6,8	8,2	1977	84,2	84,5
1943	6,8	8,3	1978	88,7	89,0
1944 März	6,8	8,2	1979	93,8	95,0
1950	9,9	11,4	1980	100	100
1951	11,3	13,1	1981	105,5	104,4
1952	12,2	14,1	1982	110,5	108,1
1953	12,8	14,8	1983	114,1	111,0
1954	13,1	15,3	1964	116,8	114,7
1955	14,0	16,4	1985	121,3	118,5
1956	15,4	17,8	1986	125,6	122,2
1957	16,8	18,7			
1958	17,9	19,6			
1959	18,9	20,5			

Note: From 1913 to 1944, figures are given for the territory of the Reich as it was at the time; from 1950–59 they are for the Federal Republic excluding Saarland. No attempt was made to allow for variations in the methods and systems used (for example, differences in the national territory, in the definition and number of industries included or employment structure). Despite these reservations, the figures give a rough idea of how earnings have changed over the years.

Source: Statistisches Jahrbuch für die Bundesrepublik Deutschland 1987, p. 481.

*e) Wage differences between the sexes in the textile industry,
1913–78 (female wages as a percentage of male wages in each
category, based on gross hourly wages)*

Year	Skilled	Unskilled
1913	78	84
1926	82	82
1932	84	79
1943	84	78
1951	(71)	75
1972	82	84
1978	84	86

Note: The 1951 figure in the "Skilled" column includes semi-skilled workers' wages.

Source: Josef Mooser, Arbeiterleben in Deutschland 1900–1970
(Frankfurt a. M. 1984), p. 91.

4. Working hours

a) *Length of the working day and working week in industry, 1800–1918*

Year	Average working day (in hours)	Average working week (in hours) acc. to	
		R. Meinert	W. H. Schröder
um 1800	10—12	approx 60—72	
um 1820	11—14	approx 66—80	
um 1830—1860	14—16	80—85	
um 1861—1870	12—14	78	
1871			72
1872			69,25
1873			68
1874			68,25
1875	12	72	68,25
1876			68,5
1877			68,75
1878			68,75
1879			69
1880			68,75
1881			68,75
1882			68,75
1883			68,5
1884			68,75
1885	11	66	68,75
1886			68,5
1887			68,5
1888			68,25
1889			67,75
1890			66,25
1891			66
1892			66
1893	10,5—11	63—65	65,75
1894			65,75
1895			65

Year	Average working day (in hours)	Average working week (in hours) acc. to	
		R. Meinert	W. H. Schröder
1896			63,5
1897			62,5
1898	10,5	61—63	62,25
1899			61,75
1900			60,75
1901			60,75
1902			60,5
1903	10—10,5	59—61	60,25
1904			60
1905			59,5
1906			58,5
1907			57,75
1908	10—10,5	58—60	57,75
1909			57,5
1910			57,25
1911			56,75
1912	10—10,5	58—60	56
1913			55,5
1914			55,5
1915—1918		ca. 60—85	

Source: Figures according to Ruth Meinert, Die Entwicklung der Arbeitszeit in der deutschen Industrie 1820–1956, dissertation (Münster 1958), pp. 5, 10, 12, 21 and 23; Wilhelm Heinz Schröder Die Entwicklung der Arbeitszeit im sekundären Sektor in Deutschland 1871 bis 1913, in Technikgeschichte, vol. 47, 1980, No. 3, pp. 252–302; these figures p. 287. Figures for the working week in 1800, 1820 and 1915–18 are from Martin Wolfsteller, Vom Vierzehnstundentag zur Vierzigsstundenwoche. Zur Geschichte und Problematik der Arbeitszeit in Deutschland (Wiesbaden 1963) (Ms), p. 115 f.

b) The length of the working week in industry, 1919–83

Year	Average working week (in hours)	Year	Average working week (in hours)
1919	48	1950	48,1
1920	48	1951	47,5
1921	48	1952	47,6
1922	48	1953	47,8
1923	48	1954	48,4
1924	50,4	1955	48,6
1925	—	1956	47,9
1926	—	1957	46,2
1927	49,9	1958	45,4
1928	48,9	1959	45,3
1929	46,0	1960	45,3
1930	44,2	1961	45,2
1931	42,5	1962	44,6
1932	41,5	1963	44,4
1933	43,0	1964	44,1
1934	44,6	1965	44,3
1935	44,5	1966	43,9
1936	46,7	1967	42,3
1937	47,6	1968	43,3
1938	47,9	1969	44,0
1939	48,6	1970	44,0
1940	50,1	1971	43,2
1941	50,1	1972	42,8
1942	49,2	1973	42,8
1943	48,0	1974	41,9
1944	48,3	1975	40,5
1945	—	1976	41,6
1946	39,5	1977	41,7
1947	39,1	1978	41,6
1948	42,4	1979	41,9
1949	46,5	1980	41,6
		1981	41,2
		1982	40,7
		1983	40,5

Source: Until 1949, R. Meinert, p. 44 f.; thereafter, Günter Scharf, Geschichte der Arbeitszeitverkürzung (Cologne 1987), p. 458.

5. Unemployment

a) Unemployment rates, 1887–1939

Year	Unemployment rate acc. to Kuczynski	Unemployment rate acc. to Galenson/ Zellner	Year	Unemployment rate acc. to Kuczynski	Unemployment rate acc. to Galenson/ Zellner
1887	0,2				
1888	3,8				
1889	0,2				
1890	2,3		1915	3,2	3,2
1891	3,9		1916	2,2	2,2
1892	6,3		1917	3,2	1,0
1893	2,8		1918	0,8	0,8
1894	3,1		1919	3,7	3,7
1895	2,8		1920	3,8	3,8
1896	0,6		1921	2,8	2,8
1897	1,2		1922	1,5	1,5
1898	0,4		1923	10,2	10,2
1899	1,2		1924	11,4	13,1
1900	2,0		1925	8,3	6,8/ 5,2
1901	6,7		1926	17,9	18,0/15,3
1902	2,9		1927	8,8	8,8/10,1
1903	2,7	4,7	1928	9,7	8,6/10,4
1904	2,1	3,6	1929	14,6	13,3/14,3
1905	1,6	3,0	1930	22,7	22,7/23,2
1906	1,2	2,7	1931	34,7	34,3/34,1
1907	1,6	2,9	1932	44,4	43,8/42,0
1908	2,9	4,4	1933		36,2
1909	2,8	4,3	1934		20,5
1910	1,9	3,5	1935		16,2
1911	1,9	3,1	1936		12,0
1912	2,0	3,2	1937		6,9
1913	2,9	4,2	1938		3,2
1914	7,2/3,2	7,2	1939		0,9

Source: Jürgen Kuczynski, Die Lage der Arbeiter in Deutschland von 1789 bis zur Gegenwart, vol. 1, Part II, 1871 bis 1932, 6th ed. (Berlin, GDR 1954), pp. 80, 82, 221 and 236. Walter Galenson and Arnold Zellner, International Comparison of Employment Rates. Reprinted from: The Measurement and Behaviour of Unemployment. Reprint No. 86 (Berkeley 1957), p. 529 ff. Collation and critical comments: Manfred Lohr with the assistance of Franz Rothenbacher, Langfristige Entwicklungstendenzen der Arbeitslosigkeit in Deutschland, in E. Wiegand and W. Zapf (eds), Wandel der Lebensbedingungen in Deutschland, pp. 237–333; these figures p. 281 f.

b) Unemployment rates, 1950–87

Year	Unemployment rate	Year	Unemployment rate
1950	11,0	1970	0,7
1951	10,4	1971	0,9
1952	9,5	1972	1,1
1953	8,4	1973	1,2
1954	7,6	1974	2,6
1955	5,6	1975	4,7
1956	4,4	1976	4,6
1957	3,7	1977	4,5
1958	3,7	1978	4,3
1959	2,6	1979	3,8
1960	1,3	1980	3,8
1961	0,8	1981	5,5
1962	0,7	1982	7,5
1963	0,8	1983	9,1
1964	0,8	1984	9,1
1965	0,7	1985	9,3
1966	0,7	1986	9,0
1967	2,1	1987	8,9
1968	1,5		
1969	0,9		

Note: Figures based on card-files of labour exchanges.

Source: Statistische Jahrbücher für die Bundesrepublik Deutschland, 1952 ff.

6. Structure of the labour force

a) Persons in paid employment by economic sector, 1882–1987 (as a percentage of all those in paid employment)

Year	Agriculture and forestry	Industry and handicrafts	Service sector
1882	43,5	33,7	22,8
1895	37,5	37,5	25,0
1907	35,2	40,1	24,7
1925	30,5	42,1	27,4
1933	28,9	40,4	30,7
1939	25,9	42,2	31,9
1950	23,7	43,3	33,0
1971	8,0	48,4	43,6
1987	5,1	40,5	54,4

Note: Figures for 1987 are provisional. Figures for 1882–1939 are for the German Reich; after 1950, for the Federal Republic of Germany.

Source: For 1882–1907 calculated according to G. Hohorst et al., Sozialgeschichtliches Arbeitsbuch p. 66; for 1925–39, D. Petzina et al., Sozialgeschichtliches Arbeitsbuch III, p. 55; for 1950, Statistisches Jahrbuch für die Bundesrepublik Deutschland 1955, p. 109; for 1971 and 1987, Statistisches Jahrbuch für die Bundesrepublik Deutschland 1988, p. 100.

b) *Employment categories 1895–1987 (as a percentage of all those in paid employment)*

Year	Self-employed	Helping in family business	Salaried employees	Civil servants	Manual workers
1895	25,0	10,0	8,0		57,0
1907	19,6	15,3	10,3		54,9
1925	15,6	17,0	17,3		50,1
1933	16,1	16,5	12,7	4,7	50,0
1939	13,9	16,4	13,6	5,3	50,8
1950	14,8	14,4	16,0	4,0	50,8
1971	9,8	5,7	30,7	7,5	46,3
1987	9,4	3,2	39,3	9,3	38,8

Source and note: see Table 6a.

II. Bibliography

1. Bibliographies

Bibliographie zur Geschichte der deutschen Arbeiterbewegung, hrsg. von der Bibliothek des Archivs der sozialen Demokratie, Bonn-Bad Godesberg I (1976) ff.

Dowe, Dieter, Bibliographie zur Geschichte der deutschen Arbeiterbewegung, sozialistischen und kommunistischen Bewegung von den Anfängen bis 1863 unter besonderer Berücksichtigung der politischen, wirtschaftlichen und sozialen Rahmenbedingungen, 3., wesentl. erw. u. verb. Aufl., bearb. von Volker Mettig, Bonn 1981

Emig, Dieter/Rüdiger Zimmermann, Arbeiterbewegung in Deutschland. Ein Dissertationsverzeichnis, Berlin 1977

Günther, Klaus/Kurt Thomas Schmitz, SPD, KPD/DKP, DGB in den Westzonen und in der Bundesrepublik Deutschland 1945—1973. Eine Bibliographie, bearb. von Volker Mettig, 2. Aufl., Bonn 1980

Klotzbach, Kurt, Bibliographie zur Geschichte der deutschen Arbeiterbewegung 1914—1945, 3. Aufl., bearb. von Volker Mettig, Bonn 1981

Literaturverzeichnis zur Gewerkschaftsgeschichte, hrsg. vom DGB-Bundesvorstand, zusammengestellt von J. Eikelmann, Düsseldorf 1977

Steinberg, Hans-Josef, Die deutsche sozialdemokratische Arbeiterbewegung bis 1914, Frankfurt—New York 1979

Tenfelde, Klaus/Gerhard A. Ritter (Hrsg.), Bibliographie zur Geschichte der deutschen Arbeiterschaft und Arbeiterbewegung 1863—1914. Berichtszeitraum 1945—1975, Bonn 1981

2. Trade Union History

Abelshauser, Werner (Hrsg.), Die Weimarer Republik als Wohlfahrtsstaat. Zum Verhältnis von Wirtschafts- und Sozialpolitik in der Industriegesellschaft, Stuttgart 1987

Abendroth, Wolfgang, Die deutschen Gewerkschaften. Weg demokratischer Integration, Heidelberg 1954; Neudr. Berlin 1972

Abraham, David, The Collapse of the Weimar Republik. Political Economy and Crisis, Princeton/N. Y. 1981

Albrecht, Willy, Fachverein — Berufsgewerkschaft — Zentralverband. Organisationsprobleme der deutschen Gewerkschaften 1870—1890, Bonn 1982

Anders, Karl, Stein für Stein. Die Leute von Bau-Steine-Erden und ihre Gewerkschaften 1869 bis 1969, Frankfurt 1969

Armingeon, Klaus, Die Entwicklung der westdeutschen Gewerkschaften 1950—1985, Frankfurt—New York 1988

Bajohr, Stefan, Die Hälfte der Fabrik. Geschichte der Frauenarbeit in Deutschland 1914 bis 1945, Marburg/L. 1979

Barthel, Paul (Hrsg.), Handbuch der deutschen Gewerkschaftskongresse, Dresden 1916

Bednarek, Horst/Albert Behrendt/Dieter Lange (Hrsg.), Gewerkschaftlicher Neubeginn. Dokumente zur Gründung des FDGB und zu seiner Entwicklung von Juni 1945 bis Februar 1946, Berlin (DDR) 1975

Beier, Gerhard, Schwarze Kunst und Klassenkampf. Bd. 1: Vom Geheimbund zum königlich-preußischen Gewerkverein 1830—1890, Frankfurt — Wien — Zürich 1966

Beier, Gerhard, Das Lehrstück vom 1. und 2. Mai 1933, Frankfurt — Köln 1975

Beier, Gerhard, Willi Richter — Ein Leben für die soziale Neuordnung, Köln 1978

Beier, Gerhard, Geschichte und Gewerkschaft. Politisch-historische Beiträge zur Geschichte sozialer Bewegungen, Köln 1981

Beier, Gerhard, Die illegale Reichsleitung der Gewerkschaften 1933—1945, Köln 1981

Beier, Gerhard, Schulter an Schulter. Schritt für Schritt. Lebensläufe deutscher Gewerkschafter, Köln 1983

Bergmann, Joachim (Hrsg.), Beiträge zur Soziologie der Gewerkschaften, Frankfurt 1979

Bergmann, Joachim/Otto Jacobi/Walther Müller-Jentsch, Gewerkschaften in der Bundesrepublik, 2 Bde., 2. Aufl., Frankfurt 1976—77

Bieber, Hans-Joachim, Gewerkschaften in Krieg und Revolution. Arbeiterbewegung, Industrie, Staat und Militär in Deutschland 1914—1920, 2 Bde., Hamburg 1981

Blüm, Norbert, Gewerkschaften zwischen Allmacht und Ohnmacht. Ihre Rolle in der pluralistischen Gesellschaft, Stuttgart 1979

Bock, Hans Manfred, Syndikalismus und Linkskommunismus von 1918—1923. Zur Geschichte und Soziologie der Freien Arbeiter-Union Deutschlands (Syndikalisten), der Allgemeinen Arbeiter-Union Deutschlands und der Kommunistischen Arbeiter-Partei Deutschlands, Meisenheim 1969

Boll, Friedhelm, Massenbewegungen in Niedersachsen 1906—1920. Eine sozialgeschichtliche Untersuchung zu den unterschiedlichen Entwicklungstypen Braunschweig und Hannover, Bonn 1981

Borsdorf, Ulrich/Hans Otto Hemmer/Gerhard Leminsky/Heinz Markmann (Hrsg.), Gewerkschaftliche Politik: Reform aus Solidarität. Zum 60. Geburtstag von Heinz O. Vetter, Düsseldorf 1977

Borsdorf, Ulrich/Hans Otto Hemmer/Martin Martiny (Hrsg.), Grundlagen der Einheitsgewerkschaft, Historische Dokumente und Materialien, Köln — Frankfurt 1977

Borsdorf, Ulrich, Hans Böckler. Arbeit und Leben eines Gewerkschafters von 1875 bis 1945, Köln 1982

Borsdorf, Ulrich (Hrsg.), Geschichte der deutschen Gewerkschaften von den Anfängen bis 1945, Köln 1987

Brandt, Gerhard u. a., Anpassung an die Krise: Gewerkschaften in den siebziger Jahren, Frankfurt — New York 1982

Brandt, Willy/Leonard Woodcock (Hrsg.), Festschrift für Eugen Loderer zum 60. Geburtstag, Köln 1980

Braunthal, Gerard, Der Allgemeine Deutsche Gewerkschaftsbund. Zur Politik der Arbeiterbewegung in der Weimarer Republik, Köln 1981

Breit, Ernst (Hrsg.), Aufstieg des Nationalsozialismus. Untergang der Republik. Zerschlagung der Gewerkschaften. Dokumentation der historisch-politischen Konferenz des DGB im Mai 83 in Dortmund, Köln 1984

Brüggemeier, Franz-Josef, Leben vor Ort. Ruhrbergleute und Ruhrbergbau 1889—1919, München 1983

Buhl, Manfred, Sozialistische Gewerkschaftsarbeit zwischen programmatischem Anspruch und politischer Praxis. Der ADGB und die freien Gewerkschaften in der Stabilisierungsphase der Weimarer Republik (1923/24—1927/28), Köln 1983

Buschak, Willy, Von Menschen, die wie Menschen leben wollten. Die Geschichte der Gewerkschaft Nahrung-Genuß-Gaststätten und ihrer Vorläufer, Köln 1985

Bußmann, Bernhard, Die Freien Gewerkschaften während der Inflation. Die Politik des Allgemeinen Deutschen Gewerkschaftsbundes und die soziale Entwicklung in den Jahren 1919—1923, Phil. Diss. Kiel 1965

Conze, Werner/Ulrich Engelhardt (Hrsg.), Arbeiter im Industrialisierungsprozeß. Herkunft, Lage und Verhalten, Stuttgart 1979
Conze, Werner/Ulrich Engelhardt (Hrsg.), Arbeiterexistenz im 19. Jahrhundert. Lebensstandard und Lebensgestaltung deutscher Arbeiter und Handwerker, Stuttgart 1981

Deppe, Frank u. a., Kritik der Mitbestimmung. Partnerschaft oder Klassenkampf?, Frankfurt/M. 1969
Deppe, Frank, Autonomie und Integration. Materialien zur Gewerkschaftsanalyse, Marburg 1979
Deppe, Frank/Ludwig Müller/Klaus Pickshaus/ Joseph Schleifstein, Einheitsgewerkschaft. Quellen — Grundlagen — Probleme. Mit umfangreichem Dokumententeil und Fotos, Frankfurt 1982
Deppe, Frank/Georg Fülberth/Jürgen Harrer (Hrsg.), Geschichte der deutschen Gewerkschaftsbewegung, 3. Aufl., Köln 1981
Deppe, Frank/Witich Rossmann, Wirtschaftskrise, Faschismus, Gewerkschaften. Dokumente zur Gewerkschaftspolitik 1929—1933, 2. Aufl., Köln 1983
Deppe, Frank, Ende oder Zukunft der Arbeiterbewegung? Gewerkschaftspolitik nach der Wende. Eine kritische Bestandsaufnahme, Köln 1984
Detje, Richard u. a., Von der Westzone zum Kalten Krieg. Restauration und Gewerkschaftspolitik im Nachkriegsdeutschland, Hamburg 1982

Eickhof, Norbert, Eine Theorie der Gewerkschaftsentwicklung, Tübingen 1973
Eilrich, Claus/Hans Otto Hemmer (Hrsg.), Die neue Mehrheit. Bilder-Lesebuch: Angestellte, Berlin — Bonn 1988
Eisner, Freya, Das Verhältnis der KPD zu den Gewerkschaften in der Weimarer Republik, Köln — Frankfurt 1977
Engelhardt, Ulrich, „Nur vereinigt sind wir stark". Die Anfänge der deutschen Gewerkschaftsbewegung 1862/63 bis 1869/70, 2 Bde., Stuttgart 1977
Engelhardt, Ulrich/Volker Sellin/Horst Stuke (Hrsg.), Soziale Bewegung und politische Verfassung. Beiträge zur Geschichte der modernen Welt, Stuttgart 1976
Esters, Helmut/Hans Pelger, Gewerkschafter im Widerstand, Hannover 1967; 2. Aufl., Bonn 1983

Feldman, Gerald D., Armee, Industrie und Arbeiterschaft in Deutschland 1914 bis 1918, Berlin — Bonn 1985
Fehrmann, Eberhard/Ulrike Metzner, Angestellte und Gewerkschaften. Ein historischer Abriß, Köln 1981
Fichter, Michael, Besatzungsmacht und Gewerkschaften. Zur Entwicklung und Anwendung der US-Gewerkschaftspolitik in Deutschland 1944—1948, Opladen 1982
Fricke, Dieter, Die deutsche Arbeiterbewegung 1869—1914. Ein Handbuch über ihre Organisation und Tätigkeit im Klassenkampf, Berlin (DDR) 1976

Geary, Dick, Arbeiterprotest und Arbeiterbewegung in Europa 1848—1939, München 1983
Gorz, André, Abschied vom Proletariat, Frankfurt/M. 1980
Grebing, Helga, Geschichte der deutschen Arbeiterbewegung, 10. Aufl., München 1980

Hamel, Iris, Völkischer Verband und nationale Gewerkschaft. Der Deutschnationale Handlungsgehilfen-Verband 1893—1933, Frankfurt 1967

Hartfiel, Günter, Angestellte und Angestelltengewerkschaften in Deutschland. Entwicklung und gegenwärtige Situation von beruflicher Tätigkeit, sozialer Stellung und Verbandswesen der Angestellten in der gewerblichen Wirtschaft, Berlin 1961

Hartmann, Knut, Der Weg zur gewerkschaftlichen Organisation. Bergarbeiterbewegung und kapitalistischer Bergbau im Ruhrgebiet 1851—1889, München 1977

Hartwich, Hans-Hermann, Arbeitsmarkt, Verbände und Staat 1918—1933. Die öffentliche Bindung unternehmerischer Funktionen in der Weimarer Republik, Berlin 1967

Haupt, Heinz-Gerhard u. a. (Hrsg.), Politischer Streik, Frankfurt 1981

Heer, Hannes, Burgfrieden oder Klassenkampf. Zur Politik der sozialdemokratischen Gewerkschaften 1930—1933, Neuwied — Berlin 1971

Heer-Kleinert, Lore, Die Gewerkschaftspolitik der KPD in der Weimarer Republik, Frankfurt — New York 1983

Hentschel, Volker, Geschichte der deutschen Sozialpolitik 1880—1980. Soziale Sicherung und kollektives Arbeitsrecht, Frankfurt 1983

Herkunft und Mandat. Beiträge zur Führungsproblematik in der Arbeiterbewegung, Frankfurt — Köln 1976

Herzig, Arno/Dieter Langewiesche/ Arnold Sywottek (Hrsg.), Arbeiter in Hamburg. Unterschichten, Arbeiter und Arbeiterbewegung seit dem ausgehenden 18. Jahrhundert, Hamburg 1983

Heupel, Eberhard, Reformismus und Krise. Zur Theorie und Praxis von SPD, ADGB und AfA-Bund in der Weltwirtschaftskrise 1929—1932/33, Frankfurt — New York 1981

Heyde, Ludwig (Hrsg.), Internationales Handwörterbuch des Gewerkschaftswesens, 2 Bde., Berlin 1931/32

Hirsch-Weber, Wolfgang, Gewerkschaften in der Politik. Von der Massenstreikdebatte zum Kampf um das Mitbestimmungsrecht, Köln — Opladen 1959

Hohorst, Gerd/Jürgen Kocka/Gerhard A. Ritter, Sozialgeschichtliches Arbeitsbuch. Materialien zur Statistik des Kaiserreichs 1870—1914, München 1975

Hüllbüsch, Ursula, Gewerkschaften und Staat. Ein Beitrag zur Geschichte der Gewerkschaften zu Anfang und zu Ende der Weimarer Republik, Phil. Diss. Heidelberg 1958

Husung, Hans-Gerhard, Protest und Repression im Vormärz. Norddeutschland zwischen Restauration und Revolution, Göttingen 1983

Industriegewerkschaft Metall (Hrsg.), 90 Jahre Industriegewerkschaft 1891 bis 1981. Vom Deutschen Metallarbeiter-Verband zur Industriegewerkschaft Metall. Ein Bericht in Wort und Bild, Köln 1981

Industriegewerkschaft Metall (Hrsg.), Frauen in der Metallgewerkschaft 1891 bis 1982. Dokumente, Materialien, Meinungen, Frankfurt 1983

Industriegewerkschaft Metall (Hrsg.), Kampf um soziale Gerechtigkeit, Mitbestimmung, Demokratie und Frieden. Die Geschichte der Industriegewerkschaft Metall seit 1945. Ein Bericht in Wort und Bild, Köln 1986

Kaelble, Hartmut/Horst Matzerath/Hermann-Josef Rupieper/Peter Steinbach/Heinrich Volkmann, Probleme der Modernisierung in Deutschland. Sozialhistorische Studien zum 19. und 20. Jahrhundert, Opladen 1978

Kern, Horst/Michael Schumann, Das Ende der Arbeitsteilung? Rationalisierung in der industriellen Produktion, München 1984

Kittner, Michael (Hrsg.), Gewerkschaftsjahrbuch 1984. Daten, Fakten, Analysen, Köln 1984 (erscheint seitdem jährl.)

Klönne, Arno, Demokratischer und sozialer Rechtsstaat. Dokumente zur Gewerkschaftspolitik, Bochum 1964

Klönne, Arno, Die deutsche Arbeiterbewegung. Geschichte, Ziele, Wirkungen, Düsseldorf — Köln 1980

Klönne, Arno/Hartmut Reese, Die deutsche Gewerkschaftsbewegung. Von den Anfängen bis zur Gegenwart, Hamburg 1984

Koch, Bernhard, Der Christliche Gewerkschaftsbund, Düsseldorf 1978

Koch, Ursula E., Angriff auf ein Monopol. Gewerkschaften außerhalb des DGB, Köln 1981

Kocka, Jürgen, Klassengesellschaft im Krieg. Deutsche Sozialgeschichte 1914—1918, 2. Aufl., Göttingen 1978

Kocka, Jürgen, Lohnarbeit und Klassenbildung. Arbeiter und Arbeiterbewegung in Deutschland 1800—1875, Berlin — Bonn 1983

Kocka, Jürgen (Hrsg.), Europäische Arbeiterbewegungen im 19. Jahrhundert. Deutschland, Österreich, England und Frankreich im Vergleich, Göttingen 1983

Kolb, Eberhard, Die Arbeiterräte in der deutschen Innenpolitik 1918—1919, 2. Aufl., Berlin 1978

Kosthorst, Erich, Jakob Kaiser, Bd. 1: Der Arbeiterführer, hrsg. von Werner Conze/ Erich Kosthorst/Elfriede Nebgen, Stuttgart — Berlin — Köln — Mainz 1967

Kurth, Josef, Geschichte der Gewerkschaften in Deutschland, 4. Aufl., Hannover — Frankfurt 1965

Kutz-Bauer, Helga, Arbeiterschaft, Arbeiterbewegung und bürgerlicher Staat in der Zeit der Großen Depression. Eine regional- und sozialgeschichtliche Studie zur Geschichte der Arbeiterbewegung im Großraum Hamburg 1873—1890, Bonn 1987

Langewiesche, Dieter/Klaus Schönhoven (Hrsg.), Arbeiter in Deutschland. Studien zur Lebensweise der Arbeiterschaft im Zeitalter der Industrialisierung, Paderborn 1981

Lattard, Alain, Gewerkschaften und Arbeitgeber in Rheinland-Pfalz unter französischer Besatzung 1945—1949, Mainz 1988

Laubscher, Gerhard, Die Opposition im Allgemeinen Deutschen Gewerkschaftsbund (ADGB) 1918—1923, Frankfurt 1979

Leithäuser, Joachim G., Wilhelm Leuschner. Ein Leben für die Republik, Köln 1962

Leminsky, Gerhard/Bernd Otto, Politik und Programmatik des Deutschen Gewerkschaftsbundes, 2. Aufl., Köln 1984

Limmer, Hans, Die deutsche Gewerkschaftsbewegung, 11. Aufl., München 1986

Löwenthal, Richard/Patrik von zur Mühlen, Widerstand und Verweigerung in Deutschland 1933 bis 1945, Berlin — Bonn 1982

Losseff-Tillmanns, Gisela, Frauenemanzipation und Gewerkschaften, Wuppertal 1978

Losseff-Tillmanns, Gisela (Hrsg.), Frau und Gewerkschaft, Frankfurt 1982

Lucas, Erhard, Arbeiterradikalismus. Zwei Formen von Radikalismus in der deutschen Arbeiterbewegung, Frankfurt 1976

Luthardt, Wolfgang (Hrsg.), Sozialdemokratische Arbeiterbewegung und Weimarer Republik. Materialien zur gesellschaftlichen Entwicklung 1927—1933, 2 Bde., Frankfurt 1978

Mai, Gunther, Kriegswirtschaft und Arbeiterbewegung in Württemberg 1914—1918, Stuttgart 1983

Mai, Gunther (Hrsg.), Arbeiterschaft in Deutschland 1914—1918. Studien zu Arbeitskampf und Arbeitsmarkt im Ersten Weltkrieg, Düsseldorf 1985

Markovits, Andrei S., The politics of the West German trade unions. Strategies of class and interest representation in growth and crisis, Cambridge, London u. a. 1986

Mattheier, Klaus J., „Die Gelben". Nationale Arbeiter zwischen Wirtschaftsfrieden und Streik, Düsseldorf 1973

Matthias, Erich (Hrsg.), Einheitsgewerkschaft und Parteipolitik. Zum 75. Jahrestag des Mannheimer Abkommens zwischen der Sozialdemokratischen Partei Deutschlands und den Freien Gewerkschaften von 1906, Düsseldorf 1982

Matthias, Erich/Klaus Schönhoven (Hrsg.), Solidarität und Menschenwürde. Etappen der deutschen Gewerkschaftsgeschichte von den Anfängen bis zur Gegenwart, Bonn 1984

Matthias, Erich (Begr.); Hermann Weber, Klaus Schönhoven u. Klaus Tenfelde (Hrsg.), Quellen zur Geschichte der deutschen Gewerkschaftsbewegung im 20. Jahrhundert, Bd. 1: 1914—1919; Bd. 2: 1919—1923; Bd. 3, I u. II: 1924—1930; Bd. 4: 1930—1933; Bd. 6 (Hrsg.: Hermann Weber u. Siegfried Mielke): 1945—1949, Köln 1985 ff.

Mayer, Tilman (Hrsg.), Jakob Kaiser. Gewerkschafter und Patriot. Eine Werkausgabe, Köln 1988

Meyer, Thomas/Susanne Miller/ Joachim Rohlfes (Hrsg.), Lern- und Arbeitsbuch deutsche Arbeiterbewegung. Darstellung, Chroniken, Dokumente, 2., um einen vierten Band erg. Aufl., Bonn 1988

Mielke, Siegfried (Hrsg.), Internationales Gewerkschaftshandbuch, Opladen 1983

Miller, Susanne, Die Bürde der Macht. Die deutsche Sozialdemokratie 1918—1920, Düsseldorf 1978

Miller, Susanne, Burgfrieden oder Klassenkampf. Die deutsche Sozialdemokratie im Ersten Weltkrieg, Düsseldorf 1976

Mommsen, Hans (Hrsg.), Arbeiterbewegung und industrieller Wandel. Studien zu gewerkschaftlichen Organisationsproblemen im Reich und an der Ruhr, Wuppertal 1980

Mommsen, Hans/Ulrich Borsdorf (Hrsg.), Glück auf, Kameraden! Die Bergarbeiter und ihre Organisationen in Deutschland, Köln 1979

Mommsen, Hans/Dietmar Petzina/Bernd Weisbrod (Hrsg.), Industrielles System und politische Entwicklung in der Weimarer Republik, Düsseldorf 1974; unveränd. Nachdr. Kronberg — Düsseldorf 1977

Mommsen, Wolfgang J./Gerhard Husung (Hrsg.), Auf dem Wege zur Massengewerkschaft. Die Entwicklung der Gewerkschaften in Deutschland und Großbritannien 1880—1914, Stuttgart 1984

Mooser, Josef, Arbeiterleben in Deutschland 1900—1970. Klassenlagen, Kultur und Politik, Frankfurt 1984

Müller, Dirk H., Gewerkschaftliche Versammlungsdemokratie und Arbeiterdelegierte vor 1918. Ein Beitrag zur Geschichte des Lokalismus, des Syndikalismus und der entstehenden Rätebewegung, Berlin 1985

Müller, Werner, Lohnkampf, Massenstreik, Sowjetmacht. Ziele und Grenzen der „Revolutionären Gewerkschafts-Opposition" (RGO) in Deutschland 1928 bis 1933, Köln 1988

Müller-Jentsch, Walther (Hrsg.), Zukunft der Gewerkschaften. Ein internationaler Vergleich, Frankfurt — New York 1988

Nebgen, Elfriede, Jakob Kaiser, Bd. 2: Der Widerstandskämpfer, hrsg. von Werner Conze/Erich Kosthorst/Elfriede Nebgen, Stuttgart — Berlin — Köln — Mainz 1967

Nestriepke, Siegfried, Die Gewerkschaftsbewegung, 3 Bde., 2. Aufl., Stuttgart 1922—23

Niehuss, Merith, Arbeiterschaft in Krieg und Inflation. Soziale Schichtung und Lage der Arbeiter in Augsburg und Linz 1910—1925, Berlin — New York 1985

Niethammer, Lutz/Ulrich Borsdorf/Peter Brandt (Hrsg.), Arbeiterinitiative 1945. Antifaschistische Ausschüsse und Reorganisation der Arbeiterbewegung in Deutschland, Wuppertal 1976

Oertzen, Peter von (Hrsg.), Festschrift für Otto Brenner zum 60. Geburtstag, Frankfurt 1967

Oertzen, Peter von, Betriebsräte in der Novemberrevolution. Eine politikwissenschaftliche Untersuchung über Ideengehalt und Struktur der betrieblichen und wirtschaft-

lichen Arbeiterräte in der deutschen Revolution 1918/19, 2., erw. Aufl., Berlin —
Bonn-Bad Godesberg 1976

Offermann, Toni, Arbeiterbewegung und liberales Bürgertum in Deutschland 1850—
1863, Bonn 1979

Opel, Fritz, Der Deutsche Metallarbeiterverband während des Ersten Weltkrieges und
der Revolution, 4. Aufl., Köln 1980

Opel, Fritz/Dieter Schneider, Fünfundsiebzig Jahre Industriegewerkschaft 1891 bis
1966. Vom Deutschen Metallarbeiter-Verband zur Industriegewerkschaft Metall,
Frankfurt 1966

Osterroth, Franz/Dieter Schuster, Chronik der deutschen Sozialdemokratie, 3 Bde., 2.
Aufl., Berlin — Bonn 1978

Otto, Bernd, Gewerkschaftsbewegung in Deutschland. Entwicklung, geistige Grundlagen, aktuelle Politik, Köln 1975

Petzina, Dietmar/Werner Abelshauser/Anselm Faust, Sozialgeschichtliches Arbeitsbuch, Band III: Materialien zur Statistik des Deutschen Reiches 1914—1945,
München 1978

Pfromm, Hans A., Das neue DGB-Grundsatzprogramm. Einführung und Kommentar,
München — Wien 1982

Pirker, Theo, Die blinde Macht. Die Gewerkschaftsbewegung in Westdeutschland,
1945—1955, 2 Bde., München 1960; 2. Aufl., Berlin 1979

Pohl, Hans (Hrsg.), Sozialgeschichtliche Probleme in der Zeit der Hochindustrialisie-
rung 1870—1914, Paderborn 1979

Potthoff, Heinrich, Gewerkschaften und Politik zwischen Revolution und Inflation,
Düsseldorf 1979

Potthoff, Heinrich, Freie Gewerkschaften 1918—1933. Der Allgemeine Deutsche
Gewerkschaftsbund in der Weimarer Republik, Düsseldorf 1987

Preller, Ludwig, Sozialpolitik in der Weimarer Republik, Stuttgart 1949; unveränd.
Nachdr. Kronberg — Düsseldorf 1978

Prinz, Michael, Vom neuen Mittelstand zum Volksgenossen. Die Entwicklung des
sozialen Status der Angestellten von der Weimarer Republik bis zum Ende der NS-
Zeit, München 1986

Protokolle der Verhandlungen der Kongresse der Gewerkschaften Deutschlands. 1,
1892—10, 1919, 7 Bde., Nachdr. Bonn — Berlin 1979/80

Rabenschlag-Kräußlich, Jutta, Parität statt Klassenkampf? Zur Organisation des
Arbeitsmarktes und Domestizierung des Arbeitskampfes in Deutschland und
England 1900—1918, Frankfurt — Bern 1983

Renzsch, Wolfgang, Handwerker und Lohnarbeiter in der frühen Arbeiterbewegung.
Zur sozialen Basis von Gewerkschaften und Sozialdemokratie im Reichsgründungs-
jahrzehnt, Göttingen 1980

Reulecke, Jürgen (Hrsg.), Arbeiterbewegung an Rhein und Ruhr, Wuppertal 1974

Richter Werner, Gewerkschaften, Monopolkapital und Staat im ersten Weltkrieg und in
der Novemberrevolution, 1914—1919, Berlin (DDR) 1959

Ritter, Gerhard A., Die Arbeiterbewegung im Wilhelminischen Reich. Die Sozialdemokratische Partei und die Freien Gewerkschaften 1890—1900, 2. Aufl., Berlin 1963

Ritter, Gerhard A., Staat, Arbeiterschaft und Arbeiterbewegung in Deutschland. Vom
Vormärz bis zum Ende der Weimarer Republik, Berlin — Bonn 1982

Roder, Hartmut, Der christlich-nationale Deutsche Gewerkschaftsbund (DGB) im
politisch-ökonomischen Kräftefeld der Weimarer Republik. Ein Beitrag zur Funktion und Praxis der bürgerlichen Arbeitnehmerbewegung vom Kaiserreich bis zur
faschistischen Diktatur, Frankfurt 1986

Röder, Werner, Die deutschen sozialistischen Exilgruppen in Großbritannien. Ein Beitrag zur Geschichte des Widerstandes gegen den Nationalsozialismus, Hannover 1968

Ross, Dietmar, Gewerkschaften und soziale Demokratie. Von der Richtungs- zur Einheitsgewerkschaft, von Weimar zur Nachkriegszeit. Untersuchungen zur gewerkschaftlichen Programmatik für den Aufbau einer demokratischen Gesellschaft, Phil. Diss. Bonn 1976

Ruck, Michael, Die Freien Gewerkschaften im Ruhrkampf 1923, Köln 1986

Rupp, Hans Karl, Außerparlamentarische Opposition in der Ära Adenauer. Der Kampf gegen die Atombewaffnung in den fünfziger Jahren. Eine Studie zur innenpolitischen Entwicklung der BRD, Köln 1970

Saul, Klaus, Staat, Industrie, Arbeiterbewegung im Kaiserreich. Zur Innen- und Sozialpolitik des Wilhelminischen Deutschland 1903—1914, Düsseldorf 1974

Schabedoth, Hans-Joachim, Bittsteller oder Gegenmacht? Perspektiven gewerkschaftlicher Politik nach der Wende, Marburg 1985

Scharf, Günter, Geschichte der Arbeitszeitverkürzung. Der Kampf der deutschen Gewerkschaften um die Verkürzung der täglichen und wöchentlichen Arbeitszeit, Köln 1987

Scharrer, Manfred (Hrsg.), Kampflose Kapitulation. Arbeiterbewegung 1933, Reinbek 1984

Schellhoss, Hartmut, Apathie und Legitimität. Das Problem der neuen Gewerkschaft, München 1967

Schiefer, Jack, Geschichte der deutschen Gewerkschaften, 3. Aufl., Aachen 1946

Schmädeke, Jürgen/Peter Steinbach (Hrsg.), Der Widerstand gegen den Nationalsozialismus. Die deutsche Gesellschaft und der Widerstand gegen Hitler, München 1985

Schmidt, Eberhard, Ordnungsfaktor oder Gegenmacht. Die politische Rolle der Gewerkschaften, Frankfurt 1971

Schmidt, Eberhard, Die verhinderte Neuordnung. Zur Auseinandersetzung um die Demokratisierung der Wirtschaft in den westlichen Besatzungszonen und in der Bundesrepublik Deutschland, 8. Aufl., Frankfurt 1981

Schmidt, Ute/Tilman Fichter, Der erzwungene Kapitalismus. Klassenkämpfe in den Westzonen 1945—1948, Berlin 1971

Schneider, Dieter u. Rudolf Kuda, Arbeiterräte in der Novemberrevolution. Ideen, Wirkungen, Dokumente, Frankfurt 1968

Schneider, Dieter (Hrsg.), Zur Theorie und Praxis des Streiks, Frankfurt 1971

Schneider, Michael, Das Arbeitsbeschaffungsprogramm des ADGB. Zur gewerkschaftlichen Politik in der Endphase der Weimarer Republik, Bonn-Bad Godesberg 1975

Schneider, Michael, Unternehmer und Demokratie. Die freien Gewerkschaften in der unternehmerischen Ideologie der Jahre 1918—1933, Bonn-Bad Godesberg 1975

Schneider, Michael, Aussperrung. Ihre Geschichte und Funktion vom Kaiserreich bis heute, Köln 1980

Schneider, Michael, Die Christlichen Gewerkschaften 1894—1933, Bonn 1982

Schneider, Michael, Streit um Arbeitszeit. Geschichte des Kampfes um Arbeitszeitverkürzung in Deutschland, Köln 1984

Schneider, Michael, Demokratie in Gefahr? Der Konflikt um die Notstandsgesetze: Sozialdemokratie, Gewerkschaften und intellektueller Protest (1958—1968), Bonn 1986

Schöck, Eva Cornelia, Arbeitslosigkeit und Rationalisierung. Die Lage der Arbeiter und die kommunistische Gewerkschaftspolitik 1920—28, Frankfurt — New York 1977

Schönhoven, Klaus, Expansion und Konzentration. Studien zur Entwicklung der Freien Gewerkschaften im Wilhelminischen Deutschland 1890 bis 1914, Stuttgart 1980

Schönhoven, Klaus, Die deutschen Gewerkschaften, Frankfurt 1987

Schröder, Wilhelm-Heinz, Arbeitergeschichte und Arbeiterbewegung. Industriearbeit und Organisationsverhalten im 19. und frühen 20. Jahrhundert, Frankfurt — New York 1978

Schröder, Wolfgang, Klassenkämpfe und Gewerkschaftseinheit. Die Herausbildung und Konstituierung der gesamtnationalen deutschen Gewerkschaftsbewegung und der Generalkommission der Gewerkschaften Deutschlands, Berlin (DDR) 1965

Schürholz, Franz, Die deutschen Gewerkschaften seit 1945. Praktische Arbeit und Reformbedürfnisse, Düsseldorf 1955

Schumann, Hans-Gerd, Nationalsozialismus und Gewerkschaftsbewegung. Die Vernichtung der deutschen Gewerkschaften und der Aufbau der deutschen Arbeitsfront, Hannover — Frankfurt 1958

Schuster, Dieter, Die deutsche Gewerkschaftsbewegung. DGB. 5. verb. und erg. Aufl., Düsseldorf 1976

Schuster, Dieter, Die deutschen Gewerkschaften seit 1945, 2. Aufl., Stuttgart — Berlin — Köln — Mainz 1974

Schuster, Dieter, Der Deutsche Gewerkschaftsbund, Düsseldorf 1977

Schwarz, Salomon, Handbuch der deutschen Gewerkschaftskongresse (Kongresse des Allgemeinen Deutschen Gewerkschaftsbundes), Berlin 1930

Sohn, Karl-Heinz, Berufsverband und Industriegewerkschaft. Organisationsprinzipien der deutschen Gewerkschaften, Köln 1964

Stearns, Peter N., Arbeiterleben. Industriearbeit und Alltag in Europa 1890—1914, Frankfurt — New York 1980

Stollberg, Gunnar, Die Rationalisierungsdebatte 1908—1933. Freie Gewerkschaften zwischen Mitwirkung und Gegenwehr, Frankfurt — New York 1981

Streeck, Wolfgang, Gewerkschaftliche Organisationsprobleme in der sozialstaatlichen Demokratie, Königstein 1981

Teichmann, Ulrich (Hrsg.), Gewerkschaften. Analysen, Theorie und Politik, Darmstadt 1981

Tenfelde, Klaus, Sozialgeschichte der Bergarbeiterschaft an der Ruhr im 19. Jahrhundert, Bonn-Bad Godesberg 1977

Tenfelde, Klaus/Heinrich Volkmann (Hrsg.), Streik. Zur Geschichte des Arbeitskampfes in Deutschland während der Industrialisierung, München 1981

Tenfelde, Klaus (Hrsg.), Arbeiter und Arbeiterbewegung im Vergleich. Berichte zur internationalen historischen Forschung, München 1986

Tennstedt, Florian, Sozialgeschichte der Sozialpolitik in Deutschland. Vom 18. Jahrhundert bis zum Ersten Weltkrieg, Göttingen 1981

Tennstedt, Florian, Vom Proleten zum Industriearbeiter. Arbeiterbewegung und Sozialpolitik in Deutschland 1800 bis 1914, Köln 1983

Thum, Horst, Mitbestimmung in der Montanindustrie. Der Mythos vom Sieg der Gewerkschaften, Stuttgart 1982

Timm, Helga, Die deutsche Sozialpolitik und der Bruch der großen Koalition im März 1930, Düsseldorf 1952, unveränd. Nachdr. 1982

Todt, Elisabeth/Hans Radandt, Zur Frühgeschichte der deutschen Gewerkschaftsbewegung 1800—1849, Berlin (DDR) 1950

Tschirbs, Rudolf, Tarifpolitik im Ruhrbergbau 1918 bis 1933, Berlin — New York 1986

Uhen, Leo, Gruppenbewußtsein und informelle Gruppenbildungen bei deutschen Arbeitern im Jahrhundert der Industrialisierung, Berlin 1964

Ullrich, Volker, Die Hamburger Arbeiterbewegung vom Vorabend des Ersten Weltkrieges bis zur Revolution 1918/19, 2 Bde., Hamburg 1976

Varain, Heinz Josef, Freie Gewerkschaften, Sozialdemokratie und Staat. Die Politik der Generalkommission unter der Führung Carl Legiens (1890—1920), Düsseldorf 1956

Vetter, Heinz Oskar (Hrsg.), Aus der Geschichte lernen — die Zukunft gestalten. Dreißig Jahre DGB. Protokoll der wissenschaftlichen Konferenz zur Geschichte der Gewerkschaften vom 12. und 13. Oktober 1979 in München, Köln 1980

Vetter, Heinz Oskar (Hrsg.), Vom Sozialistengesetz zur Mitbestimmung. Zum 100. Geburtstag von Hans Böckler, Köln 1975

Volkmann, Heinrich/Jürgen Bergmann (Hrsg.), Sozialer Protest. Studien zur traditionellen Resistenz und kollektiven Gewalt in Deutschland vom Vormärz bis zur Reichsgründung, Opladen 1984

Wachenheim, Hedwig, Die deutsche Arbeiterbewegung 1844—1914, Frankfurt — Wien — Zürich 1971

Wentzel, Lothar, Inflation und Arbeitslosigkeit. Gewerkschaftliche Kämpfe und ihre Grenzen am Beispiel des Deutschen Metallarbeiter-Verbandes 1919—1924, Hannover 1981

Wilke, Manfred, Die Funktionäre. Apparat und Demokratie im Deutschen Gewerkschaftsbund, München 1979

Winkler, Heinrich August, Von der Revolution zur Stabilisierung. Arbeiter und Arbeiterbewegung in der Weimarer Republik 1918 bis 1924, 2. Aufl., Berlin — Bonn 1985

Winkler, Heinrich August, Der Schein der Normalität. Arbeiter und Arbeiterbewegung in der Weimarer Republik 1924 bis 1930, Berlin — Bonn 1985

Winkler, Heinrich August, Der Weg in die Katastrophe. Arbeiter und Arbeiterbewegung in der Weimarer Republik 1930 bis 1933, Berlin — Bonn 1987

Wolfram, Adam, Es hat sich gelohnt. Der Lebensweg eines Gewerkschaftlers, Koblenz 1977

Zoll, Rainer, Der Doppelcharakter der Gewerkschaften. Zur Aktualität der Marxschen Gewerkschaftstheorie, Frankfurt 1976

Zwahr, Hartmut, Zur Konstituierung des Proletariats als Klasse. Strukturuntersuchung über das Leipziger Proletariat während der industriellen Revolution, Berlin (DDR) 1978

411

III. Abbreviations

Where there is an accepted English abbreviation it is given in brackets.

ADAV   Allgemeiner Deutscher Arbeiterverein
General Association of German Working Men

ADB   Allgemeiner Deutscher Beamtenbund
General Federation of German Civil Servants

ADGB   Allgemeiner Deutscher Gewerkschaftsbund
General German Trade Union Federation

AfA-Bund   Allgemeiner Freier Angestellten-Bund
General Free Union of Salaried Staff

AFG   Arbeitsförderungsgesetz
Law to Promote Employment

APO   Außerparlamentarische Opposition
Extra-parliamentary opposition

AVAVG   Gesetz für Arbeitsvermittlung und
Arbeitslosenversicherung
Law on Labour Exchanges and
Unemployment Benefit

BDA   Bundesvereinigung der Deutschen
Arbeitgeberverbände
Federal Association of German Employers'
Federations

BDI   Bundesverband der Deutschen Industrie
Federal Association of German Industry

BfG   Bank für Gemeinwirtschaft
Bank for Co-operative Economy

BGAG   Beteiligungsgesellschaft für
Gemeinwirtschaft AG
Finance Company for Co-operative Economy

CDI   Centralverband Deutscher Industrieller
Central Federation of German Industrialists

CDU   Christliche Demokratische Union Deutschlands
Christian Democratic Union of Germany

CGB	Christlicher Gewerkschaftsbund
	Christian Trade Union Federation
CSU	Christlich-Soziale Union
	Christian Social Union
DAF	Deutsche Arbeitsfront
	German Labour Front
DAG	Deutsche Angestellten-Gewerkschaft
	German Salaried Employees' Union
DBB	Deutscher Beamtenbund
	German Civil Service Union
DDGB	Deutsch-Demokratischer Gewerkschaftsbund
	German Democratic Trade Union Federation
DDP	Deutsche Demokratische Partei
	German Democratic Party
DDR	Deutsche Demokratische Republik
	German Democratic Republik
DGB	Deutscher Gewerkschaftsbund
	German Trade Union Federation
DHV	Deutschnationaler Handlungsgehilfen-Verband
	German National Union of Clerical Assistants
DIHT	Deutscher Industrie- und Handelstag
	German Industrial and Trade Association
DKP	Deutsche Kommunistische Partei
	German Communist Party
DMV	Deutscher Metallarbeiterverband
	German Engineering Workers' Union
DNVP	Deutschnationale Volkspartei
	German National People's Party
DP	Deutsche Partei
	German Party
DVP	Deutsche Volkspartei
	German People's Party
EBFG	Europäischer Bund Freier Gewerkschaften
	European Confederation of Free Trade Unions (ECFTU)
EGB	Europäischer Gewerkschaftsbund
	European Trade Union Confederation (ETUC)

413

FDGB	Freier Deutscher Gewerkschaftsbund
	Free German Trade Union Federation
FDP	Freie Demokratische Partei
	Free Democratic Party
GdA	Gewerkschaftsbund der Angestellten
	Trade Union Federation of Salaried Staff
Gedag	Gesamtverband Deutscher
	Angestellengewerkschaften
	General Association of
	German Salaried Staffs' Unions
Gesamtmetall	Gesamtverband der metallindustriellen
	Arbeitgeberverbände
	General Federation of Engineering
	Employers' Associations
Gesamtverband	Gesamtverband der christlichen
	Gewerkschaften Deutschlands
	General Association of German Christian
	Trade Unions
GNP	Gross National Product
H.-D. Gewerkvereine	Hirsch-Dunckersche Gewerkvereine
	Hirsch-Duncker Trade Associations
IAA	Internationale Arbeiter-Assoziation
	International Working Men's Association
	(IWMA) (the International)
IBCG	Internationaler Bund
	christlicher Gewerkschaften
	International Federation of
	Christian Trade Unions (IFCTU)
IBFG	Internationaler Bund Freier Gewerkschaften
	International Confederation of
	Free Trade Unions (ICFTU)
IGB	Internationaler Gewerkschaftsbund
	International Trade Union Federation
KAB	Katholische-Arbeitnehmer Bewegung
	Catholic Wage Earners' Movement
KPD	Kommunistische Partei Deutschlands
	Communist Party of Germany

NPD	Nationaldemokratische Partei Deutschlands
	National Democratic Party of Germany
NSBO	Nationalsozialistische
	Betriebszellenorganisation
	National Socialist Company Cell Organization
NSDAP	Nationalsozialistische Deutsche Arbeiterpartei
	National Socialist German Workers'
	(Nazi) Party
ÖTV	(Gewerkschaft) Öffentliche Dienste, Transport
	und Verkehr
	Public Services, Transport and Communications
	Union
RDI	Reichsverband der Deutschen Industrie
	National Federation of German Industry
RGI	Rote Gewerkschaftsinternationale
	Red Trade Union International
RGO	Revolutionäre Gewerkschafts-Opposition
	Revolutionary Trade Union Opposition
RM	Reichsmark
	(unit of currency)
SDAP	Sozialdemokratische Arbeiterpartei
	Social Democratic Workers' Party
SPD	Sozialdemokratische Partei Deutschlands
	Social Democratic Party of Germany
UGO	Unabhängige Gewerkschaftsorganisation
	Independent Trade Union Organization
USPD	Unabhängige Sozialdemokratische Partei
	Independent Social Democaratic Party
VDA	Vereinigung der Deutschen
	Arbeitgeberverbände
	Federation of German Employers' Associations
WGB	Weltgewerkschaftsbund
	World Federation of Trade Unions (WFTU)
WTB-Plan	Woytinsky-Tarnow-Baade-Plan

ZAG   Zentralarbeitsgemeinschaft der
industriellen und gewerblichen
Arbeitgeber und Arbeitnehmer Deutschlands
Central Association of Industrial and
Commercial Employers and Employees
of Germany

IV. Glossary of other organizations

Alldeutscher Verband: Pan-German League
Allgemeiner Deutscher Arbeiterschaftsverband: General Federation of German Workers
Allgemeiner Deutscher Arbeiterunterstützungsverband: General German Federation for the Support of Working Men
Allgemeiner Deutscher Verband: General German League
Arbeiterverbrüderung: Fraternity of Working Men
Arbeitsgemeinschaft Freier Angestelltenverbände: Association of Free Unions of Salaried Staff

Bund der Geächteten: League of Outcasts
Bund der Gerechten: League of the Just
Bund der Industriellen: League of Industrialists
Bund der Kommunisten: Communist League
Bund deutscher Konsumgenossenschaften: Federation of German Consumer Co-operatives

Deutscher Flottenverein: German Naval Association

Freie Vereinigung deutscher Gewerkschaften: Free Association of German Trade Unions

Generalkommission der Gewerkschaften Deutschlands: General Commission of German Trade Unions
Gewerkschaftsring deutscher Arbeiter-, Angestellten- und Beamtenverbände: Trade Union League of Workers', Salaried Staffs' and Civil Servants' Associations
Gutenberg Bund: Gutenberg League

Hauptstelle Deutscher Arbeitgeberverbände: Central Organization of German Employers' Associations

Kartell der schaffenden Stände: Cartel of Productive Classes

Rat der Volksbeauftragten: Council of Popular Delegates

Reichsbund der höheren Beamten: National Federation of Senior Civil
    Servants
Reichsverband gegen die Sozialdemokratie: Imperial Association against
    Social Democracy
Reichswirtschaftsrat: National Economic Council

Verband der Deutschen Gewerkvereine (H.-D.): Federation of German
    Trade Associations (H-D)
Verband deutscher Arbeitervereine: Union of German Workers' Associa-
    tions
Verein Deutscher Arbeitgeberverbände: Union of German Employers'
    Associations
Volksbund für Freiheit und Vaterland: Popular League for Freedom and
    Fatherland
Volksverein für das katholische Deutschland: Popular Association for
    Catholic Germany

V. Index of Names

The numerals in italics refer to pages on which biographical information is given or illustrations appear.

Abendroth, Wolfgang 256, 275 f., 285
Adenauer, Konrad 240, 250, 253, 258, 270, 279 f., *284*, 302
Agartz, Viktor 255, 261, 264, 279, 298
Albrecht, Ernst 348
Arendt, Walter 315
Arndt, Adolf 284
Arnold, Karl 176, 278 f.
Auerbach, Walter 221
Aufhäuser, Siegfried 143, *144*

Baade, Fritz 173, 195
Baltrusch, Friedrich 172
Bangemann, Martin 349
Barth, Emil 125, 131
Barzel, Rainer 312
Bauer, Gustav 93, 128
Bebel, August 41 ff., 45, 60, 89–92, 109
Beck, Ludwig 221
Behrens, Franz 121
Benda, Ernst 288, 312
Berg, Fritz 250
Berlepsch, Hans Hermann Freiherr von 67
Bernstein, Eduard 90, 123
Bessemer, Henry 16, 33
Biedenkopf, Kurt 308, 321
Bismarck, Otto von 30, 35, 49–54, 58, 61 f.
Blättel, Irmgard 339
Blüm, Norbert 353
Böckler, Hans 218, *226 f.,* 228 f., 235, 239 f., 242, 244, 248, 250, 253, 256, 278
Bömelburg, Theodor 91
Born, Stephan 24
Borsig, Ernst von 116
Brandes, Alwin 218
Brandt, Willy 289, 304, 313, 319, 326, 342
Brandts, Franz 56 f.
Brauer, Theodor 111, 175, 199

Brauns, Heinrich 164 f.
Breit, Ernst *346 f.,* 350, 369, 371
Brenner, Otto 255, 261, *262, 264,* 265, 268, 278, 280, 283, 286, 296, 298, 301, 309, 334 f.
Brey, August 56
Briefs, Goetz 276
Brümmer, Hans 264
Brüning, Heinrich 186 ff., 191, 194, 196, 345
Brusis, Ilse 339
Brust, August 78

Cohen, Adolf 116, 132, 135

Dawes, Charles G. 159
Dittmann, Wilhelm 131
Duncker, Franz 43 ff.

Ebert, Friedrich 131, 135
Ehrenberg, Herbert 315
Ehrhardt, Heinrich 153
Eichler, Willi 221
Eisenhower, Dwight D. 224 f.
Elm, Adolf von 85, 91
Engelen-Kefer, Ursula 372
Engels, Friedrich 22
Erdmann, Lothar 206
Erhard, Ludwig 239 f., 250, 274, 289, 302 f., 306
Erkelenz, Anton *76, 77, 144,* 150, 167, 172, 189
Even, Johannes 279

Fahrenbrach, Heinrich 173
Farthmann, Friedhelm 359
Fette, Christian 253, 255 f., 258, 278
Fimmen, Edo 218
Fink, Ulf 355, 372
Fitz, Alfred 218
Forsthoff, Erich 256
Franke, Heinrich 366
Freese, Heinrich 66

Freitag, Walter 218, 255, 277
Friedrich Wilhelm IV. 23
Fritzsche, Friedrich Wilhelm 39–42, 48
Fröhlich, Karl 27

Genscher, Hans-Dietrich 347, 351
George, Heimo 348
Giesberts, Johannes 96, 120, 128
Goerdeler, Carl Friedrich 221
Göring, Bernhard 218
Goldschmidt, Karl 77
Gottfurcht, Hans 218, 221
Grassmann, Peter 205, 207
Groener, Wilhelm 117, 131
Gscheidle, Kurt 309, 315
Guillaume, Günter 342
Gutermuth, Heinrich 297

Haase, Hugo 123, 131
Habermann, Max 221
Härtel, Richard 37
Hagen, Lorenz 227
Hanna, Gertrud 143, 146
Hannover, Heinrich 285
Hansen, Werner siehe: Wilhelm Heidorn
Hartmann, Gustav 150
Haussmann, Helmut 349
Hesselbach, Walter 332, 341
Heidorn, Wilhelm 221
Hilferding, Rudolf 173
Hindenburg, Paul von 117, 159, 176, 196, 201, 204, 206
Hirsch, Max 43 ff., 76
Hitler, Adolf 155, 188, 201, 204 ff., 210, 213 f., 220, 222, 230
Hitze, Franz 57
Höcherl, Hermann 286 f., 312, 367
Hoogen, Matthias 284
Hugenberg, Alfred 166, 188
Husemann, Fritz 218

Ihrer, Emma 82
Imbusch, Heinrich *145,* 167

Jäckel, Hermann 173
Jahn, Hans 218, 221
Joetten, Wilhelm 178
Joos, Joseph 166
Jungk, Robert 280

Kaas, Ludwig 166
Kähler, Wilhelmine 82
Kaiser, Jakob 198 f., 218, 221 f., 278 f.
Kaiser, Joseph H. 256
Kapp, Wolfgang 153 ff., 166, 203
Kautsky, Karl 60, 90, 93, 123
Ketteler, Wilhelm Emanuel Freiherr von 23, 34 f.
Kiesinger, Kurt Georg 304
Kirdorf, Emil 174
Kirn, Richard 220
Kloß, Carl 56
Knöchel, Wilhelm 220
Kohl, Helmut 347–351, 357
Kohlweck, Wenzel 28
Kollwitz, Käthe 182
Kolping, Adolph 23
Kopp, Georg von 95
Korum, Michael Felix 95
Krupp, Alfred 31 f.
Kummernuss, Adolph 218
Kupfer, Erhard 227

Lafontaine, Oskar 355, 367
Lambach, Walther 167
Lambsdorff, Otto Graf 345, 348
Landsberg, Otto 131
Lassalle, Ferdinand 34 f., 39 ff.
Leber, Georg *262,* 264, *265,* 280, 287, 296 f., 304, 315, 366
Leber, Julius 221
Legien, Carl 56, *70,* 80, 86, 88 f., 92, 114, 123, 136, *144,* 147, 155, 251
Leipart, Theodor 56, 135, *144, 147,* 166, 193, 201, 204–207
Lenders, Helmut 309
Leo XIII. 57, 77
Letterhaus, Bernhard 221
Leuschner, Wilhelm 207, 221 f., *223*
Ley, Robert 212 f.
Liebknecht, Karl 123
Liebknecht, Wilhelm 41, 45, 60
Lücke, Paul 289, 309, 312
Ludendorff, Erich 117
Luxemburg, Rosa 90, 92 f., 123

Mahlein, Leonard 345
Mann, Heinrich 219
Marshall, George 230, 237 ff., 248
Marx, Karl 22, 41 f.
Matthöfer, Hans 309, 315, 341

Max von Baden, Prinz   128
Meyer, Bernhard   170
Meyer, Heinz-Werner   372, *373*
Möller, Alex   319
Motteler, Julius   43
Müller, August   120
Müller, Hermann   185 ff.
Müller, Richard   125, 135
Mugrauer, Hans   220

Naphtali, Fritz   169, 173 f., 194
Nebgen, Elfriede   175
Nipperdey, Hans Carl   256
Nölting, Erik   173
Nörpel, Clemens   169
Noske, Gustav   135

Ollenhauer, Erich   280
Otte, Bernhard   *145,* 167, 189, 207

Papen, Franz von   196 ff., 201
Paulssen, Hans Constantin   286
Pius X.   95
Pius XI.   95, 199
Posadowsky-Wehner, Arthur Graf von   67
Potthoff, Erich   235
Puttkamer, Robert von   56

Raiffeisen, Friedrich Wilhelm   28
Rappe, Hermann   353, 357
Reagan, Ronald   348
Reichert, Jakob Wilhelm   115, 132
Reusch, Hermann   273
Richter, Willi   227, 277, 280, 282, 286, 296, *314*
Riemer, Horst-Ludwig   321
Rosenberg, Ludwig   221, 278, 296, *297,* 298 f., 309, *314*

Savigny, Franz von   95
Scheel, Walter   313
Scheidemann, Philipp   93, 131
Schiesser, Horst   340
Schiller, Karl   304 ff.
Schippel, Max   120
Schleicher, Kurt von   201
Schlicke, Alexander   56
Schlieffen, Alfred von   110
Schliestedt, Heinrich   218 f.
Schlimme, Hermann   218

Schmidt, Helmut   312, 341 ff., 352, 355, 358
Schneider, Gustav   150
Schob, Heinrich   42
Schöttle, Erwin   221
Schröder, Gerhard   283–286, 312
Schröder, Kurt von   201
Schulze-Delitzsch, Hermann   29, 85
Schumacher, Kurt   248, 278
Schuman, Robert   278
Schumann, Louis   42
Schweitzer, Johann Baptist von   40–43, 45
Seifert, Jürgen   285
Severing, Carl   178
Sinzheimer, Hugo   173
Stegerwald, Adam   *80,* 86, 94, 112 f., 120, *145,* 149, 167, 176, 186, 190
Steinkühler, Franz   341, 345, 357
Stinnes, Hugo   251
Stötzel, Gerhard   34
Storch, Anton   279
Strasser, Gregor   201
Strauß, Franz Josef   304
Stresemann, Gustav   159
Stumm-Halberg, Carl Ferdinand Freiherr von   31

Tacke, Bernhard   283
Tarnow, Fritz   142, 194 f., 219 f.
Teichgräber, Richard   218
Tessendorf, Hermann   49, 51
Thatcher, Margret   348
Thomas, Sidney   16
Tirpitz, Alfred von   62
Truman, Harry S.   236

Urich, Max   218

Vetter, Heinz Oskar   *314 f.,* 316, 319, 321, 347, 370
Vietor, Albert   340, 347
Vogel, Hans-Jochen   356
Vogt, Franz   220
Vollmar, Georg von 90

Weitling, Wilhelm   22
Wichern, Johann Heinrich   24
Wieber, Franz   94
Wilhelm I.   51, 53
Wilhelm II.   58, 61, 66 f., 110, 127
Winkelheide, Bernhard   279

Wissell, Rudolf   135 f., 178
Woytinsky, Wladimir   194 f.
Wulf-Mathies, Monika   339
Wunder, Dieter   354

Yorck, Theodor   42, 47

Zeiss, Carl   66
Zimmermann, Friedrich   367